From Dan to Beersheba and Beyond

Other books by Barry Blackstone

Though None Go With Me

Rendezvous In Paris

Though One Go With Me

Scotland Journey

The Region Beyond

Enlarge My Coast

From Dan to Beersheba and Beyond

A Promised Land Pilgrimage

BARRY BLACKSTONE

RESOURCE *Publications* · Eugene, Oregon

FROM DAN TO BEERSHEBA AND BEYOND
A Promised Land Pilgrimage

Copyright © 2014 Barry Blackstone. All rights reserved. Except for brief quotations in critical publications or reviews, no part of this book may be reproduced in any manner without prior written permission from the publisher. Write: Permissions, Wipf and Stock Publishers, 199 W. 8th Ave., Suite 3, Eugene, OR 97401.

Resource Publications
An Imprint of Wipf and Stock Publishers
199 W. 8th Ave., Suite 3
Eugene, OR 97401

www.wipfandstock.com

ISBN 13: 978-1-62564-669-9

Manufactured in the U.S.A.

05/07/2014

All quotes from the Bible are from the Old King James Version.

Contents

Prelude: From Dan to Beersheba—Judges 20:1 | 1

1. Israel Study Tour—1 John 1:1 | 7
2. We're Marching to Zion—Psalms 48:12-13 | 11
3. The Citadel and the Tower of David—Song of Solomon 4:4 | 14
4. Weeping at the Wailing Wall—Ezekiel 27:32 | 17
5. Views from the Bulwarks—Isaiah 26:1-2 | 21
6. Down the *Via Dolorosa*—John 19:16-17 | 25
7. An Evening at the Dung Gate—Nehemiah 12:31 | 29
8. Hezekiah's Tunnel—2 Chronicles 32:30 | 33
9. Jesus' Jerusalem—Luke 2:22 | 37
10. The Burnt House of Kathros—Luke 19:41 | 42
11. Not One Stone Left Upon Another—Matthew 24:2 | 46
12. The Beautiful Gate—Acts 3:2 | 50
13. In the Garden—John 19:41 | 54
14. Gibeon from Nebi Samwil—Joshua 9:3 | 58
15. Gibeah of Saul—1 Samuel 10:26 | 61

16	Finding a Cistern at Michmash—1 Samuel 13:23	65
17	Jericho—Joshua 2:1	69
18	Sunday Morning On Olivet—Acts 1:12	73
19	Gethsemane Garden—Matthew 26:36	77
20	O Little Town of Bethlehem?—Luke 2:4	81
21	Herod's Herodium—Matthew 2:19	85
22	A Morning on Mount Moriah—2 Chronicles 3:1	89
23	Corrie Ten Boom's Tree—Genesis 12:3	93
24	A Man Named Moses—Exodus 2:10	97
25	Western Wall Tunnel—Isaiah 7:3	101
26	A Stop in the Shephelah—2 Chronicles 26:10	105
27	Confronting Giants On Mount Azekah—1 Samuel 17:1	110
28	Picking Stones In the Elah Valley—1 Samuel 17:40	114
29	A Meaningful Stop at Mareshah—Micah 1:1	118
30	Lachish—Joshua 10:3	121
31	Disappointments and Delights in the Negev—Genesis 12:9	125
32	Beersheba—Genesis 21:31	129
33	From Arad to Avdat—Joshua 12:14	133
34	A Taste of the Wilderness—Psalms 72:9	137
35	The Oasis of Eilat—2 Chronicles 8:17	141
36	Parting the Red Sea—Exodus 10:19	145

37	The Tabernacle at Timnah—Acts 7:44	149
38	The Animals of Israel and Their Lessons—Job 12:7-9	153
39	Sleeping Under the Shadow of Masada—Psalms 127:2	158
40	A Climb Up Masada—Psalms 63:1	162
41	The Fortress of Masada—Psalms 62:2	165
42	A Message From Masada—Isaiah 25:12	169
43	En Gedi and the Dead Sea—Ezekiel 47:10	173
44	The Caves of Qumran—Joshua 15:61-62	177
45	The Abiding Word of God—1 Peter 1:24-25	181
46	Yad Ha Shmonah Guest House—Acts 10:4	185
47	The Church of the Redeemer—Psalms 19:14	189
48	The Plain of Sharon—1 Chronicles 27:29	193
49	Caesarea By the Sea—Acts 8:40	197
50	A Lesson from the Theatre at Caesarea—Acts 25:13	201
51	An Unexpected Lunch at Joel's House—1 Chronicles 4:25	204
52	Mount Carmel—1 Kings 18:19	208
53	Sleeping On Carmel—Micah 7:14	212
54	A Rolling Stone Tomb by the Road—Mark 15:46	216
55	Arriving at the First Battlefield—Joshua 12:21	220
56	Tel Megiddo and a Manger—1 Kings 9:15	224

57	Armageddon and the Valley of Megiddo —Zechariah 12:11	228
58	Jezreel and Naboth –1 Kings 21:1	232
59	Drinking at the Well of Harod—Judges 7:1	236
60	Journey to Nazareth—Matthew 2:23	240
61	Nazareth Village and Detours—Mark 1:9	244
62	Another Day In Nazareth—Luke 2:51–52	248
63	Sunset Over the Sea of Galilee—Mark 1:16	252
64	A Stranger In Galilee?—Obadiah 12	256
65	Bethsaida Brotherhood—John 1:44	261
66	Capernaum—Matthew 4:13	265
67	Unimpressed In Tiberias—John 6:23	268
68	A Mountaintop Experience—Matthew 28:16	272
69	Simon's Ship—Luke 5:3	276
70	The Sea of Galilee—John 6:1	280
71	Completing the Triangle—Matthew 11:20–21	284
72	Hazor and the Hulah Valley—Joshua 11:1	288
73	From Dan . . .—Genesis 14:14	292
74	The High Place At Dan—I Kings 12:28–29	296
75	Caesarea Philippi—Matthew 16:13	300
76	Viewing Mount Hermon from the Golan Heights —Deuteronomy 3:8–9	304
77	The New Bulls of Bashan—Psalms 22:12	308

78	A Final Salute to En Gev—Matthew 10:12	312
79	A Baptism at the Jordan River—Matthew 3:13	316
80	The River Jordan—Mark 1:5	320
81	A Walk Through Beth—Shan—1 Samuel 31:12	324
82	Hot Springs and a Dust Storm—Psalms 107:35	328
83	A Memorable Lecture—Joshua 7:2	332
84	Archeological Dig at Ai—Joshua 8:28	336
85	Doctor Merrill's Square—Psalms 22:15	340
86	The Field at Shiloh—Joshua 18:1	344
87	Overlooking Shechem—Psalms 108:7	348
88	Doctor Wood's Lecture On Jericho—Joshua 6:26	352
89	Last Day In Israel—Nehemiah 8:18	356
90	Finishing My Lists—Revelations 1:19	360
91	My Israeli Meat—John 4:32	365
92	Going Home From School—Judges 19:9	369
93	Israel Pilgrimage—1 Peter 2:11	373

Postlude: Instructive Teachings from Israel Trip—Proverbs 9:9 | 377

Bibliography | 381

PRELUDE

From Dan to Beersheba

Judges 20:1—Then all the children of Israel went out, and the congregation was gathered together as one man, FROM DAN TO BEERSHEBA, with the land of Gilead, unto the Lord in Mizpeh.

From the balcony of my Adi Hotel room on the edge of the Red Sea I watch early this morning the winds from the country of Jordan (the old land of Edom) blow across the narrow gap that is the Bay of Eilat. It has been 14-days since I left my home on the coast of Maine for this amazing adventure, and it is here where Solomon built his famous seaport of Ezion-Geber (I Kings 9:26) that I have finally realized what I will name the book that I will write recording the remembrances and reflections of my first, and hopefully not my last, trip to God's favorite land (Psalms 78:68). Bob Boyd, in his booklet, "Footsteps in Bible Lands", gives this informative description of 'this land':

> Israel, frequently called 'Palestine', since the end of the First World War when Britain received the Mandate of this mid-east territory. It lies between the Mediterranean Sea and the desert east of the Jordan River. The Southern boundary was in the area of Beersheba and the Northern boundary at Mount Hermon- from 'Dan to Beersheba'. The geography of Palestine is varied and includes the maritime plain by the Mediterranean Sea, the central mountain range with an average height of two thousand feet, desert regions, and the Jordan Valley. Eastern Palestine, a large fertile plateau, is east of the Jordan River. Because of the varied elevation (some above sea level and some below), the climate differs in various parts of the country. It has two seasons:

winter-rainy and mild, from December to March, and summer-hot and dry, from May to October. The highest temperature ever recorded was 129 degrees and the lowest was 19 degrees. Both were recorded in the Jordan Valley!

In my church today, left over from the day when a Christian School once thrived in this building, you can find an old fashion globe. If you look for Palestine on that globe you will find a tiny spot, a narrow section along the eastern tip of the Mediterranean Sea. As we learned in our travels around Israel, it is easy to drive comfortably in a single day around the borders of that land, a land mass about the size of the Island of Sicily! To this day it is an isolated island land surrounded by massive Arab nations, mortal enemies of the Jewish people. Once it linked the great Asia empires to Egypt containing two of the ancient world's great highways: the Via Maris (the way of the sea) and the King's Highway. Today, it is the thorn in the side of those who wish to make the Middle East an Islamic World, void of Jews.

Since the fragmented tribes of Israel first established a foothold in Canaan, the accepted description of the boundary of this land has been "from Dan to Beersheba". At least nine times (I Samuel 3:20, II Samuel 3:10, 17:11, 24:2, 15, I Kings 4:25, I Chronicles 21:2, and II Chronicles 30:5) the Bible makes this distinction! It finally came to me as I enjoy the warm breezes of the Red Sea that I had traveled 'beyond' these boundaries. I am on a study tour of Israel through Dallas Theological Seminary, and before our 19-day trip in country is over we will have traveled 'from Dan to Beersheba and beyond'!

Who would not desire to travel to the land of Jesus and his people the Hebrews? Since childhood I have heard the stories of the Bible. Since adulthood I have been studying the Bible and its truths. I still do not know what provoked in me to start praying for this trip in December of 1979, but I do know where I was. I had taken over the pastorate of the Calvary Baptist Church in Westfield, Maine earlier that year. I was just getting started into my second pastorate, raising a young family, and trying to stay afloat financially. I certainly didn't have the time or the money to take such a trip, but I started to pray. I claimed the promise of John 15:7:

> If ye abide in me, and my words abide in you, ye shall ask what ye will, and it shall be done unto you.

I did know a few people personally that had made the pilgrimage to the 'holy land', and their stories only added to my desire to go there myself. I read books of strangers and their observations and reflections that went, and each and every time the urge to follow in their footsteps reinforced the aspiration to go.

Years passed, decades passed! I didn't pray much for this specific request, but I kept it in my prayer journal. Periodically I would come across it again and would remind the Lord of my desire then press on with where I was and what I was doing in my life. Two more pastorates and two kids grown and on their own quickly passed by my rear view mirror! By then it was the spring of 2009 and I was 18 years into my 4th pastorate. My son was a specialist in the United States Army, a veteran of the Iraq War and heading to Afghanistan. My daughter had just finished her first semester at Dallas Theological Seminary seeking her Master's in teaching and theology, and I was in the midst of settling my father's only brother's estate. Uncle Paul had died suddenly leaving me to clean up what he had left behind. Because I was the only member of my family who didn't own a house, I got my grandparent's old home. It was during an encouraging call from my daughter that she said in passing, "Bubby (Marnie's nickname for me), do you know that DTS takes a trip to Israel at the end of every academic year?"

She went on to explain that only a limited number of people go and that it was actually a study trip, not just a tour. She could get three credit hours if she went, and that sometimes they allow people not attending DTS to participate. I quickly told her to get the information necessary to go, and that it sounded exactly what I was looking for in a trip to Israel. Most people I knew that had gone basically did the tourist things; a few days in Jerusalem, a trip to Jericho, the Dead Sea, and the Sea of Galilee with a stop in Nazareth and Bethlehem. I didn't just want to go, I wanted to learn more of that land and its history and see those places and things spoken of in the Bible. I knew that I now had the time, but a 19-day stay in Israel would be expensive, but did I have the money?

It was then that the Good Lord reminded me that along with the house my uncle had given me, he had also left behind a brand-new, New Holland tractor. My uncle had bought it the year before to plow snow and cut grass. I was living 205 miles from the property and would only be using it as a cottage at best. What did I need a tractor for? It was then I made up my mind that the Lord was starting to answer my 30-year old prayer request. The chance to go had materialized, the time to go was available, and if He would sell my uncle's tractor the money would be no problem. It was then my old prayer request had a sense of urgency to it. Marnie began to pray as well, for I had told her if all the planets would line up that I would take her along for the experience, the credit, and the thrill of sharing another adventure together (we had already done Paris and India).

Within a few weeks the tractor was sold, the money was in the bank, and the opportunity to be a part of the group opened up. I sent a deposit for the trip in August, and by early 2010 the dates were set, the money was paid, and I waited for the Good Lord to finish answering my old petition. On May 7, 2010 I left Maine for Dallas. On May 10, 2010, I left with my daughter and 33 other individuals for Israel. What you have before you are the observations and opinions I recorded in my trip journals (I wrote two). It is my prayer that this will be more than just the memories of a pastor in 'the promised land'? As with my original petition, my prayer is that some spiritual insight will be delivered as well. Oswald Chambers once wrote:

> The only reliable way to be truly guided by God is to assimilate the Word of God to your character. Yet even that spiritual truth will damage instead of help you if the Holy Spirit is not present. . . . Scripture reveals God's will only if we allow His Holy Spirit to apply it to our circumstances.

Like an unexpected trip to Israel!

I am convinced that is one of the reasons this prayer request was answered. Unknown to me, over the 30 plus years, I wasn't trying to answer the prayer myself. I simply made the request, repeated it often enough to show my true desire, and let the Good Lord through His Spirit work out the timing, the details, and the right tour. It was the great preacher and writer Charles Spurgeon that recorded this on my prayer promise:

> Of necessity we must be in Christ to live unto Him, and we must abide in Him to be able to claim the largesse of this promise (John 15:7) from Him. . . . All true believers abide in Christ in a sense; but there is a higher meaning, and this we must know before we can gain unlimited power at the throne.

I see now that 30 years was required for me to be in the right place, not only in my life, but in my relationship to Christ. Interestingly, I started praying this petition within three-months of Marnie's birth! Yet I see now that she was ready at thirty to do what I was only ready to do at nearly sixty. I had prayed over a long period of time; Marnie over a short period of time. Spurgeon went on to add this:

> The heart must remain in love, the mind must be rooted in faith, the hope must be cemented to the Word, the whole man must be joined unto the Lord, or else it would be dangerous to trust us with power in prayer!

I will never forget this trip to Israel, nor will I ever forget how it came to pass. Some might focus on the amazing supply of funds to accomplish the journey, while others will focus on how a father and daughter were able to travel together to Canaan, but as for me, I am focusing on the lesson in prayer this answer has given to me. We serve a gracious and loving Heavenly Father that loves nothing better than giving His child his or her heart's desire. Did not Jesus Himself teach us?

> If ye then, being evil, know how to give good gifts unto your children (as I did with Marnie and this trip), how much more shall your Father which is in heaven give good things (as the Father did with me and this trip) to them that ask him?" (Matthew 7:11)

I simply asked and He graciously gave!

1

Israel Study Tour

1 John 1:1—That which was from the beginning, which we have heard, which we have seen with our eyes, WHICH WE HAVE LOOKED UPON, and our hands have handled of the Word of life.

For me there is no other Bible verse that can express in a few lines what happened on Israel Study Program BE903A sponsored by Dallas Theological Seminary from May 10–30, 2010. I began to read the Bible when I began to read. I was taught the Bible stories long before I started school or could read. To say my life has been wrapped up in the pages of God's Holy Word would be an understatement. I had read it, memorized it, meditated upon it, studied it, preached and taught it for decades, but one aspect of my Biblical training was lacking: visualization. I had yet to see it, touch it, handle it, walk it, smell it, and that is what happened when I joined the Dallas Field Study team to Israel in the spring of 2010.

In the summer of 2009 my daughter Marnie began to send me information about this trip. I still can feel the excitement I felt when I read things like this:

> Picture yourself climbing through Hezekiah's ancient tunnel as it snakes beneath the city of Jerusalem . . . reading about David slaying Goliath while standing at the spot where the event took place . . . gazing out over the Judean Wilderness where 'the voice of one crying in the wilderness' announced the coming of Jesus Christ . . . looking over the Sea of Galilee from atop a cliff and review the ministry of Jesus along its shores.

I was hooked immediately, and then I read:

> This program is designed for a seminary/college-aged student. It is physically VERY strenuous and much more demanding than a normal sightseeing tour! Participants will be required to walk/hike for long hours on consecutive days, uphill, downhill, on uneven steps and over rocks. You must be able to walk 8 to 12 miles on some days. Weather conditions can be very hot!

I was far from a college student (37 years removed). I was 58 and I couldn't remember walking 8–12 miles a day, not ever, NOT ONCE! I began to rethink my desire, but deep in my soul the urge to go and the desire to see for myself 'the promised land' quickly overcame my fear that I couldn't do it.

I soon realized that the opportunity to see Israel up close and personal could not be compared to walking in the hot weather I might have to endure. Nevertheless, I started to prepare for the physical aspect of this trip by walking around the lanes and back roads of my coastal community of Ellsworth. Interestingly, within three months of leaving for Israel I would be fulfilling a planned missionary trip to India; what better place to train for the heat of Israel than the 100 degree days I would experience there? How many people get to train for a trek through Israel in India?

On a 30-day journey through three states in India (Kerala, Tami Nadu, and Andrah Pardesh), I prepared for the strenuous aspect of my Israel adventure. Every day in India I experienced temperatures that reached as high as 124 (the hottest we saw in Israel was 105 at the Dead Sea). After India, Israel was a piece of cake, and for the miles we had to walk (100 miles in 19 days), the surrounding sights were so interesting and inspiring I didn't even notice the miles slipping by, either uphill or downhill! Just to be clear, one of my companions on the trip had a walk-a-meter and he recorded the miles we actually walked each day. The most we ever did was seven and a half miles in one day; so the warning had more teeth than the actual trip had bite.

On May 10, 2010, the study tour actually began at the Dallas/Fort Worth Airport where we meet Dr. John Hilber and his wife Charlotte and the other members of the group for our first flight to Newark, New Jersey. My daughter did recognize a few names on the team list, but we were strangers that first day. Most were students of DTS, either at the main campus in Dallas, or at one of the many extension campuses around the country. In actuality, Dallas Theological Seminary was partnering with IBEX (Israel Bible Extension) of The Master's College of Santa Clarita, California to provide the expertise for the Israel Study Program. Dr.

Hilber, from the Old Testament Studies department at DTS, and his wife would be our primary travel host and hostess, but once we got to Israel we would be met by Dr. Greg Behle, a professor of the IBEX Institute located in Israel itself. He would be our primary instructor and guide for our travels throughout Israel.

We left Dallas around seven in the morning and arrived in Newark about eleven. By 2:30 PM we were on El AL flight #28 for an overnight (Israel is seven hours ahead of east coast time) flight to Tel Aviv. The travel was uneventful including the very strict Israeli security. We arrived on time (8:20 AM on May 11) at the Ben Gurion International Airport on the shores of the Mediterranean Sea. It was an amazing sight and a much deeper emotional experience than I expected to actually be in my Lord's country. Even the strict security didn't dampen our spirits as we made our way through immigration and customs towards our waiting bus, a bus that would drive us to Jerusalem; yes, Zion itself! My eyes were beginning to see, and I was starting to look upon 'the miracle of Israel'.

One of the interesting aspects of the timing of this trip was the fact that we would be in the land of promise on the 62nd anniversary of the rebirth of the nation of Israel (May 14, 1948). I was born less than three years later, so in my lifetime the Jews have literally transformed a barren land into an Eden. From the edge of Tel Aviv I could see the thriving coastal city. Within days I would see parts of the desert blossoming in vineyards, olive yards, date groves, orange groves, amazing farms, and a score of other agricultural enterprises. I had come to see firsthand what God had done through His people in my lifetime. Granted, as someone once described, modern Israel is

> Not a melting pot but a pressure cooker.

I too saw the soldiers with their loaded machine guns everywhere. I knew I was coming into a hostile land, but I was finally there, and the Jew had returned. One of the first books (1973) I ever read of a man's travels in Israel and his observations was Vance Havner's "Song at Twilight". In a chapter he called, the Miracle of Israel, he wrote this:

> Thirty years ago a college president said, 'Israel will never return to Palestine. Jews love the cities where they can make money. They would never go back to that rock pile.' Back at the turn of the century (the twentieth century) some Bible scholars saw Israel's return as unlikely (to quote Dr. Carl Henry) as a Swiss navy. They put it into the Scofield Bible which was laughed at

in some circles. They were as right about it as they were about the rise of Russia as a commanding figure in the last days. True, Israel is back in unbelief but it is there and the stage is set.

And I was now set to see it for myself!

2

We're Marching to Zion

Psalms 48:12–13—WALK ABOUT ZION, and go round about her: tell the towers thereof. Mark ye well her bulwarks, consider her palaces; that ye may tell it to the generation following.

From the window of our bus, I watched with anticipation for the first Biblical site to be pointed out to me. The Ben Gurion Airport had been built on the Plain of Sharon (I Chronicles 27:29), a fertile valley that runs from Joppa in the south to Caesarea in the north along the Mediterranean Sea. Before Greg made his first explanation, I saw a signpost for the Old Testament city of Lod (I Chronicles 8:12) and the New Testament city of Lydda (Acts 9:32). My heart skipped a beat as I realized that I was going through the same area that Peter had traveled (Acts 9:35, 38) in the early days of the Church. In the back of my travel journal I started recording these sites, and before our Israel journey was finished I would record over 120 such places.

Lod or Lydda was not our destination, but the mountaintop city of Jerusalem. The plains very quickly turned into rolling hills as we made our way up the Aijalon Valley (Joshua 10:12) where the moon stood still for Joshua. From a distance we were pointed out the hilltop fortress of Gezer (I Chronicles 20:4), one of my disappointments for this trip. (Places I knew and read about but had no time to actually visit. Before the trip was over I would have to add Petra, Hebron, Samaria, Cana, En Gedi Falls, and many others to that list)! Despite the quick trip through my first section of Biblical country, I was blessed to see the sunflower fields, the ancient knolls, the steep valleys as we wound our way through the 28 miles of Route One to old Jerusalem. The rolling hills as quickly turned into steep inclines and even deeper canyons. Nevertheless, within an hour we had climbed the 2,500 feet to Zion Ridge. I will never forget my first impression of Jerusalem as we worked our way through the busy, late morning traffic up the Hinnom Valley (Joshua 18:16) towards the Jaffa Gate.

I was finally here. I had arrived at the ancient capital of Israel. I was now within sight of one of the most important, if not the most important city of the entire world. Scripture began to flow through my mind as I remembered that this was the place that the Almighty had chosen to put His name (I Kings 14:21), and, if you believe like I do, chose to dwell first on earth in the person of Melchizedek (Genesis 14:17–24). It was called Salem then, and the Christ was the incarnate priest/king that met Abraham after the slaughter of the kings (Hebrews 7:1–4). Then it was called Jebusi (Joshua 18:28) in the days of the Amorites, and by the time of Joshua's conquest better known as Jerusalem (Joshua 15:63). When David captured the town, he named it 'the city of David' (II Samuel 5:7, 9). And there before my eyes were the hills of Jerusalem (Zion, Acra, Moriah, and Bezetha):

> As the mountains are round Jerusalem, so the Lord is round about his people from henceforth even forever. (Psalms 125:2)

And there on top of those hills was the old city of Zion and spread out on all sides the new city of Jerusalem. As the bus slowly made its way up the final ascent, I was moved by the Scriptures that flooded my memory. The countless times I had read of this place, but now a reality in cut-stone. The new part of town quickly faded and all I could see were the gates and walls and ramparts and bulwarks and towers of the Old City, but just how old?

I knew what my eyes had long since desired to see were not the walls of David's Jerusalem, nor Solomon's city gates, neither Herod's fortress, but the 1540 masterpiece of the Ottomans. Oh, there was still a lot of the ancient city as we would discover, but as I got off the bus just above Jaffa Gate and under the shadow of the Citadel and David's Tower I was content to know that whether Ottoman or Almighty, I had arrived and for me I was walking on 'holy ground'. As I picked up my bag and started to walk up to New Gate Isaac Watts old hymn and Robert Lowry's wonderful refrain began to float through my mind creating a meaningful step; one might even call it a march:

Come, we that love the Lord, and let our joys be known, join in a song of sweet accord, join in a song of sweet accord, and thus surround the throne, and thus surround the throne.... The hill of Zion yields a thousand sacred sweets before we reach the heavenly fields, before we reach the heavenly fields or walk the golden streets, or walk the golden streets.... then let our songs abound and every tear be dry; we're marching through Immanuel's ground, we're marching through Immanuel's ground to fairer worlds on high, to fairer worlds on high.... We're marching to Zion, beautiful, beautiful Zion; we're marching upward to Zion, the beautiful city of God.

Granted, I knew that Watts and Lowry were writing of the heavenly Jerusalem, the New Jerusalem, but for me as I followed my companions up my first Jerusalem hill, through my first Jerusalem gate, around my first Jerusalem corner to the Knight's Palace (our resting place for the next seven nights), and on my first Jerusalem street, the old stone pavement might as well have been covered in gold. Every eyeful was a 'sacred sweet' to my soul, every noise was a glorious song, and every step was on Immanuel's ground!

3

The Citadel and the Tower of David

Song of Solomon 4:4—Thy neck is like THE TOWER OF DAVID builded for an armoury, whereon there hang a thousand bucklers, all shields of mighty men.

After we got settled into our medieval home away from home (the Knight's Palace was located in the Latin Patriarchate in the Christian Quarter of the Old City and was built into the old Ottoman walls; the high ceilings and wide ornate halls were decorated in ancient artifacts from the days of the knights), our first order of business was to get orientated to where we would live for the next week. It was also lunch time, so where to eat and what to eat? (All meals on the trip were provided with the exception of our noon meal because there was no telling where we would be at any given noon hour.) Greg took us down to the Jaffa Gate and pointed out a few eating places with instructions to meet in front of the Citadel in an hour for our first walk-about in Jerusalem. It was like the blind leading the blind as we wandered like sheep without a shepherd between the Knight's Palace and the Jaffa Gate. Most of us were not ready to buy the unknown food we saw at the very expensive prices the vendors were asking. So what do Americans do when they find themselves in a strange place with a strange menu? We find a pizza place, and sure enough, just up a side street was Jacob's Pizza! (It wasn't bad for the price.)

I must admit I had a hard time waiting the hour before the official start to our tour of the Old City. From every place I stood I saw high walls, massive gates, impressive bulwarks, and beautiful towers. Destroyed in 70 AD by the Romans, the city was not fully rebuilt until 1540

AD under the Turks and there fabulous leader, Sultan Suleiman the Magnificent. When he ordered the walls and gates to be rebuilt there was one section of the old structure still there. When Herod built his Jerusalem, he constructed a fortress to guard what is now the Jaffa Gate. This was the only section the Romans left when they fulfilled Jesus' prophecy of Jerusalem's destruction (Matthew 24:2). The fort is now a museum; filled with old stones, bronze busts, and wonderful descriptions and mockups and models of Old Jerusalem. As we waited for Greg to arrive for our first expedition into the past, I could only imagine what we would find behind the huge, entrance gate?

It was nearly one o'clock when we started to wander through the vast rooms, central courtyard, and towers of this ancient fortress. It seems that the Crusaders were so impressed with the fort that they were the ones that gave the citadel the name of 'The Tower of David'. Some even believe that the tomb of David is located on site, but because of the location of the citadel, nearly on the opposite side of Jerusalem where the hill of Ophel (II Chronicles 27:3) is found, the facts are against this place. Despite the historical evidence the name and place retain the title. On this very first afternoon in Jerusalem I learned that there was a great gulf fixed between truth and tradition in Jerusalem, as well as in most of what is Israel today. The sepulcher of David that Peter mentions in Acts 2:29 were probably destroyed by the Romans in 70 AD. These differences of opinions and interruptions did not take away from the amazing sights we saw and the places we explored in the Citadel, tower of David or no tower of David, that warm Tuesday afternoon. This adventure included a hike up the staircase leading to the roof of the fortress.

It was from the top we actually got our first panoramic view of Jerusalem. We could see both inside and outside the city. It was from this magnificent height (there was only one other place we found better to view the city than from the top of the citadel and that was from the top of the tower of the Lutheran Church of the Redeemer) that we got our first look at Temple Mount, the Mount of Olives, the Kidron Valley, the Dome of the Rock, the Holy Sepulcher, and countless other famous places. From where we stood we could see a dozen or more churches and half a dozen mosques. Way in the distance we could make out the Wilderness of Judea and the infamous West Bank Wall could be seen snaking its way across sections of the ridge line to the east. We got some memorable photographs of Marnie and me with the Old City behind us. We finished the tour by working our way down through the courtyard and back into the streets of the city. My highlight for the afternoon was a bust of my favorite emperor, Hadrian. I had a chance to visit his famous wall in Scotland, but I didn't know that he had such an impact on Jerusalem during his reign. Marnie took a picture with me and the bust of Hadrian in the Citadel in Jerusalem, the first of many a historical favorite, both people and places. Another bit of history getting filled in for me, and on site is the best way to study and enjoy the past.

We finished our afternoon in the business section of the Christian quarter getting our bearings along St. Francis Street and the Christian Quarter Road. The streets of Jerusalem are only for walking, few vehicles are allowed in the Old City. We were shown where it was safe to shop and of course exchange our dollars into shekels. I wrote this in my personal journal at the end of our first full day in Israel:

> Our walk-about took us through the shopping section of old Jerusalem, and, yes, The Money Changers Are Still Alive And Doing Well In Jerusalem!

I was reminded as we exchanged (we got 3.6 shekels for every American greenback) our money with a man named Shaaban at Ali Baba Souvenir (that should tell you all you need to know) that Jesus also encountered the money changers in His trips to Jerusalem (John 2:15). My first negative impression in Israel was that business was still number one and that everything and anything connected to our faith has either been turned into a business or a business opportunity. Merchandizing and making money still holds an important place in this place that the Almighty once said:

> But I have chosen Jerusalem that my name might be there. . . .
> (II Chronicles 6:6)

The shekel and not the Saviour is still the real god of Jerusalem!

4

Weeping at the Wailing Wall

Ezekiel 27:32—And IN THEIR WAILING they shall take up a lamentation for thee, and lament over thee, saying, What city is like Tyrus, like the destroyed in the midst of the sea?

One of the blessings of our Israel trip was the free time and down time we enjoyed in the evenings. Our days were filled with scheduled stops, but most evening remained open to do what we wanted to do, or to go where we wanted to go. This fit in very nicely with my daughter's and my personality. We love adventure, doing our own thing, going where angels fear to tread so to speak! Top on our list was to see the Western Wall, better known to most as the Wailing Wall. We had noticed on our program schedule that we would make a daytime stop, but for us we didn't want to wait.

One of the interesting aspects of this trip was the presence of another similar group from Master's Seminary out of California. They had arrived at the Knight's Palace shortly after we had gotten back from our afternoon orientation walk around the Christian Quarter of the Old City. To get them used to the area, Michael Grisanti, their leader, we learned, was going to take a small group to the Western Wall after supper. Getting to the wall was beyond our understanding of the city, so Marnie and I decided with a couple other female members of our team to tag along at least until we got to the Wall; then we were going to explore the city from the Wall back to the palace ourselves. This expedition would take us into the Jewish Quarter, and to the most sacred site of modern Judaism. The wall was probably built in the 4th century and is the closest the Jews can get to Temple Mount, the site of the temples built there in the past. So for centuries Jewish pilgrims have come to this spot to mourn the destruction of the last temple, and pray for the rebuilding of a new Temple. Most non-Jews call it 'the wailing wall', but the Jews call it 'Kotel Ha Maaravi', or the Western Wall.

One of the aids given to us when we arrived at the Knight's Palace was a map of the old city. I put that map in my pocket as we followed the Master's group through the narrow streets of Jerusalem. Our journey took us through some of the streets we had traveled that afternoon; St. Francis Street to Christian Quarter Road to David's Street, one of the main lanes through the heart of the city. David's Street is the dividing line between the Christian Quarter and the Armenian Quarter. The end of David's Street runs into the Ha-Shalshelet the dividing line between the Jewish Quarter and the Moslem, or Arab Quarter. Within fifteen minutes we were standing on a ledge overlooking the plaza in front of the Western Wall. It was nearly eight and the entire area was lit up with soft spotlights. The brighter lights on the Dome of the Rock highlighted the top of the wall, but it was the sacredness of what was happening at the base of the Wall that drew Marnie and me to separate from the group.

After passing through security, we slowly made our way to the short wall that separated the upper plaza from the area just in front of the wall. The area was segregated, men on the left and women on the right. Marnie and her two girlfriends from Dallas went their way and I walked alone into the sea of men chanting, wailing, reading, and singing near the Wall under Wilson's Arch; named after the archeologist that discovered this old entrance onto Herod's Temple Mount. What caught my eye first were the massive stones that make up the wall. From top to bottom the stones grew larger signifying the different sections of the wall and when the stones were laid. The experts believe the larger stones come from the 2nd (Zerubbabel's Temple-Ezra 1:5) Temple and the 3rd (Herod's Temple-John 2:20) Temple and the lowest rough stones from the 1st (Solomon's Temple-II Chronicles 2:1) Temple. As I got closer to the sacred stones, I noticed pieces of paper in the cracks. I would only learn later that they were the written prayers of Jews who are not able to make a pilgrimage to the Western Wall. Their relatives in Jerusalem place the letters in the wall so God will hear their petitions. I learned that some even believe that God dwells in the Wall. The moisture that collects between the huge slabs of stone will eventually destroy the prayer petitions leaving room for others to be added. An old Jewish tradition believes that the nightly dew (Psalms 133:3) is the tears of the Wall weeping for the exiled people of God.

As I wandered under Wilson's Arch, I noticed that I too was crying. I rarely cry. I am not by my very nature a weeper. Yet there I was walking through strangers in a strange place hearing strange sounds with tears falling down my face. It would not be the last time I would cry in Israel, but it was the first and most memorable time. It was then I realized that my heart had become very sad over what I was witnessing. After that night in the shadow of the Wailing Wall I decided I knew the answer to Ezekiel's question printed above: the city of Jerusalem! Between 1948 and 1967 the Jews had been denied access to the Wall because it had come under Jordanian rule. After Israel regained control of the Wall there has been a constant vigil at the Wall. During our seven-day stay in Jerusalem we walked to the Wall or near the Wall many times and there was always a crowd. Each time a tear came to my heart if not to my eye. Jeremiah also wrote:

For a voice of wailing is heard out of Zion...." (Jeremiah 9:19)

I heard that voice while I was there and what made we weep was their Messiah had come to take that weeping and wailing away. I looked into the empty faces of the men who were at the Wall that night; simply going through the motion as if by "their much speaking" and "vain repetitions" (Matthew 6:7) they would be heard. I know now why my Saviour the Lord Jesus Christ had wept over this place and its people. (Luke 19:41) I left the plaza after about twenty minutes, but on our way back to the Knight's Palace we stopped at another place closer to my faith that would also cause my spirit to wail.

Our walk back took us up Muristan Street past the Church of the Redeemer (a site we would return to later in the trip) and into another plaza. As we passed under the archway into the courtyard of the Holy Sepulcher (the church contains the Chapel of Golgotha, where Jesus was believed to have been crucified, the Stone Unction, were Jesus' body was believed to have been washed after his death, the Chapel of the Holy Sepulcher, where Jesus was believed to have been laid in a tomb, the Greek Cathedral, the Chapel of Apparition, where they believe Jesus appeared to Mary, and the Chapel of Invention of the Cross, where they believe the 'true cross' was discovered) it was nearly nine in the evening. Marnie and I had been traveling for nearly two days now with little sleep and that could have added to the depression that ascended on me. The courtyard was barely lit, and the crowd was small. The ancient church (the first church was built in 336, demolished in 614, rebuilt in 616 and destroyed in 969 to be rebuilt again in 1037; in 1056 the Crusaders erected a large Romanesque church embracing all holy places and chapels; this church was destroyed in 1244, rebuilt in 1310, restored in 1400 and 1717, destroyed again in 1810 and rebuilt in its present form in 1810) was cold and lifeless. I watched as an Arab (the story is that the various Christian group that claim this site could never agree on who would have the responsibility to open and close the church, so they chose a neutral party to do the job, and for a number of generations this certain family has possessed the keys to the church!) climb an old ladder to lock the front door of this famous church. The same lifeless expressions I saw at the Wall were there as well. Motions created after years and decades and centuries of rites and rituals to a Saviour believed in without the joyous experience of a personal relationship. Isaiah described these Jews and Christian's best when he records the Almighty saying:

> Wherefore the Lord said, Forasmuch as this people draw near to me with their mouth, and with their lips do honour me, but have removed their hearts far from me. . . . ." (Isaiah 29:13)

Is there anything sadder than a religious individual with no concept of the relationship his God wants to have with him?

5

Views from the Bulwarks

Isaiah 26:1-2—In that day shall this song be sung in the land of Judah; we have a strong city; salvation will God appoint for WALLS AND BULWARKS. Open Ye THE GATES that the righteous nation which keepeth the truth may enter in.

As I stood looking out the window of our 405 room at the Knight's Palace, I noticed that our morning walk would take us past the courtyard of our ancient motel. According to our trip schedule, we were to walk the ramparts of the old city this morning. It was an early six a.m. as I watched Jerusalem rise after another peaceful night's rest, only one of few she has had over her thousands of years of a turbulent history. It was then I was overwhelmed with the reality that I had just awakened in Jerusalem. Now before my very eyes was the greatest concentration of history that I had ever personally witnessed. I was actually where so many of my favorite Biblical and historical events had taken place. The wall that I would walk to view this famous city was just outside my window. I had for years read about the famous individuals, who had come 'here', but now I was 'here'; and as I was to discover on this trip, it is inspiring to be 'there', and being 'there' makes all the difference in truly understanding 'how', and yes, even 'why'? Here within the confines of my view were the answers to so many of Biblical mysteries, and I couldn't wait to see my questions answered.

Before we could start walking the Bible, however, we had to listen to our first official lecture of the trip. This was an actual college level course so there had to be classroom time. That first lecture was an overview of the history, geography, and topography of Jerusalem. Despite the desire to go walking, I did enjoy the lesson. I was not taking the class for credit as was my daughter and many others on the team, but for me the information was helpful. I had studied the material for years, even taught a class on the geography of Jerusalem in one of my Evening School courses, but the subject matter is so vast you can always learn and that morning in the Knight's Palace conference room I learned a lot. In particular, I was interested in the next part of our travels into the old city, or should I say on top of the old city. We were about to embark to the Jaffa Gate where we would climb up to the top of a walkway that snakes its way around the circumference of the Ottoman bulwarks: thirty-four towers, two and a half miles of walls, and eight gates make up the fortress that surrounds Old Jerusalem today!

Our walk began at the Jaffa Gate, or 'the gate of the friend' (Isaiah 41:1) and would end at the Lion's Gate (named because of the stone lions craved near its mouth), or sometimes called 'Stephen's Gate'. Church tradition teaches that it was through this gate that the Church's first martyr was taken to be stoned outside the city. (Acts 7:58) A church has been built on a site just down the hill from the entrance of the gate to remember the death of the Church's first deacon (Acts 6:5). We would actually only walk on the wall for half of its length, but what sights we saw and what memories still linger from that mid-morning walk back through time.

As Greg began to point out the places within our line of sight, the Bible began to shrink in my mind's eye. I had been raised to recognize the places of the Bible, but for me they were always huge in nature and great in distance. Jerusalem was a New York to me, but on Wednesday May 12, 2010 my Biblical world got smaller, actually very small. As we worked our way along the western side of the city leaving the Citadel and Jaffa Gate behind, we passed the Knight's Palace and turned the corner onto the northern wall by New Gate (created in 1887 to give pilgrims easy access to the Holy Sepulcher). From the northern wall we could see the new city growing and expanding, but as I reminded my fellow pilgrims often on the trip, I had not come for modern but antiquity! It wasn't long after we turned another corner that the old became very clear to me. By the time we had arrived at the tower over the Damascus Gate my mind had relived the history books I had read; about how many times this series of knolls had been captured and sacked and destroyed only to be rebuilt to be captured and pillaged and razed again and again. I recalled the Biblical invaders like Shishak of Egypt (II Chronicles 12:9), Sennacherib of Assyria (II Chronicles 32:1), and Nebuchadnezzar of Babylon (II Chronicles 36:7). Then there were the little known invaders like Antiochus Epiphanus, Pompey, and Titus each leaving their mark on this city. Even after its destruction in 70 AD; there followed a series of invaders to this isolated, rocky mountaintop between the surrounding valleys; the Persians, the Saracens, the Turks, the Crusaders, the Ottomans whose ramparts and bulwarks I was walking upon. They had all come and gone, but the city remains. As Vance Havner once put it:

> Gory is its past, glorious is its future!

And there before my eyes as we turned the corner from the northern wall to the eastern wall I was viewing Nob (I Samuel 21:1) where David first fled to escape the wrath of King Saul. It was so close, and there just a short distance away was the Mount of Olives. What I had imagined as miles was only feet away; all visible on a clear, cloudless day. A Mediterranean breeze kept us comfortable as we stopped and viewed the city, both its insides and its outsides from high on top of the Ottoman walls. We had crawled over countless towers and passed over four gates. We were shown famous chapels and churches, modern buildings like the King David Motel, and as we made our way off the rampart by the Lion Gate, but I have one more view to record. How you view Jerusalem depends greatly on your guide, and I am not talking about Dr. Behle, or Dr. Hilber.

What I witnessed from the roof of Jerusalem was the triumphal entry of Christ from the Mount of Olives through the Kidron Valley and into the city by the eastern gate. I watched as the Passion Week played out in the streets on the top of Mount Moriah—seen from just about every angle from off the rampart. I watched my Saviour die on Golgotha's knoll (now covered by a dome), but from just a few yards away from a borrowed tomb He rose again on the most famous 'third day' in history. From the view, I saw Christ's ascension back to the Father, and watched as the Holy Spirit descended to this very hilltop to start the Church. Everything I think important, not only of the past, but also of the future could be seen from where I walked and gazed that morning in Jerusalem. I read a lot of the importance of having a clear view through 'the window on the world'. It is not that window we should be concerned about, but 'the window of the Word'. Some might think I was impressed with dusty old Jerusalem, the rocks and rubble, the walls and gates, ramparts and bulwarks, but if you think that, you will have missed what stirred me so. My views from the walls were not of an ordinary tourist taking a tour, a foreign student taking a class while on a trip through a beaten and battered city ravaged by centuries of abuse and misuse. What I relived was my spiritual past in living color and my spiritual future in living hope. I have seen where my Lord will return, and where I will rule and reign with Him for a thousand years! (Zechariah 14:1–4 and Revelation 1:6, 20:6). From that wall that day I viewed eternity, and with Vance Havner I agree:

> I came a long way to see this view but what a distance He traveled to provide it!

6

Down the *Via Dolorosa*

John 19:16–17—Then delivered he (Pilate) Him therefore unto them to be crucified. And they took Jesus, AND LED HIM AWAY. AND HE BEARING HIS CROSS WENT FORTH INTO A PLACE called the place of the skull, which is called in the Hebrew Golgotha.

It is hard to put together a first century story even in a sixteenth century place. One of my goals during my Israel trip was to retrace the steps of Jesus on that meaningful Friday of His monumental death. I knew in my heart that the trail He trod was under layers and centuries of time and turf, but as we left the ramparts at Stephen's Gate (some believe the old sheep's gate of Nehemiah 3:1) we stepped onto the most famous lane in history: the Via Dolorosa.

Within feet of our exit, we turned into a lovely garden and church (Saint Anne's) complex known in the Biblical text as 'the pool of Bethesda' (John 5:2). Again modern man has turned the area into a shrine and a money maker, but it was still a quiet and pleasant interlude from the busy streets of the Arab Quarter. We only stayed a short while; long enough to read the story of the healing of the palsy man and wander the area looking for the pool. They have dug up the ruins (some of the five porches can be seen in the rocks), but no water remains and with it seemingly the miracles. The chapel was very simple unlike many of the other Jerusalem churches. I did enjoy a European group as they sang hymns, and psalms, and spiritual songs in the chapel of Saint Anne's Church. As I left the church area for the stone covered street of the Via Dolorosa, I imagined in my mind what I knew from Scripture of Jesus' famous walk.

We know that Jesus left the Antonia, (I believe that scholarship backs up tradition in the belief that Christ's trial took place in the Fortress of Antonia. Unlike the other sides of Jerusalem which are protected by deep valleys, the northern approaches to the city are defenseless. Even in the days of Nehemiah a strong fortress was built north of the Temple (Nehemiah 2:8). Years later the Maccabeans built a fort there, and when Herod came into power he rebuilt on the site the Antonia, named after his good friend Mark Antony (of Cleopatra fame!), and in particular the Praetorium (Mark 15:16) or the Pavement (John 19:13) or Gabbatha) sometime about mid-morning on that fateful Friday (John 19:14). The modern day Via Dolorosa is very near the site of this old fortress. When we came off the wall we were just a few yards from the northern retaining wall of the Temple Mount. There remains to this day an arch (Ecce Homo-Behold, the Man (John 19:5) in Latin) built by Hadrian (told you I liked this man) in a palace he built there in 135 AD. Also the traditional 'walk' begins in front of the Franciscan Monastery of Flagellation. So it is at least in the general area where no doubt Jesus was condemned. The question that remains to be answered is: did Jesus walk north or west?

If you travel north today up the Al-Calisaya through the Arab Quarter to Herod's Gate, you exit the city very near to a place they call Gordon's Calvary which is outside the 16th century city. According to the Bible the place of Christ's death was outside the walls of the city and near a highway with a garden nearby (Luke 23:33, John 19:17, 18, 41, Matthew 27:33). This site wasn't recognized as Calvary until the nineteenth century, despite the fact that it looks and feels more like Calvary than the traditional site at the Holy Sepulcher. But a western turn took us down the Via Dolorosa (the way of suffering or the way of the cross) through the old city and to a place most feel was located outside the old walls in the days of Jesus; to a rocky knoll that is now well within the walls and covered by a cathedral and a number of chapels. Because the current street is much higher than the early first century street, it is impossible to verify the traditional 'stations of the cross'. There are markers that recognize the arch over the street where Pilate gave Jesus to the crowd, (John 19:5) where Jesus received the cross, (Luke 23:26) where Simon of Cyrenean was enlisted to help Jesus, (Matthew 27:32) where Jesus spoke to the women of Jerusalem (Luke 23:27–31) and the like. The last five stations are found inside the Holy Sepulcher itself. Because the first chapel was built over this site in the 3rd century most hold that despite the appearance this is probably the original Calvary.

Together we walked down the Via Dolorosa until we came to a major intersection of streets. (On the corner was a small chapel (3rd station of the cross) commemorating where Jesus fell under the load of the cross. There is a marble relief over the door of this chapel picturing this scene.) It was just after noon so we stopped again for lunch. It was under the shadow of the Holy Sepulcher that I ate my first Falafel, considered the national snack food of Israel. It was only proper that we would stop our sacred pilgrimage to the most holy site in Christendom to shop and snack. I was deeply moved by the commercialism that surrounds Christianity in Jerusalem (they even put us Americans to shame on Sunday) and nothing illustrates this concept more than deep fried chick-peas! Consisting of ground chick-peas blended with coriander, garlic, cumin, cayenne pepper, and salt, this mixture is then formed into small balls about an inch and a quarter in diameter. The ball is then deep fried for two to three minutes; placed in pita bread and garnished with whatsoever your imagination can think up. As we waited to walk the final yards to Calvary, we ate Jewish and thought Christian. (My falafel on the corner of Al-Wad Road and the Via Dolorosa was my first and last!)

After lunch we continued our trek through the narrow Via Dolorosa and the increasing crowds. We first passed the Armenian Church of Our Lady of the Spasm which had been built over a Crusader church supposedly honoring the time Mary met Jesus on the road. There is no Biblical evidence that Mary saw Jesus until Jesus was on the Cross (John 19:25–27). We then passed the Franciscan oratory (a small chapel) celebrating the place Simon of Cyrene started helping Jesus carry the Cross. Just a few feet further was another Franciscan chapel were Jesus was believed to have fallen again (no Biblical evidence for this event). The next event to be commemorated was Jesus' consoling the women of Jerusalem (Luke 23:28). Today, a Latin cross on the wall of a Greek Orthodox Monastery marks the supposed spot? Just before the courtyard of the Holy Sepulchre is an Ethiopian Monastery where Jesus was believed to have fallen a third time; once again there is no Biblical evidence for this event either.

By the time we arrived at the courtyard, the vendors were so thick we could hardly get through. Unlike the night before, there was a huge crowd both inside and outside the massive domed structure. Entering through the single door we came across the station called the rock of preparation; where they believe Jesus body was prepared for crucifixion; women were weeping and washing the stone with their tears as we entered. Walls were lined with burning candles, and the place was covered in icons and lamps and altars beyond imagination. For me the whole atmosphere felt idolatrous, even verging on blasphemous. Inside the huge church was a smaller chapel which we were told actually contained 'The Tomb'. The line was so long we never got a chance to step inside. There were a few other tombs in the back they claimed were like the one in the small chapel, and as for Calvary? The line was so long leading to Golgotha that Marnie and I were only able to get a picture on the steps leading to its top from the outside of the church. I did get a postcard of the inside of the chapel at Calvary, and it was just more of the same.

You have to imagine with me, the entire area is covered in churches, chapels, sanctuaries of every form of Christianity invented since the first century. Even the Ethiopians have a presence on top of the buildings. I was saddened by what I saw, heard, touched, smelled, and experienced. I John 1:1 came flooding back to me, and I realized that my Israel journey would produce both blessed and bitter experiences. A bitter taste came to my spirit not because of the seemingly dedication and devotion of these people, but because they have changed the glory of what my Saviour did for us in this place into images made by man. Like Paul wrote of the ungodly, they have

> . . . changed the truth of God into a lie, and worshipped and serve the creature more than the Creator . . . (Romans 1:25)

Needless to say, my trip down the Via Dolorosa was not the most memorable of our pilgrimage, for I am afraid I will have to call it the most meaningless walk of the tour! I loved going to Israel, but some aspects of my faith I wish could have remained the way I imagined them to be. Now when I hear that grand Easter song, "Down The Via Dolorosa", I no longer watch my Saviour as I once did, but instead I see a vendor and merchant lined street where selling is the center of attraction, not the Saviour!

7

An Evening at the Dung Gate

Nehemiah 12:31 — Then I brought up the princes of Judah upon the wall, and appointed two great companies of them that gave thanks, whereof one went on the right hand upon the wall toward THE DUNG GATE.

After the disappointing discoveries at the Holy Sepulcher, we continued our walk through the old city making these stops:

1. At the Cardo (more about this place in another observation) where the Romans had their market place, we stopped at the four quarters (where the Christian, Armenian, Moslem, and Jewish Quarters meet). We actually went up on somebody's roof for the four-corner view of the old city.

2. We stopped at the traditional site of the Upper Room (an ancient Gothic building-all that is left of a large church constructed by the Crusaders, but Church tradition maintains that under this site was where Christ shared his last meal with His disciples). It was an upper room, but only another attempt by someone to make a Biblical place a tourist attraction!

3. At David's Tomb (located beneath the Hall of the Last Supper), but once again the place was far from David's Jerusalem, and most feel the grave is that of a crusader of the 11th or 12th century.

4. We walked outside the city walls at Zion Gate to see the grave of German-born Oscar Schindler, of "Schindler's List" (Steven Spielberg's 1993 movie) fame, but the cemetery was closed. Schindler was a business man who, during the Second World War, went out of his way to

use Jewish prisoners in his factory. He is given credit for the saving of over 1000 Jews from the gas chambers. When he died in 1974, he asked to be buried in Jerusalem!

5. We then followed the wall back towards our motel passing again Jaffa Gate before we entered New Gate.

We had walked from 9:30 AM to 4:30 PM in the up and down streets and walls of the old city. We had seen a lot on our second day in Jerusalem, but Marnie and I were not through walking or exploring.

As we set at supper in the dining room of the Knight's Palace, we began to discuss our options for our second free evening in Israel. We certainly had walked a lot and seen a lot on this day around the walls of the old city. Most of our group was going to rest, but Marnie and I decided that we hadn't come to Israel to rest. There were still sections of the wall and a number of gates we hadn't seen that day; so after our evening meal we decided to walk to a section of the wall we hadn't seen and in particular the section from the Dung Gate to the Lion Gate which would also include the Eastern Gate. Who would ever spend an evening looking for a dung gate?

One of my fascinations of the Bible has been 'the gates of Jerusalem'. "The Lord loveth the gates of Zion more than all the dwellings of Jacob." (Psalms 87:2) When you study the Bible you will discover that Jerusalem's 'gates' are more famous than its geography, its hills, yes, more famous than its walls. What makes these gates so unique is the history of their names:

Ephraim Gate (II Kings 14:13)

Corner Gate (II Chronicles 26:9)

Joshua Gate (II Kings 23:8)

King Gate (I Chronicles 9:18)

Shallecheth Gate (I Chronicles 26:16)

Foundation Gate (II Chronicles 23:5)

Horse Gate (Jeremiah 31:40)

Valley Gate (Nehemiah 2:15)

Fish Gate (Zephaniah 1:10)

Fountain Gate (Nehemiah 12:37)

Sheep Gate (Nehemiah 12:39)

Old Gate (Nehemiah 3:6)

Water Gate (Nehemiah 8:1) (no, not the one in Washington D.C.)

East Gate (Jeremiah 19:2)

Miphkad Gate (Nehemiah 3:31)

Prison Gate (Nehemiah 12:39)

High Gate (Jeremiah 20:2)

New Gate (Jeremiah 36:10)

Benjamin Gate (Zechariah 14:10)

Middle Gate (Jeremiah 39:3)

First Gate (Zephaniah 14:10)

And the infamous Dung Gate (Nehemiah 3:13, 14)

Even the New Jerusalem (Revelation 21:10) will have gates (Revelation 21:13), and each of these gates will be named after the twelve tribes of Israel (Revelation 21:12), so we must add to our list of names: Reuben Gate, Simeon Gate, Levi Gate, Judah Gate, Issachar Gate, Zebulun Gate, Dan Gate, Naphtali gate, Gad Gate, Asher Gate, and Joseph Gate; and Benjamin Gate has already been listed above.

Today's Jerusalem contains only eight gates with only seven of them actual entrances into the city: Jaffa in the west wall, Lion and Golden in the east wall, Herod, Damascus, and New in the north wall, and Dung and Zion in the south wall. Marnie and I were off to find the Dung Gate and exit through it to find the most famous gate of all, the Golden, sometimes called the eastern, or Beautiful Gate (Acts 3:2). Some people believe that when the Turks closed off this gate it ties into the fulfillment of Ezekiel's prophecy which has to do with the second coming of Christ (Ezekiel 44:1–3)!

Our evening walk to the Dung Gate took us through the Armenian Quarter past the Cathedral of Saint James, another massive church. Once we hit the southern wall near Zion Gate, we turned eastward toward the Jewish Quarter. We hadn't gotten into that section very long when we noticed the crowds were increasing and everyone looked like a teenager. Little did Marnie and I know that day (May 12, 2010) was the beginning of Jerusalem Days: an annual celebration in which young people from all over Israel are brought to Jerusalem to highlight the significance of the city to their country? We were soon to realize that the main entrance to the Western Wall plaza was through the Dung Gate, go figure!

From Dan to Beersheba and Beyond

The flow of people only got worse the closer we got to our goal. We even left the street to walk on the wall as we had done in the morning, but the crowds of young people milling around only got worse. As the sun was setting, we watched from the ramparts the groups of young people singing and marching their way to the Wall. We barely got through the Dung Gate as we attempted to walk the roadway toward the Eastern Gate. Israeli security guards had blocked off all streets around the old city and the roadways had become walkways to the thousands now streaming towards Israel's most famous shrine. For a few minutes we tried to fight the flow coming in our direction, but we eventually gave up the fight and turned (the Eastern Gate would have to wait for another day) and we were carried along by the river of people heading back to the Dung Gate. We knew our goal for the evening was beyond reach so we headed back the way we came to the Knight's Palace.

Each street back to the palace was literally blocked with hundreds upon hundreds of teenagers and tourists. Marnie and I decided that it was the worst crowd we had ever been in. We took St. James Street to Ararat Street hoping to bypass the main lane up through the Armenian Quarter. We finally made David's Street but once again we were met with a flood of people celebrating. It was then our attention was drawn to an elderly couple trying to make their way through the sea of humanity. Their speech told us they were from Europe, and our common problem bound us together despite the fact we couldn't understand each other. I told Marnie to take my hand, and she in turned motioned to the couple to take her hand and we slowly crawled our way up David Street hugging the wall on the left side of the lane. After about 10 minutes we emerged at the Jaffa Gate, just a few corners away from our home away from home. The couple gave us a big smile and I took a photograph of Marnie and the husband and wife before they headed back to their place of rest; then we made our way quickly up the side alley to the Knight's Palace.

That night from our motel window we watched and heard the celebration fireworks of Jerusalem Days from the Jewish Quarter, a fitting salute to our evening walk to the Dung Gate and beyond!

8

Hezekiah's Tunnel

II Chronicles 32:30—This same Hezekiah also stopped THE UPPER WATERCOURSE OF GIHON, AND BROUGHT IT STRAIGHT DOWN to the west side of the city of David. And Hezekiah prospered in all his works.

After another wonderful night's rest at the Knight's Palace, we were off again to explore the ancient ruins of old Jerusalem. I was excited beyond measure because today I would fulfill an age old dream of actually walking through one of the great engineering wonders of the ancient world: Hezekiah's Tunnel.

Before we headed for 'the city of David' (which is now located outside the current walls of Jerusalem), we walked our way through the Cardo to an archeological site just discovered. With the Jews modernizing Jerusalem, they have unearthed some amazing sites from the Jerusalem of the past. One such site was the discovery of Hezekiah's 'broad wall':

> And he (Hezekiah) strengthened himself, and built up all the wall that was broken, and raised it up to the towers, AND ANOTHER WALL WITHOUT, and repaired Millo in the city of David, and made darts and shields in abundance." (II Chronicles 32:5)

A section of this wall has been left as they found it, and it was a marvelous introduction to where we were heading next.

Our morning journey took us once again past the Western Wall and through the Dung Gate, little did we know! Unlike the night before the streets outside the wall were filled with cars and trucks and buses and few people. We were heading for Ophel, the eastern hill that overlooks the Kidron Valley, directly south of Temple Mount. Many believe this is where the ancient city of Jebus was located, the original conquest of David. King Jotham rebuilt much of the wall in his day (II Chronicles 27:3) and King Manasseh only added to it in his kingship (II Chronicles 33:14). Nehemiah would also repair the walls on its ridge after the Babylonian Captivity (Nehemiah 3:26–27). The famous Spring of Gihon is located on the eastern side of this hill, our destination.

The City of David today is a massive archeological dig. All along the ridge people are digging. One of the objects of their search is for the real tomb of David, and maybe, some of the other kings of Israel. We were on a schedule because we had a start time to walk through the most amazing discovery on the tel, the fully restored water tunnel mined by King Hezekiah's men. Groups can only walk through the tunnel by appointment, so as we waited our turn we wandered around the site and heard details about 'the heart-beat of Jerusalem': Gihon Spring.

It was through a water shaft from the Spring Gihon that David's men lead by Joab were believed to have gained entrance to the impregnable fortress of Jebus (II Samuel 5:6–8). I had read about Warren's Shaft (the man who first discovered it) for years, and now I was going to be able to see it for myself. Greg took us to a site just over the spring where the Bible tells us that Solomon was crowned king (I Kings 1:32–40). Throughout the history of Jerusalem, the spring of Gihon had provided water to the people behind the walls. It was in the days of King Hezekiah that an attempt was made to actually bring the water into the city. Hezekiah's engineers planned to cut a tunnel through solid rock, and if done correctly, the natural slope of the hill would allow the water from the spring to flow unobstructed to a pool Hezekiah would build at the base of the hill:

> And the rest of the acts of Hezekiah, and all his might, and how he made A POOL, AND A CONDUIT, and brought water into the city, are they not written in the book of the chronicles of the kings of Judah? (II Kings 20:20)

We know that pool today by the name Siloam (John 9:7)!

At 11 o'clock we entered the tunnel leading to the spring. Our descent took us through sections where the exploration is still going on, including the massive walls Hezekiah built around the spring to protect it. Eventually we made our way past Warren's Shaft, and then under our feet was the spring itself, still flowing crystal clear as it has done for thousands of years. It was at this point we literally stepped into the spring and began walking through this amazing tunnel-stream. As I walked along in complete darkness, the tunnel only illumined by my headlight and the flashlights of those ahead and behind me, I recalled the story of the 'tunnel'. History tells us that Hezekiah ordered his men, one group starting at the spring and the other at the newly created pool to dig towards each other. Periodically the groups would stop to listen for the other group changing their course periodically. I noticed as we walked that the tunnel changed direction at times. We don't know how long it took, but eventually the two groups met and the water flowed downhill emptying into the pool. The 1800 foot conduit took us about 25 minutes to travel. Sometimes we were in hip deep water, but most of the time just above our ankles. Sometimes the tunnel was so narrow that you brushed your shoulders on each side, and at other times two people could stand side by side. Sometimes the tunnel was so low you had to bend down to get through and at other times the roof of the conduit seemed 15 feet high. As you walk through the subterranean tunnel, you sense the S-shaped course as it makes its way through solid rock. A modern engineer has determined that if the builders of the tunnel could have constructed the tunnel in a straight line they could have saved nearly 700 feet of difficult digging!

When we emerged we were at an old Byzantine pool. The original Pool of Siloam is just being dug out today. They have uncovered stone steps leading to the pool, but the water of the Gihon has been diverted in another direction. Years ago as some experts were examining the passageway we had just travelled through, they noticed through the light of their torches an inscription (one of the oldest ever found written in the Hebrew language) carved on the rocks just a few feet from the entrance of the tunnel by the Pool of Siloam. This is what it said:

> The boring through is completed. And this is the story of the boring: while yet they plied the pick, each toward his fellow, and while yet there was three cubits to bored through, there was heard the voice of one calling to the other that there was a hole in the rock on the right hand and on the left hand. And on the day of the boring through the workers in the tunnel struck each to meet his fellow, pick upon pick. Then the water poured from the source (Gihon Spring) to the pool (Siloam Pool) twelve hundred cubits, and a hundred cubits was the height of the rock above the heads of the workers of the tunnel.

The Turkish government removed this inscription before the First World War and it can be seen in a museum in Istanbul to this day!

What inspired me so much about this walk is the fact that after thousands of years this piece of Biblical history is untouched. They have changed Calvary, the gates of Jerusalem, the Upper Room, but the tunnel of Hezekiah remains a testimony to the marvelous things recorded in the Bible. While waiting our bus ride back to our motel, Marnie and I ate magnum bars (ice cream has always been Marnie's and my way of celebrating a great adventure together, whether under the Eiffel Tower in Paris, an eating place in Kerala, India, or at the foot of Hezekiah's Tunnel in Jerusalem) and concluded that so far for us Hezekiah's Tunnel was the best part of the trip!

9

Jesus' Jerusalem

Luke 2:22—And when the days of her purification according to the Law of Moses were accomplished, they brought him (Jesus) TO JERUSALEM, to present him to the Lord.

After our amazing journey through Hezekiah's spectacular tunnel, we boarded our bus for another breath-taking experience. We were off through the traffic-filled streets of the new city; our destination was the Jerusalem Museum (built in 1965 on a ridge overlooking West Jerusalem, containing some of the country's finest pieces of art and archaeology). We were to see the famous collection of Dead Sea Scrolls (more later when we visit Qumran), and a large scale-model of Jesus' Jerusalem.

Many years ago a Mr. Kroch began the construction of a 1/50 scale-model of Herod's Jerusalem, the Jerusalem that Jesus would have visited first as an eight-day old baby (Luke 2:21), then as a 12-year old child (Luke 2:42), and many times as an adult (Luke 4:9). The archaeological and topographical data was supplied by a Professor M. Avi-Yonah of the Hebrew University, who also supervised the building of this amazing model of Old Jerusalem. This model was first built on the grounds of the Holyland Hotel before it was moved to its present site at the Jerusalem Museum. Over the years with each new archeological discovery this model has been changed to reflect the current understanding of what Jerusalem would have been like in the early days of the first century. There beside the unique structure (its roof looks like the lid of a clay pot) built to house the Dead Sea Scrolls is this massive model of ancient Jerusalem as it once sat on top of Mount Zion and Mount Moriah; to the west the

Kidron Valley and to the east the Hinnom Valley. Surrounded by walls and ramparts and towers (our tour started at the octagonal Psephinus Tower, situated at the northwestern corner of the Third Wall, and according to Josephus one could see both the Mediterranean Sea and the mountains of Arabia from its 115 foot height) this model highlights the old sections of the city, like the city of David or the Ophel Ridge. Located south of Mount Moriah, where Herod built his colossal temple, David's city was where we had just been in our walk through Hezekiah's underground world. It was here Herod had also built his impressive Hippodrome, like the Roman circus, for chariot races. The spectators would sit on stair-like seats around the central space, and the horses would race around them!

Also clearly seen in the model was the lower city, where thirty to forty thousand of the poorest people might have lived. It was in this section of the city that the Pool of Siloam was built at the bottom of the Tyropoeon Valley, or Central Valley. (Most recognize the Kidron and Hinnom Valleys, but Jerusalem once contained a third valley. The Tyropoeon Valley once ran down through the middle of Old Jerusalem separating the western hill (Zion) from the eastern hill (Ophel), until over time it was filled in!) Tyropoeon means "valley of the cheese makers" and may be the 'mactesh' of Zephaniah 1:1, or the 'valley' mentioned in Nehemiah 2:15. This valley was still very distinct in the day of the Jewish historian Josephus, for he mentions in his book on the Jewish Wars this valley as separating the upper and the lower city and ending at the Pool of Siloam. It was as if Marnie and I had been transported in a time machine to the very spot we last explored to this bird's eye view of how it was two thousand years before our visit.

To the west of the lower city was a perfect model of the upper city where the rich and famous had their homes built on Mount Zion; even Herod had built a fabulous palace (where Jesus was taken on the night of His trial-Luke 23:7–12) on the brow of the hill that overlooked the entire city. It was very distinct because of the three massive towers on its northern wall. The Phasael Tower was named after Herod's brother and rose 148 feet above the skyline. Then there was the Hippicus Tower, named after a friend of Herod standing 132 feet above the ridge. Finally, there was the Tower of Mariamme (it was 74 feet high), named after Herod's beloved wife whom he had murdered because she had become more popular than him in the eyes of the people! Herod's Palace consisted of two main buildings, each with its own banquet halls, baths, and room for hundreds of guests. It was surrounded by groves of trees, canals, and ponds studded with bronze fountains. It was also separated from the city itself by a wall and towers. Herod feared his own people most! It was also in this section of the town that Herod built a beautiful theatre, and near by the archaeologists believe was Ananias' palace, where Jesus was first taken after his arrest (John 18:13). In the same area was Caiaphas' palace, where Jesus was tried before the Sanhedrin (Matthew 26:57). Behind this palace was a monument built marking the site of the tomb of David (yes, another place) because the location of the real tomb on the south-eastern hill (Ophel) had been lost!

Dividing the two southern sections of the city from the northern part of the city was a wall called the First Wall. (To the north of Jerusalem, the city was defended by three walls because this was the most vulnerable side of the city. While a single wall was sufficient on the remaining sides because of the deep valleys surrounding them, the northern side had to be protected in depth.) This separated the residential part of the city from the business section of the city. The newer area of the city in Jesus' day was being expanded to the north of the business district, and there before our eyes we could see the entire northern ridge enclosed by a wall and the new homes being constructed. With each discovery an additional part of the model is being built, so different sections are being added periodically as each archeological dig discovers something new about Jesus' Jerusalem.

Dominating the entire model is the massive temple area on Mount Moriah. Herod literally reshaped the ridge and hill line to make room for his version of God's Temple. The southern retaining wall would eventually rise 200 feet ("the pinnacle of the temple" [Matthew 4:5] were Jesus was tempted of the Devil). The area would enclose a flat surface of 1,200 feet long and 800 feet wide. There in the middle was the beautiful structure known as the Third Temple. If one didn't look around, one would think that they were back in Jesus' day traveling through the streets and lanes of the city of Herod. All the recognizable buildings beside the Temple could easily be seen from any side of the model. There just to the north of the temple mount was the Antonia, Herod's famous fort, and just north of that the famous Pool of Bethesda with its five porches (John 5:2). The architects of this model left nothing to the imagination, and as Greg took us around the model and pointed out the various Biblical places well known to us through the Gospels; it was like we were walking with Jesus and seeing for the first time what our Saviour saw when He would travel to Jerusalem. There in the shadow of the Knesset (constructed with the red stone native to the area, this is where the Israeli parliament of 120 members meet) Building (finished in 1966 at a cost of seven million dollars, the structure was paid through a gift from the family of James de Rothschild of England), we could look down and see old Jerusalem and look up and see the modern state of Israel developing before our eyes.

Around 4:45 PM, we boarded our bus for the fifteen minute ride back to the Jaffa Gate and supper. As we snaked our way through rush-hour traffic, I had time to reflect on what I had just experienced at the Jerusalem model and how it had forever changed my understanding and imagery of Jesus' trips to Jerusalem. I like most am a hostage to my western ways. I think like a westerner and I interpret mostly everything with a distinct western slant. I come from a large land and big cities, but Israel is both small and tiny. To shrink my Biblical world to a 1/50 scale was exactly what I needed to bring into perspective my Saviour's world. They say that Jesus never traveled more than 200 miles from his birth (even including the trip to Egypt). I once knew of that kind of world. When I was a kid I stayed within 60 miles of my birth for the first 18 years of my life, except for a weekend trip to Boston to see my beloved Red Sox play. One of the things I have forgotten since I headed off to South Carolina for college is that there is a difference between a world view and a local view. Don't get me wrong, Jesus came to die for the sins of the whole world, but while He was waiting to die He lived within the boundaries of a very small world. All my life I have been trying to escape my local restrictions for the freedom of that far off and distant place, why?

Was Jesus trying to teach us something by the limitations He put on Himself? Was He trying to show us that our world is local and not distant? That we ought to be working and living within the confines of Barry's Ellsworth, Barry's Hancock County, Barry's Maine as He did in His Jerusalem, His Galilee, His Israel? As Marnie and I ate our supper at the Knight's Palace that third night in Jerusalem, we realized that we were beginning to change our thought patterns in relationship to what we once understood to be Biblical; that we were being radically changed in how we understood not only the Scriptures, but our Saviour as well. Our walk around a model had made us rethink just how our Christ ministered as well as died, because for me the most sobering aspect of the model could be seen in the very middle of this impressive site. Just outside a gate to the north of Herod's Palace and to the west of the Antonia the creators of this model had placed a single rock. It stood out because it was isolated from any other structure. At first I didn't notice it because I was taken aback by the sheer beauty and size of the city. I had walked the entire circumference of the model before I was moved by the simplicity of the stone. Unlike the other sacred sites we had traveled to, this spoke to me. I had finally, after 50 years in the Faith, come face to face with Calvary. In the scope of this unbelievable model, the insignificance became to me the most significant of all!

10

The Burnt House of Kathros

Luke 19:41—And when he (Jesus) was come near, he beheld the city, AND WEPT OVER IT.

Our 4th day in Jerusalem began with breakfast at the Knight's Palace, and a morning stroll to our first stop of the day: the burnt house of Kathros. I am always surprised by what moves me and what I am so unmoved by! After three full days in Jerusalem, I was beginning to establish in my heart an opinion on what I saw as commercial and entertaining and what I saw as spiritual and meaningful. I thought I would be moved by the Upper Room, the Holy Sepulcher, the Shrine of the Book, and the Tomb of David, but I wasn't. They were just sights, stops, and sites. I was beginning to realize that it was the unexpected, the unknown, and often unnoticed places that were really touching my heart and soul on this trip, like the unexpected emotion I exhibited in an archeological site in the old upper city!

The tour of the Jerusalem model the day before had prepared me for what I would experience as we stopped to wait the opening of The Burnt House Museum on the Cardo early that warm morning in the old city. Where we were standing that morning was two thousand years before a part of the Upper City section of Jerusalem. It was given that name because it stood higher than the Temple Mount which still can be seen from its slopes. Between the two famous spots was an important commercial area called 'the cheese makers valley', where the Western Wall Plaza is located today. As we waited for the doors to open, we had a marvelous view down onto this active plaza. Historically, this area of the city withstood the 70 AD siege of the Romans an additional month after the Temple was destroyed.

One of the reasons this section held out longer was the sophisticated drainage system running under the rich homes located there. During the Great Revolt these tunnels were used to hide Jewish soldiers and this network of underground passageways was used for communicating with other parts of the city and eventually escapes for some. Josephus Flavius, the famous Jewish historian, writes this in his monumental book, The Jewish War:

> The rebels . . . escaped . . . one by one they disappeared into the tunnels . . . the Romans were puzzled because they could not find their enemies . . . they burnt the houses with all who had taken refuge within . . .

Interestingly, one of the artifacts found in 'the burnt house' we were to explore was an iron Roman spear. As with the rest of the city, eventually, the Romans captured this part of Jerusalem, and it wasn't until after the Six-Day War of 1967 that this area once again came under the control of the Jews. In 1970 they began to rebuild, and as they rebuilt this section of the city they uncovered the sad history of those final hours in the Upper City.

This area was home to the rich people of Jerusalem as well as many of the priests who serviced the Temple. These were the homes of those that confronted Jesus and no doubt made up the group that condemned Jesus to death. Known for their corruption and isolation from the masses, they were the last to yield to the Romans despite their earlier alliance with them. The revolt forced them to choose and they chose to put their trust in the empty hope that Jehovah would never allow Jerusalem or the Temple to be taken. They were as wrong as the people of Jeremiah's time when it was the Babylonians and not the Romans attacking their town. Jehovah had left with His Son; no wonder Jesus wept over the city. It was while digging new foundations for the resettlement of the Upper City that the workers came across a home; a house with a paved courtyard, four rooms, a kitchen area, and stairs leading down to a ritual bath. As the workers removed the debris, the remains of this home began to appear. They noticed immediately that the stones were blackened by soot. There were burnt articles, charred timbers, and soot-covered walls. Slowly the picture became clear that this was one of the houses burned by the Roman legionnaires in 70 AD. Professor Nachman Avigad led the group of archeologists painstakingly through the site. It appeared that the house had been put to the flame and eventually collapsed in on itself. There saved in time were the remains of a home that faced the horror of the Roman siege, but whose house?

As the archeologists dug deeper into the remains of this burnt house, they began to find articles of pottery and other household items. Among the findings was a stone weight and on that weight was engraved the words "Bar Kathros", or son of Kathros. Kathros can mean 'oak tree' or 'a lyre like instrument'. The Kathros family was a prominent aristocratic family during the first century with a lineage that can be traced back deep into Hebrew history. They were known for their abuse of power and corrupt status in the administration of the Temple, including the position of High Priest. The Talmud, the collection of writings making up the Jewish civil and religious law, says this about the Kathros Family:

> Woe is me because of the House of Kathros, woe is me because of their poison pens . . . for they are the High Priests, and their sons are treasurers, and their son-in-laws are trustees, and their servants beat the people with staves.

Josephus tells us that 110,000 people were casualties of the great siege and 97,000 more taken into captivity. Also discovered among the ruins of the Burnt House was a skeleton of a young woman's hand leaning on one of the walls of the house. As we sat in seats overlooking the ruins of that house, a film was shown tells of the last days of the Kathros family. The film revealed their hope that Jehovah would somehow save them, and it was at that moment I felt the tears touching my cheeks again! Caught up in the moment, I pondered why they had been killed and their world burnt? Was this not the place of the Torah and the Temple? Were these not the People of God, those chosen out of all races to be given the Commandments of Jehovah? Yet were they not the same people that had deliberately rejected their own Messiah just a few short decades before? What I was witnessing in that underground museum that spring morning in May was a fulfillment of Jesus' own prophecy:

> And there followed Him (Jesus) a great company of people, and of woman, which also bewailed and lamented Him. But Jesus turning unto them said, 'Daughters of Jerusalem, weep not for me, but weep for yourselves, and your children. For, behold, the days are coming in the which they shall say, Blessed are the barren, and the wombs that never bare, and the paps which never

gave suck. Then shall they begin to say to the mountains, Fall on us; and to the hills, Cover us.' (Luke 23:27–30)

Was one of those "children" the young girl that died in The Burnt House? Or, was the young maid the daughter of one of the "women" Jesus met as He carried His cross to Calvary? I wept because of the countless women and girls I was seeing in Jerusalem still without Christ! Unsaved souls are still worth our tears.

11

Not One Stone Left Upon Another

Matthew 24:2—And Jesus said unto them, See ye not all these things? Verily I say unto you, There shall NOT BE LEFT HERE ONE STONE UPON ANOTHER, that shall not be thrown down.

After the emotion of The Burnt House Museum, we were off to another section of the old upper city and the Wohl Archeological Herodian Quarter Museum. We toured one of the richest homes discovered in the area with its multi-level construction (4 of them) and the expensive mosaic floors. The space was so great it took us an hour to walk around. In my journal that night I wrote:

> Rich people haven't changed much in these two thousand years!

The saddest part of this stop was we were not able to take pictures. By the time we were finished it was time for lunch, and what better place than the Cardo with all of its shops and stores, a taste of a modern Jerusalem built over an ancient past.

One of the first couples we connected with on this trip was the mother and son team of Barb and John Nuxoll. John was a student at Dallas Theological Seminary like my daughter Marnie, and Barb was along for the ride and experience like me. On this noontime stop we decided to eat together. I had yet to find something Israeli that I liked, so I settled for the first American food I could find: French fries (they are American aren't they?). Marnie got falafel and Barb got shawarma, but John was determined to find an American hamburger. The three of us discovered our food quickly and found a pleasant eating area overlooking the Western

Wall plaza. I was through my French fries and soda and part of Barb's shawarma (I knew I had found my favorite Israeli food) by the time John got back. In his hands was the biggest hamburger I had ever seen. He told me he had paid over $10 for it, but it would be worth it if it tasted like home. One bite and I could tell (I wish I could show you the photograph Marnie took of John's face) it wasn't the best hamburger John had ever eaten. It was then he offered me a bite, to which I immediately agreed, anything is better than falafel I thought? I was soon to learn that an Israeli hamburger is worse than falafel! I can honestly say that it was the poorest excuse for a hamburger I have ever eaten, and like John, after one bite I had had enough! After exchanging $100 for 367 shekels we were off to The Jerusalem Archeological Park.

Our first stop was another walk about the Western Wall area, for those who had yet to experience the site. I did return to the tunnel under Wilson's Arch for a few more pictures, but I was not as moved emotionally as I had been that first night in Jerusalem. Surprising how fast we hardened to the troubling experiences in our lives. Within the hour we were through the gates leading to an archeological site still under exploration; the southern stair area of Herod's famous retaining wall. To literally stand and step onto stones that Jesus once walked upon was thrilling. As we prepared for some free time around the area, Greg instructed us again in what had taken place in this part of Jerusalem. I will always remember these words:

> If you are looking to walk where Jesus walked, this will probably be the only site you can be confident that Jesus probably did walk on these stones!

This would have been where Mary and Joseph would have brought the baby to enter the Temple area for his circumcision and naming; Bethlehem is just a few miles away. There were two main entrances to the Temple Mount from the west; up the staircases which created Robinson's Arch and Wilson's Arch (named after the two archeologists who discovered them). Only Wilson's Arch remains, but it is buried under hundreds of years of history and dirt. Only the stones used to attach the arch to the retaining wall remain of Robinson's Arch, but one can imagine just how magnificent the staircase must have been. In the Citadel, we saw an artist concept of what it might have looked like, and it wasn't hard to imagine the holy family climbing the stairs. The tragedy today is that people still associate climbing stairs with godliness, as the Lateran staircase in Rome.

I saw it in Saint Anne's Cathedral outside Quebec City, Canada shortly after my wife and I were married. A throng of pilgrims laboriously toiling to climb a set of stairs stopping at each step and supplicating thinking by this they will be heard by God. As we had seen already in Jerusalem hundreds enslaved to a miserable bondage that thinks by doing something, like climbing stairs, one can merit divine favor of some kind. When will mankind realize:

> They that are in the flesh cannot please God? (Romans 8:8)

As we walked along Herod Street (a main artery that use to run the complete length of the western side of the massive retaining wall of the Temple Mount), scattered here and there were piles of huge stones. We were told that the archeologists that uncovered this pile of rocks left them just were they were found in testimony to Jesus' prophecy printed at the beginning of this remembrance. These stones had been thrown down by the Roman legionnaires after they captured the Temple area. One could see that the wall had been repaired with smaller stones, but the closer you go to the street the larger the stones (some 15 feet long and 5 feet thick). We would only see larger stones when we got a chance to walk through a tunnel under the Western Wall. Marnie and I got our picture taken on a mound of stones high up against the wall. As I sat there I was moved by the realization that I was setting on the very stones Jesus drew the attention of His disciples to. I don't know if I felt any closer to an actual Biblical event than there. I was within sight, not only of Jesus' great theme in His Olivet Discourse (Matthew 24–25), but where Peter preached his famous sermon on Pentecost (Acts 2). It was at that moment I realized just how easy it was for some to exchange the place, for the Person, the event for Emmanuel.

One of the lessons I learned that day on the street that Jesus walked was the danger in replacing the substance for the spiritual. I could see how I could easily become a stair-climbing pilgrim instead of a Jacob's ladder saint. I left the stone-lined Herod Street with this song in my heart:

> I'm pressing on the upward way, new heights I'm gaining every day, still praying as I'm onward bound, 'Lord, plant my feet on higher ground. Lord, lift me up and let me stand by faith on heaven's tableland; a higher plain than I have found. Lord, plant my feet on higher ground.

What made me the happiest was the fact that my feet are no longer on unstable stones, even stones as large and solid as those we found on Herod's Street? It just reminds us that anything of man will be thrown down eventually, and only the streets of Glory and the walls of the New Jerusalem will last forever!

12

The Beautiful Gate

Acts 3:2—And a certain man lame from his mother's womb was carried, whom they laid daily at the gate of the temple, which is called BEAUTIFUL, to ask alms of them that entered into the temple.

For the third time in my short stay in Jerusalem I walked out the Dung Gate into the busy walkways along the eastern wall. We had just finished a walking lecture through The Jerusalem Archeological Park, including as our last stop, an explanation of a first century ritual bath site. Very close to Herod Street, a huge bath complex had been unearthed by the archeologists working in the area. I got some wonderful pictures of Marnie descending down the stone staircase into a carved out bath area and then ascending up the other side of the staircase. One of the blessings of our Israel trip was the opportunity to experience firsthand Biblical practices. The ritual bath on Herod Street would be added to the list I was recording in my journal under the caption: Biblical Events We Were Able To Experience. As we neared the end of our 4th day in Israel, there was only one area of the wall of Jerusalem we hadn't covered, the section between the Dung Gate and the Lion Gate, either on our rampart walk or our evening walks.

Marnie and I had tried to walk to the Golden Gate on our second evening in Jerusalem, but were turned back by the crowd celebrating Jerusalem Days. We had walked near the famous gate on our third day, but instead had turned south to visit David's City and walk through Hezekiah's Tunnel. Now we would not be stopped as we slowly worked our way around the southeast corner of Herod's retaining wall. We stopped periodically to be told of the extensive excavations being done on this part of the old city. Even a 9th gate through the wall had been added to aid the workers in uncovering the mysteries still trapped in the ruins along the eastern wall and under Temple Mount (we were told they have found Solomon's stables (II Chronicles 9:25) under the southern end of the mountain). From the western ridge of the Kidron Valley, we had a bird's eye view of the fabled hillside to our east, the Mount of Olives (a future walk I was looking forward to). Within moments of our turning the corner, the first interesting object before us was Absalom's Pillar. There at the base of the largest Jewish cemetery in Israel was a huge stone monument in an area called the King's Dale. Many believe that David's son Absalom built the tomb, but Biblical history tells us that Absalom was buried in the woods of Ephraim (II Samuel 18:1–18). Most historians believe that a Maccabean leader by the name of Alexander Janaeus who died in 75 BC is actually in Absalom's tomb. Jewish tradition also believes the tomb of the prophet Zacharias (Matthew 23:35) is located nearby. Church tradition says that the grave of its 2nd martyr, the apostle James (Acts 12:2), is located in this dale as well.

It was then our guide directed our attention westward, for there before us stood the only double gate of Jerusalem. Sometimes called the 'golden' gate, or better known as the 'eastern' gate, this section of the wall is perhaps the most photographed area of Jerusalem. What drew my attention first was the fact that the Arabs had built a cemetery just in front of the gate. In actuality, the cemetery ran just about the entire length of the eastern wall, starting just before the eastern gate and running along the ridgeline to the Lion's gate. Quickly however, I was reminded of the importance of this place in the history of my Faith, for it was through the 'beautiful' gate on which the golden gate was built that Jesus made His famous triumphal entry into Jerusalem (Matthew 21:1–12). It was here, or just below where I was standing that Peter healed the lame man sitting in the 'beautiful' gate (Acts 3:1–10). And as we looked up into the sealed gates (the Turks had blocked off the gates centuries before), I heard for the first time the interruption of Ezekiel 44:1–3:

> Then he brought me back the way of the gate of the outward sanctuary which looketh toward the east; and it was shut. Then said the Lord unto me; This gate shall be shut, it shall not be opened, and no man shall enter in by it; because the Lord, the God of Israel, hath entered in by it, therefore it shall be shut. It

is for the prince; the prince, he shall sit in it to eat bread before the Lord; he shall enter by the way of the porch of that gate, and shall go out by the way of the same.

In my long exposure to Biblical prophecy, I had never had anyone show me these verses before until I was standing under the shadow of the eastern gate. For me it was an epiphany! I was standing where my Lord and Saviour Jesus Christ, the Prince of Peace, was coming back; the first person through those sealed gates will be Him at His Second Coming. It was also at that moment that I realized the significance of the reference to 'the porch'. Could this be the famous portico where the early church first met? (Acts 3:11 and 5:12) I had for most of my life been taught that the early church met in the upper room, but when I first came across Luke 24:53:

And were continually in the temple, praising and blessing God.

I changed my belief. Was I standing in one of the places the early believers would gather to fellowship and worship the Lord? It had only been days, weeks, or months since He told them that He would return to the spot He had left them from (Acts 1:11). What a better place to wait and watch for His return. From where I was standing I could see clearly the Mount of Olives and the hill of Ascension. (Remember, the disciples had returned to Jerusalem after Jesus' departure 'a Sabbath's day's journey' (Acts 1:12). According to tradition, a Sabbath day's trip was 1000 yards, the distance that separates Olivet from Jerusalem. There is a small chapel on site today that was built as an edifice in the courtyard of a church built by the Crusaders in the 12th century. The legend is that the sanctuary was built over the site where the footprints of Jesus were left before His ascension; why it is called the Church of the Ascension today!) No one dreamed that Jesus would wait 2,000 years to return. The disciples lived in the expectation and anticipation that Jesus would come back soon, so what better place to witness His return than in front of the eastern gate?

We continued our walk along the wall until we arrived at the Lion's Gate, the place we had gotten off the wall during our rampart walk two days before. We had finally finished the circumference of the old city. Along the way Greg pointed out three great Churches: the Church of Nations (built between 1919 and 1924 with the combined contributions of 16 nations, thus the name), the site of the Garden of Gethsemane, Stephen's Church, located on the tradition spot of his stoning and death, and Mary Magdalene's Church, a Russian Orthodox Church (built in 1888 by Czar Alexander III in memory of his mother) with its seven golden onion-shaped spires, perhaps the most spectacular of any church I have seen. As we entered the Lion's Gate and headed back to our motel by way of the Via Dolorosa, I couldn't get my mind off the feeling I had at the eastern gate. I had seen it in pictures and was thrilled the first time I heard the Gaither Trio sing 'the King is coming' from that very spot, but being near it brought the reality of my Lord's return home. In my mind's eye I can now see it for myself, and to think when He comes back to that place I will be with Him, and I will think:

> I have been here before!

13

In the Garden

John 19:41—Now in the place where he was crucified there was A GARDEN; and IN THE GARDEN a new sepulcher, wherein was never man yet laid.

After nearly seven hours of walking, we were back to the Knight's Palace. As we entered the lobby area, Greg told us we only had an hour to rest because we had one final hike to make before supper. We were going to walk over to Gordon's Calvary and the famous Garden Tomb. Despite the fact the site was a recent (1883) addition to the Biblical story of Christ's death, burial, and resurrection, it was worth a visit. I had been a General Gordon fan for many years, and whether or not it was the real Golgotha or not mattered little to me. I wanted to see up close and personal what we had witnessed from the walls of Jerusalem on our second day walking the ramparts.

Charles George Gordon was commissioned a lieutenant at the age of 19 at the Royal Military Academy in Woolwich, England and then began one of the most amazing military careers in English history. He fought in the Crimean War, and following that he spent two years surveying the Russo-Turkish border. By 1860, Gordon was a captain and helped capture Peking for the British in China. Three years later he was given charge over the army that would eventually put down the infamous Taiping Rebellion. For his leadership and courage the Chinese emperor gave him the highest military rank in China, and henceforth, he would be known as "Chinese Gordon." From there he went to Egypt where he establish British rule in the upper Nile region. In 1877, he was appointed governor-general of the Sudan. When Gordon retired, he visited Israel and made claims to the alternative site for Calvary: a knoll just outside Herod's Gate. (Gordon noticed a rocky hill which resembled a human skull (it does), and made the first suggestion that this might be the true site of Calvary. Nearby he found a Roman tomb quarried in the hillside. The simplicity and solitude of the site helped cement in many minds this alternative site to the Church of the Holy Sepulcher for Calvary. In 1892 an organization was formed to clear the site and the tomb, and the rest as they say is history.) Since that time Gordon's Calvary has been on the agenda of most pilgrimages to Jerusalem. Asked by the British government in 1884 to return to the Sudan, Gordon was killed when the city of Khartoum fell to the rebels. Nevertheless, this dedicated Christian's lasting legacy remains in a garden and on a rugged knoll affectionately called 'Gordon's Calvary'!

We left at 4:30 PM for the twenty minute walk to the Garden Tomb. After passing through the New Gate, we walked downhill toward the Damascus Gate. Once we arrived in the Arab Quarter, we crossed the street working our way through a busy market area before heading up a side street just across from Herod's gate. Within a hundred yards, we came to a rock wall and an obscure entrance. It was so unlike the other religious site we visited. It was quiet and peaceful. There were no vendors peddling their wares, and there was no admission cost. After the constant noise of the milling crowds and street sounds, my first impression was that I was going to love this place. I had come to the conclusion why the Holy Sepulcher was probably the real Golgotha and garden tomb, but instantaneously I knew why General Gordon had fallen in love with this alternative!

Our first stop in the garden area was to the rock face that overshadowed the garden. It was easy to see the skull in the hillside (Matthew 27:33), a rocky mask, and an eerie image in stone. It was Golgotha at its best in my imagination, and when you added to it the nearness of the garden (within yards) why wouldn't you see the possibilities of the site? We walked on through wonderful shade tree and beautiful flowers. Beside the sights, the smells were divine. That later afternoon visit also happened when there were very few tourists, or pilgrims. It seemed at times we had the place to ourselves. Not since I arrived in Israel had I felt alone, but my stroll through this garden reminded me of the words to Austin Miles classic Church hymn:

> *I come to the garden alone, while the dew* (there was no dew, but there was roses) *is still on the roses; and the voice I hear, falling on my ear, the Son of God discloses. He speaks, and the sound of His voice is so sweet the birds* (yes, we did hear birds for the first time since we arrived in Israel) *hush their singing; and the melody that He gave to me within my heart is ringing. I'd stay in the garden with Him through the night* (for us to the night was falling) *around me be falling but He bids me go thru the voice of woe, His voice to me is calling. And He walks with me, and He talks with me, and He tells me I am His own; and the joy we share as we tarry* (Marnie and I also tarried longer than most) *there none other has ever known.*

For the first time in my long Christian life, I finally understood the deep spiritual meaning of that memorable song.

We continued our wandering through the shrub-lined paths and flowered lanes until we came to the heart of this garden. There before us was the 'tomb'. I had certainly seen pictures of the place both in books and on television. I had watched others being there, but now I was there. I had all I could do to convince myself that this wasn't the place of my Lord's burial. It was tranquil and true to what it might have been like, and eventually I gave up on the intellect and gave in to the emotion. For a few moments I believed that I was in the right spot, walking through the opening into that place 'wherein was never man yet laid'. Each of our party was allowed a few minutes alone in the tomb. Marnie and I went in together. It was solemn and sober and spiritual. You will have to go yourself to understand how I felt. I tell people it is like explaining salvation. How do you express it, put it in words, only the experience can explain the moment.

We left the garden tomb to wander for another half an hour or more. Eventually, everybody left to return to the Knight's Palace and supper. Because we knew our way back Greg let some of us stay a bit longer. Marnie and I and a few others lingered. I breathed in the sweet fragrances and enjoyed the quiet solitude for a bit longer. As I left another, not so famous, Church hymn came to my mind and came out on my lips. Eleanor Schroll wrote the words and J. H. Fillmore composed the melody. If you know it sing along as we leave the most beautiful garden in Jerusalem:

> There's a garden where Jesus is waiting, there's a place that is wondrously fair; for it flows with the light of His presence, 'tis the beautiful garden of prayer'. There's a garden where Jesus is

waiting, and I go with my burden and care, just to learn from His lips words of comfort, in the beautiful garden of prayer. There's a garden where Jesus is waiting, and He bids you to come meet Him there, just to walk and to talk with my Saviour, in the beautiful garden of prayer. O the beautiful garden, the garden of prayer, O the beautiful garden of prayer; there my Saviour awaits, and He opens the gates to the beautiful garden of prayer.

With a warm chill in my spine and a peaceful interlude in my heart, I left the garden of Gordon and walked slowly back to the old city. Without a doubt I knew in my mind I was not at Calvary or the garden, but my spirit was having a hard time accepting the reality of either.

14

Gibeon From Nebi Samwil

Joshua 9:3—And when the inhabitants of GIBEON heard what Joshua had done unto Jericho and Ai.

Our 5th day in Israel would take us on our first bus ride outside the city limits of Jerusalem and our first expedition into the West Bank. Because of the ongoing conflict between the Palestinian Arabs and the Israeli Jews, we could not travel safely in all regions of the West Bank. Many places like Hebron and Samaria and Gibeon were off limits, but this didn't mean there were no ways of seeing some of these places.

Catching our tour bus just north of the Jaffa Gate, we traveled just a few miles before being stopped by the impressive high walls and guard towers that separates Israel from the West Bank. This wall was built by the Jews to govern who comes in and who goes out of Jerusalem and other parts of Israel. This extreme measure of defense was necessary after decades of terrorist attacks. We had no trouble getting through the checkpoint, but one could clearly see the difficult nature the wall now brings to those who wish to harm Israel. Our journey wasn't long (5 miles) before we started a steep climb to the top of a high hill that would give us a bird's eye view of Mount Ephraim, the Beth Horon Ridge, and Gibeon.

Our destination was Nebi Samwil, the traditional, but not Biblical, burial site for the prophet Samuel. (The Bible states clearly that Samuel was buried at his house in Ramah—I Samuel 25:1. Ramah is located just a few miles from Nebi Samwil, but is not the Biblical site of Ramah.) Nevertheless, located on the brow of a hill overlooking Gibeon is a stone chapel that raises high over the surrounding landscape. From its height one can see back into Jerusalem (you can clearly see the Dome of the Rock from the roof of the building on a clear day and we were experiencing a mighty fine day) and looking straight down to Tel Gibeon with its neatly kept circled mount. We had come to understand one of the main routes into Jerusalem, the Beth Horon Ridge Route. There are those who do believe that this knoll does have Biblical significance, and that being the possible site of the 'high place of Gibeon' where Solomon is recorded to have asked for wisdom after God granted him the desire of his heart! (I Kings 3:3–15 and II Chronicles 1:1–13).

After climbing the stone stairway onto the top of the chapel, we understood immediately why this was a stopping off place for our instructors. It was ideal, a visible illustration of what we had learned in class the night before. Each time we ventured out into an area of Israel we always received a lecture on where we were going and what we would see. This prepared us for what we needed to look for and the lessons we were to learn. Maps and pictures and diagrams are great, but actually being there and seeing with one's own eye is certainly the best. From the top of Nebi Samwil we had a 360 degree panorama platform to see in all four directions. To the north we could see Mount Ephraim (I Chronicles 6:67) and Shechem beyond (a place we would see on our next to our late day in Israel). To the south we could see Mount Moriah and Jerusalem beyond. But our primary purpose for coming was within direct sight, almost at our feet: Tel Gibeon and Beth Horon.

Gibeon (hill or height) has a colorful history in the Biblical account. This Hivite city decided not to fight the Israelites like the other 'royal' cities in the Amorite alliance (Joshua 10:1–2). In order to escape total destruction, the inhabitants tricked Joshua into a peace treaty with a very clever plan (Joshua 9:1–15). Pretending to have come from a far off and distant country, they put on old, worn-out clothes and had old, dried-out bread in their sacks. Joshua fell for the deception, but put them under slavery and they became 'hewers of wood and drawers of water' (Joshua 9:21) from that day after. Eventually, Gibeon was given to Benjamin (Joshua 18:25) and was made a Levitical city (Joshua 21:17). It was also known for a famous well of water (Jeremiah 41:12) and Joab's men and Abner's men fought a famous battle at the 'pool of Gibeon' (II Samuel 2:12–15) during the Civil War between the house of David and the house of Saul. Archaeological discoveries in the area have revealed huge cisterns and irrigation ditches which fit in nicely with the work Joshua set the Gibeonites to do.

Also from the top of the church on Nebi Samwil we would see westward down the Beth Horon Valley towards the coast. As a matter of fact, the day we were there we could clearly see the Mediterranean Sea to the west 35 miles away! The sky was so transparent we could see the Jordanian Plateau to the east 35 miles away. From where we were standing we could see the entire width of Israel!!! But it was the Beth Horon (the place of the hollows) Ridge that drew most of my attention; both because of Biblical history and military history, which I love. Divided into two sections, the Upper Beth Horon (Joshua 16:5) and the Lower Beth Horon (II Chronicles 8:5), this is the best and most direct way to reach Jerusalem from the northwest. As we learned in our first lecture, the best way to strike the city of Jerusalem is from the north. One of the bits of history I learned while viewing Beth Horon from Nebi Samwil was that Richard the Lionheart used Nebi Samwil for his staging area just before his unsuccessful attempt to recapture Jerusalem during the Third Crusade. The ruins of a crusader fort can easily be seen from the roof of the chapel on Nebi Samwil to this day!

As I looked down the Beth Horon, I saw in my mind's eye the Amorites fleeing from Joshua as large hailstones from God mowed them down (Joshua 10:11). I also watched as the Philistines were routed back down the Beth Horon in the days of Samuel (I Samuel 7:5–11), in the days of Saul and Jonathan (I Samuel 14:31), and in the days of David (II Samuel 5:25). It wasn't long before those that defended Jerusalem understood that Beth Horon had to be fortified as well (I Kings 9:15–17). It was this route that Pharaoh Shishak took to attack King Rehoboam at Jerusalem (II Chronicles 12:2–4). It was in this same area Judas Maccabees defeated the Greek, and even as late as 1917 the British used this route to capture Jerusalem from the Turks. How many that I had read about had stood on this same knoll overlooking the Beth Horon? I felt that day as I wandered around the rim of that hill that I too had become part of history, not because I had fought a battle there, or witnessed some struggle from there, but because I had simply been there. As I had felt before on this trip and as I would feel again, I was living history, experiencing history, and I was reliving and understanding the strategy of why: why the Egyptians, the Philistines, the Amorites, the Greeks, and the Crusaders came to Jerusalem the way they did, for it was the best way to get to Jerusalem, their final goal. I watched in my mind's eyes the armies parade past Nebi Samwil in full battle gear, confident of victory, what a sight; what a memory!

15

Gibeah of Saul

I Samuel 10:26—And Saul also went home to GIBEAH; and there went with him a band of men, whose hearts God had touched.

We left Nebi Samwil after about an hour of lectures and viewings, of wanderings and remembrances of Biblical and world history. Our next stop would be another famous place in the Old Testament story, the hometown of Israel's first king, Saul.

Our bus took us back down the hill onto the very impressive road system around Jerusalem, and the more impressive defense system surrounding Jerusalem. We passed through the Upper Sorek (Judges 16:4) Valley, better known as the 'Jerusalem Mote', as we headed east. We were not going far, but we were going deeper into the West Bank and the traffic would slow our progress as we passed through one Arab village after another. On our short journey we also saw our first Israeli settlement, the flashpoint for most of the conflict between Arabs and Jews right now! It was shortly after ten o'clock in the morning when our bus driver dropped us off on a sidewalk in the middle of what seemed to be a residential area in one of those numerous towns, but was it Arab or Jewish? Greg told us that we would have to walk the final hundred yards or more to Tel Gibeah. As we worked our way up hill (it seemed to me that anything important in Israel was always uphill, a fitting testimony of the struggles of this land), I noticed we were in an Arab village. The area reminded me of the housing developments my wife and I had seen in the hills of Southern California while visiting our missionary friends, the De La Hayes. Built on a steep slope, the homes seemed to defy gravity, but as I pondered this later that day I came to this conclusion and wrote in my journal:

Where else would they build? For the Israel I knew, to this point, was nothing, but side hills!

Eventually, we reached the end of the street and started up a sandy knoll. By now the sun was up and the temperature had reached into the 90s. We were hot, but the minute we reach the summit a cooling Mediterranean breeze greeted us (this was how it was throughout our travels in Israel; the weather was always ideal). Before us was a very strange sight. I expected to see old rock walls, but instead I saw the concrete shell of a mansion. I expected to view the ruins of an archeological dig, but instead I saw the skeleton of an uncompleted house. I expected to see some kind of shrine, but instead I saw the unfinished summer home of an Arab king. There on an isolated knoll overlooking an Arab village in the heart of Israel was what remained of a palace started before 1967 by King Hussein of Jordan. My first thought was what are we doing here, but it wasn't long before I discovered that just below my feet were the remains of the ancient Benjaminite city of Gibeah and before my eyes was a wonderful view of God's land.

In 1951, three years after Israeli statehood, King Abdullah of Jordan was assassinated, and two years later his grandson, Hussein, was crowned king. In the early years Jordan controlled the region we call the West Bank, including Jerusalem. Just before the famous Six-Day war of 1967, King Hussein had started building an elaborate summer home on the site of old Gibeah. From its summit he could see back to Jordan. He could also see into Jerusalem, even Nebi Samwil could be seen a few miles away, and there in the distance was the blue horizon of the Mediterranean Sea. Hussein only got the concrete frame of the two story mansion completed when the '67 war began. After it was over not only had Israel gained control over Jerusalem but the Jordanian territory known today as the West Bank. The unfinished edifice was left as it was. What it has become is a wonderful observation post to see the surrounding area. The Jordan Rift, the Wilderness of Judea, the Hills of Jerusalem, and countless towns and villages can be seen from the roof of the second story of Hussein's deserted palace. Famous Biblical towns like Bethel (where Jacob had his vision-Genesis 28:29), Mizpeh (where Samuel called Israel to prayer-I Samuel 7:5), and Ramah (Samuel's hometown—I Samuel 25:1) can also be seen from Gibeah, but the town's fame comes from two Biblical events.

First, there was the infamous, inhuman crime committed against the concubine of a Levite that provoked a Civil War between the tribe of

Benjamin and the other tribes of Israel (Judges 19-21). For the first time I could finally see the geography of that story because I was in line sight of the places of that story: Bethlehem (Judges 19:1), Jerusalem (Judges 19:10), Gibeah (Judges 19:13), and Mount Ephraim (Judges 19:16). This route along the ridges of central Canaan was the main traveling route of the patriarchs (Abraham, Isaac, and Jacob). Once again the old stories were coming alive, and a new understanding of the significance of the places was being realized. If you remember that Civil War nearly wiped out the tribe of Benjamin which is important because Saul was from that tribe (I Samuel 9:1). This place is a part of the watershed ridge (rain that falls on the east side flows to the Jordan River and rain that falls on the west side flows to the Mediterranean Sea) that cuts the nation of Israel in two from north to south.

Second, this was the site of Israel's first capital (I Samuel 15:34) under the rule of Saul. The name means 'height', and once you climb to its top and see that the land slopes downward from all sides you understand its meaning. Only once is a Gibeathite mentioned in Scripture (I Chronicles 12:3—a man named Shemaah), but Saul was also a Gibeathite (an inhabitant of Gibeah). Before it became the capital of Saul's monarchy, it was known as the 'Gibeah of Saul' (I Samuel 11:4). Even hundreds of years later when the Assyrians were threatening King Hezekiah this place was still known as "Gibeah of Saul" (Isaiah 10:29). Pretty much the entire life of Saul is seen from Gibeah (I Samuel 10-26). We found Gibeah a simple rocky mount with a few scrub trees and bushes growing on its summit. All evidence of the once important town is now buried under layers of dirt and time. The only other important historical event that happened there was that Titus (the Roman general that destroyed Jerusalem) gathered his forces at Gibeah before his final assault on Jerusalem in 70 AD, or so says the famous Jewish historian Josephus. When Titus was in Gibeah he was a mere four miles from Jerusalem!

We stayed less than an hour on Gibeah. We took a few pictures, and enjoyed the cool breezes. As we slowly worked our way back to the bus, I thought of how so many stories in the Bible seem to happen on a hill or mountain; of just how many of God's men were 'mountain men', not men of the valley! Hills seem to have by their very nature an upward pull, not only for our feet but our faith as well. As I was writing this chapter I got a call from my Israeli companion, my daughter Marnie. She was calling from Dallas just to say, "Hi!" She asked what I was doing and I said, "I'm at Gibeah!" She understood what I meant because she knew I was writing of our adventure together. Her next response was, "I really didn't like Gibeah; there was nothing there." On this we disagree, for me the hill was enough, the view was sufficient, because I believe in Vance Havner's philosophy:

> God had more in mind than mere geography when He mixed the peaks and the plains!

You can't stay on any hilltop for long as Peter, James, and John discovered with Jesus (Matthew 17:4), but you can enjoy the time there high above the grime of a racial war, the gloom of a hostile world, and the grind of living in the same old, same old repetition of history. I can honestly write that many of my most positive experiences in Israel took place on high ground. My old bifocals seemed to see so much farther, and so much clearer from places like Gibeah!

16

Finding a Cistern at Michmash

I Samuel 13:23—And the garrison of the Philistines went out to the passage of MICHMASH.

Our third stop on our first adventure outside the eternal city was a roadside adventure I will never forget. Don't get me wrong, I loved our special stops in Jerusalem and Nebi Samwil, but after the isolation of Gibeah I was really feeling the sweetness of rural Israel. Away from the crowds and cities, I was beginning to feel at home where the people weren't! When our bus suddenly stopped between two hills, and Greg said we were going on a hike I knew I would like this place. Our destination was a lonely, shepherd's hillside from which we could see from afar 'the passage of Michmash'.

As I looked over the itinerary for this trip certain places simple jumped off the page and immediately excited my Biblical wish-list. One of those places was the mention of Michmash. This Old Testament place isn't as well-known as Beersheba or Bethlehem, Jericho or Jordan, Carmel or Canaan, but for me, it is the place where one of my favorite Old Testament characters became famous. Michmash was where Jonathan, Saul's son, won an important victory over the Philistines:

> And between the passages, by which Jonathan sought to go over unto the Philistines' garrison, there was a sharp rock on the one side, and a sharp rock on the other side: and the name of the one was Bozez, and the name of the other Seneh. The forefront of the one was situate northward over against Michmash, and the other southward over against Gibeah. And Jonathan said to the young man that bare his armour, Come, and let us go over unto

the garrison of these uncircumcised: it may be that the Lord will work for us: for there is no restraint to the Lord to save by many or by few. . . . And Jonathan climbed up upon his hands and upon his feet, and his armourbearer after him: and they fell before Jonathan; and his armourbearer slew after him. And that first slaughter, which Jonathan and his armourbearer made, was about twenty men, within as it were a half acre of land, which a yoke of oxen might plow. (I Samuel 14:4-6, 13-14)

This is not the most famous battle in the Bible, or the biggest battle described in God's Word, but for me it shows the courage of a man of God who trusts in the Lord alone and for me that is valuable. I have known the detail of this encounter since childhood, and have studied its importance since adulthood, but now I would see with my own eyes the cliffs of Bozez and Seneh, the passage of Michmash, and the field of Jonathan's most famous exploit.

We worked our way along a rocky side hill trail climbing with each step. It was nearing high noon when we finally came around a small outcropping and there it was in the distance. We were many miles from the actual passage of Michmash, but we could see clearly the two cliffs and there on the Michmash side was Jonathan's Field. It was exactly as the Bible described the scene. I guess one of the reasons I love places like Hezekiah's Tunnel and Michmash Pass was the reality that man hasn't altered these places in all these years. The place was exactly like the day when Jonathan climbed the cliff to attack the Philistine garrison in Michmash. We had just traveled over the ridge from Gibeah, and now just seven miles from Jerusalem I was witnessing another Biblical happening in my mind. This was probably the 'passage' Joshua took when he traveled over night from Gilgal to Gibeon to save the Gibeonites from their allies (Joshua 10:1-5). This became the border between Israel and Judah in the days of King Asa (I Kings 15:22), and Isaiah tells us the Assyrians used this passage to gain access to Jerusalem (Isaiah 10:28) in the days of Hezekiah, but the most famous story of Michmash in the Bible is the story of Jonathan and his armourbearer and their solo attack on the Philistine garrison on Michmash Ridge. As Greg shared the history, I began to roam because once I got my eye off Michmash Pass I realized I had been taken back in time to witness and experience more than a famous battle, but a personal reassurance.

It wasn't long before I noticed we were viewing Michmash from an old hill side which contained small wheat fields scattered among the rocks and boulders sown up and down the slope. We found sheep's wool everywhere in the thorny bushes scattered about. Leaving the group I worked my way down the hill to the base a few hundred feet in the descent. It was then I noticed something strange; two rocks that had been carved out on their tops as if to form a trough, a manger. Looking around I saw it, on the top of another rock a metal cover and there beside that rock a bucket. Lifting the cover I discovered a cistern about six feet deep. Looking into the cistern I saw the light reflected back by the water below. I had discovered an ancient shepherd's cistern. I took the bucket and lowered it into the pool of water at the bottom. Once I had it filled I brought it up and deposited the crystal, clear water into the two stone troughs. It wasn't long before others in our group noticed what I was doing and came to explore. I showed them my discovery and they in turn played water boy and water girl for a few minutes. I know to most this wouldn't seem to be much, but to me it was as if I had discovered a gold mine; I had, a Biblical gold mine!

One of the sheer delights of this trip was to actually do Biblical things. Walking through Hezekiah's tunnel was the first, watching my daughter taking a ritualistic bath was the second, and drawing water from a cistern was the third. I was doing what David had done, and Abraham before him. We did not see any sheep or shepherds while overlooking Michmash, but when the shepherd returned with his flocks that evening his watering troughs would be full—by my hand! For just a few minutes I pretended to be an ancient shepherd watching from afar two men scaling the cliff of Bozez. As my sheep graze in the small wheat fields I have planted, I watch two soldiers back to back fighting off the onslaught of scores of Philistines on a piece of land about a half-acre in size. Then in a moment of triumph I see them lift their swords in victory as their final opponent falls and the rest flee in fear. As we retraced our steps to the bus, I took one final glance over my shoulder at the passage of Michmash, the cliff of Bozez, Jonathan's field, and to a shepherd's cistern hidden away among a group of rocks at the foot of a Canaanite ridge, and I thought of the way God works 'by few'. Whether a soldier like my son, or a shepherd like myself, there are different callings but the same Lord over all. I will never forget my discovery at Michmash, for it reminded me of who I am and what I am, even though I dreamed and desired to be a soldier like Jonathan most of my early life!

At Michmash I rediscovered my calling. Despite the battlefield before me, I was quickly distracted by a cistern, why? Because I am not a soldier by my nature, but a shepherd! A shepherd leads his flock by 'still waters' (Psalms 23:2), like the cistern at Michmash. He draws them water from a well just like I do on a weekly basis, but my cistern is the Word of God (Ephesians 5:26). We cannot be what we are not even if we are drawn to that life. I admire the Jonathans of history, but a Jonathan I am not! I admire the work my son has done in Iraq and Afghanistan, at times I even envy his adventures, but I fight a different foe, a different battle. My weapons are spiritual (II Corinthians 10:4–5) and my battle plan comes from God, not the Joint Chiefs.

17

Jericho

Joshua 2:1: And Joshua the son of Nun sent out of Shittim two men to spy secretly, saying, Go view the land, even JERICHO . . .

Since boyhood I have heard the thrilling story of Joshua and Jericho and 'the walls coming tumbling down'. Probably, only the story of David and Goliath has been in my collective thoughts more than the famous battle of Jericho in which the children of Israel defeated this Amorite city by simply walking around it. As our bus left Michmash for Jericho, I knew that I was just a few minutes away from making that walk!

Our first descent into the Jordan Rift took place on a warming spring day in the middle of May. Jesus was certainly right when he had the victim of his famous parable 'going down to Jericho' (Luke 10:30). With Jerusalem nearly 2,300 feet above sea level and Jericho nearly 820 feet below sea level, there is only one way to Jericho and that it 'down'. A steady decline could be felt and observed as we followed the main road into the Jordan Valley. What we saw from our bus windows also changed from rolling hills with olive groves in the dales and small settlements on the ridges to a bleak, barren desert. We had entered the infamous Judean Wilderness. We had seen glimpses of it from Jerusalem, but until one actually is swallowed up by it, one can't fully understand how desolate the area really is—mile after mile of nothing but treeless terrain, and a landscape that was nothing short of a moonscape. I had only been in two other areas that were more barren than this: the desert areas of Western Australia and the deserts of Andrah Pardesh in India. The only aspect that makes these places worse is their size. Within a half an hour we were into the lush green of Jericho. While the deserts of Australia and India cover hundreds of miles, it is only 15 miles between Jerusalem and Jericho!

What a contrast when we came around a sharp corner and there before us was 'the city of palm trees' (Deuteronomy 34:3). It certainly came by its name naturally, for within our vision was a settlement of buildings literally engulfed in palm trees and fig trees and date trees. The road into town took us by three recognizable landmarks of Jericho. First, on the east side of the highway was the 'fountain of Elisha', a spring made famous by Elisha's miracle recorded in II Kings 2:18–22, when with a handful of salt he turned the deadly water sweet. There beside the road this waterway flows to this day in a concrete canal that feeds the town and its fields with life-giving water. Second, on the west side of the roadway was the distinctive shape of the Mount of Temptation, the traditional site of Jesus' famous test by Satan recorded in Matthew 4:1–11. Nobody can be sure of the sites except for the test at the Temple, but traveling through that wilderness certainly gives one a moment of pondering of just how one could spend 40-days in that wilderness? Third, we passed Tel Jericho on our left as we turned into an Israeli mall beside the famous site. It was well after lunch, so the first order of business was our customary hour lunch break. The businessmen of Jericho were ready for us, as they were for the dozen or more other tour busses that were there that day.

While the others sought something for their stomachs, I sought a better view of the city. I have never been much for tours things, so I quickly walked through the gift shops and restaurants and headed back up the way we came for a look beyond the palm trees. I walked over to the west side of the Tel, but the tall trees blocked just about every angle. I will admit, Jericho was the only town in which I had this problem. Sometimes it was a hill or mount, but there are few places in Israel where trees will block your view! Unable to get the pictures I wanted I returned to the mall. As I entered the second time, I ran into Seonhee Park, one of the younger ladies on our trip. She asked me if I had seen the view from the roof. It seems that the businessmen who created the mall of Jericho had put an observation deck on the roof of the structure. I thanked Seonhee for her suggestion and headed up the four flights of stairs to the top of the roof. What a vista awaited me there!

To the northeast I could make out the Jordan River, my first of many angles on this classic waterway. To the southeast I could make out the Dead Sea, also my first sighting but not my last. What amazed me most was just how close the children of Israel were to Jericho when they made their miraculous crossing of the Jordan (Joshua 3:14–17). The watchmen on the walls of Jericho could have seen them, so why didn't they attack when Israel was so exposed? (Joshua 6:1) Another aspect of how the Lord protected the Israelites could be seen from atop that mall. To the southwest and northwest the barren wilderness of Judea came again into focus, and then there was below me Tel Jericho. My first impression was just how small it was! I had always wondered just how so many people could walk around its walls because in my mind's eyes it was a big city, but it wasn't. Even on a hot day, and it was by far the hottest day we had yet experienced in Israel (about 100 degrees), one can literally walk round Tel Jericho in minutes, not hours! By the time I found Marnie and took her to the top of the mall for some family pictures, it was time to walk around old Jericho.

Jericho is still considered the oldest walled city ever discovered in the world. It is also one of the most explored archeological sites in the world. Work continues to this day, and we were able to see the excavated wall, even sections that appear to have fallen out, not in! We saw gateways, rooms, and even in some of the archeological holes, ash layers from the day Joshua burned the city (Joshua 6:24). This certainly is the more famous story about Jericho, but as I wandered around the sand pile and rock pile that is ancient Jericho today, I remembered these Biblical stories as well; despite the curse (Joshua 6:26) Jericho was rebuilt in the days of Ahab (I Kings 16:34); it was here that David's ambassadors stayed until their hair grew back after their insult by the Ammonites (II Samuel 10:1–5); it was here that Elijah established a prophet's school and eventually left from to be taken up in a whirlwind (II Kings 2:4), and it was here that Jesus healed the blind Bartimaeus (Matthew 20:29–34) and saved the publican Zacchaeus (Luke 19:1–10). Interestingly, some of the trees we saw in Jericho were sycamore trees!

After Hiel the Bethelite rebuilt Jericho there has been a string of builders place their mark on this ancient city. Herod the Great was the builder of Jesus' Jericho, which included an amazing winter palace (we got to visit the ruins on the way out of town) on the edge of town and a fortress on a hilltop just southwest of town called Cyprus, named after his mother (Herod died in that fort and his body was taken to the Herodian for burial). Later the Romans, the Byzantines, and the Crusaders all left their handiwork, and the modern Arab town is built on the ruins of them all. After our walk-about around Jericho, we enjoyed a refreshing juice (grapefruit and orange) drink from one of those Arabs. We found the dates (the best I ever had) sweet, the citizens friendly, the weather hot, and the experience Biblical. We ended out stay in Jericho with a camel ride, another unforgettable thrill. Marnie and I had ridden an elephant together in India and our camel ride in Jericho was just as memorable. I followed this camel ride with a donkey ride down a hillside after searching for Saint George's monastery (one of my disappointments of the trip was not being able to see the famous monastery myself, or walk the twenty minute trail to see it up close and personal) in the Wadi Kelt (an ancient retreat founded in 480 and carved out of the steep rock wall of the narrow gorge) on our way back up the Jericho Road to Jerusalem. Two other Biblical experiences that only added to my understanding of Jesus' donkey ride (Matthew 21:1–11) down the Mount of Olives into Jerusalem, and Rebekah's camel ride from Haran back to marry Isaac (Genesis 24:25–67). I was not only walking the Bible, I was riding the Bible as well!

18

Sunday Morning On Olivet

Acts 1:12—Then returned they unto Jerusalem from the mount called OLIVET, which is from Jerusalem a Sabbath day's journey.

I woke on my sixth day in Jerusalem to the battle of the bells. It was the Lord's Day and the competing sects of Christianity were trying to outdo the other in announcing Sunday. What most don't realize is that when music isn't unified it simply makes a noise. I still remember the music in the bell of the Baptist Church of Perham, my hometown as a boy. It sounded heavenly as it echoed off the surrounding hills on a May Sunday morning. Its sweetness and harmony came because it was the only one sounding (Perham had only one church then). My first Sunday morning in Israel began with a racket, not a round; a din, not a doxology; a sound, not a strain!

Marnie and I had enjoyed another pleasant evening and night at the Knight's Palace after our exhausting day of travel to the east of Jerusalem. We had eaten our supper and breakfast in the coolness of the courtyard, and talked of what we had experienced and would experience. We also had a chance to call my wife who was visiting a dear friend fighting cancer in California. Our adventures on this new day would take us again outside of Jerusalem, but this time to the south; however, before we could travel to Bethlehem we had to go to church and what better place to go to church on a Sunday morning than to the churches on the Mount of Olives?

I know now what 'a Sabbath's Day's journey' is. Within minutes we had traveled by bus from our place of rest to the ridge that lies due east of Jerusalem. Our plan was to walk down Olivet and pick up our ride to Bethlehem at the base. The Mount of Olives rises to a height of almost 2500 feet which makes it a couple hundred feet higher than Jerusalem. The famous mountain has never been a part of the more famous mountains to the west, but it will forever be inseparably connected to the eternal city both geographically and historically and spiritually. This ridge got its name because it was at one time covered in olive groves, and though a few remain, most of the side hill is now covered with Jewish graves and Christian churches, chapels, and shrines (even the sects have arrived on the Mount). The 'mount' is about a mile long and runs pretty much from north to south. It is separated from Jerusalem by the Kidron Valley (John 18:1). Our trip down its slopes started on an observation platform directly over the Jewish cemetery located on its southern end. From there I came to an understanding of what Jesus meant when he spoke of 'whited sepulchers' (Matthew 23:27). The thousands of grave sites and grave markers were bleached white by the years of exposure to the sun, beautiful, but still a graveyard. Little could I imagine the 'whited sepulchers' I would discover in the Christian section of Olivet?

Once we got a good look and some marvelous photographs of old Jerusalem, we started down the traditional path of Jesus' triumphal entry (Mark 11:1–11). The donkey ride the day before gave me a better understanding of just how difficult that ride was. The slope was steep, and unbeknownst to me there was a man halfway down that would have given me a ride on his donkey. Instead of buying a ride down, I gave some money to a bagger at the head of the route. He was only the third that I had seen in six days, which surprised me? The road was lined with rock walls that separated us from the cemetery on our left and the first church complex on our right. Halfway down the hill we walked through a stone gate into an olive grove. We were heading for the Church of the Tear Drop, and what Greg said was the best picture taking spot on the entire mount.

As I have written in other articles, there is hardly a story in the life of Christ where somebody hasn't determined where that event took place. Jesus' connection to the Mount of Olives was extensive. He not only rode a donkey down its west side, but He is recorded to have prayed over the city of Jerusalem from its slopes (Luke 19:41), and somebody has found the exact spot and they have built a church over it! When we arrived, a church service was already going on, so we didn't interrupt them. But we were able to look directly across the Kidron Valley to the Eastern Gate, and what a sight! There were plenty of people there, but for me it was more a tour atmosphere than a worship atmosphere. I knew I would have to find another place to worship, and there were plenty of choices on Olivet.

From where I was standing in front of the Church of the Tear Drop, I could see high on the hill the Church of the Ascension, the place of Jesus' return to Heaven (Acts 1:11)? Just below me and to my right was the Church of Mary Magdalene (Luke 8:2), a Russian Orthodox Chapel with seven distinctive golden domes; in my opinion the most beautiful of all the church building I saw in Israel. Below and just in front of the Lion Gate I could see the Church of Stephen, built on the spot where they believe he was martyred (Acts 7:58). Directly below me I could see the roof of the Church of Nations, built next door to the Garden of Gethsemane (Matthew 26:36). How many other chapels and churches were out of my sight? I knew that even the Mormons had built a shrine on the northern end of Olivet to my utter amazement and shock. The more I stayed on Olivet the more I wished to be removed to the slopes overlooking Michmash again, for a quiet place to worship the Christ on a Sunday morning in Israel.

I think it is time for us to stop for a moment and consider 'the test of the true'. I must admit that I too have been deceived by the ability of mankind to make something artificial look like the genuine thing. I still remember the first time I saw a pot of flowers and was tricked by the exquisite texture, the skillful coloring, and the natural shape of the presentation. It was only as I got close enough and took a deep breath that I knew I had been admiring artificial. In our synthetic age we have been able to deceive even the so called expects at times, and what is true in the world has become true in the Church. Satan is the Master Duplicator (II Corinthians 11:14). The world is filled with the Jannes and Jambres (II Timothy 3:8) of our times, and I saw their product on Olivet. What scares me at times is that the artificial of today is often more attractive than the real. Mankind has developed places of worship that are spiritually cleaner, humanly fresher, more symmetrical and uniform than the godly. I saw a lot of dedicated, devoted, disciplined disciples on Olivet that Sunday morning, but how many were genuine believers? I saw a lot of beautiful places and beautiful people but something didn't smell right to me. Remember, Jesus began His Church with a weather-beaten, double-minded, recently-defeated Peter, not the perfectly-dressed, phylactery-wearing, spotless-robed Pharisee.

I was disappointed in the Mount of Olives, but there was one place yet to visit. Would the Garden of Gethsemane be different, was there still a place that I could really worship the Lord on Olivet? I had put each place and each site to the test of the true and so far I had only found the artificial hand of man trying to make something historical into something profitable. I was still looking after an hour for that quiet and tranquil place where I could *"be still, and know that"* (Psalms 46:10) *God was still God and Christ was still Christ, and that He could still be exalted among the heathen and in the earth; especially on a hill He went to so often to communicate with His Father!* (Luke 22:39–40).

19

Gethsemane Garden

Matthew 26:36—Then cometh Jesus with them unto a place called GETHSEMANE, and saith unto the disciples, Sit ye here, while I go and pray yonder.

From the upper ridge of Olivet, Marnie and I reached the lower slopes of the Mount of Olives about mid-morning. There to our left was a stone doorway and over it's lentil the word 'Gethsemane'!

Most of my life I have been singing Jennie Evelyn Hussey's classic communion hymn, "Lead Me to Calvary". Its chorus still haunts me every time I remember its exhortation:

> Lest I forget *Gethsemane*; lest I forget Thine agony; lest I forget
> Thy love for me, lead me to Calvary.

I was taught from a very young age that before you can go to Calvary you need to stop first at Gethsemane. (The teaching was that at Gethsemane Jesus made the commitment to Calvary, and before we accept Jesus' pardon paid for at Calvary we need to commit ourselves to the price we must pay to serve Him after salvation. Salvation costs us nothing but service costs us everything-Luke 14:33—as it did for Christ!) On this trip we had reversed that philosophy, but now that I have been to both places I think my childhood teachers were right.

Once we entered the garden of Gethsemane, I not only felt something different, but smelled something different. Unlike so many of the other Biblical spots there were no vendors in or outside the gate. Was it because it was Sunday? I know not. All I know is that on the morning I visited Gethsemane the crowd was quiet, the garden was peaceful, and the atmosphere was spiritual. Once inside the courtyard you could see the hand of man as he had surrounded what was left of the olives trees by a stone walkway. We were told the eight ancient trees that remain have roots that can be traced back to the time of Christ. There in the middle of this rock courtyard, surrounded by high stone walls, the olive trees stood as sentinels to what happened somewhere on that side hill nearly 2000 years ago. Among wonderful flower beds and other blooming bushes and shrubs, the twisted roots and branches of the olive trees mirror the agony that took place when Jesus cried:

"Not My Will, But Thine Be Done." (Mark 14:36)

I too had found my place of worship.

When did mankind decide that it was better to worship God inside instead of outside? Don't get me wrong, I am not condemning the worship of God in churches, chapels, or cathedrals. I believe we can worship the Good Lord anywhere and at any time. As I wandered around Gethsemane garden, my entire being changed. I took pictures, but I also took in the serenity and softness of what they had done to make Gethsemane sobering and spiritual. And was that a bird singing? I had heard very few natural sounds on this trip so far. I was beginning to realize why the Lord loved to come to this place. In my mind's eye I began to imagine the garden free from walls and chapels and stone walkways. There under the shadow of the olive trees Jesus found solitude He couldn't find even in the Temple, His Father's own house. The noise of the city was lost in the forest that was Gethsemane, and even when He did come He insulated Himself from His disciples by moving further into the grove of trees. I couldn't do that for there was only so far to go, and I was sharing this experience with a hundred people or more. But on this day they were respectful to the place and the time, and maybe, just maybe, like me they too were looking for that place to worship on a Sunday morning.

Only twice is Gethsemane mentioned in the Gospels (Matthew 26:36 and Mark 14:32). Located about a mile from the walls of Jerusalem, this garden or orchard was a regular stopping off spot for Jesus. There is no mention of Jesus ever staying in Jerusalem over night, but He would often leave the city for Bethany which is located on the backside of the Mount of Olives. For me the lesson is clear. We need on occasion to leave the city and head for a country spot, like Gethsemane. Most today have no appreciation for the finer things found in the woods, under the trees, among the branches. I know we are sacrificing these places today for progress and the advancement of society. If I were asked whether or not we need to give up a peaceful gethsemane for another parking garage I say no! We have replaced Jesus in Gethsemane for an astronaut in space. We so soon forget that God created man and put him in a garden, not a gutter. There are very few gardens left, and I must admit it did my heart good to find at least three still in Jerusalem (the garden tomb, Gethsemane garden, and the garden at the holocaust museum-we will go there tomorrow). I left Gethsemane with a full heart and a revived spirit, but my morning worship service wasn't over yet. Gethsemane was the preamble, the worship music, the reading of Scripture, the special musical number, but it was in the Church of Nations that I heard the morning message.

Next to the Garden of Gethsemane is the massive, but simple Church of the Nations. As we waited to board the bus for Bethlehem, I wandered through the huge doors of this old church. I expected to see a repeat of the Holy Sepulcher, but how wrong I was. I thought my Olivet experience was over with the blessing of Gethsemane, but instead the joy continued. To my happy surprise the church building was as quiet and solemn as the garden. As I soon learned the church was built beside the garden to give pilgrims like me from any nation a place to worship and pray. It was not like most of the other church connected with some Christian sect, denomination, or brand of Christianity. Inside I found a medieval-like structure; much like the churches my wife and I found when we did a tour of England, Scotland, and Wales for our 30th wedding anniversary. There were beautiful stained-glass windows, tall marble pillars, and tasteful murals. Each one seemed to tell a certain part of the story of Christ in the garden. There was the betrayal of Judas, the Lord praying, and the arrest by the soldiers. I wandered the cavern that was the Church of Nations for fifteen minutes or more. When I left to see if the bus had yet come, I found that it hadn't so I wandered some more, and it was then I heard my sermon for that Sunday.

On the other side of the church structure was another small area, a place for the overflow of pilgrims I suspect. The flowering bushes surrounding the stone patio were beautiful and fragrant. It was then I was reminded that I am a migrant, a pilgrim, a stranger at best in this old world (I Corinthians 4:11), and whether I am at home in Maine, or in Gethsemane the Lord will always find for me a place to worship Him. We sometimes forget that we are not citizens of earth, but our citizenship is in Heaven (Ephesians 2:19). That one day there will be no Baptist,

Methodist, Presbyterian, Episcopal, Pentecostal, or another other of the Heinz 57 varieties of churches now found on this planet. One day the only Church will be the Church of Nations, the bride of Christ, the royal priesthood, a brotherhood of mankind!

20

O Little Town of Bethlehem?

Luke 2:4—And Joseph also went up from Galilee, out of the city of Nazareth, into Judaea, unto the city of David, which is called BETHLEHEM; because he was of the house and lineage of David.

When we left the Mount of Olives we only had a five mile ride to Bethlehem, but it seemed to take us forever to get there. Traffic slowed our progress, pilgrims or tourists? We made a side visit to Kirth Himmon, an ancient Jewish gravesite from the 1st century located behind the Menachem Begin Heritage Center. Our guide and instructor seemed to be fascinated by ancient cemeteries; we rarely passed one by on the trip! As we climbed out of the Himmon Valley onto the ridge that would take us to Bethlehem, we stopped at a park that overlooked the valley with a northern looked at the old city. I still don't understand the delay to this day, but over an hour was wasted that we could have spent in Bethlehem, or was it? Did Greg know something he wasn't sharing? I will never forget Greg's words as we passed through another Israeli checkpoint, through another impressive section of the West Wall, and passed another set of huge guard towers into the West Bank:

> I will warn you now that after you see Bethlehem you will never sing "O Little Town of Bethlehem" the same way again.

I was thinking that my visit to Bethlehem would thrill me and chill me each and every time I sang that Christmas classic, but now I know what Greg was talking about! So before I ruin it for you as well, sing it with me, Phillips Brooks' classic Christmas carol and Lewis Redner's haunting melody one more time as you picture our childhood Bethlehem:

> O little town of Bethlehem, how still we see thee lie! Above thy deep and dreamless sleep the silent stars go by. Yet in thy dark street shineth the everlasting Light; the hopes and fears of all the years are met in thee tonight. For Christ is born of Mary, and gathered all above, while mortals sleep, the angels keep their watch of wondering love. O morning stars together proclaim the holy birth, and praises sing to God the King, and peace to men on earth. How silently, how silently the wondrous gift is given! So God imparts to human hearts the blessings of His Heaven. No ear may hear His coming, but in this world of sin, where meek souls will receive Him still the dear Christ enters in. O holy Child of Bethlehem! Descend to us, we pray; cast out our sin, and enter in; be born in us today. We hear the Christmas angels the great glad tidings tell; O come to us, abide in us, Our Lord Emmanuel.

I feel I must put a warning label on this chapter, and tell you that if you really don't want your mind changed about Bethlehem stop reading now and go on to the next chapter; this will be your final warning!

From a distant hill I had my first look at Bethlehem sitting on a high ridge over 2,000 feet above sea level. It was larger than I imagined (a rarity on this Israel trip), but why wouldn't it be after all these years? I was so focused on Bethlehem I missed the white-domed structure known as the tomb of Rachel (Genesis 35:19-20) and King David's Well were his brave soldiers got him a drink of water (II Samuel 23:14-17). I was thrilled that I was coming into Ruth and Boaz's town, David's village, 'the house of bread', the place that Micah would prophesy that the Messiah would come from (Micah 5:2), the birthplace of my Lord and Saviour Jesus Christ. As we entered the city proper, the bus began to laugh as we passed a sign that said "Stars and Bucks." The logo was familiar, and then it hit me, it was a coffee shop that had adapted the more famous label; it was then and there a knot came to my stomach and a sadness sweep over my soul. A terrible question began to ascend from deep in my mind:

> They haven't spoiled the place of His birth, too?

I had seen what men had done to mar the significance of His death and resurrection by false traditions, godless shrines, elaborate pomp, and meaningless ceremony in Jerusalem. I had witnessed the costly edifices built over spots where Christ may or may not have even been on Olivet, but surely not Bethlehem, too?

Our first stop in Bethlehem was at The Church of the Nativity. It is said to have been built over the cave where Mary delivered the baby Jesus by Emperor Constantine nearly 10 years after he made Christianity the Roman State Religion in 321 AD. (In my opinion one of the greatest tragedies ever inflicted on Christianity in its history!) Because of the nature of the place (Bethlehem is located on the West Bank and a hotbed of Arab resistance to the Israeli occupation), we were instructed not to gather as a group and only enter the church in twos and threes. Despite the hostility by the Arabs, their entire economy seemed to be based on this place. In the basement of the church is a grotto and there you will find a silver star that is supposed to mark the very spot of Christ's birth. The crowds were so large when we arrived we would have had to wait for hours to see the 'star'. There were shrines and altars throughout the space much like at the Holy Sepulcher. We did take time to visit Jerome's Chapel where the famous Church father spent 30 years of his life translating the Bible from Greek and Hebrew into Latin. The Vulgate was the Church's only Bible for over 1000 years until the days of Wycliffe. I had come thousands of miles and waited all my life to see Bethlehem and I spent less than a half an hour in the Church that honored the most famous birth in history, why?

I couldn't get over the commercialization of the 'little town'. I couldn't stand the hucksters on the streets. I couldn't stand the fanfare that celebrated a 'faith' I couldn't understand. All that was now Bethlehem disgusted my reverent heart for the place and the Person of that place. We stayed long enough to eat a noon meal together in a new restaurant, perhaps, the worst food I ate on the entire trip, which didn't help my attitude about Bethlehem. We stopped at a 'nativity' gift shop for those who wanted to buy a remembrance of Bethlehem. The carvings were beautiful in olive wood, or so they said, but the price was far beyond most of us; again, commercialization gone mad. We even stopped to take a look at the Shepherd's Field which only added to my disappointment. The so called place of the Christmas shepherds is now surrounded by houses and housing developments. They said that within a few years even this land will be swallowed up by the Arabs. I believe the hope of most that live there now is to somehow erase what happened there so very long ago. It has been a masterful strategy of the Wicked One to mix this monumental event with pagan holidays, heathen practices, and modern economics until the average Christian worshipper is bewildered with a mixture of fact and fancy. It has been a winning tactic of the Devil to create a modern Bethlehem that looks more like a mall than the place of

Messiah's birth and obscures the real business of the Lord with the local business fortunes of the Arab Christians until tourists and not pilgrims are the majority of visitors on a Sunday morning in May! Satan has won in Bethlehem because he has blinded the minds and eyes (II Corinthians 4:4) of most lest 'the everlasting Light' which once brightened 'thy dark streets' would shine in their hearts. Lucifer will do whatever it takes to keep mankind from facing his sin, his need of a Saviour, and from singing *'cast out our sin and enter in, be born in us today!'* Until I went to Bethlehem, I didn't realize just how good our Adversary was!

I think it is about time we stop returning to Bethlehem and start rediscovering the Babe of Bethlehem. I left Bethlehem about one-thirty, and as we left I turned my head away mournfully singing *O little town of Bethlehem*.

21

Herod's Herodium

Matthew 2:19—And when HEROD was dead...

My sad countenance only remained with me for about three miles of travel through the foothills surrounding Bethlehem. The minute I saw the Herodium my mind quickly told me that I was about to visit a place that has been on my 'bucket list' since high school.

One can't visit the holy land without traveling under the shadow of one of 'the greats'. History is filled with mighty men, but on only a few has history placed the phrase 'the great' behind their names. Men like Alexander the Great, Cyrus the Great, Fredrick the Great, and Herod the Great. (Note, these men were 'great' in the eyes of the world, not the Lord!) To this day Herod can still be seen in Israel. We had already explored parts of Herod's Jerusalem. We had witnessed his handiwork in Jericho, and would see it again in Caesarea and Masada, but for me the best example of this man's amazing ability to build was at the only place he named after himself: the Herodium. It is also interesting to note that this impressive engineering masterpiece was located in the shadow of Bethlehem. It was here the great Herod came the closest to earthly immortality when he tried to kill the Great King (Matthew 2), but failed.

Herod was an Arab by birth, an Idumaean, what we know from the Bible as an Edomite, a race linked to Jacob's brother Esau (Genesis 36). The territory of the Edomites was in southern Palestine. History tells us that Herod's grandfather adopted Judaism and his father, Antipater, was rewarded for his support of the Romans in the region by Roman citizenship and the rule over the entire area of Judaea. When Antipater died in

43 BC his sons, Herod and Phasael (who Herod named the tower in his Jerusalem palace after), became joint-governors of Palestine. In 40 BC, Phasael died when the Parthians (Iran) invaded the area. Herod had to flee to Rome for safety. While in Rome, Herod made friends with powerful people like Mark Antony (who he named the fortress in Jerusalem after-the Antonia), and Octavian (the future Caesar Augustus-Luke 2:1). Once Rome reestablished control over the country of Judaea, they appointed Herod king in 37 BC. Herod would be king until 4 BC and would rule his kingship with a rod of iron. With the riches he gained as ruler, he began rebuilding the country; including a series of forts to protect him from invasion as well as from his own people. Herod was not only a great builder, but he was capable of great cruelty which include killing his beloved wife as we have seen. He killed his firstborn son because he thought he was plotting against him, as well as members of the Pharisees. Is it any wonder that he put a price on the head of a baby when he heard that the King of the Jews had been born in Bethlehem?

Caesarea is impressive as we will see, but there was at least water for a seaport. Masada is impressive as we will see, but there was already a mighty rock. Temple mount is impressive as we have seen, but there was already Mount Moriah. What makes the Herodium, in my opinion, so impressive is that there was no hill there. Yes, Herod built a mountain first then he put a round fortress on its top! Located about ten miles from Jerusalem, the Herodium would guard Herod's southern flank. In order to keep in touch with his outlying forts he needed line of sight, so that the signal fires could be seen. In order to do that he had to make a manmade mount high enough for his purpose. About half way into his kingship Herod started this most ambitious building project that when finished would be his summer palace, a district capital, a mighty fortress, and his burial plot!

Built between 23 and 20 BC, the immense Herodium complex is still standing today, if only in piles of rocks, but even in its ruins it speaks of its glory days. Located near the ancient road to the Dead Sea, the project was completed in two sections: the Upper Herodium found on the mount and the Lower Herodium found at the base of the mountain. The Lower Herodium contained a large palace with many rooms, terraced gardens, and one of the greatest swimming pools (over 210 feet long and over 135 feet wide) of ancient times. We could clearly see the pattern of the walls of the palace and the pool from high on top of the hill. The Upper Herodium contained a palace set within the walls of a circular fort on the cone-shaped, artificial mountain. The fort was constructed with a double cylindrical wall, a semicircular western tower, a semicircular southern tower, a semicircular northern tower, and the Great Tower which looked eastward standing high above them all. There was a surface staircase from the lower palace to the upper palace of 200 steps of the purest white marble. Marnie and I and the rest of the group took the snake path around the outside of the cone to the volcano-shaped top. The archeologists have only uncovered sections of the staircase, and about halfway up they believe they have found the actual burial tomb of Herod the Great. (They say Herod was buried in a bier which was of solid gold studded with precious stones and had a covering of purple embroidered with various colors!)

Once we were at the top we got to see the surrounding country from what is left of the great tower. Greg told us that on a clear day (it was a bit hazy that day) you can see the towers on the Mount of Olives where we had been that morning towards the northwest. The 'little' town of Bethlehem could be seen clearly to the west. We turned east and the Wilderness of Judean was at our feet. Greg told us again that on a clear day you could see all the way to the Dead Sea and Masada. We got to climb down into the center of the structure and walk into the storage rooms and guest rooms of the fortress. There was a synagogue and a bath room, but for Marnie and me the most impressive part of the Herodium still standing couldn't be seen from on top. As Herod's engineers built the mountain they literally honeycombed the middle of the hill with thousands of feet of tunnels. From just below the Great Tower you enter into the subterranean world much like we experienced in Hezekiah's tunnel, but the Herodium didn't have a Gihon Spring, so what were they to do for water? You start the 500 foot decent into the heart of the Herodium and along the route you discover vast cisterns, both upper and lower. The upper or intermediate cistern would collect the water that fell naturally, but Herod also built a backup system into his plans with three lower cisterns that were filled by Herod's servants carrying water in skins, jars, or buckets. It is estimated that the lower cisterns could hold upwards of 400,000 gallons of water. A walk through the tunnels of the Herodium was a cooling and refreshing reprieve after the heat on top of the hill.

We learned that after the Herodium was completed Herod used it until his death. Turned over to his son Archelaus, the fortress only remained in his hand until the Romans took it over. In 66 AD the Zealots controlled the Herodium until they were defeated in 70 AD. There is no record that any major battle was ever fought over it, even in the Revolt of 135 AD. Hundreds of years after the Herodium was abandoned a group of Byzantine monks established a community there. Other groups established a few churches (churches that worshipped the Baby, Herod wanted to murder; isn't God's humor amazing?) there until the Arabs came, and only in the days of the Crusaders (the Herodium is sometimes called the 'mount of the Franks') was the fort occupied again. For nearly a thousand years it was abandoned and major archeological work didn't begin until 1962. It is a national park today, and its message is clear to me. The iconic symbol of a great king lies in ruins while ironically the Great King is still worshiped. The Herodium is simply a cemetery of a great king, while the cemetery of the Great King is empty!

22

A Morning On Mount Moriah

II Chronicles 3:1—Then Solomon began to build the house of the Lord at Jerusalem in MOUNT MORIAH, where the Lord appeared unto David his father . . .

Olivet was inspiring, Bethlehem was disappointing, and the Herodium was interesting. We got back to the Knight's Palace after another exhausting day exploring outside the city walls late in the afternoon of May 16th. After six days on the run Marnie and I decided to take a break from walking and get caught up on our journals and turn in early. The last day of our first week in Israel would be just as busy and just as blessed as the others had been. We were planning an early morning accent up Mount Moriah.

As a child in children's church, I still remember Lily Harris telling the story of Abraham and Isaac's climb to Moriah (Genesis 22:1-14), of the gracious substitution of the ram, and the thrilling return of that same father and son back off that sacred mountain. Because of the sensitive nature of the area, we didn't know until our last day in Jerusalem whether or not we would be able to go to Mount Moriah. That area of Jerusalem has been a flashpoint between the Jews and Arabs since 1948 and even more so since 1967 when Israel took control of Jerusalem. There is an unsettled coexistence to this day and sometimes it is dangerous to tour the area. No Jews are allowed any religious freedom on the top, and all Bibles and Christians symbols are taboo as well. We were going to make an early morning attempt before the crowds got large and the area got busy. We were hoping to get in and out stealthily as a tour group rather than a Bible study class.

We left the Knight's Palace around 7:30. It took us a half an hour to walk to the Western Wall and pass through security. To gain the summit we had to snake our way through a man-made wooden tunnel that rose from the floor of the plaza of the Western Wall just north of Robinson's Arch and just south of the Wailing Wall itself. The incline eventually brought us to a small stone gate that opened up to the massive courtyard (35 acres, or a 6th of the entire area of the Old City) that Herod had built to support his temple complex. Two huge structures are there today. Upon entering the area you are confronted by the Aqsa Mosque (beneath this mosque they have discovered Solomon's stables) which stands on the southern end of the esplanade. This is the primary worship place of the Moslems of the area, and it was first built between 709 and 715. Little remains of the original structure for it was destroyed and renovated many times. During the Crusader era, the Al Aqsa was used as a palace for the Latin kings, and later headquarters for the Knights Templar. The building today is large enough to hold 5,000 worshippers! It was very quiet the morning we were there, almost eerie. As we gathered to get orientated, I saw less than 100 people in the immediate area. There seemed to be other small groups like ours gathered here and there, and most people were talking in a whisper. Once Greg explained the history and what we could see, we were encouraged to split up in groups of twos and threes. We had about an hour or so to explore. Then we would meet together again on the far side of the courtyard before our decent off Mount Moriah.

Of course the most famous building (maybe, one of the most recognizable structures in the whole world) on Mount Moriah is the Dome of the Rock (interestingly, it took all the taxes of the province of Egypt for seven years to pay for the building of this mosque), or sometimes called the Mosque of Omar. (This building is a rectangular octagon with each side measuring 63 feet with a diameter of 180 feet. Above it raises a dome on a cylindrical drum to a height of 108 feet from the ground; this has a diameter of 78 feet. The dome is made of a special aluminum bronze alloy which makes it shine like gold under a bright Jerusalem sun.) I recalled its history as Marnie and I began to take pictures from different angles. Built in the 7th century by Caliph Abd el-Malik, supposedly directly over the top of the peak of Mount Moriah, and because we were not allowed to enter the building we didn't get to see the famous rock. Interestingly, as I was writing this book I came across a series of slides taken by my Uncle Paul who traveled to Israel nearly thirty years before me. My uncle passed away 18 months ago and I was left as trustee of his estate which

A Morning On Mount Moriah 91

included going through his belongings. As I was sorting through his pictures I discovered one of the 'Rocks' (it is 15 yards long, 12 yards wide and rises to a height of 2 yards above the ground). My Uncle must have been able to actually enter the Dome of the Rock, so I have seen the top of Moriah through his photographs. (Although the mosque was designed and built by Byzantine artists, all its decorations are Oriental. The interior of the building has a beautifully decorated Cupola, and the richly colored stain glass windows are beyond description. There are lovely mosaics on the walls and wonderful woodwork in the arcades.) After the Crusader's conquest of Jerusalem in 1099 the dome became a church. When Saladin recaptured Jerusalem in 1187 the golden cross on the top of the dome was replaced with the Crescent of Mohammad. In Islam, the Dome of the Rock is the third holiest spot in the Moslem world only behind Mecca (the place of the birth and tomb of the prophet Mohammad) and Medina (the place of his first conquest). The Moslem fable is that Mohammad took his so called 'night ride into heaven' on a white horse leaving earth from Mount Moriah!

My interest in our walk-about was to visualize the three temples that once stood on this site. The verse I have printed above is the only mention of Mount Moriah in the Bible, and this scripture makes it clear that the original structure on this mountaintop was a temple, not a mosque. David planned it, but Solomon built the first Temple on this site. On our last day in Israel, Marnie and I with a number of other members of our group returned for one last look at the old city. In our final walk I came across Solomon's quarries at the base of the city wall just east of the Damascus Gate. A huge cave known as Zedekiah's Grotto is located there. Jewish legend reports that this was the last king of Judah escape route from a dying city in 586 BC (II Kings 25:1-21). The cave is filled with white limestone, and Josephus, the Jewish historian, calls it the royal caverns in his writings. Most feel this is where David and Solomon got the hewn stones for the Temple (I Kings 6:7). Because Moses prohibited the cutting of stone near the altar (Exodus 20:25), most feel the closeness to Temple Mount is ideal (I Kings 5:15-18). This final expedition allowed me to see how they built the Temples on Mount Moriah.

Most feel, including our guides, that Solomon's Temple (II Samuel 7 and I Chronicles 22) was located on the northern end of the plaza. I have read estimates of upwards of 100 billion dollars to replace the original temple in all its glory and with gold over $1,200 an ounce today that might be an underestimation. That Temple was plundered, set on fire, and utterly destroyed by Nebuchadnezzar's army in 586 BC (II Kings 25:8–11). It was another hundred years plus before another Temple was raised from the ashes. When Cyrus issued a decree allowing the Jews back into their land after 70 years (Daniel 9:1), one of the first things the Hebrews did was to plan to rebuild their beloved Temple. It followed the basic pattern of Solomon's Temple, but was not as magnificent (Haggai 2:9). Even some of the scared vessels plundered by Nebuchadnezzar were returned (Ezra 1:1–4), but the most precious of all the articles, the Ark of the Covenant, had disappeared! Eventually this Temple, known in history as Zerubbabel's (Ezra 5:2) Temple, named after the man who above and beyond any others got the second temple built, was polluted by Antiochus Epiphanes of Syria during the age of the Maccabeans (what we called the inter-testament period, or between Malachi and Matthew), and restored more or less by the Maccabeans until Herod the Great decided to rebuilt it in 20 BC.

The huge plaza Marnie and I walked around on May 17, 2010 was built by Herod to support his grand temple. Forty-six years (John 2:20) in construction, this area once included an outer court for Gentiles, a woman's court, and an inner court which contained the Holy Place and the Holy of Holies. This completed temple only stood for less than fifty years when in 70 AD Titus and his army destroyed Herod's Temple, or the third temple in fulfillment of Jesus' prophecy (Matthew 24:1–2). Before I was through I viewed the area from all four corners. I walked to the door of the Dome of the Rock, the staircase leading up from the Eastern gate, and the northern area which overlooked the site of the Antonia. We were off Mount Moriah by mid-morning, safe and inspired, for I now have seen where the final Temple will be built, and when it is finished I will be able to go inside!

23

Corrie Ten Boom's Tree

Genesis 12:3—AND I WILL BLESS THEM THAT BLESS THEE...

Our last morning staying in the old city of Jerusalem was filled with breakfast, our first quiz (remember, this was actually a graduate level course from Dallas Theological Seminary and with the lectures and study tour there was a weekly quiz), a trip up Mount Moriah, and our first extended free-time of our journey. We had six hours to do what we wanted before the last official walk in the old city took place (we were going to explore the tunnel that runs along and under the Western Wall). What to do? Some went shopping; some walked over to the Mount of Olives again, and others stayed in the motel to rest. There was no doubt what Marnie and I were going to do: visit the Holocaust Museum in Jerusalem. Marnie had been moved by a visit to the one in Washington D.C. and the minute she heard about our free-time in Jerusalem the Yad Vashem (meaning "a name and a place" taken from *Isaiah 56:5-6"Even unto them will I give in mine house and within my walls a place and a name better than of sons and of daughters: I will give them an everlasting name, that shall not be cut off."*) Holocaust History Museum was on her "to-do" list. As we talked about taking a cab into Jerusalem others in our group decided to come along. I was going along because a good friend of mine, Mark Honey, asked if I would visit the museum for him. Mark has MD and has been confined to a wheelchair for nearly half his life. A serious student of history, the minute he heard about my trip, he called and his first question was, "Are you going to the Holocaust Museum in Jerusalem?" Today, I was!

Twelve of us met at the cab stand at the Jaffa Gate to find a ride to the museum. It took a bit of doing by our appointed representative Steve Peacock, our Uncle Paul of the trip, but he eventually hired three taxis to take the dozen of us on the 15-minute ride to the Yad Vashem located on a tree-covered side hill on the western side of modern Jerusalem. It cost us about five dollars each and we arrived safely around ten o'clock. We agreed that we would meet back at the cab stand in front of the museum in two hours; we should have agreed on more time for little did we realize what we were about to experience!

There is no way I would ever try to explain in words what I saw in the massive triangle shaped building that was the Yad Vashem (an archive, a research institute, a museum, and more importantly, a monument to the everlasting memory of the more than 6,000,000 Jews that died in the Nazi holocaust). As we wandered from room to room the history of the Jews in Europe from 1930 to 1948 came alive in pictures, in murals, in artifacts, and eye-witness testimonies. The horror of the holocaust was described and defined through the personal tragedy of individuals who survived and who died. I was moved by 'the hall of names', a dome covered in over 600 photographs of people who died plus an archive of books containing over 3 million names (the goal of the museum is to record every name that was lost). This part of the museum was motivated by men like David Berger who wrote in 1941:

> I should like someone to remember that there once lived a person named David Berger!

After wandering through history, we exited on the other end to more of the same on the outside. One of the buildings that moved me most was the Children's Museum. Walking down a narrow incline you enter a dark cavern. The only thing in the high ceiling room is a single candle in the middle of the room. However, the creator of this museum had placed a thousand mirrors at different angles so that one candle looked like a thousand, and as you weave your way through the pathway created a looped tape recites the names and ages of the estimated 1,500,000 kids murdered in the holocaust! Another tomb-like chamber that impressed me beside the museum was the Ohel Yizkor (the Hall of Remembrance), a structure lined with unhewed boulders where the visitor will find the names of the twenty-one death camps of Europe written on flat, black, basalt slabs on the floor. An eternal flame burns next to a vault containing the ashes from the cremation ovens of those camps of some of the victims of the great holocaust of the Twentieth Century.

After this moving experience Marnie quietly said:

> I want to find Corrie ten Boom's tree!

In our wandering through the museum we had learned about the Court and Avenue of the Righteous Among Nations, a garden created to honor the gentiles (nearly 16,000 individuals are recognized, people like Oskar Schindler) that tried to help the Jew in Europe during the holocaust. One of my daughter's spiritual heroines is the Dutch lady who along with her family tried to save the Jews in the Netherlands before she was arrested and almost died in the holocaust herself. Many years ago I did some research on a subject I called 'The Lord's Ladies', a short biographical sketch on some of the great women of the Church. This is what I wrote about Corrie:

> I have to add this woman's name to my 'Lord's ladies' list because of my daughter. She is one of Marnie's favorite authors, and has been a role-model for her most of her life. She is one of the Lord's most amazing works of grace; her name is Corrie ten Boom.
>
> Corrie was born in Haarlem, Netherlands in 1892. She lived a very sheltered and happy life with her family, devout Dutch Reformers. Corrie's father and his father before him ran a watch shop; a very simple existence for the drama that would bring this family into the horror of Nazism. Because of their contacts with Jewish suppliers in Germany, the ten Boom family learned early of the terror that was afflicting the German Jew in the 1930s. Willem, Corrie's brother, was the first to join the Dutch underground, who was involved with helping Jews escape Nazi Germany. The roots of helping the Jews in the ten Boom family can be traced back to Corrie's grandfather who as far back as 1844 had established a prayer meeting for the sole purpose of praying for the salvation of Israel. As only the Good Lord can time things, it was exactly 100 years later the Gestapo raided the ten Boom residence and arrested the family for helping Jews (the Jews hiding in the ten Boom house were never found by the Gestapo).
>
> What happened next has been told in books and even on the big screen in the wonderful movie called 'The Hiding Place'. The horror of imprisonment in the Ravensbruck death camp is now the thing of legend in Church history. Within a short

time Corrie's father died leaving Corrie alone to take care of her sick sister, Betsy. The year and more she spent in that notorious death camp cost her her sister, but strengthened her trust into something our Saviour called 'great faith' (Matthew 8:10). Despite her simple life, when her faith was tried and tested beyond imagination, she was found to be one of the great ladies of Christianity. When she was finally released alone in 1945, Corrie was ready for a world-wide ministry of love and forgiveness.

Over the next 38 years of her life (1945–1983), Corrie would span the globe telling her story in the light of His Story. With the publishing of her book, she was even able to meet former camp guards and show them 'the forgiveness of Christ' by her own forgiveness of them. Only Christ can take a simple lady and take her through a bitter misery and keep her sweet!

Outside the garden there is a towering column dedicated to the memory of all those who resisted Nazism, with the word "ZKOR" at the top: Remember! It took us the final fifteen minutes we had at Yad Vashem, but after checking the name tags on scores of trees we eventually found (should I say John Nuxoll found) Corrie's Tree: a small pine on the backside of the garden. Some of the most meaningful pictures of the entire trip are of my daughter kneeling by the name tag next to that tree holding a pinecone in her hand. The plaque simply reads:

Corrie ten Boom, Father Casper, and Sister Elizabeth. Holland.

We left the Holocaust Museum realizing that despite the horror and terror of those years God is able, even in the midst of the worst mankind can imagine, to keep not only his people alive but work a good work through a Gentile who in turn blessed not only her Church but the world.

Good always wins in the end because God is its champion!

24

A Man Named Moses

Exodus 2:10—... And she called his name MOSES ...

Around noon we left (As it turned out we also left a member of our team behind. Beth Horn had gotten so caught up in the grandeur of the place that she was late getting back to the rendezvous spot. After waiting awhile and sending others back to see if she was around we concluded that she had come out early and had taken a cab back to the Knight's Palace herself. She eventually did just that but only after waiting a few hours for us.) The Yad Vashem Museum and by 12:30PM were back to the palace. Marnie took a nap and I caught up on my journal which took me into mid-afternoon. When Marnie woke up she said, "Let's go shopping." There were still a few items on our list and we knew that the next day we were leaving Jerusalem for the southern Israel part of our tour and we didn't know if we would ever get back into the city again? After a week in the old city we knew the layout pretty well and were comfortable in walking alone in the area. So we headed for the business section of the Christian quarter.

Our steps took us over familiar stone walkways as we left the Knight's Palace along St. Francis Street. It was a busy crowd we encountered when we made the right at Christians Quarter Street. We were heading for the only merchant we knew in the city, Shaaban A. Amer. We were looking for a memory card for my digital camera (why did I think that only one would do, I still had 12 days left on the trip and my only card was nearly full), a nativity set for Marnie, some Israeli tea for my wife, and we needed to exchange some dollars for shekels to purchase any of these things. We found Shaaban on his corner right where we left him the last time we visited his shops. As usual he was ready to exchange our dollars for his shekels, and he was also knowledgeable to where we could find what we were looking for. He soon had us off to a shop where Marnie was able to buy a beautiful nativity set for about a fifth of the price they wanted in Bethlehem (it appeared to be the very same item we saw in the expensive shop in Bethlehem)! As we made our way back to check on tea and a memory card, Marnie got distracted by a few other treasures that caught her eye. I had an eye on postcards and was waiting on the outside of a shop Marnie had entered when a pleasant American voice asked:

Where are you from?

I looked around but saw nobody that looked American so I returned back to my quest of finding the perfect postcard for my wife (each day of the trip I bought a postcard that best explained my day in Israel and sent it home).

Where are you from?

I heard again. Turning for the second time I did notice a dark-haired Arab man setting in a chair on the opposite side of the stone street. He was looking straight at me, but the voice and the accent didn't fit the appearance, and yet there he was speaking to me in perfect American English. Without a brogue of any kind, you would have thought he was from the United States. We soon struck up a conversation after I apologized for not responding to his original question. Come to find out he had just gotten back from California where he had lived and run a business for years; thus the perfect English. He was so unlike the other merchants I had met, seemingly more interested in conversation than commercialization, and what a story he had.

One of five brothers, his father an Arab Moslem and his mother an Arab Christian, he had left Israel years before to make his fortune in the United States. Opening a jewelry shop in Venice, California he had settled into a life and lifestyle he thought he would enjoy for the rest of his life. His Arab wife was homesick for Israel, but his kids were enjoying California and the American dream. Then one day he got a call from his mother telling of the sudden and unexpected death of his Dad. His other brothers had also left Israel for other parts of the world, some to England and Germany and the others to the States. As they all returned for the funeral of their father, they knew that one of them would have to return back to Jerusalem to run the family business (two jewelry shops on Christian Quarter Street) and take care of their mother. After the funeral the brothers and their wives met and came up with a plan; that whichever son the mother chose he would leave his life wherever he was and return to Jerusalem no questions asked! The only other arrangement was that the four sons that didn't return would have to help the brother that did financially because business in Israel was slower than business in England, Germany, or the United States. Not knowing who the mother would choose, the brothers and their wives agreed. To which Moses (and she called his name Moses) concluded:

> Now you know who our mother's favorite child is!

Then he laughed, and said, "Truthfully, my mother loves my wife, and my wife really wanted to return to Jerusalem."

By the time Moses finished his story we had moved into his small shop just across the lane. He was showing me his handmade (Moses is also quite the artist when it comes to taking the nature stones of Israel and making them into jewelry.) jewelry when Marnie came into the shop thinking she had lost me. Once I introduced her to Moses and she heard his American accent she too was hooked. It wasn't long before Moses had Marnie trying on Roman Glass earrings. As we talked Moses sold and it was only then I realized his angle in merchandising. The saddest aspect of our conversation was the fact that being raised in a mixed 'faith' family Moses was still very confused about his relationship with Christ. He had as he told us tried them both, but had come to the conclusion that religion wasn't for him. He was however still open to us sharing our testimony. He told us that one of his brothers, the one living in England, was a devout Christian and was continually witnessing to him. Marnie and I were happy to add our watering (I Corinthians 3:8) to Moses' field. For over an hour we stayed and talked, and, yes, bought. We headed back to the palace with a craved box to put all my Israeli treasures in, an Eilat Stone from the Red Sea for my wife, and Marnie did get those Roman Glass earrings. We didn't get everything on our list, but we did get a few things not on our list because of a man by the name of Moses; the best was an opportunity to witness for our Saviour!

Perhaps, one of the best spiritual experiences and one of the best ministerial experiences I had in Israel was my time spent with Moses. Both Marnie and I agreed that before we left Israel we would try to reconnect with Moses, and we did. Our last day in the land allowed us to return to the old city and look Moses up. He was just were we had left him selling his custom made jewelry in his father's shops on Christian Quarter Street. Because we don't know the hearts of men we can only share our Saviour and pray for their salvation. Fanny Crosby's old lines come to mind when I pray for Moses:

> Feelings lie buried that grace can restore;
> Down in the human heart crushed by the tempter
> Touched by a loving heart wakened by kindness,
> Chords that are broken will vibrate once more.

Marnie and I touched Moses with both love and kindness during our shopping trips into the Christian Quarter, and while his business was jewelry and while he tried to sell us his wares what better business have we than the business of trying to give Jesus to him?

25

Western Wall Tunnel

Isaiah 7:3—Then said the Lord unto Isaiah, Go forth now to meet Ahaz, thou, and Shearjashub thy son, AT THE END OF THE CONDUIT OF THE UPPER POOL in the highway of the fuller's field.

We got back to the Knight's Palace around four o'clock. Once we deposited our purchases in our room we had just enough time to meet our study group for our last official visit in the old city. We were returning to the Wailing Wall, but this time we had an appointment with a man who was going to take us under the wall. We had already experienced the deep emotion generated by touching the stones of the Western Wall; even just standing near the ancient structure provokes feelings and yes, sometimes tears. For some it creates a hope, for others lamentation, and still others joy. To this day one can witness the frustration of the Jews in not being able to go on top of the wall and worship at the holy site where the temples use to rest. In 1967, the Ministry of Religious Affairs undertook the task of creating a place for Jewish pilgrims to gather. The result of that project was the Western Wall Plaza. At the same time they began to tunnel under the wall starting at Wilson's Arch. Tons and tons of dirt and soil have now been removed so that one is able to walk nearly 1500 feet at various depths beside that wall. As the archeologists dug deeper, more interesting bits of history were uncovered. Here is a sample of what we were able to see in our walk underground beneath and beside and below the Western Wall.

We entered into what used to be a secret, vaulted passageway built as a substructure to support the street that once ran along the wall. Interestingly, the lane was once called 'the street of the chain', but nobody seemed to know why? Then we entered a huge Hashmonaem Hall from the third Temple period. This room was found at the end of the secret passage and contained stones hewed in the typical Herodian style of the period. Then we entered an even larger hall. This subterranean structure was made up of four interlocking vaults built either in the 13th or 14th century during the Ayyubid or Mamluk periods. The most interesting aspect in this section of the walk was a computerized model of Herod's Temple. We sat around the model as the different aspects of the temple were revealed. After seeing the model at the Jerusalem Museum, it was helpful to see it close to where it actually stood. I was drawn to the model, but I couldn't keep my eyes from wandering to what was directly in front of us!

The massive cut stones before me were some of the largest stones ever uncovered in Jerusalem; an entire section of the Western Wall made up of just a few stones. The largest of them all is 45 feet long, 14 feet thick and 10 ½ feet high. Greg told us that it weighed more than the 777 we flew to Israel on. How they were able to move that stone to this spot is still unknown? If it were a bottom stone it would be one thing, but it is high up on the original wall. That section of the wall is called 'the master's course', and contains the largest cut and hewn stones ever found in Israel. Needless to say, we had our picture taken beside 'the mother of all stones'! When I returned to the United States I found this verse in connection to Solomon's building of the first temple:

> All these were of costly stones, according to the measures of hewed stones, sawed with saws, within and without, even from the foundation unto the coping, and so on the outside toward the great court." (I Kings 7:9)

Did we see some of these costly, hewn stones on our walk by the wall?

We then moved into the section of the wall I had been able to visit on my first evening in Jerusalem: Warren's (named after Charles Warren who uncovered it in 1867) Arch or Gate. There were four entrance gates into the Herod's Temple at the time of its completion. This section is called 'the cave' today, but in the early days of Israel's statehood it contained a synagogue because of its proximity to the Holy of Holies. Very close to this spot is what they call 'the foundation stone'. Jew's tradition states that this is the site from which the world was created and would eventually become the resting place of the Holy of Holies, the most sacred site in all Judaism. And right next door to this famous stone is a medieval cistern that once supplied water for the buildings above. One of the reasons I chose the Biblical verse at the beginning of this chapter is the realization that this tunnel complex was at least in part a conduit, or an aqueduct!

As we travel further into the tunnel we eventually came upon a section of bedrock. The natural rock served as the foundation for that section of the Western Wall. We had finally come upon a piece of the original Mount Moriah. What was above us was man-laid, but what we touched there was God-made. It was there we also found the Hashmonaem cistern that supplied water to the large groups of people that came to the temple area to worship. It was here we also began to walk on a section of the street that once ran the entire length of the Western Wall: Herod's Street. When we explored the southern end of this street it was open; remember the road that had all the boulders still piles beside it? This was the road that Greg said that if we wanted to walk where Jesus walked this might be the best place. Now we were walking on the northern part of that road, but we were doing it underground.

Our next stop was to visit an underground quarry. Some of the very stones still in the Western Wall were extracted from this quarry. Then we entered the Hashmonaem water tunnel that once brought water into the temple mount area before the time of Jesus. We had finally come to the northernmost end of the Western Wall, but we were not as yet through the tunnel. The room from there led us upward and it winds a bit through what is called 'Antonia Hill'. Of course we have discovered on this journey that Herod built a famous fort in honor of his good friend Mark Anthony in the northern end of the Temple Mount. All that remains today of this fortress is the bedrock upon which it was built and I had the privilege to stand on that foundation during our western wall tunnel walk.

What we saw next was very interesting to me: an underground dam? The explanation that was given was that Herod's engineers built a dam to stop the water in the original water tunnel from flowing. Which must have continued to flow even after the expansion of the temple mount, so in order not to have any further problems a dam was constructed. This doesn't mean that the water in the upper section was stopped because it became a source of water for the Antonia. As a matter of fact, a pool was created and given the name 'lark'. It was here we also saw a section of the moat of the Antonia which defended the fortress in case of an attack from the north. The Emperor Hadrian turned this section above the moat into a marketplace building two vaults above the pool; there was still water in the pond when we passed by it on our wandering walk along the wall!

Our walk only ended when we climbed a stone staircase from the Roman era to Bab al-Ghawanimah Street next to Lion Gate Road, or the upper end of the Via Dolorosa. We knew exactly where we were, and our walk back to the palace was over similar terrain, and on our way back I finally found a new card for my digital camera. The one I brought from home was nearly full and tomorrow would find us heading south into the Negev for a four-day journey from Jerusalem to Eilat by way of the coastal route and a return trip to Jerusalem by way of the Dead Sea. Our week in Jerusalem was over with a spectacular walk through layer after layer of history along the Western Wall. A fitting testimony to what we had seen and learned about God's city. No matter how much time passes, God's Word will forever be revealed even if we have to at times dig for it, one verse at a time!

26

A Stop in the Shephelah

II Chronicles 26:10—Also he built towers in the desert, and digged many wells: for he had much cattle, both in THE LOW COUNTRY, and in the plains: husbandmen also, and vine dressers in the mountains, and in Carmel: for he loved husbandry.

A cool wind was blowing through our third story window at the Knight's Palace as I awoke before six. We had opted to leave the windows open and turn the air-conditioner off for our last night in Jerusalem. As with the nights before, I slept soundly. The fresh air and the difficult hikes of the day caused a healthful exhaustion which results in a restful and refreshing night's sleep. I was excited with the prospects of the new day as I wrote Day Eight at the top of a new page in my journal. Within two hours Marnie and I would be off on the southern expedition of our Israel study trip; we were off to the 'shephelah'. "Shephelah" is the Hebrew word for 'low country'. We were going to explore the Land of Israel to the south of Jerusalem, all the way to Eilat on the Red Sea!

Around 7:30 AM we boarded an Asia Tour Bus just north of the Jaffa Gate outside the old city walls. We were introduced to our bus driver, Soffer, by Greg. We would be on and off this bus for the next four days (a very good driver and a very modern bus, but with a temperamental air-conditioner). As we worked our way back along the highway that had first brought us into Jerusalem, we made our first stop at the Yad Hashmona Guest House, our home away from home when we returned from this part of our trip. This was also the headquarters of the IBEX Campus in Israel. We stopped to pick up some equipment we would be using on our trip south. The first leg of our 8th day in Israel took up halfway back to Tel Aviv before we took a turn off Route 1 to Route 30, the main road heading into the shephelah, the Negev, and eventually into the wilderness of southern Israel.

We had travel barely 15 miles as the crow flies from Jerusalem when Soffer stopped and parked in a dusty parking lot beside the road. As with Michmash, we were going on a short hike up a small hill to a tel that overlooked the Sorek Valley. My Old Testament history began to flood through my mind as we reached the summit. The site was deserted, though we could see that some archeologists had been there long before us. (The only visible ruins were of an ancient Byzantine monastery, but below us there was a city gate area and a water source; a vital ingredient for any ancient city site.) Only when we got to the top of the knoll did we see why we had stopped. On the summit of Tel Beth Shemesh, we could see well back into the pages of the books of Judges and I Samuel, and relive a few more Sunday school stories from our childhood.

"Beth Shemesh", or 'house of the sun' was one of the towns that marked the northern border of the land given to the Tribe of Judah (Joshua 21:16) and the Tribe of Dan (Joshua 15:9-10—when you read these verses you should note the geographical difference in the elevations between the hill country and the low country). Naphtali is rebuked in Judges 1:33 for not driving out the Canaanites from Beth Shemesh, but the land was allotted to Dan who also failed to drive out the inhabitants (Joshua 19:40-47). When the Danites were forced out of this region (Judges 1:34-35), they used the Kirjath Jearim ridge route to escape and to reestablish themselves in northern Israel (Judges 18:1-31). (We will travel to that site on our northern trip.) Because the Shephelah had no natural defenses like the hill towns of Judah, it was difficult for the children of Israel to hang onto this section of the Promised Land. Instead of trusting in God, they left themselves open for occupation by the former residents and their biggest threat, the Philistines. One of the great lessons I relearned on this trip was:

> Trusting in the Lord and not the land is the key to survival in the Promised Land!

What made this stop so interesting to me were the places I could see from the top of the mount mentioned in the life of Samson. Most of Samson's tragic story could be seen within eye sight of Beth Shemesh. Delilah, the woman who defeated the world's strongest man, came from the Sorek

Valley (Judges 16:4) which ran northeast to southwest before us. We could make out Zorah and Eshtaol (Judges 13:25), where Samson's family was from, on the ridge across from Beth Shemesh. We could see well down the valley towards the great Philistine plain only two miles away. We were only seven miles away from the great Philistine city of Ekron of Philistia. The valley before us was one of five valleys (Aijalon, Sorek, Elah, Guvrin, and Lachish) that snake their way up from the coastal plain through the shephelah into the hill country of Judah and Benjamin. The Sorek Valley eventually connects with the Valley of Rephaim (giants), a valley we passed through in our travels around Jerusalem (II Samuel 5:18) many times. And as we would learn, every valley needed a guard city to protect is, and for the Sorek Valley Beth Shemesh was that guard city!

One of the eye-opening revelations of stopping in the Shephelah was a better understanding of Philistia, the country along the coastal plain settled by the powerful, sea-people, the Philistines, in the five city-states of Ashdod, Gaza, Askelon, Ekron, and Gath (I Samuel 6:17). From the days of Moses when God lead the Israelites away from 'the land of the Philistines' (Exodus 13:17) to the giants of Gath that kept the first generation of Israelites out of the Promised Land (Numbers 13:33), Philistia was a major player in Canaan throughout the early history of the Jews in Palestine (actually a name derived from Philistine) and far into the kingship age. Only after conquest of Judah by Nebuchadnezzar did Philistia disappear from the pages of history. And Philistia's history revolves around these five important cities:

1. ASHDOD—where the god Dagon was worshipped (I Samuel 5:1–8). It wasn't until the reign of King Uzziah that this city was finally conquered (II Chronicles 26:6–7). The Ashdodites had intermarried with the Israelites by the time of Nehemiah for which they were rebuked (Nehemiah 4:7–8, 13:23–25).

2. ASKELON—was originally a Jewish possession (Judges 1:18), but was lost to the Philistines. Herod the Great was born in Askelon.

3. EKRON—where the god Baal-zebub was worshipped (II Kings 1:1–16). This was the last place the Ark of the Covenant was taken (I Samuel 5:10—6:1) before it was sent back to Israel.

4. GAZA—is one of the oldest cities in the world (Genesis 10:19 and Deuteronomy 2:23) and sometimes called Azzah. Originally a possession of Judah but lost to Philistia (Joshua 15:47). Samson first carried its gates to Hebron (Judges 16:1–3) and then Samson was carried to Gaza

to eventually die under the rubble of its temple (Judges 16:21–31). It was near Gaza that the Ethiopian eunuch had his famous encounter with Philip (Acts 8:26–39).

5. GATH—where the great giant family of Goliath was from (I Samuel 17:4 and II Samuel 21:15–22). Goliath had at least four other brothers just as big or bigger, and each of them would eventually be defeated by David and his men. Gath would only be conquered in the days of King Uzziah (II Chronicles 26:6–7).

But perhaps Beth Shemesh's best call to Biblical fame is the events described in First Samuel 6:1—7:2, when the Ark of the Covenant was captured by the Philistines at the Battle of Ebenezer (I Samuel 4). After being taken around to a number of the Philistine cities, the Ark of the Covenant was returned to Israel because of the plagues that broke out on the citizens of the city-states of Philistia (I Samuel 5). From Ekron (I Samuel 5:19), the Ark was placed on a cart pulled by two cows. After seven months (I Samuel 6:1), the Ark was back in Jewish hands when the residents of Beth Shemesh spied it coming up the valley during the wheat harvest (I Samuel 6:12). I now can visualize that heart-stopping event in my mind! The residents of Beth Shemesh rejoiced, but within a short period of time the people of Beth Shemesh also transgressed (I Samuel 6:19) and the Ark had to be moved again. The Bible tells us that the men of Kirjath Jearim (I Samuel 7:1) came and got the Ark and it would remain in their care until the days of David (II Samuel 6:3). Interestingly, when we left the IBEX Campus we were pointed out the hill of Kirjath Jearim under the shadow of the Yad Hashmona Guest House. We had traveled the distance the Ark traveled thousands of years before that morning.

The only other call to fame of this town was the defeat of King Amaziah of Judah by King Joash of Israel at Beth Shemesh (II Kings 14:7–14 and II Chronicles 25:14–24). After his victory, King Joash continued up the Kirjath Jearim route to Jerusalem where he broke down part of its defensive wall. Once again the smallness of Israel was driven home to me. That the majority of the Biblical story takes place in a tiny little section of this land, and that the distance between places is so small! I also began to realize just how much topography and geography plays in the Biblical text. The classic stories of Israel's first years in Canaan came alive as I saw why certain battles were fought where they were fought and why the people took certain routes when they traveled. The Shephelah with its low hills and wide valleys changed my understanding of the books of Joshua, Judges, and Samuel. Now when I reread this historical text I can see in my mind the hilltop of Beth Shemesh and the context of the stories beyond. We were only on the tel about half an hour, but a lifetime of Scriptural study became so much clearer. Our springtime journey into the Shephelah was turning out to be a trip down ancient miles where valiant men fought and died thousands of years ago to secure an exposed border against hostile forces. Whether Samson's wars with the Philistines, or Israel's wars with itself and others, the battle ground was the Shephelah.

Even to this day Israel is aware of the threat to their national security that comes from a small strip of land called Gaza. In the Old Testament it was the Philistine that was a thorn in their side, and today it is the Palestian that threatens their Shephelah!

27

Confronting Giants
On Mount Azekah

I Samuel 17:1—Now the Philistines gathered together their armies to battle, and were gathered together at Shochoh, which belongeth to Judah, and pitched between Shochoh and AZEKAH, in Ephesdammim.

If there is anywhere a lovelier spot in all of Israel than the Valley of Elah, I do not know where it is? Being a country boy from the hills and valleys of Northern Maine, I instantly feel in love with the shephelah because it reminded me of home. The rolling fertile knolls and wide fertile dales are similar to the terrain of my home county of Aroostook. As we stopped to climb Tel Azekah, was that a pine tree (the Maine state tree is a pine) I saw?

It is a cool late-summer Saturday morning on the coast of Maine as I put these remembrances of the Elah Valley into my old laptop. Sitting on a shelf just to my right is a group of three pinecones. The first I picked up in California while on a visit to see old friends; the second I picked up in North Carolina on a visit to see my soldier boy son at Fort Bragg. The middle cone I picked up on the southern slope of Mount Azekah. It is my visual reminder of a late morning ascent to view the Elah Valley, and it was from that hilltop I looked out onto the most famous battlefield in all of history; a field in which a young shepherd boy confronted the Rambo of his age and won!

Since childhood I have known of the story of David and Goliath, but it was only on Mount Azekah that I finally saw the battle unfold in the geography of its setting. The historical context is printed above, but this is not the only Biblical reference to this important hill. Joshua conquered Azekah in the early days of the Canaanite campaign (Joshua 10:10), and it was at Azekah that the Lord hurled the large hailstones on the fleeing Amorites (Joshua 10:11) after the Battle of Gibeon. Solomon saw the importance of Azekah as a strategic site during his reign and fortified it (II Chronicles 11:9). It was still an important fortress by the time of the invasion of the Babylonians for Jeremiah 34:7 tells us that the Babylonians fought against Azekah, and it was one of the last towns of Israel to hold out against the onslaught. Hearing of the Biblical importance of Azekah as shared by Greg on the run (just a few miles) over from Beth Shemesh, I couldn't wait to visit the site and see Elah Valley from its summit, but wait we would because unknown to us there was still giants in the area!

Upon our arrival at the parking area on the slopes of Azekah, we were confronted with a group of individuals that told us that we would have to wait until a television crew finished filming. At first we thought they were some news crew, so we waiting patiently for them to get done; or should I say some of the group waited patiently. I, on the other hand, have a hard time waiting on something that I really want to do, like climbing a steep hill to see the Elah Valley. So while the others waited I went wandering. Greg had told us that from the western slope (Elah was on the eastern side) of Azekah you could make out Gath (Goliath's hometown-I Samuel 17:4) in the distance. I went for a look up a pine lined, boulder infested trail. Sure enough from a rocky outcropping halfway up the path I saw the knoll that once was Gath, but it was on my way back to the group I saw them. There on the trail in front of me were two huge men, and I mean huge! By my estimation they appeared to be 400 to 500 pounders anyway, and they were carrying a large pole between them? (My spiritual imagination kicked in and all I could see was two Goliaths and a massive spear.) And there directly in front of them, like an ancient armourbearer, was a short little lady hardly a fourth their size with a notebook in one hand and a megaphone in the other, but what could this be, and where was the shield?

Unlike David I didn't confront the 'giants' but let them pass by quietly, for they seemed to have another target in mind as they rushed by. Working my way back to the parking lot I found that my daughter Marnie had figured out the puzzle of the 'giants' of Mount Azekah and the reason we were being delayed. As Marnie looked around her eye caught the emblem on the side of the television trucks. At first it didn't make any sense then she realized she had seen the symbol before. As with the 'stars and bucks' in Bethlehem, it seems that the Israelites have also copied another American product: The Biggest Loser! What they were doing on Mount Azekah was filming a segment of an Israeli television reality show, and the big men I saw on the trail were two of the contestants. When we finally got a chance to climb to the top of the mount, we came across huge tractor tires along the trail. We watched from afar as two-man teams put a steel rod through the center of a tire and then they rolled the tire over a set course to see which team would win. The giants of Mount Azekah were only over-weight men trying to lose a few pounds!

Realizing we didn't have to fight any giants to gain the summit (besides, we hadn't picked up our stones yet), we slowly walked our way around The Biggest Losers props, and eventually made the top after about a half an hour or so delay. The view from the perch on the northern edge of the hill was spectacular. Majestic pine-tree covered hills rolled out before us beyond our sight. The clear morning that welcomed us in Jerusalem was now cloud covered, but the low sky only added to the amazing vista before us. I will not attempt to describe what I saw other than to say I now understand why the Valley of Elah is a main route into the hill country of Israel. Jerusalem was only 17 miles to the northeast, and Bethlehem was much closer than that. The Plain of Philistia could be seen to the west, and it was not hard to imagine the gathering hordes of Philistines with Goliath in the lead as they worked their way up the Elah. At the same time, we could see how Saul positioned his army to block the advance of the Philistines into the heart of his kingdom. It was all there before us because of our ascent up Azekah.

How many of my companions saw the glory before us I know not, but I believe most of them had a similar spiritual experience? Yet just a few yards away was another group of individuals, Jews, who now saw the mount and the view as only a good place to film a reality show. They had come for fun and funds and to maybe get rid of a little fat, and in all their attempts to create a 'show', they failed to see the significant of The Biggest Lesson of all. Faith not fat was on display before them and they couldn't see it. Throngs of television viewers will watch the 'giants' of Azekah push their big wheels (in an ironic twist to the encounter, we watched as we drove through the Elah Valley one of those tires get loose and literally roll down the side of the hill) up and over and down Azekah, and be so caught up in the entertainment they will miss the lesson David tried to teach his nation both then and now; for pretty much the same reason mankind has missed the glory of the relative of David, Jesus.

Blinded by the 'giant' Satan (II Corinthians 4:4), familiarity breeds disrespect. As with all Biblical spots in Israel I sensed a reverence and respect, but all I saw on Azekah was irreverence and disrespect. Because they live in Israel they have become so accustomed to the places of God and the events of their history they see its historical sites as only backdrops for a TV program. People who live near great historical sites seldom see what the tourist sees, and yes, we on the coast of Maine sometimes wonder why people come from all over the world to see our shoreline? Because we see it every day we don't admire it as much as the stranger that only sees it once. I guess that is what happened to me on Azekah as I looked down into the Elah Valley. The lesson I learned on Azekah was not to lose the glory and the lesson of the Biblical story just because of my familiarity with it.

28

Picking Stones In the Elah Valley

I Samuel 17:40—And he (David) took his staff in his hand, and chose him FIVE SMOOTH STONES OUT OF THE BROOK, and put them in a shepherd's bag which he had, even in a scrip; and his sling was in his hand: and he drew near to the Philistine.

I first heard of David and his famous stones through a simple childhood chorus:

> *Only a boy named David*
> *Only a little sling.*
> *Only a boy named David*
> *But he could pray and sing.*
> *Only a boy named David*
> *Only a rippling brook.*
> *Only a boy named David*
> *And five little stones he took.*
> *And one little stone went in the sling*
> *And the sling went round and round.*
> *And one little stone went in the sling*
> *And the sling went round and round.*
> *And round and round and round*
> *And round and round and round and round.*
> *And one little stone went up in the air*
> *And the giant came tumbling down.*

As we made our way off Mount Azekah, Greg asked how many of us would like to pick five stones out of Elah stream.

Under the shadow of Azekah and just across the Valley of Elah is a small Wadi called Sumt. Because of the geography of the hills most Biblical scholars believe it was here David stopped to pick up the stone that would eventually knock down a giant (remember Goliath was eventually killed by his own sword—I Samuel 17:51). The day we stopped to walk that Wadi, the terrain hadn't changed much since David's first visit. We saw no houses or any other development except for the fields along the road that follows the valley floor from west to east. The fields beside the Wadi had just been harvested, probably a winter wheat of some kind. As we got off the bus, I felt like I was walking the head rows of one of my father's fields back in Maine. The area looked similar to the Blackstone homestead, but what we saw when we finally got to the streambed wasn't familiar at all.

I have never seen a streambed in Aroostook County void of water. Because we came to Israel during their dry season, the Wadi Sumt was dry as a bone. Even at its height we could see that it wasn't much of a waterway, just a small creek at best. I was one of the first to descend into the channel and saw almost at once that many others had been there before us. The streambed was without any rocks of any size. At first I thought to myself this is strange and then I realized that thousands of pilgrims just like me had come and had done exactly what I was about ready to do; take home a souvenir from David's famous 'brook'. If everybody did that, then there wouldn't be many stones left. And sure enough the further I walked down the streambed the more stones appeared, but I wasn't looking for just any five stones, but the smoothest five stones I could find.

In one of the museums we toured in Jerusalem, we saw 'slinging stones' for the first time (Judges 20:16). They were bigger than I imagined and rounder, but when I heard the explanation I understood why David chose the stones he did. In order for them to be effective they had to have weight as well as the ability to fly straight and true. As we all know David had become an expert in the use of the ancient sling, the favorite weapon of the wilderness shepherds. With these simple weapons even a small boy could fight off a lion or a bear which would with each encounter build a courageous confidence that one day could take on even a giant.

As I wandered about the Wadi Sumt in search of my 'five stones', I recalled the outline of a favorite sermon I had prepared years before, but now the characteristics of A GIANT KILLER came alive as I searched for the ammunition necessary for a kill-shot:

1. They are Consistent Despite the Routine-I Samuel 17:12-16.
2. They are Challenged Despite the Risk-I Samuel 17:20-23.
3. They are Committed Despite the Ridicule-I Samuel 17:28-30.
4. They are Courageous Despite the Roar-I Samuel 17:31-37.
5. They are Confident Despite the Restrictions-I Samuel 17:38-39.
6. They are Careful Despite the Rocks-I Samuel 17:40.
7. They are Conquerors Despite the Rage-I Samuel 17:41-51.

David believed that like the stone in his sling, he himself was but a servant in the hand of the Almighty. Oh, that we would learn that lesson as well.

Peter writes:

> Ye also, as lively stones, are built up a spiritual house, an holy priesthood, to offer up spiritual sacrifices, acceptable to God by Jesus Christ." (I Peter 2:5)

The same characteristics of the stone must be found in the characteristics of the servant. In another sermon on David I noted these qualities that were found in David and his stone:

1. Obedient—I Samuel 17:17
2. Responsible—I Samuel 17:20
3. Faithful—I Samuel 17:35
4. Believing—I Samuel 17:45
5. Aggressive—I Samuel 17:48

I suggest to you that all of these were found in 'the stone' that took down a giant because all of these were found in 'the slinger' that killed Goliath. If we are to meet our 'giant' head on, we too must mirror these spiritual qualities in our actions. Philip Bliss once wrote:

> *Many giants, great and tall, staking through the land, headlong to the earth would fall, if met by Daniel's Band* (why he used Daniel and not David I know not). *Dare to be a Daniel, dare to stand alone! Dare to have a purpose firm! Dare to make it known!*

These were all the characteristics of a young shepherd boy not by the name of Daniel, but David! And these should be the qualities found in our lives as well.

29

A Meaningful Stop at Mareshah

Micah 1:1—The word of the Lord that came to Micah the Morasthite (an inhabitant of MARESHAH) in the days of Jotham, Ahaz, and Hezekiah, kings of Judah, which he saw concerning Samaria and Jerusalem.

Our journey through the shephelah of southern Israel took us next to the Bet Guvrin-Mareshah National Park (30 miles from Jerusalem). There are 63 parks in Israel's national park system, and before we finished our travels we would visit nearly half of them. Most of our stops were Biblically familiar to me, but when we drove into the Bet Guvrin-Mareshah National Park and had our universal passes punched, I drew a Biblical blank on why we had stopped here?

I had heard the word Guvrin in our lecture in preparation for this phase of our trip, but Mareshah was an unknown place, or so I thought. Guvrin is one of five valley routes from the low lands of coastal Israel to the hill country of Judah and Benjamin. We had already seen the Aijalon, Sorek, and Elah valleys in our morning travels into the Shephelah, and now we were in the Guvrin Valley. The open country surrounding this park fell away to the coast to our west (we were only 15 miles from the Mediterranean Sea), but as with our other stops in the Shephelah, we could see the foot hills to the east beginning to rise. We had already passed the main routes into Jerusalem and Bethlehem, and now we were in one of two valleys that lead to Hebron, the city of Caleb (Joshua 14:14). This would be the closest I would get to one of my dream stops. Located in that ancient city is the Cave of Machpelah (Genesis 25:9), the burial site of the patriarchs. Because Hebron is now a hotbed of Palestinian unrest on the West Bank, it is an extremely unsafe place to be, so we never got closer than Mareshah to its famed cave.

Once off the bus we climbed another tel (hill) to visit the pigeon caves of Mareshah, a collection of vast underground caverns where the people of the region used to keep pigeons for food and sacrifice. Before we entered the stone stairway leading into these caves, we had a chance to view the surrounding area and reflect on some unfamiliar Biblical events that took place here:

1. Mareshah is first mentioned in the Scriptures as one of the cities conquered by the tribe of Judah in the Promised Land—Joshua 15:44.
2. Mareshah is numbered among the cities Rehoboam fortified during his kingship in Judah—II Chronicles 11:8.
3. Mareshah is the site of a great battle when Judah was attacked by Zerah the Ethiopian and ultimately defeated by King Asa—II Chronicles 14:9–15.
4. Mareshah is the hometown of the prophet Eliezer, a seer in the days of King Jehoshaphat—II Chronicles 20:37.
5. Mareshah is also the hometown of the prophet Micah that wrote the Book of Micah—Micah 1:15.

One of the reasons I had come on this trip was to be exposed to Biblical knowledge that had escaped me all these years. I had read many times all five verses before mentioned, but had not stopped once to ponder where this place was. Now I knew, and now each and every time I come across these scriptures they will have a different meaning and significant to me now that I have visited the ancient city of Mareshah.

As we ascended out of the mouth of the vast underground complex, we were reminded of other Biblical sites within our view. The one that drew my closest attention was the fact that we were just a few miles away from the famous Cave of Adullam (we never got to visit it as with the Cave of Machpelah, maybe next time). You will recognize this as being the gathering place for David and his army of men that would eventually put him on the throne of Israel (I Samuel 22:1–4). This was the backdrop of three of David's well-known psalms (Psalms 35, 57, 142). Now I know why Micah wrote:

> The glory of Israel shall come to Adullam" (Micah 1:15)

because Adullam was in his backyard. David's three mighty men left Adullam for Bethlehem (about 10 miles away) to get the most famous cup of water in history (II Samuel 23:13-17). Joshua had captured this city as one of 31 major city-states in Canaan (Joshua 12:15, 24), and had in turn allotted the town and area to the tribe of Judah (Joshua 15:35). No wonder David was familiar with this territory, for it was in his backyard! When David fled Saul for the Cave of Adullam no doubt he had grazed his father's sheep on the shephelah we were walking over in the national park of Guvrin/Mareshah. There was one last stop we had to make before we left Mareshah for Lachish, and that was at the Columbarium (a vault with niches that contain bodies, or a multi-chambered tomb) Caves.

As we made our way to the well-excavated Hellenistic and Idumaean (Edom) city of Bet Guvrin to see the preserved caves, olive presses, cisterns, and tombs we also realized that we were within sight of another ancient, Hebrew city: Keilah (I Samuel 23:1-14). This was the town David saved from the Philistines, but he was paid back by the men of Keilah when they informed King Saul about his whereabouts in the region. Our descent into the tombs was similar to other tunnels we had climbed into on our trip, but when we got to the tomb itself what a surprise waited us. I can honestly say that it was the most beautiful (if a gravesite can be beautiful) grave complex I have ever been in! There were no bodies left (no doubt grave robbers) in the vaults, but the well-defined chambers and the artful artwork on the walls was amazing. There were pictures of animals (I even found an elephant) and birds throughout the entire cave, as well as pictures of people at play. We took our time taking pictures of each other, even some of us lying in the tombs themselves. It reminded me of the 'white-washed sepulchers' (Matthew 23:27) of Jerusalem. Why is it that man spends so much time (these hand-carved tombs would have been very expensive) and money on a dead body and so little time and money on a living soul? Jesus was right when he proclaimed:

> For whosoever will save his life shall lose it: and whosoever will lose his life for my sake shall find it. For what is a man profited, if he shall gain the whole world, and lose his own soul? Or what shall a man give in exchange for his soul?" (Matthew 16:25-26)

30

Lachish

Joshua 10:3 —... of LACHISH ...

After a quick lunch at a local gas station near Mareshah, our bus driver took us on the winding roads to the major archeological site of Lachish. I had desired to visit this site for a long time. I had read about the history of Lachish since boyhood through many books, and being mentioned over twenty times in Scripture makes it one of the significant cities of ancient Israel. What I wasn't prepared for was the massive size of this tel, and the rockwork that still reminds on site; including the Assyrian siege ramp of 701 BC!

My first surprise upon arrival was just how isolated Lachish now is. The day we came to Lachish the place was empty: no tourists, no archeologists, no guards, nobody, we had the place to ourselves the entire time we were there. You could see instantly that a lot of work had been done at the site, but nothing is happening now. Off the beaten path (about 32 miles from Jerusalem, where we had left from just a short six-hours before and 15 miles from Beersheba, our next destination), Lachish was once the center for all things in the region and along the coastal highway (the Via Maris—the way of the sea, the major coastal trading road) to Egypt.

The first mention of Lachish in the Bible is a reference to the Amorite city-state that once occupied the hilltop. In a confederacy with cities like Jerusalem, Hebron, Jarmuth, and Eglon, Lachish tried to resist the advance of Joshua into central Canaan (Joshua 10:5). Their combined armies were defeated by God (Joshua 10:11–14), and their kings killed

(Joshua 10:23). Eventually, Joshua and the army of Israel besieged Lachish and took it (Joshua 10:31–32). As we stood in the parking area of the tel, I looked up into the mound that was now Lachish and recalled the lecture by Greg about what the archeologists had uncovered on its summit; at least nine layers of civilization before the time of Christ:

1. 13th century—Egyptian control—unfortified city—major temple area found.
2. 12th century—Philistines destroy city but Egypt under Ramesses keeps control.

   (Nobody seemed to live here through the 11th century.)
3. 10th century—Israeli control—destroyed by Egypt 925 BC—Judean palace found.
4. 9th century—Judean control—two walls and a gate found—major defense city.
5. 8th century—Judean control, but destroyed by Assyria in 701 BC.

   (Nobody seemed to live here through 7th century.)
6. Early 6th century—Judah rebuilds, but destroyed again by the Babylonians 586 BC.
7. Late 6th century—Persian control—part of the palace complex discovered.
8. 4th century—Greek control—Alexander—city walls and solar shrine found.
9. 2nd century—basically what we were standing on when we made out ascent.

The first major discovery at Lachish was an amazing gate complex located on the southern slope of the hill. We had a chance to walk up through the massive walls that protected the way into the heart of the city. Many believe that King Rehoboam, the son of Solomon, was the first to make Lachish into a major fortress (II Chronicles 11:5–12). His fortifications were impressive because Lachish would resist one of the greatest sieges of history, and one of the best recorded battles of the entire Bible (II Kings 18–19, II Chronicles 32, and Isaiah 36–37). Five chapters of God's inspired word are given to the description of the invasion of Assyria and their famed king Sennacharib. I believe the reason so many pages are given to this encounter is the faith of King Hezekiah and his willingness to trust God and God alone in the defense of his country.

Despite the fact that Lachish would eventually fall to the Assyrians, Jerusalem would survive and Sennacharib and his army would leave and Lachish would be rebuilt.

Beside the Biblical account, there is a secular account of this famous siege in the "Sennacherib's Letter to God", and on his palace Sennacherib had great murals created depicting the victory at Lachish; most feel that he did this to cover up his defeat at Jerusalem; Lachish being his final victory in Judea. As we walked by the Assyrian siege ramp that eventually was used to break into the city, I saw only a hollow victory. For me the six-chamber gate complex, typical of Solomon's construction (one can see the same in Megiddo as we would see) was the most impressive part of our walkabout Lachish. The sheer size of the walls and the slope of the hill cause one to understand why the Assyrians built their ramp. On top we were able to see the counter siege ramp the Jews built to resist the entrance of the Assyrians into the city. On the very brow of the hill we were able to go into the palace-fort complex, the last defensible part of the city. We only spent an hour roaming around; I could have stayed there the rest of the day!

When I got back to the States, and in preparation for writing this book, I found these other significant Biblical happenings at Lachish:

1. When King Amaziah was threatened by his own people in Jerusalem, he fled to the fortress of Lachish for safety, but the people of Lachish slew him—II Kings 14:19.

2. When the Babylonians attacked Judah and took its cities one by one, one of the last cities to fall was Lachish—Jeremiah 34:7.

3. When the children of Israel returned after the Babylonian Captivity, one of the cities they rebuilt was Lachish—Nehemiah 11:30.

4. When Micah preached against the sins of Israel, he said this about Lachish: "O thou inhabitant of Lachish. . . . she is the beginning of the sin to the daughter of Zion: for the transgressions of Israel were found in thee." (Micah 1:13)

It was an evil age and Micah called it just that. He could not have picked a time when that message was more out of step with the times. Business was booming in Lachish. Everything was looking up. People never had it so good. Lachish was on the borderland of the Promised Land. It closeness to the world's trade route only exposed it to the wickedness of the world. Micah's condemnation reminded me that places like Lachish can be dangerous to one's spiritual health. I recalled Paul's admonition:

> For Demas hath forsaken me, having loved this present world, and is departed unto Thessalonica ... (II Timothy 4:10)

In Micah's days they seemed to be heading to Lachish, but the party town today is nothing but an empty hill surrounded with rubble, void of people and in ruins. Lachish ought to be a warning to Atlantic City, Las Vegas and any other 'sin-city'!

31

Disappointments and Delights In the Negev

Genesis 12:9—And Abram journeyed, going on still toward the south (NEGEV).

With Lachish in our rearview mirror, we headed farther into the south country of Israel. My hope had been for a westerly direction and warm, blue waters. In the print out of the itinerary for this trip our next scheduled stop was supposed to be Askelon National Park, one of the five Philistine cities (I Samuel 6:17). These five city-states have been a fascination of mine most of my Biblical life. Because of my love of military history, I was hoping that I would at least get to visit one of these cities on our trip into southern Israel. I had seen Gath from Mount Azekah and Eglon from Tel Lachish (the two inland cities of Philistia), but the three coastal cities (Gaza, Askelon, and Ashdod) would have to wait another trip. (Some feel Askelon was the birthplace of Herod the Great, and we know from the Bible this was the place Samson came to get the thirty changes of clothes—Judges 14:19. Askelon is known for its wonderful beaches, and I was looking forward to my first swim in the Mediterranean Sea!) Greg said it was a time factor, our encounter and delay with The Biggest Loser at Azekah, but I wondered if there was not another reason; the closeness to the Gaza Strip?

At Lachish, we were just a few miles from this infamous strip of land along the Mediterranean Sea. Our original plans were to swim in the Mediterranean late on our first day in the Negev (south). When we arrived at Beersheba at 4:15 PM, I knew it wasn't the delay at Azekah that had cost us our one chance to swim in the Mediterranean Sea. Askelon is the middle city of the three coastal cities of ancient Philistia, and is located on the northern tip of the Gaza Strip today. Like with Hebron and later on with Shechem, there are places in Palestinian controlled Israel were it is dangerous to travel. It wasn't until we returned to the States that we learned just how quickly unrest in Gaza can happen, like when the Israeli armed forces stormed a supply ship heading for Gaza. It was probably the reason for our sudden turn south on May 18, 2010. The Philistines are no longer in the land, but Philistia remains a war-like region to this day!

The Philistines were one of the great military powers of history. The word Philistine is made up of two words: 'migrate' and 'aliens'. Genesis 10:14 tells us that they were descendants of Ham by his son Mizaim. Amos 9:7 and Deuteronomy 2:23 tell us they originate from 'Caphtor', the ancient island of Crete. By the time of Abraham, they had already settled along the coastal plain in Gezar in the southwest Negev (Genesis 20), and there great lord Abimelech interacted with Abraham on a number of occasions (Genesis 21:34, 26:1). By the time of the Exodus (1446 BC), the coastal route into Canaan was called 'the way of the Philistines' (Exodus 13:17). Interestingly, the Philistines were not on God's hit-list of nations to be removed from the land. The Bible gives this explanation:

> Now these were the nations which the Lord left, to prove Israel by them. . . . only that the generation of the children of Israel might know, to teach them war, at the least such as before knew nothing thereof; namely, five lords of the Philistines . . . (Judges 3:1–30)

As we traveled away from Gaza, the old Philistia, all that I could think of is the Lord is still using the same strategy today!

As we traveled the final miles into Beersheba, the terrain changed rapidly. From the tree-covered hills and fertile valleys of the shephelah, we entered the treeless grass lands of the northern Negev. We saw flocks of animals grazing on the sweeping plains on both sides of Route 6. It was then one of the biggest shocks of the trip took place. I had pictured Beersheba in my mind as a lazy frontier town, but instead we entered late that afternoon a modern expanding city. I never heard how large Beersheba is today, but from where I come from it is a big city. Only Jerusalem or Tel Aviv could compare to the community before us. We traveled through the heart of the city to a hostel on the southern edge of town. The streets were crowded, and there were people everywhere. It was Pentecost Eve, and little did we know the change that was about ready to take place?

After getting settled into the Beersheba Hostel, our first hostel on the trip and a completely different experience to the Knight's Palace—yes, we had been spoiled; a group of us (Kristen George, Cristin Marposon (she is a major in the army), Barb and John Nuxoll, Diane Mich, and Marnie and I) decided to explore Beersheba on our own. By the time we left the hostel it was after six o'clock, and the holyday of Pentecost (yes, the famous Jewish holyday (celebrated 50 days after Passover) that ushered in the Holy Spirit (Acts 2:1, 20:16 and I Corinthians 16:8) was underway. The streets were void of cars and the sidewalks were empty of people. All the shops were closed and the bustling city we entered just a short time before was deserted. However, even in the disappointment of the sudden change of events, a blessing for me appeared.

We turned a corner about two blocks from the hostel and a familiar military hero was looking me straight in the face. I have mentioned a number of times in this record of my trip to Israel of my love of military history. Though not as famous as his Battle at Megiddo, British General Allenby is known in the annals of the First World War for his defeat of the Turks at the Battle of Beersheba (to this day the major crossing from the country of Jordan into Israel at Jericho happens over the Jordan River by way of Allenby Bridge), a battle that laid the ground work in 1917 for his victory at Megiddo on September 19, 1918. There, in a park, was a bronze statue of the man himself, and a memorial plaque of the strategy he used at Beersheba. It was an unexpected surprise to actually visit this old battlefield that I had read so much about in my military history books, but our surprises were not over yet on this spontaneous side trip into the streets and lanes of Israel's southern border town-'from Dan to Beersheba'.

As we walked on we debated whether or not we should turn back seeing nothing was opened. Cristin was looking for an ATM machine to withdraw some funds. We found a number along the way but none were working. After nearly a mile of walking and seeing nothing, we finally decided to turn back. It was then that John persuaded us to walk another block. His American stomach (remember he was the young man in Jerusalem that had to have an American hamburger) was getting the best of him again, so we pressed on in hopes of finding something American to eat. To our delight and absolute surprise, we came to a major junction in the road and there on the opposite side of the highway was a Domino's Pizza, and to our further shock the 'open' sign was flashing!

In one of the best turns of events for us, the Dominos chain in Israel doesn't close for holidays or holydays. We quickly crossed the street, walked into the store, ordered the biggest pepperoni pizza they made and bought the largest container of Coke they sold. After fifteen minutes the pizza was cooked and we set down around a table outside the store and ate, in my opinion, the best meal of the entire trip. There in the town of Beersheba we conquered a terrible onslaught of hunger pains for something American, with an assault of our own on a large Domino's pizza. The pizza didn't have a chance. We walked back to the hostel with our lips still tasting the sweet flavor and savor of home. When we got back to the hostel and told our story just about everyone wanted to know where we had found the pizza joint. I don't know if any others made the trek back to the Domino's Pizza place in Beersheba, but for me my first impression of Abraham's town was a positive one. Not because of the place, but because of the pizza!

32

Beersheba

Genesis 21:31—Wherefore he (Abraham) called that place BEERSHEBA; because there they sware both of them.

Located about 45 miles southwest of Jerusalem, Beersheba has a rich Biblical history that can be traced back to Father Abraham himself. It was the great patriarch that actually gave this place its name, 'well of the oath', after the covenant agreed to by Abraham and the Philistine lord of Gerar, Ahimelech (Genesis 21:22–34). Beersheba is also about halfway between the Mediterranean Sea and the Dead Sea. Abraham and Isaac spent a lot of time in the area grazing their flocks and using the water from the wells (tradition numbers them at seven, why it is called Beer Sheva today-the well of seven). Isaac had to redig the wells in his lifetime after the Philistines had filled them in (Genesis 26:17–33), and like his father before him made a pact with the lord of Gerar. Our overnight stay in Beersheba gave me plenty of time to remember my Bible school lessons from childhood. The stay was pleasant, the room was air-conditioned, the food in the cafeteria was ok, but the best part was an early morning trip on our 9th day in Israel to Tel Beersheba.

After a 9:00PM to 6:00 AM rest (the longest on the trip so far) and a 7:00 AM breakfast, we were on the bus by 7:45 AM for the ten minute ride to another National Park. We were the first tour bus of the day to arrive, so we had the place to ourselves for the hour and a half we were there. It is a massive tel with plenty of rock walls, and a marvelous view of the Negev. We saw shepherds in the wadis grazing there sheep. We saw herds of camels and goats and even cows in the surrounding fields. The first stop that morning on site was a stone-horned altar, similar to the ones they used for sacrifice in the Old Testament. What made the altar unrealistic to me was it was built with cut stones, whereas the Bible warns against that (Exodus 20:25)! We then made our way up the southern slope of the mound until we came to Abraham's well. Tradition says the very one Abraham himself dug? Again I question the instruction, but we were certainly in the right area. After an extensive lecture on Beersheba and where we were going next (Arad), we had a chance to roam the tel and see for ourselves the ancient town that grew up around Abraham's well. As I walked the grounds I recalled some of the other Biblical events that took place here:

1. After the patriarchs, the town was occupied by many of the nations of the Negev that is until the Jews returned and the town was taken over by the sons of Simeon (I Chronicles 4:28).
2. Samuel's sons would judge Israel from Beersheba in the days of the judges, but not righteously (I Samuel 8:2).
3. Elijah would stop in Beersheba on his great flight from Jezebel (I Kings 19:3).
4. The tribe of Judah would occupy Beersheba when the Israelites returned to the land after the Babylonian Captivity (Nehemiah 11:27).

Beersheba would be the guard city of the central Negev basin throughout Biblical times.

The site we explored that morning was basically a rock and mud based structure that was dated back to the United and Divided Kingdom era of Hebrew history. The archeological work on Tel Beersheba included the uncovering of the outer gate, a well, and drainage channel to the outside. Further into the complex you came to the main gate consisting of two thick-walled towers that protected this vital entrance. There was a massive city square, or plaza. There was a peripheral street that paralleled the main wall and followed it all the way around the city limits. This street was about six feet wide. We found the governor's palace and numerous other homes laid out in a well-defined pattern. The casemate walls were built along the edge of the mound, and from the top of the mound a tower. The Beer Sheva Valley cuts southward and during the rainy season would be filled with water. The main storage area was a set of three long storerooms, but for me the highlight of the tour was another trip down through time in the water tunnel of Beersheba.

When the fortified city of Beersheba was built, the water system was built into the structure itself. The water system of Beersheba was made up of three parts:

1. A shaft nearly 70 feet deep lined with rocks with a flight of stairs along the side. We were able to climb down those stairs.
2. A reservoir was hewn out of the surrounding rock and divided into five sections, each section plastered, so the combined capacity was thousands of gallons of water. We all enjoyed just how much cooler it was under the tel verses on top of the tel!
3. A winding feeder channel that allowed the flood waters of Hebron Stream to flow into the reservoir. We climbed out this channel to exit the tel where we came into the tel earlier that morning.

The Bible tells us that Abraham's final days (after he offered up Isaac on Mount Moriah) were spent in Beersheba (Genesis 22:19). His body was taken to Hebron (about 25 miles away) and the Cave of Machpelah for burial, but I think he left his heart in Beersheba. This place was the oasis of the wandering pilgrimage that was Abraham's life. The Bible tells us that Abraham

> looked for a city which hath foundations, whose builder and maker is God! (Hebrews 11:10)

It was from Beersheba that Abraham sought that city, so that is why I believe he left his heart there. It is told in Church history that the great missionary David Livingstone left as a final instruction before his death: the removal of his heart from his body. Upon his death his heart was buried in his beloved Africa and his body was carried by two of his faithful servants to the ocean and then taken by sea back to England before his body was finally buried under the floor of a chapel at Westminster Abby. For me Livingstone and Abraham come from the same stock. Men of God, lone Christians, who walked a different path, that traveled a different way, who cared more for what was before them than what was around them. When Abraham found the well at Beersheba, we know, spiritually speaking, he had already found the well of life (John 4:14). As I climbed out of the tunnel that morning that runs today under Tel Beersheba, I thought of Jesus' admonition concerning the heart:

> For where your treasure is, there will your heart be also."
> (Matthew 6:21)

I believe Abraham's treasure was not in his flocks, but in his faith. A faith that allowed him to live on the edge of a wilderness and still find pasture and plenty from the One who had called him to his lifestyle. Who says you can't make a covenant with God concerning everlasting water, and not keep it and drink from it for the rest of your life? Abraham did, and so can we!

33

From Arad to Avdat

Joshua 12:14—... the king of ARAD ...

Once we left Tel Beersheba, our travels south would take us into the territory best known for the wilderness wandering of the children of Israel during their infamous 40 years of death and dying. Instead of heading directly south, we journeyed east along Route 31 until we came to the ancient wilderness settlement called Arad. Located halfway between Beersheba and the Dead Sea, this site featured a fortified mound, an extended temple area, a palace complex, a beautiful gate structure, high city walls, numerous excavated residential buildings, and an impressive well.

The Biblical history of Arad is very simple:

1. Numbers 21:1—During the years of wandering the Israelites journeyed northward through the Wilderness of Zin into the lower Negev until they came to Arad. The king of Arad resisted their northern migration and defeated them, and as it says: 'and took some of them prisoner'!

2. Numbers 33:40—It appears a second attempt to enter the Promised Land from the south was tried later in the wandering, but once again the king of Arad blocked the advance of the Israelites and they had to turn south again, eventually invading Canaan from the east.

3. Joshua 12:14—When Joshua was listing the city-states he conquered in his Canaanite campaign the 12th 'one' named was Arad.

4. Judges 1:16—After the control of the country was achieved, the Kenties, the relatives of Moses' father-in-law, Jethro, who had journeyed with the Israelites to Canaan, settled in this area.

I can't even believe I am writing this so anybody could read it, but I must acknowledge that despite my years of fascination with Lachish, I liked Arad better!

Our ninety minute stay at Arad started with a walk up to the hilltop fortress probably built by the Judean kings to protect their southern border. This wilderness stronghold was eventually captured by Pharaoh Shishak in 925 BC during the reign of King Rehoboam (I Kings 14:25–28). We do not know this fact from Biblical sources, but from Egyptian history which lists Arad on an accounting of cities subjugated by Shishak after his advance into Judah in the days of Solomon's son. As we wandered the ruins, we stopped at an excavated site that appeared a lot like the layout (one of the best found in all of Israel) of the Jerusalem Temple. There was a stone altar and a holy of holies area. We stopped for a short lecture by Dr. Hilber on the mingling of the religions of Canaan with the Hebrew faith. In the holy of holies were two standing stones, one on the right and the other on the left of the enclosure. The higher stone represented Jehovah and the lower stone Ashtaroth (Judges 2:13), the female fertility god of the Philistines and Phoenicians. As we had seen in other places, the towns along the borderland of Israel seemed to be the first to yield to the temptations of conformity and coexistence with the Canaanites.

The strategic importance of Arad could be seen from the fortress walls. Located in the eastern basin of the Negev, it controlled the road from the hill country of Judah to the land of Edom across the Jordan Rift. Arad is within line sight of Masada just a few miles to the east, and less than 15 miles from Hebron and a mere 34 miles from Jerusalem. We could also see into the Wilderness of Judah. From on top of the mound we caught the cooling breezes from the Mediterranean across the southern Negev. Even Greg remarked just how good (normally this region is very hot in May) the weather was, and again the view was crystal clear. We could have seen to the Dead Sea, if only the wilderness hills had not been in the way. Again our stay was too short as we worked our way through the ruins of the Canaanite Arad at the bottom of the hill on our way back to the bus. This day would be the longest day in road miles (100 mile) we would travel in Israel, and we still had many miles to go before we could sleep on the shores of the Red Sea.

From Arad to Avdat 135

Leaving Arad, we actually traveled back towards Beersheba until we came to the junction of Route 31 and Route 50. We turned south on 50 until it merged with Route 25. Route 25 is a major route from Beersheba to Route 90, the main north/south highway along the Dead Sea and the border with Jordan. We traveled 25 until we came to the small isolated town of Dimonia. This is the location, or so they say, of Israel's atomic research center (this would be Israel's Area 51); the place they believe Israel created their first atomic bomb, the worst kept secret in the Middle East! Just before we passed by Dimonia we turned south again on Route 224 for a short trip over to Route 40, the main roadway into the Paran Desert area. On the way, we made three stops in the Wilderness of Zin (Numbers 13:21):

1. Ben Gurion National Park, the final resting place of modern Israel's first prime minister. It was said that he wanted his fellow citizens to see the potential in the Negev, so he chose to live out his final days there and to be buried there.
2. En Avdat National Park, the grand canyon (a white-walled gorge 656 feet deep) of Israel. This was one of the most impressive stops we made in Israel. The deep gorge was spectacular, and the picture taking opportunities were limitless. Once again we only stayed ten minutes, so we didn't have much of a chance to enjoy the beauty of the canyon, but we did see the two pools of water on the canyon floor but not the waterfall! Time did not allow us to walk the canyon trail to the bottom, another thrilling hike I hope to make in my next trip.
3. Avdat National Park, a major ancient city (built by the Nabataeans in the 2nd century) on the famous incense highway from Petra to Gaza. We actually had lunch at the foot of this hilltop fortress before driving to the top for another marvelous trip back through time.

Avdat was a lot like Arad; it sits on a high hill dominating the area. Its walls and gates were the best I had seen since Jerusalem. The archeologists had uncovered well defined streets, buildings, temples, tombs, pillars, arches, and the best and largest wine press site uncovered in Israel. The eight-section press and holding tanks, all made of stone, were amazing. I saw my first huge millstone at Avdat, and once again the view from the walls into the Wilderness of Zin that surrounded the area was awesome. If you like desert landscapes, then I recommend a trip to Avdat. We even got a chance to see a few old churches that had been created from the old temples in the Christian era. We had the place to ourselves for the hour we spent in the fortress of Avdat. One of the blessings of the trip had been the times we had the places of our stops to ourselves. Greg told us when we started the class that we would be going to the sites most tourists never go. He was right on this, and I was enjoying every 'alone' moment.

As for the Biblical significance of Avdat, there are some who believe it is the Biblical site of Adar mentioned in Joshua 15:3. If you read carefully Joshua 15:1–3 and the description of this area it does fit into the other geographical places mentioned (check out Numbers 34:1–4 as well). I was beginning to understand just how hard it must have been for the Israelites to move through this area, and the divine way God provided for them, but more evidence of this was just down the road!

34

A Taste of the Wilderness

Psalms 72:9—They that dwell IN THE WILDERNESS shall bow before Him ...

There are twenty 'wilderness' areas mentioned in the Bible:
1. Beersheba—Genesis 21:14
2. Beth-Aven—Joshua 18:12
3. Damascus—I Kings 19:15
4. Edom—II Kings 3:8
5. En Gedi—I Samuel 24:1
6. Etham—Numbers 23:8
7. Gibeon—II Samuel 2:24
8. Jerval—II Chronicles 20:16
9. Judah—Judges 1:16
10. Kadesh—Psalms 29:8
11. Kedemonth—Deuteronomy 2:26
12. Maon—I Samuel 23:25
13. Moab—Deuteronomy 2:8
14. Paran—Genesis 21:24
15. Red Sea—Exodus 13:18
16. Shur—Exodus 15:22
17. Sin—Exodus 16:1

18. Sinai—Exodus 19:1
19. Zin—Numbers 13:21
20. Ziph—I Samuel 23:14

Marnie and I, along with the other wanderers in our group, had a chance to spend an afternoon in two of them: the wilderness of Zin and the wilderness of Paran. Before we arrived at the Wilderness of Zin, we had already traveled through the Wilderness of Beersheba and on our trip to Jericho, the Wilderness of Judah! Before our Israel journey was over we would either travel through or get to see 12 of these 20 wilderness areas!

We continued our bus ride down Route 40 towards the Israeli National Park at Mitzeph Ramon (a crater 25 miles long and 5 miles wide and 1,300 feet deep), our next scheduled stop. There was no way we were prepared for what we would see when we got off the bus and climbed a small hill that overlooks the Machtesh Ramon. There below us was a vast desert that looked more like the surface of the moon, or the landscape of Mars. Even the deserts of Australia and India hadn't prepared me for what I saw and experienced. Before we actually drove through the wilderness of 'the wilderness wandering of the children of Israel', Greg wanted us to see the desolation and isolation of the terrain that can only be seen from the cliffs at Mitzeph Ramon; called Israel's most spectacular natural phenomenon. This is the largest of three craters in the Negev!

The Wilderness of Zin is located on the southern boundary of the Promised Land and on the northeast side of the Wilderness of Paran. The desert oasis of Kadesh-barnea (Numbers 32:8) was located about 15 miles to the east of our observation ridge at Mitzeph Ramon. Most feel that this famous stopping off place of the children of Israel during their exodus from Egypt to Canaan is the dividing line between these two vast desert areas. I recalled my Biblical history:

1. It was from this area that the twelve spies were sent out to explore the Promised Land in advance of the invasion—Deuteronomy 1:2.

2. It was here that Moses' struck the Rock instead of speaking to the Rock and whereby lost his chance to enter the land—Numbers 20:1–13.

3. It was here the people rebelled and were cursed until the old generation was removed and a new generation was prepared to enter the land—Numbers 33:36.

4. It would be here that the Almighty would establish the southern border of Israel's kingdom—Numbers 34:3-4.

Space fails me to tell of Caleb and Joshua, the Korah Rebellion, the countless days of manna, and the daily funerals that marked every step through this moonscape of unbelievable misery and death.

After a few spectacular photographs from the edge of the gorge, we drove down the roadway that lead into the Wilderness of Paran and began our long trip through its barrenness. Geographically, the wilderness straddles the central section of the Sinai Peninsula, south of the Wilderness of Zin. Nobody has yet completely defined the borders of this vast desert, it is generally recognized to be between the Wilderness of Shur to the west and the Arabah (the name given to the valley on both sides of the Jordanian Rift—Joshua 18:18) to the east. Our trek through this wasteland brought these other Biblical stories to mind:

   1. The kings of the east attacked through this region before defeating the Sodomite alliance and capturing Lot—Genesis 14:6.
   2. When Hagar was driven from the household of Abraham, she brought her son Ishmael here—Genesis 21:21.
   3. David spent some of his wilderness wandering time from King Saul in this desert—I Samuel 25:1.
   4. Hadad the Edomite, an archenemy of King Solomon, fled to the Paran after an unsuccessful revolt against Israel—I Kings 11:18.

My daydreaming came to a sudden end when about halfway through our wilderness trek the bus stopped just north of the Route 40 and Route 13 junction, but why?

From over the microphone Greg said:

> I now want you to taste what it was like in this desert for the children of Israel. I am going to let you off the bus for about fifteen minutes. I want you feel for a few minutes what it must have been like to wander in the Paran!

The first thing that hits you is a blast of hot air. It was well over 100 when we disembarked the bus and started our 'wilderness wandering' experience. As we had seen for mile after mile there was nothing before us but a barren, rocky plain. To our west there were a few ridges, but they were just as rocky and barren as the flatlands that surrounded us. The only object that stood out in the vast wasteland was a lone acacia tree (the

Biblical Shittim tree—Exodus 25:5) about a hundred yards from the bus. As my companions wandered about, I headed for the shade of the Shittim tree. If there was one thing I have learned from my three trips to India and my one trip to Australia, it is to find shade, and that a little shade is better than no shade at all.

One of my treasured souvenirs from Israel is a small piece of acacia wood taken from that wilderness tree. It is for me a reminder of just what the Lord did for Israel as they wandered helplessly through the wilderness of Sin, of Sinai, of Shur, of Paran, and of Zin to finally arrive forty years later in a land 'flowing with milk and honey'. You know about the water (Exodus 15:27), the manna (Exodus 16:4), the quail (Exodus 16:13), the shoes and clothes that never wore out (Deuteronomy 29:5, but what about the shade? I was able on that afternoon to understand for the first time Psalms 121:5–6:

> The Lord is thy keeper: the Lord is thy shade upon thy right hand. The sun shall not smite thee by day . . . !

I have come to believe that one of the benefits of the 'pillar' (Exodus 13:21–22) that lead Israel could have been the shade that it might have provided during those 100 degree days in the Paran, and other wilderness areas!

35

The Oasis of Eilat

II Chronicles 8:17—Then went Solomon to EZION-GEBER (modern day Eilat), and to Eloth, at the sea side in the land of Edom.

We left our self-imposed wilderness wandering spot around five o'clock in the afternoon of our 9th day in Israel. We still had a two hour run to Eilat (Israel's only town on the Red Sea), our overnight destination, ahead of us. As we slowly made our way through the stark sand, I had time to reflect a bit more on my day in the desert world of southern Israel.

After our visit to Paran and being swallowed up in the vastness and barrenness from every side, I soon felt dizzy and dazed by why anyone would want to spend more than fifteen minutes in this place? Why would any person, let alone a group of people choose to stay any longer than necessary? Why would you wander aimlessly through such a no-man's land when there was a shephelah to the north? Oh, I know the reasons why the Israelites rebelled (giants, walled-cities, and a difficult land- Numbers 13:32–33), but after already experiencing two years (the little known conception about the wilderness wandering is that the Israelites had already been two years from Egypt to Kadesh, so the actual wandering time in Paran was 38 years) of wilderness living, why would you stay any longer than you had to in a terrible terrain, a waterless world you had already traveled through? Personally, I couldn't wait until we were through Paran; anywhere would be better than this, and to think an oasis waited me on the other side!

How does one escape the reality of rebellion, disobedience, rejection of God's will? As I look around my world I see more and more people making the same choice as the Israelites. Oh, they try to make their world look better, feel better with their Disney World, Bush Gardens, Six Flags, Broadway Play, Las Vegas, and Atlantic City. They live like Alice in a Wonderland created by their own hands, a Wizard of Oz world with their yellow brick roads leading to a Cinderella ending, but what they never realize is they have never gotten out, or will ever get out of the wilderness of Paran. They escape in their mind through movies and operas and video games and ball games but when they come back to reality all around them is an empty wasteland of a desert without end. Around and around they go not realizing they have been there before; that the footsteps they see in the sand are not somebody else's, but their own. The wrong road they took at Kadesh always leads them back to Kadesh, and the drugs and alcohol and sex along the way is just another trap that keeps them from moving on to Beulah Land. One doesn't have to visit the wilderness of Southern Israel to understand that there are two worlds of reality in this old world: man-made and God-made.

For those who feel or wish this was the Shangri-La, like Ben Gurion, of Israel, are still of the attitude of those that escaped Egypt only to be captured by Paran. Paul teaches us that 'the things which are seen are temporal; but the things which are not seen are eternal." (II Corinthians 4:18) Also wandering in the desert of Paran with the lost generation of Jews were two men, Caleb and Joshua. When the wandering was over, they alone would be alive of their generation, why? They wandered more than anyone else, yet they lived while everybody else died, why? I believe they learned that one can live in another world while living in this world. Caleb lived in a spiritual reality that allowed him to endure untold misery and madness without falling or yielding to the despair and depression that engulfed his companions. While the others had become citizens of Paran, Caleb and Joshua never gave up their citizenship in the Promised Land, a citizenship they earned the day they stepped into the Promised Land on their spy mission and believed. I love these words from Caleb to Joshua in the final days of their lives:

> . . . but I wholly followed the Lord my God. . . . and now, behold, the Lord hath kept me alive, as He said, these forty and five years, even since the Lord spake this word unto Moses, while the children of Israel *wandered in the wilderness:* and now, lo, I am this day fourscore and five years old. As yet I am strong this day

as I was in the day that Moses sent me: my strength was then, even so is my strength now, for war, both to go out, and to come in. (Joshua 14:9–11)

As others grew weaker, Caleb and Joshua grew stronger!

Halfway to Eilat we made a pit stop at a place called Yotvata. We had left the worst of the Paran exiting Route 40 for Route 90. We had once again entered the Arabah that continues down the giant rift that runs all the way from northern Israel into southern Africa. Despite the Jordan ending in the Dead Sea, the valley continues down the entire length of eastern Israel, the great borderland between Israel and Jordan. Our stop at Yotvata was to try the most famous milk in Israel? A huge dairy herd, the largest in Israel, was known for its milk products, and they said the chocolate milk was the best in the world. Because I am a sixth generation son of Maine dairy farmers, I had to put the claim to the test. I am afraid that Israel hasn't come close to the milk my grandfather and father once produced. I will leave it at that. With another hour to travel, I went back to reflecting on my trek out of the Wilderness of Paran.

I too have discovered that my true citizenship isn't in the wilderness of America, but in a heavenly citizenship purchased for me by Jesus Christ Himself (Ephesians 2:19). Like Abraham, I too look for a city (Hebrews 11:10) not made with human skill and craftsmanship, but by God Himself. As we made the final drop into Eilat, I couldn't believe the contrast between the dirty brown of Paran and the beautiful blue of the Red Sea. We had not only traveled through the Wilderness of Beersheba, Zin, and Paran, but we had also paralleled the Wilderness of Moab and Edom on our final descent into Ezion-Geber. Surrounded in such stark landscape, the lush trees and bushes of Eilat reminded me of Jericho; a green land in the middle of a wasteland. Eilat reminded me that waiting for me at the end of my wilderness wandering on this planet is a new city by a wonderful body of water (Revelation 22:1) lined with the tree of Life (Revelation 22:2). I believe I was shown on this trip from Beersheba and 'beyond' to Eilat that we need a new brand of pilgrim in Christianity today. One who makes their way through the wilderness by looking ahead as Jesus did (Hebrews 12:2), and is always on their tiptoes waiting with expectation and anticipation for the oasis of Eilat (Heaven) to come into view. I can't describe the wonderful delight I felt as we drove into Eilat around seven o'clock after a full day of wandering through wilderness after wilderness. The contrast was that dramatic, a heaven verses earth dramatic!

There will be days of hardship and deserts as strangers and pilgrims. As exiles and aliens we must work our way through the wilderness of Paran through faith and focus. The good news is, if we only walk through, there awaits us an oasis of God. The danger is to fall in love with the desert of disobedience and to never try to escape its grasp. We must live through such days as this with 'a foretaste of glory divine' in the Heavenly Eilat before us!

36

Parting the Red Sea

Exodus 10:19—And the Lord turned a mighty strong west wind, which took away the locusts, and cast them into THE RED SEA . . .

We arrived in the paradise of Eilat just in time for supper, but early enough so we had time afterward to walk down through this coastal town (in 1948, Israel was given this seven-mile long coastline and it rapidly developed into a trading port and tourist resort). We also arrived in time to watch the sun set over the Red Sea from our third story room in the Adi Hotel. We had a wonderful view of the Gulf of Eilat and the cliffs (yes, they looked red in the sun) of Edom, Jordan today, on the far shore (just 4 miles away). After a traditional Israeli dinner, Marnie and I left our companions to walk the two blocks to the Red Sea. I had known the story of the children of Israel walking through the Red Sea all of my life, and I was determined to at least walk in its waters; little did I know what the morning would bring, but for that moment an evening walk to its shore would wash the dust of the wilderness off my feet!

Since my return from Israel a lot of people have asked the question, "What was it like?" For those that have asked me about Eilat, I have replied, "It was a lot like walking down through Bar Harbor!" I live about twenty miles from this world-famous, tourist town on the coast of Maine. Located next door to one of the most popular national parks in America, Acadia National Park, Bar Harbor is what we in Maine call a 'tourist trap'. Its only reason for existing is to draw visitors from around the world to witness the seascape that is Maine; rocky shores, boiled lobster, and downeast hospitality. Just a few days ago we were asked by some friends of ours to dine with them at the Jordan Pond House, a very popular eating place in Acadia Park. When we arrived the parking lots were full, and we didn't see a Maine license plate on one car until we left; even the car we were in was from Pennsylvania. Few Mainers spend much time on Mount Desert Island in the summertime because of all the tourists, but the rest of the year the place and its beauty is all ours. Eilat was exactly like that. As Marnie and I tried to find the water, we had to wade through hundreds upon hundreds of vacationers. Eilat is the Atlantic City of Israel, and we soon discovered our paradise in the wilderness had a dark side!

We had left traditional Israel in Jerusalem and Beersheba (remember, this was the Jewish holyday of Pentecost; from what I saw in Eilat, Pentecost, whether Jewish or Christian, was not being celebrated). Eilat was secular Israel in every way! Our Eden had discovered and tasted of 'the tree of the knowledge of good and evil', but unlike Adam and Eve, there seemed to be no shame! The women and men walked around nearly naked. The boardwalk had its fine shops, but also the bad shops. Eilat was a party town, and the lifestyle of the rich and famous could be seen everywhere. Marnie and I walked by the neon and naked in search of the sea (both Marnie and I love the sea, whether the Gulf of Maine (the Atlantic Ocean), the Pacific or Indian Ocean, where we have traveled, we have best loved our times by the sea), and sure enough after about a ten minute walk we could hear it lapping on the beach, even over the noise of the revelers and rioters. It was pitch dark by the time we found the shore, and few were on the sandy beach enjoying the cooler night air, and the refreshing water. Most had been drawn to the city lights as the prodigal of Jesus' famous parable, but for Marnie and me it was the water that called us. I took off my shoes and waded knee deep into its famous stream and for a few brief moments heard nothing but the rolling surf and felt the soft sand engulf my weary feet!

Returning to Room 304, Marnie and I caught up on our journals, wrote postcards, and prepared to get another good night's sleep. Before I drifted off, I rethought in my mind just where I was spending my 9th night in Israel. The Red Sea lies between Egypt and Arabia, and has two very distinct arms. The western body of water is called the Gulf of Suez, where the famous 'canal' is located, and where the children of Israel crossed from Egypt to Sinai, or so the tradition says, but did they? This section of the Red Sea is 190 miles long. The eastern branch is called the Gulf of Aqaba (Arab name), or the Gulf of Eilat (Jewish name). This section of the Red Sea is 112 miles long, and I have come to believe that it was here, about 50 miles south of Eilat that the children of Israel actually crossed the Red Sea at a place called Pihahiroth (Exodus 14:1, 9) from Sinai into the land of Madian (Acts 7:29)! There archeologists have discovered a beach and a land bridge just under the surface of the Aqaba Straights, and coral formations in the shape of chariots wheels. If God told Moses to return to the mountain of Horeb (Exodus 3:1–12) and he was in Madian then Horeb, or Mount Sinai must have been in Madian! So the Red Sea crossing must have been somewhere through the Gulf of Aqaba and not the Gulf of Suez? In the Bible 'red' is Edom (Genesis 25:25, 36:1), and the wilderness of Edom runs along the eastern shore of the Gulf of Eilat. At the tip of the gulf is a very narrow piece of land claimed by both Israel and Jordan. On the eastern shore is the Jordanian town of Aqaba and on the western shore is the town of Eilat. The children of Israel actually visited this place during their wilderness wandering (Deuteronomy 2:8). It was on this site many years after their brief stay that King Solomon created Israel's first navy (I Kings 9:26–28), and it was from the seaport of Ezion-Geber that Solomon in partnership with the Phoenicians sailed to the gold mines of Africa, or maybe, even India? Years later King Jehoshaphat tried to do the same thing, but his fleet was destroyed in a storm (II Chronicles 20:35–37). Over the following years Eilat was lost and recaptured as in the days of King Uzziah (II Chronicles 26:1–2), only to be lost again to men like King Rezin of Aram (II Kings 16:6). Today, Israel has a naval base there, and it is a major seaport as well. While we were there we watched a huge car-carrying ship sail into port, and our tenth day in Israel began near the spot where those cars were being unloaded. What we did that morning quickly jumped into one of the top five things I experienced in the entire trip: snorkeling in the Red Sea.

We left the Adi Hotel for the Coral Reef Beach National Park around eight. Now I knew why we had stopped at the IBEX (actually, on our way into Eilat the night before we saw the Ibex deer roaming the hills along the highway) Campus. We had picked up scuba gear for our morning of snorkeling. We left the commercial section of Eilat for a rural stretch of beach about three miles up the western shore. We stopped just short of the Israeli checkpoint that would take us into Egypt (another dream trip to trace the Exodus). From the sandy beach we could see back into Eilat with all the high rise hotels along its narrow shore. We could see Aqaba across the gulf with the red cliffs behind it. The water off shore was a sky blue, but the water near shore was a greenish-blue, we would soon find out why? Neither Marnie nor I had snorkeled before but there was in our midst a man who had been raised in Bermuda. Ron Shearer and his wife Daphne were on the trip as a graduation present for just finishing Dallas Theological Seminary, and he had snorkeled all his life. After a few quick instructions, I was off on my first snorkeling adventure over the reefs of the Red Sea.

You must understand that I am not a water lover, or a swimming fan; never have been. At first I thought I wouldn't do it, but eventually decided that I was here and this was the Red Sea, so why not. I am so glad I didn't back out. For the first time I witnessed God's beauty in the sea. As I rode on the back of the Red Sea, the wind (it was a windy day so they only let us swim with the tide) carried me from the northern pier of the reserve to the southern pier. The colors were brilliant and the fish were friendly. The bottom of the sea floor was covered with multicolored coral. The water was so clear nothing escaped my eye. I saw small colorful fish everywhere, and they were not afraid to check me out; swimming right up to my facemask. The colors of the fish and coral were a rainbow with deep reds, violet purples, many a shade of orange, and blues beyond imagine! The noise of the world was lost and the peaceful solitude was divine. I will say it was the most relaxing and quiet hour of the trip. As I parted the water of the Red Sea with my swimming strokes, a new world opened up to me. As I dove under the surface, a new reality of God's aquatic creation filled my senses. Marnie followed in my wake enjoying every wave as well. I now understood what the Psalms was praising God for when he wrote:

> When I consider. . . . the work of Thy fingers. . . . the fish of the sea, and whatsoever passeth through the paths of the sea. O Lord our God, how excellent is Thy name in all the earth! (Palms 8:3, 8, 9)

I can now say that I have taken a trip through one of the paths of the sea, and what an amazing trip it was, and to think the Almighty parted this same sea for His children to walk across on dry land (Exodus 14:21–22).

37

The Tabernacle At Timnah

Acts 7:44—Our fathers had THE TABERNACLE OF WITNESS IN THE WILDERNESS.

After a thrilling swim and snorkeling experience in the Red Sea at Eilat, one would think that nothing could top such an event on this our tenth day in Israel! As we got back on our bus and heading out of Ezion-Geber, I realized that we were at the midway point of our great Israeli adventure. The trip was half over, but the surprises and blessings would continue with our next stop. About twenty miles north of Eilat, we once again drove off the main highway along the Israeli/Jordanian border. We were heading to a place called Timnah. When I saw this place on our itinerary, I looked it up in my concordance but I found no Biblical references. The schedule simply said we were going to visit the tabernacle of Timnah. I knew it couldn't be the original Hebrew tabernacle, so what was in Timnah?

The first thing I noticed as we moved from an asphalt highway to a dirt road was that we were back in the wilderness. The greens and blues of Eilat and the Red Sea were gone; replaced with that brownish, bleak desert color that bring with it an instant foreboding. We slowly worked our way through miles of dusty paths just wide enough for our bus to pass. Within a short time we moved from flatland to desert canyons, with impressive cliffs and crags on both sides. Greg began to explain that the Egyptians had first come here to mine for copper. He also pointed out a rock formation called "Solomon's Pillars". Even though there is no historical evidence that suggests that Solomon mined for copper here, there is a Jewish tradition that says the Phoenicians who helped him build Ezion-Geber and a fleet of ships also helped him establish a copper refining center at Timnah. The refinery was laid out so that the prevailing winds from the north would help draft the fires in the smelting pots. Greg also told us that anything in Israel that is larger than life is more often than not given the name of Solomon, like Solomon's Pools north of Mamre (Ecclesiastes 2:6) which served as reservoirs for the city of Jerusalem in the days of the Romans. The chances are Solomon had nothing to do with the 'pools' or the 'pillars', but they were impressive. We had not come to Timnah for the copper mines that once drew people to this isolated spot in the Wilderness of Paran, but to another marvel with a Biblical twist.

We turned our final corner and there it was; a full-scale model of Israel's original wilderness tabernacle. A group from the United States have reconstructed the tabernacle and put it in a desert setting. Timnah Park is a tourist attraction with a gift store, a restaurant, a small pond (yes, they have found water), and the tabernacle. Of course, it is not made of gold and the fine materials used in the original tabernacle, but it looks like it fits in the geography and topography that is Timnah. It wasn't hard for me to imagine what the Israelites did when they raised this first house of God at the foot of Mount Sinai (remember in Madian not Sinai). The tabernacle of Timnah is also situated under a hill! I wish I could show you the pictures. I was thrilled with this chance to see the tabernacle, if only a model, up close and personal. I, like you, have been a part of building a model of the tabernacle. In my second church a master carpenter built us one for a Daily Vacation Bible School we ran one summer. As I write this chapter our children's church kids have just finished their own version of this ancient tent, but to literally walk around a life-size model changed many things that I had believed about the tabernacle.

The first thing that struck me was how small it was. Despite the fact the builders constructed the model on a 20 inch per cubit scale verse the traditional 18 inch per cubit scale, it seemed small. Everything was there: the gate (Exodus 27:16) in the outer court fence (Exodus 26:1–6), the brazen altar (Exodus 27:1–8), the laver (Exodus 30:17–21), and the tabernacle itself with its boards (Exodus 26:15), bars (Exodus 26:26–28), base (Exodus 26:19), and of course the four coverings (badger skin, ram's skin dyed red, goat's hair, and fine linen—Exodus 26:1, 7, 14). After passing through the door (Exodus 26:36) we saw the table of showbread (Exodus 25:23–24), the golden candlestick (Exodus 25:31–39), and the altar of incense (Exodus 30:1–5); and there standing in the corner was Aaron himself decked out in the fine attire of the high priest. There was also a lowly priest in his simple garb standing beside the candlestick. With a bit of concern (I remembered Nadab and Abihu—Leviticus 10:1-2), we moved through the veil (Exodus 26:33) and there before us was the most famous piece of furniture of the Tabernacle: the ark of the covenant (Exodus 25:10-16), and its cover, the mercy seat (Exodus 25:17), and sure enough inside the golden box was Aaron's rod that budded, a bowl of manna, and the two stones with the ten commandments written on them (Hebrews 9:4). Remember, the two tables of stones were actually copies of the same commandments; a popular misconception is that the first five commandant were written on one stone and the five others on the other stone. In actuality, God gave Moses both copies of the covenant, His and theirs (Exodus 32:15-16)!

As I wandered I remembered the long history of the Tabernacle, made at Mount Sinai from blueprints given to Moses by God Himself, the tabernacle was moved through the wilderness in six covered wagons pulled by two oxen (Numbers 7:3-9) and the rest of the pieces carried by the Levites. Each time the Israelites camped it was set up (at least 42 times according to Numbers 33) and each time they moved it was taken down piece by piece. It was first pitched at Gilgal in the Promised Land (Joshua 4:19), and when it was safe, to Shechem between Mount Ebal and Mount Gerizim (Joshua 8:30-35) where the people pledged their loyalty to God and His Word. Finally it was taken to Shiloh (Joshua 18:1) where it was (on our next to the last day in Israel we got to visit Shiloh), to my belief, to have been its last resting place. In the days of Samuel the tabernacle was still at Shiloh (I Samuel 1:3, 9, 3:3) and remained there until the Philistines captured the ark of the covenant (I Samuel 4:10-18). By the time of David the ark and the tabernacle were separated with the ark resting at Kirjath-Jearim (I Samuel 7:1) and the tabernacle at Nob (I Samuel 22). Then we are told that in the days of Solomon the tabernacle was at 'the high place at Gibeon' (I Chronicles 16:37-43). After that the tabernacle is lost in the pages of the Bible, but the last piece of it, the ark of the covenant, is finally moved to the first Temple, but only 'the two tables of stone' (I Kings 8:9) remained under the mercy seat!

I have come to believe that the Old Testament Tabernacle is the best portrait of Christ before He came to earth. The Tabernacle was a 'figure' (Hebrews 9:8, 9, 24), a 'shadow' (Hebrews 10:1), and a 'pattern' (Hebrews 8:5) and I believe that if you look carefully into the furniture and instruments and makeup of the tabernacle you see His love (Deuteronomy

7:7–8), the life He wants us to live (Exodus 25:8), and the wonderful lessons He wanted us to learn (Hebrews 8:5) from the Life of Christ. On a number of occasions over my forty years in the ministry I have had a chance to teach the Tabernacle, but so much will change in my next opportunity (an opportunity I got in India in the autumn of 2012) because I have had a chance to visualize that important Old Testament structure in its natural setting in the Wilderness of Paran. There is no evidence that the children of Israel ever pitched that sacred tent there, but the one now there is a living testimony to the Tabernacle of Testimony (Numbers 1:53); to a Living God who's only real desire is to dwell with us. Interestingly, the same reason Jesus came (John 1:14) to live with us and the same reason the Holy Spirit now lives in us (I Corinthians 3:16–17)!

38

The Animals of Israel and Their Lessons

Job 12:7–9—But ask now the BEASTS, and they shall teach thee; and the FOWLS of the air, and they shall tell thee: or speak to the earth, and it shall teach thee: and the FISHES of the sea shall declare unto thee. Who knoweth not in all these that the hand of the Lord hath wrought this?

We left the Tabernacle of Timnah, for the Hai-Bar Yotvata National Park Reserve and the opportunity to get up close and personal with some of the animals of the Promised Land. Ever since my father pointed out the three verses I have printed above, I have been a watcher of just about every creature in nature (Dad is a hunter, as I was in my youth, but since adulthood I prefer seeing an animal in its natural habitat versus shooting an animal in the wild!). One of the lists I had started in the back of my first journal shortly after we arrived in Israel was an accounting of the animals we saw on the trip. The only animals we saw in our seven days in Jerusalem was the cat and the chicken, but once we left the confines of the city, the country of Israel was full of a variety of birds, animals, and fish.

Wildlife has been a joy all of my life. The State of Maine is still home to the occasional opportunity to see an animal in its natural setting. I still rejoice each and every time I see a bull moose, a black bear, a white-tailed deer, a red fox, a Canadian goose, or an eagle in flight and my greatest joy is watching a trout or salmon swimming in a stream. One of my hopes for

Israel was to see Biblical animals while touring the out-of-the-way places of the Promised Land. By the time we got to the 3000 acre animal reserve at Hai-Bar Yotvata, we had already seen camels, donkeys, horses, sheep, ants, cows, goats, dogs, sparrows, ravens, peacocks, and of course those Jerusalem cats and chickens. The Hai-Bar would add these species to my animal list: red fox, wolf, hyena, jackals, ostrich, viper, leopard, cobra, turtle, porcupine, conies, vulture, ibex, owl, asp, gazelle, ass, and a variety of other snakes. As you will notice from the list that follows, we also saw a few more members of the animal, bird, and fish kingdoms after we left Hai-Bar!

Huge numbers of Biblical animals had become totally extinct in Israel by 1960, so measures were taken to protect the vanishing species still around. In 1968, the Hai-Bar Yotvata was set up to reintroduce ancient desert animals back into the region. The fenced in area is also home to many acacia trees and an abundance of natural pasture land. Many of the animals run free in the enclosed area, and as we drove into the parking area we could see a number of ostrich running behind the fence. I hadn't seen ostrich in the wild since my days in the deserts of Western Australia. We also saw a herd of onagers (wild ass) behind the fence as well as the gazelle. We walked through the caged areas of the reserve, including the predator's center, on a warm afternoon near the Jordanian border. Only when I got back to the States did I take the time to revisit the animals I saw and the Biblical stories and verses that made my encounter with them memorable and educational.

Here is my list of animals I had a chance to interact with in Israel and the spiritual lessons they reminded me of:

ANIMAL	WHERE SEEN	SCRIPTURE	SPRITUAL LESSON
Sparrow	Beersheba	Matthew 10:31	more valuable than many of them
Raven	Jericho	I Kings 17:4	God can use even a raven to help
Peacock	Jericho	I Kings 10:22	symbol of Solomon's pride
Fox	Hai-Bar	Song of Solomon 1:15	got to watch out for the little fox

The Animals of Israel and Their Lessons 155

ANIMAL	WHERE SEEN	SCRIPTURE	SPRITUAL LESSON
Coney (a small animal that lives in the rocks and caves, probably the hyrax; rodent-like)	Chorazin	Proverbs 30:26	feeble but wise
Vulture	Hai-Bar	Isaiah 34:15	mate for life
Chicken	Jerusalem	Matthew 23:37	how Jesus would gather us
Sheep	Negev	Psalms 100:3	we are God's sheep
Owl	Hai-Bar	Psalms 102:6	when we cry to God, we are like
Hart	Hai-Bar	Psalms 42:1–2	how we are to pant after God
Horse	Jericho	Psalms 33:17	a vain thing for safety
Wolf	Hai-Bar	Matthew 7:17	what a false prophet is like
Camel	Jericho	Matthew 19:24	hard for the rich to get saved
Leopard	Hai-Bar	Jeremiah 13:23	hard for the evil to change
Ass	St. George	Proverbs 26:3	a rod for a fools back
Mule	Nazareth	Psalms 32:9	not to be like one
Fish	Banias Stream	Matthew 7:9–10	our gifts verses God's gifts
Viper	Hai-Bar	Matthew 23:33	ungodly are like snakes
Asp	Hai-Bar	Isaiah 11:8	how safe the kingdom will be
Cow	Negev	Isaiah 11:7	how safe the kingdom will be
Goat	Shephelah	Matthew 25:33	the symbol of the lost

ANIMAL	WHERE SEEN	SCRIPTURE	SPRITUAL LESSON
Dog	Advat	Proverbs 26:11	a sinner returns to old ways
Ostrich	Hai-Bar	Lamentations 4:3	a symbol of cruelty
Ant	Jericho	Proverbs 6:6–8	a symbol of wisdom/work
Lizard	Yad Hashmona	Leviticus 11:30	a symbol of the unclean
Musht (a catfish type of fish, sometimes called St. Peter's Fish, biggest fish in sea at 17 in, 4.5 lbs)	Sea of Galilee	John 21:11	Christ's great blessing
Sardine (the smallest fish found in the Sea of Galilee—probably what the lad had at lunch)	Sea of Galilee	John 6:9	Christ's multiplication
Biny (a fish sometimes called "barbels," for the barbs at the corner of its mouth; middle size)	Sea of Galilee	Matthew 17:27	Christ's great provision
Stork	Golan Heights	Jeremiah 8:7	inborn instinct
Bull (sometimes called "the bulls of Bashan" (Psalms 22:12); the biblical name for the Heights)	Golan Heights	Isaiah 51:20	symbol of the fury of God

Even Jesus pointed out at times the birds of the air for a lesson (Matthew 6:26). Whether the hills of Jerusalem, the valleys of the Shephelah, the wilderness of the Negev, the waters of the Jordan, or the animals of the Promised Land, there was always a teaching, an instruction, a declaration,

The Animals of Israel and Their Lessons 157

a telling of some kind as we walked and worked our way through this grand land. Isaiah, perhaps, records this lesson best when he writes:

> That they may see, and know, and consider, and understand together, that the hand of the Lord hath done this, and the Holy One of Israel hath created it." (Isaiah 41:20)

39

Sleeping Under the Shadow of Masada

Psalms 127:2—... for so He giveth his beloved SLEEP.

We left the Hai-Bar Yotvata Animal Reserve around four in the afternoon of our tenth day in Israel. We had a nearly three hour northern run ahead of us paralleling the border with Jordan along Route 90 to Masada. Before we could travel to far north, we had to make one more stop at Yotvata for their world famous milk, and our afternoon surprise. My opinion about their milk didn't change with my second stop. If you want good milk, you need to come to Maine!

The winding road took us through the small Jewish villages of Ketura and Lotan and Yahel as we traveled again through the Paran Wilderness along the western side of the Arabah (the Scriptural term for the whole rift valley from the Sea of Galilee to the Gulf of Eilat—Deuteronomy 2:8). It was on this stretch of the highway we heard the daily question from Greg: "What time is it?" To which we always replied: "It's cookie time!"

It was the daily routine of Professor Greg Behle to treat his students each afternoon about four or so to a favorite Israeli cookie (they were not Opal's (my mother-in-law) or Coleen's (my wife) cookies, but they were ok). He had bought our May 10th cookies at the Yotvata rest stop. As the cookies were passed around, we watched our world once again being swallowed up by the depressing expanse of the Paran. We could see the high ridge of the Jordanian Plateau to our east (the ancient lands of Edom and Moab where the children of Israel traveled to flank the wilderness they had wandered in so long) and the endless desert of the Paran to our west. We enjoyed our late afternoon snack as we wandered again in the area they call the Arava (Arabah—Joshua 18:18) today!

It was also along that road that we got a chance to see again the Ibex deer on the high ridges that often ran alongside the roadway. Greg said that they were a rare sight in the wild, so to enjoy a taste of life in a seemingly life-less place was refreshing. We continued to pass small settlements like Paran, Bildad, Tzofar, Merkaz Sapir, and Ir Ovot; most seemed to be farming areas with vast fields under plastic. What they were growing and where they were getting their water was a mystery, but there they were. After nearly two hours of travel, Greg told us that we were coming to the southern tip of the Dead Sea near a place called Ne'ot Hakikar (also near the southern tip of the Dead Sea was the ancient town of Tamar, fortified by Solomon—I Kings 9:15–17). I was anticipating this part of our trip because of my interest in the destroyed 'cities of the plain' (Genesis 13:12): Sodom, Gomorrah, Admah, and Zeboim (Deuteronomy 29:23).

The best accepted theory of where this 'plain' used to be is under the waters of the southern tip of the Dead Sea. What is now the shallow bottom at the southern end of the Biblical Salt Sea probably was once the fertile valley of Siddim (Genesis 14:10). This is how the Bible described the region before God's great judgment:

> And Lot lifted up his eyes, and beheld all the plain of Jordan, that it was well watered everywhere, before the Lord destroyed Sodom and Gomorrah, even as *the garden of the Lord (Eden)*, like the land of Egypt, as thou comest unto Zoar. (Genesis 13:10)

Over the years this unique body of water has been given many names, including 'the sea of Lot', but its most infamous call to fame is the story of God's 'brimstone and fire' (Genesis 19:24–25) destruction during the days of Abraham. I thought the terrain couldn't get any worse after Paran, but there on the edge of the Wilderness of Zin was the worst landscape I have ever experienced in my entire life!

As we came within sight of the Dead Sea (sometimes called the sea of Arabah, the east sea, and the sea of Sodom), we began to see huge mineral plants. Besides the natural salt found there that provoked the first international war (Genesis 14) and other conflicts recorded in the Bible (II Samuel 8:13), the sea is a major producer of potassium chloride (used for the manufacture of fertilizers and explosives) and magnesium bromide (used in making light alloys). It is estimated that trillions of dollar's worth of minerals can still be found in the Dead Sea. This Dead Sea is one of the richest areas in the entire world for minerals. As we traveled up its western shore we also learned that the Dead Sea isn't completely dead! Scientists have found a single-cell creature that survives in the saltiest water in the world; ten times saltier than the ocean! This example of organic life is for me a testimony to the amazing creativity of the Creator, for what man sees as 'dead' the author of Life can make life live, both naturally and spiritually (Ephesians 2:1—John 1:4)!

Soon after we left the mineral plants behind, we started to climb what they call Mount Sodom. There at the brow of the hill was a town named Never Zohar, the Old Testament town of Zoar (Genesis 19:20-23, 30). If you remember the story, Lot saved this town from destruction because he didn't want to flee to the wilderness (a perfect example of my opinion about the wilderness). Nevertheless, after he moved into Zoar with his daughters, he left Zoar to live in a cave in 'the hills'! It was also along that stretch of highway we passed, but did not see, "Lot's Wife", a pillar named for the unique death of the woman who looked back (Genesis 19:26; Luke 17:32). It was also at this junction we passed the boundary between the southern basin and the northern basin of the Dead Sea. The two are connected today by a man-made canal that allows water from the northern basin to flow into the southern basin. The southern section of the Dead Sea is very shallow now (30 feet to 3 feet), and without the canal it would be totally dry in just a short time.

We were now just a few short miles away from another place being taken off my to—see list before I die. I had, like so many of the other places of Israel, read about Masada. I had seen the movie, seen the documentary, but I knew I couldn't understand its place in history or its topography completely until I could see it and experience it for myself. We still had a few more tourist spas to pass (we were told that the mineral water in the Dead Sea was good for a variety of ailments and that people around the world come to the sea for treatments) before I got there, but I did enjoy the Dead Sea journey. I was surprised just how many resorts we saw along the shore of the Dead Sea as we made our final ascent to the foot of Masada. Greg told us that some people spend thousands of dollars a day to visit some of the more famous spas. For me, I wasn't looking for a spa, but a sanctuary; not a resort, but a refuge to rest my tired feet and prepare me for Masada.

And there at the foot of Masada was the Masada Guest House. We arrived with just enough sunlight to see the distinct shape of the summit. The hostel was modern, the food was ok, the night's sleep was restful, and the dreams were of tomorrow's climb. I would need all the rest I could get to accomplish the trek I would take the next day. Little did Marnie and I imagine just how tough it would be to climb to the top of Masada? Sleeping under the shadow of Masada was the easy part of the adventure.

40

A Climb Up Masada

Psalms 63:1—O God, thou art my God; early will I seek Thee: my soul thirstest for Thee, my flesh longeth for Thee in A DRY AND THIRSTY LAND, WHERE THERE IS NO WATER.

The prelude to this psalm in the old King James Version of the Bible records this:

A Psalm of David, when he was in the wilderness of Judah.

Masada is located in the wilderness of Judah about 40 miles south of Jericho and 33 miles, as the crow flies, from Jerusalem. There on the shores of the Dead Sea is one of the best recognized symbols of Israeli freedom. The Hebrew word for 'stronghold' is metsudah. It is used in this eye-opening verse:

> And he (David) brought them (David's family) before the king of Moab: and they dwelt with him all the while David was in THE HOLD. (I Samuel 22:4)

Some believe that 'the hold' mentioned here was the cave of Adullam (I Samuel 22:1) located about twenty miles northwest of Masada, but I have come to believe this 'hold' might have been Masada because Masada is located directly across from the land of Moab where David took his family members to keep them out of the hands of King Saul. Could David have found this mountain-top plateau in 'a dry and thirsty land' and used it as a refuge and stronghold? In the numerous psalms in which David invoked the term 'stronghold' could he have been referring to Masada? En Gedi can be seen from the summit of Masada, a place

David went for safety (I Samuel 24:1). There is certainly plenty of evidence that David was in the region, and I can't believe he wouldn't have seen the military value of a place like Masada!

I must admit that my rest under the shadow of Masada was, as I believe, much like the Roman soldiers of 73 AD before their climb up Masada to conquer it: anticipation and excitement and foreboding. Unlike the legionnaire, I was not going to climb the ramp they had built to ascend to the top of Masada. I wasn't going to take the easier and modern way to the summit (a cable car). I was going to take the most difficult way of all: the snake path along the eastern slope to the top of the hill, and I had talked my daughter Marnie into joining me; a trail I believe David could have taken to get to the top? As it turned out about half our group decided to also climb versus ride, and to me it felt like one of those challenges in the popular reality show "The Amazing Race."

> This is a task that both members of the team must complete. You must find 'the snake path' up mount Masada and travel its length till you find the fortress of Masada at the top. Once you get to the top you must find Phil (Greg), for this is the pit stop for this leg of the race. The last team to arrive maybe eliminated from The Amazing Race: Israel.

I was up by 6:30 AM and full of energy. We had been warned the night before that this might be the most difficult climb of the trip. The hills of Jerusalem were challenging, but short (the climb up Masada might take an hour). We had ascended many a tel, but on this climb we would be walking up from 1300 feet below sea level (the lowest place on earth is the Dead Sea basin) to sea level on top of Masada. Most of our climbs before Masada had happen during cooler times, a nice sea breeze, but on the morning of our ascent it was nearing 100 degrees with no breeze whatsoever. We were warned to take plenty of water, and get plenty of sleep the night before. Marnie and I were as ready as we thought we needed to be when we boarded the buses (the study group from Master's Seminary had joined us—58 in all with 39 making the climb and the rest taking the cable car) for the short ride to the foot of Masada around 7:45 AM.

To my disappointment, we had to endure a fifteen minute lecture before we were free to start our climb. Don't get me wrong, it was interesting, but I had read and studied Masada for many years and there was nothing in the lecture I hadn't already learned. I knew we only had three hours to tour Masada, and I felt I needed every minute to see what I wanted to see and to experience what I wanted to experience. It was 8:20 AM before Marnie and I were at the head of the Snake Path (a winding serpentine trail that cuts back and forth along the side of the ridge that makes up the eastern side of Masada). Most believe this is not the original path that the Jews used at the time of the Jewish Revolt of 70 AD. I too believe that the original serpentine path is found on the northern slope next to where the Roman's built their famous siege ramp, but there is clear evidence from history that two of these paths once existed! Despite the difference, as I would see from the top, we had picked the most difficult place for our ascent there is at Masada.

As with "The Amazing Race", Marnie and I were the first to leave. I had positioned us near the door at the lecture hall so we would be the first out the gate. As we walked to the starting line we could see the Dead Sea through the early morning haze (heat haze if you are wondering). We passed the rock walls of an old Roman camp, one of eight built to keep the Jews on the top of Masada from escaping. We could see the Jordanian Plateau across the sea and the wilderness of Judah before and around us. I felt the heat and tasted the dust and knew what I was about to do was beyond what I had ever dreamed possible. To climb up Masada was certainly a physical challenge, but for me it was more of a spiritual exercise. I had come to Israel to witness the dramatics of the land in relationship to the story of the land. I knew that the story of Israel didn't end with the defeat of the Jews in 73 AD and the suicides of the defenders of Masada. That story goes on and will go on until the Lord comes back and rules and reigns in Israel as the 'King of the Jews'. Masada was a part of the past, and is a part of the present.

To the modern State of Israel, Masada is an emotional and meaningful symbol of a few standing against the many, the weak against the strong, the importance of freedom above life itself. To this day when the young men and women of Israel pledge their allegiance to Israel they come to Masada, and when the oath is over and the swearing is completed a defiant shout echoes off the canyon walls that surround Masada:

Masada shall not fall again, never again!

Fifty minutes later, Marnie and I finally arrived at the summit. We had covered one and a quarter miles of switchback trails. We had climbed the 720 stone steps along the way. We had to stop numerous times to rest and drink. (Marnie will tell you it was the most difficult physical event of her life.) Though we started first, we were the last to arrive. The good news—this was a non-elimination leg of "The Amazing Race": Israel.

41

The Fortress of Masada

Psalms 62:2—He only is MY ROCK and my salvation; He is MY DEFENSE...

Despite the exhausting hike up Mount Masada, I hit the summit running (that is after I refilled my water container at a water fountain near the gate where we entered the fortress). I left Marnie behind in the shade of a rampart wall to catch her breath and recover from the ascent. The others in our group that had come up the cable car, or beat us up the snake path, had already gathered with Greg for another lecture in the administrative section on the northern end of the plateau. I had my own agenda for the hour and a half I had left on top of Masada. For years I had studied the charts and maps of the layout of Herod's Masada, and I knew what I wanted to personally explore.

What makes Masada an impregnable fortress is first its unusual height compared to the other ridges in the area. Second, it is cut off from all other hills by deep dales that fall away sharply on all four sides. It stands alone in a region isolated and inhospitable far away from major highways and important places. In the only history we can be certain of (there is some evidence by the way of the pen of Josephus, the Jewish historian, that the first known fortress to be built at Masada was by the High Priest Jonathan somewhere between 161 and 143 BC and then the Maccabean king, John Hyrcanus refortified it in 135 BC), Herod chose this place for a major fort because of the topographical characteristics that would make it an ideal refuge, a defensible position that few would attempt to attack. King Herod had two major fears during his kingship—one, his own people (really not his own with him being an Edomite) might depose him as their king; and second, the threat from Cleopatra's Egypt, perhaps, his greatest fear. We had already traveled to the Herodium and had seen the fortress that was Jerusalem in the days of Herod, but for "a last stand" Herod picked Masada!

First, Herod built a white stone wall 18 feet high and 12 feet thick all the way around the top of the plateau that is Masada (a mile in circumference). Second, Herod built 38 towers on that wall, some of them as high as 75 feet. There were only two entrances into the fortress of Masada—one from the east (somewhere along the snake path we had climbed to gain entrance) called 'the snake path gate', and the other on the western wall called 'the western gate'. Access through this gate was by a similar kind of path found on the east side of the plateau. In front of the western gate Herod built the first of three palaces on Masada which was also a fort within the fortress. The palace walls were high and thick and on each of the corners was a tower 90 feet high! What God had already created in the natural formation that was the rock of Masada, Herod's engineers added to make the fortress of Masada invincible and impregnable to any assault by any army of his day; Herod knew how good the Romans were in siege warfare!

So besides the walls and towers and ramparts and gates and forts, Herod dug huge cisterns into the mountaintop and diverted the little rain that fell in the area to these massive holding caverns. He created big store rooms which he filled with grain, dates, wine and oil that would be sufficient for him and his guards for many years. There were even areas on the top of the plateau that could be cultivated, so the people could provide a supplemental food supply during a lengthy siege. Then Herod stocked the fortress with an amazing supply of arms; Josephus says there was enough for an army of 10,000 men! But for those who might think this was only a military base, you must also remember that Herod was used to a certain lifestyle, a very lavish and splendid lifestyle. It was in that spectacular section of Masada I was determined to see it before I explored any other aspect of Masada; and as Greg and the group lingered in the storeroom and administrative buildings of Masada, I headed for the three-tiered, northern palace-villa.

Like the Herodium, Herod commanded his engineers and workmen to do something that defies explanation. It is one thing to build a hill where there is no hill, and it is something entirely different to build a three-terraced palace on an outcropping nearly 1,500 feet above the ground! Access to this fancy villa today is by way of a 350 step staircase made along the western wall of the plateau. I found the entrance to the round-about entrance and found I was alone. Herod's plan was to build his Masada villa in three levels. The first level was located on the very brow of the plateau, the highest site on the top. This section contained a cistern, a bath, and a pathway leading to the other two sections of the villa below (this passage is no longer safe so the pathway has been blocked). Far below on a rocky outcropping Herod created the second terrace of his elaborate villa; a circular platform. From here Herod could catch the cooler breeze in the evening and see the Dead Sea and anything that would approach his fortress from the north. There was also a hidden staircase leading to the heart of this villa.

Below the second terrace, Herod's builders constructed a third terrace, another circular platform. This terrace was supported with plastered columns and the floors and walls had colorful frescos. There was even a private bath area, and the view was unbelievable. I had the privilege to stand on that platform for over ten minutes alone. From the top terrace my traveling companions looked down on me as I looked up to them. They wondered how I had gotten to the spot, and of course I had to tell them. It was beyond description the time I spent alone in Herod's villa, but if I was to fulfill my list of sites on Masada I had to leave my villa to those who would come after me!

Once I reached the top of the villa Marnie and I reconnected. She was feeling much better after her difficult climb up the snake path. Some fresh water and a little time out of the sun brought a second breath and a renewed step. She was ready for me to show her around Masada. Once again we broke from the crowd and wandered on our own. Our first stop was to the synagogue on the western side just north of the western gate area. Also along that wall we walked through the small rooms the Zealots had built to stay in during the Roman siege. From that rampart we were able to look over the wall and see the siege ramp still visible after nearly 2,000 years lying against the western slope. Far below we could still make out the outlines of the major Roman camp of Silva. We than walked over to the small palace situated in the very middle of the plateau (yes, number three!). From there we walked over to the eastern wall and followed it until we came to the southern watchtower. It was here we had our picture taken with the Dead Sea in the background. For me, it was the best picture of Marnie and me of the entire trip. I got that picture blown up and it now graces a wall in my study. When I think of Israel I see Marnie and I seated on the ramparts of Masada overlooking the Salt Sea. We then went to the southern tip to another tower complex, where we listened to our echo off the surrounding ridges. As we worked our way back to the cable car, I stopped and went into one of the great cisterns to see for myself just how much water could be stored on the summit, and into a Roman-style bath complex. Masada might have been built to be an impregnable fortress, but from all indications it was also a playground for the rich and famous—Herod-style.

42

A Message From Masada

Isaiah 25:12—And THE FORTRESS OF THE HIGH FORT of thy walls shall He bring down, lay low, and bring to the ground, even to the dust.

As Marnie and I waited on Masada to take the five-minute cable car (we didn't have time to make the walk down as some of our group did because of our extra wanderings around Masada) down from off the tabletop fortress, I scanned again the ruins that remain of this once mighty fort and remembered its most infamous event.

When Herod was named King of Judea by the Romans in 37 BC, the Jews rebelled and he was chased into the Wilderness of Judea by those that opposed his rule. He and his family found refuge in the old Maccabean fortress, or what was left of it. After the Romans gave him enough soldiers to reclaim the throne, Herod realized after his brief time in Masada that it would be a perfect place of refuge if he would ever need it again, so, as we have seen, he built (between 37–31 BC) a seemingly impregnable fortress on top of Masada. Until recent excavations and archaeological explorations, the only information historically about Masada is provided by the Jewish historian Josephus, who interestingly was working for the Romans during the siege of Masada.

After the death of Herod, Masada was turned over to a Roman garrison. In 66 AD, a group of Zealots under the command of Manachen Ben Yehuda captured Masada from the Romans (I have always wondered how, but few details are given). Known as "The Great Jewish Revolt", the struggle to throw off the oppressive yoke of the Romans would fail by

70 AD with the destruction of Jerusalem and Herod's great Temple, but the banner of freedom would fly over Masada for another three years—why? Herod had not only fortified the top of the thirty acre rock, but the twelve enormous underground cisterns filled with tens of thousands of gallon of water gave the defenders of the fort a great advantage against any attacker. Despite the great difference of numbers—967 men (some feel fewer than a couple hundred soldiers), women, and children versus 15,000 crack legionnaires of the Tenth Legion; how could Masada hold out against such a number?

When the procurator Silva arrived at the foot of Masada late in 72 AD, he immediately had his soldiers and the slaves he had brought along to help in the siege build a six-foot thick wall all the way around the hill. This created a two-mile barrier against any rebels escaping. Intermittently, along the wall, he built eight camps to house the soldiers and the auxiliaries in his force (some of the outlines of these camps can still be seen today as well as sections of the wall). Once this impenetrable ring was completed, the siege could begin. The Romans soon realized that the defenders of Masada had more water and food and time than they did. Even the most advanced catapults and siege engines the Romans had brought were useless because of the sharp slope of the mount. Every attempt proved futile including a direct assault up the snake paths. Silva soon realized that the fortress of Masada would only fall by breaching the upper wall and attacking through that breach with an infantry assault. It was then he ordered his engineers to construct a dirt ramp up the western face, the only accessible place around the entire mountain. This ramp would have to rise nearly the 1000 feet to the summit. It took the builders nine months to create the siege ramp with each foot built under attack, so the arrows and stones of their siege weapons had to guard the workers from the arrows and rocks thrown down on them from above.

While the ramp was being built, Silva had his skillful carpenters construct a 90 foot tower entirely covered in iron that would be used to climb the ramp and attack the wall. In the tower were placed catapults that could and would keep the defenders at bay while the battering-ram at the base of the tower would knock the wall down thereby opening a gap for the Romans to gain entrance into Masada. However, by the time the Romans got everything in place, the Jews, under the command of a man by the name of Eleazar, had also been at work building an inner flexible wall of wood and dirt which nullified the destructiveness of the mighty ram. The Romans countered by setting the wooden wall on fire, but at the risk of the flames actually burning down the siege tower. At first the wind was in the favor of the Jews, but when the afternoon winds shifted the fate of the defenders of Masada was sealed. The rest, as they say, is history. The end of Eleazar and his rebel band has been glorified in books (Josephus being the first) and movies, as they took their own lives rather than become slaves of the Romans. We know of the end (April 15, 73 AD) because of the eyewitness testimony of two women and five children who decided that life was better than death. The process was simple, each man killed his own family, then ten men were chosen to kill the others, and one was chosen to kill the nine. Finally, the last survivor killed himself. The seven to escape the slaughter of Masada had hid in one of the many water tunnels eluding the final assassin!

Even the battle-hardened Roman legionnaires were touched by the statement of the defenders of Masada. It is recorded as Silva walked the top of Masada some of his soldiers came up to him to congratulate him on his great victory; to which he is reported to have said:

> We have won a rock in a wasteland by a dead sea!

After the dramatic siege of Masada, the fortress remained virtually unknown until 1838 when a group of Americans touring the area spotted Masada through a telescope from En Gedi, located ten miles to the north. After that it was periodically visited by others who traveled through that area, but after 1948, when Israel gained its statehood, Masada became the most visited archaeological sites in all of the Promised Land.

I can understand the significance of Masada to the national makeup of Israel. Masada is to them what the Alamo is to America. However, as Marnie and got on the cable car to exit my most memorable morning in Israel, a different message came to me. I chose Isaiah's verse printed above because of the reality of the defeat at Masada. When mankind places their trust in a rock instead of The Rock destruction will eventually come. As I mentioned in an earlier chapter, I do believe David probably at least visited this site around 1000 BC (I Samuel 23:29), but unlike the Maccabeans and Herod the Great, and yes, even the Romans, he came to a different conclusion:

> Hear my cry, O God; attend unto my prayer. From the end of the earth will I cry unto Thee, when my heart is overwhelmed: lead me to *The Rock that is higher than I!* For Thou hast been a shelter for me, and a strong tower from the enemy. I will abide in Thy

Tabernacle for ever: I will trust in the covert of Thy wings. Selah (pause and consider this). (Psalms 61:1–4)

Was I impressed with Masada, surely you have gotten that from my experience, but I was more impressed that David could walk away from this impregnable place and put his confidence in his God. Messiah not Masada became his shelter, refuge, rock, and tower. Oh, that we would realize that a man-made fortress holds no real safety or security for us. Masada is a high fort in a weary land, but it is at best a rock in a wasteland; while Jesus is the Rock that is higher than David, Herod, Eleazar, Silva, or any other man, including me!

43

En Gedi and the Dead Sea

Ezekiel 47:10—And it shall come to pass, that the fishers shall stand upon it (DEAD SEA) from EN GEDI even unto En Eglaim; they shall be a place to spread forth nets; their fish shall be according to their kinds, as the fish of the great sea (Mediterranean Sea), exceeding many.

Our trip from Masada took us up Route 90 another ten miles. By eleven o'clock we were stopping at a tourist center for lunch and a dip in the Dead Sea. It was not until after we left the Dead Sea that I found we had stopped at the Biblical site of En Gedi (one of my great disappointments of the trip)!

En Gedi, like Hebron and Petra, was one of the places I really wanted to visit on our Israeli tour. I had seen the wonderful pictures of the spring of En Gedi and the oasis David found there in his wilderness (I Samuel 24:1) wandering from King Saul. (Some believe that David wrote his 57th Psalm from there.) It was in a cave not far for where we had stopped that David saved Saul's life for a second time (I Samuel 24:2–15). I wanted to experience for myself 'the spring of the goat' (En Gedi), the two beautiful waterfalls (Nahal David and Nahal Arugot), and perhaps, see the amazing array of wildlife (the Ibex is known for haunting the area) that it draws to the spring that never runs dry (just like the Gihon Spring). The first mention of this oasis in this bleak and barren land is in Genesis 14:7. It is called Hazezon-Tamar, or the 'row of palms' in the story of the kings of the east invading the city-states (like Sodom) along the Dead Sea. II Chronicles 20:2 tells us that Hazezon-Tamar and En Gedi are one and the same. After the heat and dust of Masada, I, like David, wanted to enjoy the lush vegetation and the cooling waters that was En Gedi. To finish off my Masada experience I wanted to see where the slaves of Silva carried the water that quenched the thirst of the legion that conquered Masada. I wanted to work my way through the narrow entrance that separated the tropical paradise of En Gedi from the torturous landscape that was the Dead Sea, but instead of the refreshing waters of En Gedi, our leader chose for us to experience the bitter waters of a dead sea!

After another terrible lunch that cost a fortune, Marnie and I got ready with the rest of our group to experience the waters of the Dead Sea. Don't get me wrong concerning what I have already written, for you must remember I didn't know just how close we were to En Gedi, so I was excited to witness for myself the impossibility of sinking in the Dead Sea. As we changed into our bathing suits, we realized that our stay in the water would have to be short. Both Marnie and I are fair-skinned and we burn very easily. It was over 100 degrees when we stepped out of the dressing rooms about 300 yards from the shore of the Dead Sea. The walk to the water revealed what we were up against. It was hot, not humid, a very dry heat but overpowering. The Sea we were getting ready to sit in (you don't jump in for it is important you keep the water out of your eyes, so you simple back into the water and sit down) was at the lowest point on the planet (1279 feet below sea level, for a contrast Death Valley in California is only 282 feet below sea level). We were nearly half-way down the western shore of the Dead Sea which is 48 miles long and 10 miles wide, and in the northern basin the water can reach a depth of 1300 feet. We would see through the haze of the heat at mid-day the Jordanian Plateau on the eastern shore. Land locked and without any outlets, the water from the Jordan River (and as I learned after our float, the waters of En Gedi as well) flows into the sea but only through evaporation does any water leave the sea; the high levels of salt and other minerals creates a buoyancy resulting in a swimmer's inability to sink!

A little after noon on May 21, 2010, Marnie was the first to back into the Dead Sea and sit down. I took a few pictures of her bobbing around before I followed her example. What I found the strangest was the difficulty I had trying to get my feet down. Sure enough you actually feel like you are sitting in a recliner with the footrest up. To keep you in an upright position seemed at first complicated, for I felt like I would roll over. The only way to kept from flopping over was to get your feet down in the water to act as a rudder. In my first tries I simply couldn't force my legs to sink. Only when I realized I had to tuck my legs close to my body was I able to drive them into the water. I was surprised just how clear the water was. Even twenty feet off shore you could see the rocks on the bottom clearly. The water had a milky look to it compared to the perfectly clear water of a Grand Lake Stream in Maine, but clear enough to see deep into the Dead Sea. There was a slight sulfurous odor in the air, as we enjoyed the sensation of floating in 'a thick, warm, tub of salty soup', as one commentator put it. We floated and bobbed around for about fifteen minutes. I had given my camera to Ike Spiker and he recorded our brief swim. I tried to get Marnie to cover herself in the black mud (lots of people come to the Dead Sea just to cover themselves in what they believe to be the healing agents found in the minerals in the mud) of the Dead Sea, but her skin was already itching; a taboo to Marnie!

I did get some pictures of other people caked in mud as we waited to wash the salt of the sea off our body by the fresh water showers. It was then I learned that the water we were using to wash ourselves off came from the spring of En Gedi. So we first showered on the shore then we walked back to the changing rooms to shower again. Marnie and I literally threw away our bathing suits and anything else we wore in the Dead Sea because the chemicals were that strong. After getting cleaned up we returned to the picnic area and shared our impressions with the rest of the group. Most took the opportunity to experience the Dead Sea, but some just relaxed before our journey continued. About mid-afternoon we left En Gedi for Qumran, the home of the famous Dead Sea scrolls.

It was only after I returned to Maine and was pondering my disappointments and delights at the Dead Sea at En Gedi that I discovered Ezekiel 47:6–11. Read these verses carefully and then consider the amazing prophecy that is being predicted here! The Dead Sea will one day be fresh water, and it will be filled like the Mediterranean (means 'middle of the earth') Sea (the Bible calls this sea 'the sea of the Philistines'—Exodus 23:31, 'the sea'—Numbers 13:29, 'the uttermost sea'—Deuteronomy 11:24, or in our key verse printed above 'the great sea'—Numbers 34:6) with fish! It says that the fishermen will spread their nets in En Gedi; I didn't see any fishermen at En Gedi, just swimmers. What this promise tells me is that there is hope for the most desolate. There is hope for the dead, and that we serve a God who is able to restore even a dead sea to life. As I thought on this concept I was reminded of these verses from the pen of Joel the prophet:

> And I will restore to you the years that the locust hath eaten, the cankerworm, and the caterpillar, and the palmerworm, my great army which I sent among you. And ye shall eat in plenty, and be satisfied, and praise the name of the Lord your God, that hath dealt wondrously with you: and my people shall never be ashamed. And ye shall know that I am in the midst of Israel, and that I am the Lord your God . . . (Joel 2:25–27)

I look forward to the day when I will fish rather than float again in the Dead Sea; when this sea is filled with the fresh water of En Gedi the whole world will know who my Christ really is!

44

The Caves of Qumran

Joshua 15:61-62—In the wilderness, Betharabah, Middin, and Secacah (QUMRAN), and Nibshan, and the city of Salt, and En Gedi; six cities and their villages.

We left En Gedi Pundak (restaurant and gift shop) on the shores of the Dead Sea just before two o'clock on the last day of our southern expedition into the wilderness of Israel. We had one last stop to make before we returned to Jerusalem. We were off to visit the site of the greatest archaeological discovery of the twentieth century:

The Dead Sea Scroll At Qumran.

Our travels would take us nearly twenty-five miles further north along the western shore of the Dead Sea to another national park located about seven miles south of Jericho. We had a chance at the Jerusalem Museum to see fragments of the famous scrolls, now we were going to get a chance to see where they were found in 1947.

As Greg reminded us of the history of Qumran, I remembered back to our short stay at the Shrine of the Book (the Shrine was designed by two Americans, Frederik Kiesler and Armand Bartos, and the white dome contrasted by the black basalt wall was to symbolize the battle between the Sons of the Light, as Essenes saw themselves, and the Sons of Darkness, the rest of humanity) on the third day of our trip, eight days before. The time had gone by quickly and I realized that there wasn't much time left to cross my Ts and dot my Is, and here we were at a place that could answer a myriad of questions I had about the people who had compiled these amazing scrolls and left them for us as a magnificent legacy to the durability of the Word of God. The most profound revelation I learned at the Shrine of the Book was the truth that since their discovery at Qumran Israel has spent a small fortune trying to preserve the fragile documents, but the ways of modern man to keep them safe from decay is not working. They would have been better off to have been left in the caves of Qumran: God's museum!

As with so many other tels on our travels, the Tel at Qumran was well defined and wonderfully excavated. As we wandered around the various section of the ancient town, Greg and John shared different aspects of the Essenes' (the pious ones—some believe that John the Baptist might have been one?) lifestyle. For those who are not familiar with this group let me give you this quick summary. Most feel this fundamentalist group of Jews fled Jerusalem (about twenty miles to the northwest) during the Maccabean Era (140 BC) and lived a communal life of self-reliance. Their goals were the purification of the priesthood by living a daily lifestyle that would please God, the preservation of the Scriptures by making copies of the Word of God for posterity, and watching and waiting for the return of the Messiah (the tragedy is that the Christ did come on their watch but they missed him because of their isolation) at the end of days. Their history seems only to have lasted about two hundred years. When Vespasian was sent by Rome to put down the Great Jewish Revolt in 66 AD he passed through Jericho and then went on to wipe out the Essenes' village at Qumran, and nothing was heard of them thereafter (there is some evidence that a few of the group might have escaped to Masada, but of course if they did in 73 AD they committed suicide to escape capture by the Romans). This group is not mentioned in the Bible, and the only historical evidence we have of their existence is through two ancient authors.

Josephus mentioned the Essenes in two of his books describing them as a Dead Sea sect that lived south of Jericho. Pliny the Elder, a Roman geographer (23–79 AD), writes of the Essenes in his book, Natural History. He says they lived on the northeast side of the Dead Sea. Both Josephus and Pliny write of their holy habits and verify the characteristics of their lifestyle archaeological discoveries have uncovered. They were an isolationist group of religious people that found a way to survive (that is until the Romans showed up) in an unforgiving land. For me the most amazing aspect of Qumran, next to the scrolls, was the way the Essenes provided for themselves a supply of water. For miles around their settlement they dug trenches so that any water that fell in the region would be channeled back to the village by way of small aqueducts. When we entered the complex, to our right was the aqueduct entrance into the city. This waterway ran into a huge cistern for holding rain water and then to a series of reservoirs (seven cisterns in total) that could allow water when needed to flow into just about every section of the town. We walked along these man-made channels to different homes and of course the Essenes most recognizable monument, the ritualistic bath areas, of which there were many in Qumran. We also visited the kitchen area (over a thousand ceramic bowls have been found here), the assembly hall (120 feet long by 90 feet wide-where they ate their communal meals), the pantry, the mill, the Sciptorium (the writing room with desks and benches and inkstands with one containing dried ink), the pottery (where they made the jars to put the scrolls in) workshop, a laundry room, the kiln, the cattle pen, and a defensive tower before we headed off out of town to view for ourselves the trademark of Qumran: the caves (of which 30 have been excavated and explored)!

As the Romans were descending on Qumran (the experts feel that up to 4,000 people might have lived here at the time) the Essenes offered up their last minute prayers and hid their scared scrolls in the caves within sight (about 100 yards away) of their village. There must have been hope that they would return and rebuild as they did in 31 BC when their town was destroyed by an earthquake. But there would be no return and their legacy remained hid from the world until 1947 when a shepherd boy was searching for a stray sheep in the cliffs near the site. The lad simply did what most boys do in their spare time; he picked up a rock and threw it into the mouth of one of the caves. The rock found its mark breaking one of the clay jars inside. The noise provoked another attribute of a typical country boy, curiosity. Entering the cave he discovered jar after jar filled with ancient scrolls. It had been 1,879 years since the Essenes had placed them there for safety. The discovery provoked a worldwide interest in not only the Essenes, but their Bible (books of the Old Testament, including a full book of Isaiah-the biggest scroll of all measuring 24 feet long and 10 inches high, the Apocrypha, as well as the sect's own writings-the Discipline Manual of the Essenes). A study of the area in 1949 by Professor Harding, director of Antiquities in Jordan, and Pere de Vaux, director of the Ecole Biblique in Jerusalem, resulted in seven priceless scrolls being uncovered. In 1951 a team of French archaeologists started to dig at Qumran, and over the next five years found additional scrolls (to date over 800 scrolls, either in part or in whole have been discovered at Qumran, including every book of the Old Testament, except Esther, is part of the collection) in other caves. We were off to see the most famous cave of the group: number 4!

The caves and crevices that dot the steep slopes surrounding Qumran not only served the Essenes, but their library as well. The reason that the scrolls survived for nearly two thousand years is the arid climate of the area. Placed in jars and out of the sunlight, the scrolls endure to this day, that is if modern man doesn't destroy them by taking them out of the preservation chambers the Essenes put them in. After about a hundred yard walk we were standing directly in front of Cave #4, where most of the hidden manuscripts were found. I got some wonderful pictures of Marnie in front of the cave, but our stay at Qumran was coming to the end. When Greg said we only had less than an hour before heading back to Jerusalem, I was determined to visit at least one of the cave myself. I asked where the closest cave (a deep canyon separated us from Cave 4) was and I was told #11. Before I knew it I had a small group including John Nuxoll, Mark Trahan, Jeremy Pendergrass (a young man who made the climb to Masada in under twenty minutes), and Chris Hanchey ready to climb with me up the hill behind Qumran to explore one of its caves.

45

The Abiding Word of God

I Peter 1:24–25—For all flesh (ESSENES) is as grass, and all the glory of man (QUMRAN) as the flower of grass. The grass withereth, and the flower thereof falleth away: BUT THE WORD OF THE LORD endureth forever. And this is THE WORD which by the gospel is preached unto you.

I mentioned at the start of this travel log that we would share more than just the places we visited and the sites we saw. I am by my very nature a preacher. I have been sharing God's Word in sermon form since I was fifteen (I am over sixty now). I would like at this junction of our travels to highlight the greatest lesson I learned at Qumran, a lesson that is being ignored today by most Christians. As I climbed with my Israel companions up the hillside to cave #11, it hit me like a lighting strike to my soul. The mighty miracle of Qumran isn't the fragments of Biblical truth found there, nor the preserved pieces of the Bible at the Shrine of the Book in Jerusalem. The universal message of Qumran is stated simply above!

As I struggled to reach my goal (yes, a harder climb than Masada, even Marnie wouldn't follow me on this ascent), I recalled what Greg had said about the importance of the find at Qumran. Until Qumran, the oldest known manuscripts of the Old Testament had been copied by scribes about 916, and that is AD not BC! This would make the Dead Sea Scrolls over a thousand years earlier than the oldest known manuscripts. To the best of their ability the experts in this field feel the scrolls of Qumran were written and compiled between 1 and 68 AD. The wonderful reality of comparing these 2000 year old documents with their 1000 year old cousins is just how alike they are. There are those who are critical of our trust in the Bible for accuracy and reliability. I have preached for years and believed most of my life that the miracle of the Bible isn't as much that it is the Word of God, but that "The Word" has endured for so long. My favorite verse on this subject is:

> For the Lord is good; His mercy is everlasting; and His truth endureth to all generations (including ours today, the Qumran generation)! (Psalms 100:5)

There have been those who have disallowed the great books of Psalms, Daniel, Isaiah, and other prophetic books for being written after the fantastic events prophesied in them. They argue that there is no way Daniel could describe the great empires of Persia, Greece, and Rome as he did writing from the time of the Babylonian Empire. Now with the scrolls of Qumran we have further proof that these Old Testament books as well as others precede the era between the two testaments—not that I myself need any proof. As I have preached for decades, whether or not they find Noah's ark on Mt. Ararat makes no difference to me for I will always believe in the ark and the flood. Whether or not a man was swallowed by a whale in the days of the whalers makes no difference in my belief of the historical Jonah and his fish story! And whether or not the Dead Sea Scrolls were found in Qumran or not makes no difference in my belief in the authenticity of the Word of God!

I climbed up to Cave #11 not to discover some new scroll (that would have been a thrill), but to experience the view of Qumran as the Essenes did when they deposited their scrolls. I wanted to say I had at least been near one of the caves that had shocked the religious world into the realization that we do have a genuine book despite how many times it has been copied and translated. The caves of Qumran only verified to my already deep-rooted belief that the Word of God will always endure. If four thousand years couldn't wipe it out, another four thousand years will have similar effects. The ruins of Qumran will be dirt again, before the Word of God is dust!

I know you are all waiting for me to tell you what we found in Cave #11. After a fifteen minute, exhausting climb to the mouth of Cave #11, we went in only to find a very shallow hole in the side of a hill. It could hardly be considered a cave, and there is no evidence that any of the hundreds of pieces of parchment (interestingly, written on Hebrew leather, Egyptian Papyrus, and even two scrolls were written on copper) were even found in Cave #11. Unlike the more famous caves, number eleven has an easterly exposure open to whatever rain might fall and the wind that might blow. I must admit I was a bit disappointed in our find; we even pressed on up to the top of the hill in hopes of finding something better, but we didn't. It only reassured me that my hope in the Scriptures and my belief in the Bible are not based on cave discoveries from Qumran. My belief is not because of my profession (preacher), nor my parentage (my parents were believers), but by providence (God-given). For most of my life I have not debated the Bible with those who don't believe or won't believe, for I believe the Bible is its own best promoter. I have claimed for years this great promise by Isaiah (also found on a Dead Sea Scroll):

> So shall MY WORD be that goeth forth out of my mouth: it shall not return unto me void, but it shall accomplish that which I please, and it shall prosper in the thing whereto I sent it. (Isaiah 55:11)

Certainly 'the thing' of Qumran is now fully known, or is it? Does God still have some hidden sacred stash still undiscovered that will make the world stand up and notice?

If Paul could get his spiritual training in the desert of Arabia (Galatians 1:17) by the Word of God, why not a settlement of scribes in Qumran copying the Scriptures for a future time when the Church needed to know that what they had been preaching and teaching for two millennium was older still? As I climbed down the hillside west of Qumran, I looked again at the site and I realized that though the place was in ruins, God's Word wasn't. Though the caves are empty, the Word of God still contains 'Thus Saith The Lord' and "It Is Written'! There in a wilderness by a dead sea the Word of God is still live and doing just fine in the purpose for which the Almighty sent it. The Essenes might have been mixed up in their theology, but they still understood the importance of the Word of God. They might have missed their Messiah, but they didn't miss the importance of preserving the Word of God. Their methods might have seemed unorthodox, but they left for the rest of us an example that it isn't the town, the water supply, or even life itself that is most important; just the Word of God! The atheists deny it, the liberals reject it, the false teachers mishandle it, the average Christian ignores it, the cults reword it, and still it endures! The Devil has yet to build a fire to consume it, the demons have yet to formulate an argument to refute it, the wicked have created no law to destroy it, and the world has yet to come up with a way to wipe it from its history. Qumran is just another example of the durability and dependability of the Word of God: *"But the Word of the Lord endureth forever!"*

46

Yad Ha Shmonah Guest House

Acts 10:4—...Thy prayers and thine alms are come up for a MEMORIAL before God.

We left Qumran for Jerusalem about mid-afternoon on our eleventh day in Israel. We did make one more stop in Jericho (where we had ridden the camel on our fifth day) to get a cool drink. It was nearly 100 (the bus air-conditioner was still not working to capacity) as we made our way up the western shore of the Dead Sea to the city of the palms. The weather was clear as we made the final ascent up Route One to finish the southern circle of our journey. We had been on the road for four days and most of us couldn't wait until the bus finally stopped rolling. We were going to spend two nights at the Yad Ha Shmonah Guest House just outside Jerusalem—our fifth home on the trip.

After a week at the Knight's Palace in Old Jerusalem, I thought nothing could beat the atmosphere of the old city. The Beersheba Hostel was nice as was the Adi Hotel in Eilat, and the night at the Masada Hostel under the shadow of the fortress will always be special in my mind. Despite the fact the Yad Ha Shmonah had no Biblical connection, (we could see Kirjath-Jearim—I Samuel 7:1—from the guesthouse) its location and unique makeup out did every place we had stayed up to this point in Israel. This was probably because I am a man of trees and templed-hills. After the barren, bleak landscape of Southern Israel, the terrain around Yad Ha Shmonah was like coming home to Maine. The rocky knoll is covered in forest and flowers, beautiful bushes and shrubs, and the buildings on site are all made of Finnish pine. But even more impressive was the reason this place was there in the first place!

This isolated hillside off Route One was founded in 1971 by Finnish immigrants who believed in the Bible and wanted to help the Jewish people settle the Promised Land. It started out as a communal village, a hilltop armed camp (the old bomb shelters are still in use today), and another claimant to a piece of Palestine that once was controlled by the Arabs but now occupied by the Jews. The name was chosen to remember the eight Jews who were sent to Germany by the government of Finland during World War Two. In the winter of 1940 Russia attacked Finland, and despite a valiant defense was eventually forced to give up territory to the Soviet Union. When Germany attacked Russia in 1941, the Finns allied themselves with the Germans to regain their lost lands. This was also the time the Nazis were rounding up every Jew in Europe they could get their hands on for 'The Final Solution'! To appease the Germans, the government of Finland turned over eight Jews; all who would die at the hands of the Nazis. Yad Ha Shmonah (the memorial to the eight) is a testimony and apology to the Jewish nation for those souls. The entire complex is constructed on a log cabin style. When you drive into the yard you might imagine you are entering a Finnish settlement, or like we also do in Maine, a log house development!

The Knight's Palace was located in a busy, noisy section of a big city. The Beersheba Hostel was located on a city street at the edge of a wilderness. The Adi Hotel was located in the heart of a bustling coastal, tourist town. And even though the Masada Hostel was isolated, it was located on a rugged, desolate ridge overlooking a dead sea. Yad Ha Shmonah's log-cabins are nestled in a peaceful, wooded Judean hilltop. From the summit you can make out the Mediterranean Sea about 25 miles away. The first night we were there Marnie took some great sunset pictures from a veranda overlooking the valley that cuts down to the coastal plain. By the late 1970's a log house dining hall and log cabin welcome center were added. Over the years many more air conditioned guest rooms were constructed. Marnie and I had our own room in a log house on the side of one of the ridges. Each room had a bedroom, a private bath, and a balcony with a spectacular view of the surrounding hills. There was also a conference hall made in the same Finnish pine (all the lumber was furnished by Finland as a further example of regret over their World War Two mistake), a restaurant, and spacious plazas throughout the complex. The walkways and pathways were lined with native trees and shrubs. Nature was in full bloom while we were there and the sights and smells were divine and the birds and their songs were heavenly.

It is here that the IBEX (Israel Bible Extension Study Program) has their campus. They rent rooms in the complex for the students and staff when the program is in session. So it would be here (remember, we had made a quick stop at Yad Ha Shmonah on our way to the shephelah but didn't get a chance to walk around) that we would prepare ourselves for the last leg of our trip into Northern Israel and it would be here we would finish our days out in Israel at the end of our journey. Also at Yad Ha Shmonah an interesting Biblical garden has been constructed. Built on the backside of the property, one can wander through ancient displays including a winepress, an olive oil manufacturing plant, a threshing floor, various grinding stones, a watchtower, a Galilean-type synagogue, an outdoor theater, a rolling-stone tomb, olive trees, a shepherd's tent, vineyards, and numerous other Biblical objects scattered periodically along the trail. Mingled with these Biblical items are the flowers and plants and trees of the holy land. It was a wonderful place to walk and meditate. The weather was ideal when we arrived and would remain that way throughout our stay!

Once we got settled into our cozy room, Marnie and I made our second call home just before supper. Marnie and Coleen talked for about 25 minutes. It was during that conversation we learned that our son, Scott, had made squad leader (Scott was a specialist in the United States Army stationed at Fort Bragg North Carolina in their heavy transportation division, but was then deployed to Camp Leatherneck in Southern Afghanistan)! Following supper we had a special lecture (one of two) by Dr. Eugene Merrill, a professor at Dallas Theological Seminary on the archaeology of Jericho. It was one of the extras we received on the trip. It was an eye opening explanation to an old familiar Biblical story. Because we had already visited the site earlier on our trip, what Dr. Merrill said only tied together the site with the scripture. The story of Joshua and Jericho came better into focus over the hour Dr. Merrill discussed the Biblical truth that is being discovered in the ruins of Jericho. Doctor Merrill is the same Doctor Merrill who wrote the well-known Old Testament text book (A Kingdom of Priests) I used at Bob Jones University in the early 1970s. A man nearing ninety, Dr. Merrill was in Israel leading a group of students from DTS, an archaeological team, digging at Tel Ai (on our next to the last day in Israel we would join him for a morning dig). He was one of the unexpected joys of this trip; more about him and our attempt to be archaeologists in another chapter.

By nine Marnie and I were snuggled in our room reading and writing in our journals. Eleven eye-opening days in Israel had passed, and the next day would be our second free day in Israel; that is free after we had taken our second quiz on the places we visited on the southern leg of our travels. We had already decided to return to the old city of Jerusalem to see a site we missed. There were also some purchases we needed to make and more memories to add to our journey beyond 'memory lane'! Truly, a fitting place to recall and remember and reminiscence on the glorious events of this Promised Land we had seen and experienced. We had been to Beersheba and beyond, now it was time to prepare for 'Dan' and beyond!

47

The Church of the Redeemer

Psalms 19:14—Let the words of my mouth, and the meditation of my heart, be acceptable in Thy sight, O Lord, my strength, and my REDEEMER.

One of my desires for this Israeli trip was not to hurry it. I wanted to enjoy, take in, relish every minute, every second; I could not, would not say with Job:

> When I lie down, I say, when shall I arise and the night be gone?
> And I am full of tossings to and fro until the dawning of the day!
> (Job 7:4)

Instead my nights were sweet and restful, as was my first night at Yad Ha Shmonah, and my days were unhurried. I felt more like the Psalmist who wrote:

> My soul waiteth for the Lord more than they that watch for the morning: I say, more than they that watch for the morning.
> (Psalms 130:6)

I woke on my 12th morning in Israel to 'the voice of the bird' (Ecclesiastes 12:4) and to the anticipation of what I would see and learn on this another unhurried day in the Promised Land.

How unhurried was our second Saturday (Sabbath) in Israel? Marnie and I slept in until 8:15 AM, our latest so far on the trip. The night was so cool at Yad Ha Shmonah we didn't even use the AC. As I left our room to find the washing machines, I instantaneously noticed the difference in the air. I noticed some of my traveling companions had on sweaters, but for me it was Maine air in Israel. I did find the two washing machines by one of the bomb shelters and managed to get a load of washing started. By the time it was done Marnie and I had breakfast and got ready for our trip into the old city. The quiz had been put off until the evening just before our lecture on the northern part of our journey. With a last minute check on my funds, and making sure I had the map of the old city in my pocket, we boarded the bus for the Jaffa Gate.

We first dropped off those who were going to visit a Sabbath church (Jerusalem Assembly Fellowship) in the new city. The bus was going to pick them up after church and take them into the old city, and return for us all later in the afternoon. Marnie and I had partnered up with Chris Hanchey, a youth pastor from Louisiana, and Jeremy Pendergrass, Chris' best friend, and our hope to only stay in the city for a few hours. We still had more laundry to do and needed time to prepare for the quiz and pack for our northern trip. We decided we would finish our lists, have lunch in the city, and hire a taxi together back to Yad Ha Shmonah. By 9:40 AM, we were back to our old stomping ground near the Knight's Palace. As Chris and Jeremy headed for the shopping (presents for their wives) district, Marnie and I had one last site to see: The Church of the Redeemer.

We had first passed this old church on the way to the Holy Sepulcher on our very first night in Jerusalem, but it was closed. On two other occasions we stopped by to get in, but again it was closed. The reason for our perseverance was the massive tower connected to the main sanctuary. We had noticed the tower while standing on the roof of the Citadel on our first day in the city. We were told that from the top of the Lutheran Church of the Redeemer you could get the best view of the old city. We had seen the ancient town from just about every angle except from on top of that tower, so before we met the boys in the Christian Quarter we were determined to climb the tower of the Church of the Redeemer and take in the vista from above its bell tower.

Aren't you glad that there are still some things man can't hurry? One of the blessings of our Israeli trip was God's timing. Instead of having to share the climb up the tower with others this would be Marnie's and my time. There were so many things Marnie and I just shared on this trip because of the Lord's timing. And here we were again alone together in Jerusalem with plenty of time to explore and experience and sure enough as we came around the corner the two massive wooden doors of the church were wide open! Isn't it great that mankind hasn't been able to get control of the 'time' machine? As impatient a creature as we are we would not do well with such power or control! God takes time with things, seasons or saints, or the speed by which we get to do something, like climbing a steeple. Our week's wait was well worth it, as we entered the church to find the staircase to the top of the belfry.

Inside the lobby of this stone church was a man who gave us a book that told of the history of this unique structure. The foundation of the church was laid on the site of the medieval Saint Mary's Church. Once that church fell into ruin a Muristan (the Persian word for hospital) was built. There is some historical evidence that the Crusaders used the site and in particular the Order of the Knights of Saint John; whose job it was to care for the pilgrims that traveled to Jerusalem during the days of the Crusades (1099–1187). When Saladin conquered Jerusalem the hospital was not destroyed but continued to serve the same purpose but now for Islamic pilgrims. From the 16th to the 19th century, the holy city was nearly forgotten and places like the Muristan fell into ruin. By 1840 there was a renewed interest in Jerusalem, especially from Europe and in particular England and Prussia. In 1869 the old site was purchased by Prussia and on October 31, 1898, Kaiser Wilhelm II (of World War One fame) helped dedicate the Church of the Redeemer. Today, the church is a series of buildings including the main sanctuary, a north portal, the chapel of peace, a cloister, the chapel of Saint John, a refectory, and of course the tower.

After we paid a few shekels for the privilege of climbing the stairs to the platform above the bell tower, Marnie and I started up the 180 stone steps to the top. The narrow spiral staircase was divided into three sections (51 in the first flight, 59 in the second flight, 70 in the third flight, yes I counted them). When we got to the top we were able to walk completely around the top floor of the steeple and view Jerusalem in all four directions, was the climb and the sights worth the wait? What we saw wasn't new (we had a bird's eye view of Temple Mount and other major sites in the old city) to us, for we had seen them up close and personal, but what was new was the angle we got to see them from, and for me it was well worth the wait. We climbed down and met the boys at the Cardo, and finished our shopping. We left the old city for lunch at a McDonald's the boys had found on a previous trip. We found a taxi and were back at the Yad Ha Shmonah by two o'clock. Laundry was next and after that a one and half hour nap. By six we were at supper, by seven we were preparing for our quiz, and by eight it was over. It took Greg 90 minutes to tell us about our northern trip that would start in the morning, and by 9:40 Marnie and I were back in our rooms with another day behind us.

I was so glad I hadn't hurried my day off in Israel. No there were no amazing discoveries like at Michmash; no amazing experiences like at the Western Wall; no amazing sights like at Masada; no amazing blessings like at Timnah; no amazing rides like at Jericho; no amazing dawns like at Eilat, but on May 22, 2010 I witnessed an unhurried dawn, an unhurried day, an unhurried duo. Marnie and I enjoyed our time together going where we wanted to go and doing what we wanted to do. In the end we were glad the Good Lord left the Church of the Redeemer for an unhurried day. The more I read the Bible the more I find the word 'wait'. It is certainly a Biblical concept, not a worldly precept. The world wants everything now. It is well worth the wait when God's involved:

> But they that wait upon the Lord shall . . . (Isaiah 40:31)

48

The Plain of Sharon

I Chronicles 27:29—And over the herds that fed in SHARON was Shitrai the Sharonite . . .

I woke on my last Sunday in Israel to a cool wind blowing over the hillside at Yad Ha Shmonah. The visibility was once again as far as the eye could see. I had mixed feelings as Marnie and headed for an early breakfast because I had enjoyed deeply the peace and tranquility that was built into the guest house we had occupied for two days. On the other hand I was excited to be heading out on a five day tour of northern Israel. It was time to explore the world of Jesus and the towns and villages that I had known about since my childhood. A little after eight o'clock we were traveling west then north for a nearly two hour bus ride through the plain of Sharon; our destination, Herod's famous seacoast port of Caesarea on the Mediterranean Sea.

Our journey took us back towards Tel Aviv on Route One until we came to the crossroad of Route One and Route Six. Route Six is the north/south highway through the coastal plain. We had traveled this route south to Beersheba, now we were heading north to Carmel. On the way we would pass a number of important Biblical sites I would have loved to visit, but time wasn't on my side once again. We drove by Lydda (Acts 9:32) where Peter healed Aneaus as we had done after leaving the Ben Gurion Airport on our first day in Israel. We then passed Joppa (Jonah 1:3) where Jonah began his fateful Mediterranean cruise. After that we traveled through the plains of Ono (Nehemiah 6:2) where Nehemiah refused to meet with his enemies. Then we traveled through

Antipatris, another building site of Herod the Great on the main trade route between Egypt and Syria. This became a major agriculture center in Herod's day; a river encompassed the city itself and grove after grove of trees surrounded the complex. To this day this region of Israel is still known for its groves and orchards. Herod named the city after his father Antipater. Paul would stop here (Acts 23:31) on his way from Jerusalem to Caesarea. Once again I felt like I was retracing Biblical events through Biblical places!

The famous battlefield of Aphek (I Samuel 4:1) was our next non-stopping site. It was also here that David had marched from Ziklag only to be turned back (I Samuel 29:1–5) by his Philistine bosses as they consolidated their forces before heading further north to Mount Gilboa (a place we would visit on this trip) to defeat King Saul and his army and his sons (I Samuel 31). It was also here that King Ahab fought an important Biblical battle against the Arameans/Syrian army (I Kings 20:26). We also passed to our east the capital of Northern Israel at Samaria, another disappointment (another hotbed of Arab resistance to the Jewish occupation and a very dangerous place). Samaria is located about 30 miles north of Jerusalem, and we still had another twenty miles to Caesarea. Once we crossed the Jarkon River we came into the Plain of Sharon proper as we pretty much followed the ancient road (the Via Maris—the way of the sea) towards Megiddo.

I can tell you that my knowledge of Sharon was first provoked by spiritual songs that used the phrase 'the rose of Sharon' (Song of Solomon 2:1). The Bible seems to use the place as a picture of beauty and bounty, as in this verse:

> It shall blossom abundantly, and rejoice even with joy and singing: the glory of Lebanon shall be given unto it, the excellency of Carmel and Sharon, they shall see the glory of the Lord, and the excellency of our God. (Isaiah 35:2)

This plain runs along the Mediterranean shore from Joppa to Caesarea. It is first mentioned in the Bible in relationship to a city-state Joshua conquered during his rampage through Canaan (Joshua 12:18). In the days of David, he appointed a caretaker over his herds in Sharon (I Chronicles 27:29). So from ancient times the plain was known for its rich pasture land and vegetation. The Jews occupied this region through the tribe of Gad (I Chronicles 5:16) and to this day find it an ideal place to settle. They told us on this trip that the vast majority of the population of

Israel today lives on the Plain of Sharon. As we traveled through the final miles of this picturesque and pasturage landscape, I came to an understanding why the commentators have connected this plain to Christ. For me, Charles Spurgeon, the famous British pastor and writer said it best in this classic "Morning and Evening" devotional:

> Whatever there may be of beauty in the material world, Jesus Christ possesses all that in the spiritual world in a tenfold degree. Amongst flowers the rose is deemed the sweetest, but Jesus is infinitely more beautiful in the garden of the soul than the rose can be in the gardens of the earth. He takes the first place as the fairest among ten thousands. He is the sun, and all others are the stars; the heavens and the day are dark in comparison with Him, for the King in His beauty transcends all. 'I am the rose of Sharon.' This is the best and rarest of roses. Jesus is not 'the rose' alone, He is 'the rose of Sharon,' just as He calls His righteousness 'gold', and then adds, 'the gold of Ophir'—the best of the best. He is positively lovely, and superlatively the loveliest. There is variety in His charms. The rose is delightful to the eye, and its scent is pleasant and refreshing; so each of the senses of the soul, whether it be the taste or feeling, the hearing, the sight, or the spiritual smell, finds appropriate gratification in Jesus. Even the recollection of His love is sweet. Take the rose of Sharon, and pull it leaf from leaf, and lay by the leaves in the jar of memory, and you shall find each leaf fragrant long afterward, filling the house with perfume. Christ satisfies the highest taste of the most educated spirit to the very full. The greatest amateur in perfumes is quite satisfied with the rose; and when the soul has arrived at her highest pitch of true taste, she shall still be content with Christ, nay, she shall be the better able to appreciate Him. Heaven itself possesses nothing which excels the rose of Sharon. What emblem can full set forth His beauty? Human speech and earth-born things fail to tell of Him. Earth's choicest charms commingled, feebly picture His abounding preciousness. Blessed rose, bloom in my heart forever!

As I reflect back on my morning on the Plain of Sharon, I realize that I had an amazing visible reminder of just how beautiful my Saviour really is to me. The sights that I saw and the smells that I smelled were but an earthly beauty that will fade into nothingness when I finally see and smell my Lord and Saviour 'face to face'!

For a couple of hours on May 23, 2010, I felt like Shitrai the Sharonite having been left in charge of the Sharon. My King allowed me for a few fleeting moments to witness the unimagined beauty of the Israel's coastal plain. I was beginning to realize that the best of the land had been left for last on this trip and that I was just beginning to get a new insight into the fertile place that would house my Saviour for most of His earthy life. They say:

> Beauty is in the eye of the beholder?

Well for me that morning I beheld great beauty, a beauty that took me far from the Plain of Sharon to the very presence of my Lord and Saviour Jesus Christ!

49

Caesarea By the Sea

Acts 8:40—But Philip was found in Azotus: and passing through he preached in all the cities, till he came to CAESAREA.

Just before ten o'clock our bus, with Joel at the wheel, pulled into Caesarea National Park, the archaeological remains of Herod the Great's amazing seaport.

    I had been impressed with Herod's temple mount in Jerusalem and his forts at the Herodium and Masada had also wowed me, but I was not ready for the sheer size of work I found when we explored the elaborate complex of Caesarea. What made Caesarea special was its location. They say, "Location, location, location!" Well, Herod picked well his spot to build one of the best seaports of the ancient world. Herod knew there was money to be made if he could tap into the trade routes of the Roman Empire. He had a monopoly on a variety of products wanted by the Romans, but how to get them to them? If he had his own seaport he could cut out the middle man and deal directly with markets around the Mediterranean Sea. If Herod could build a hill where there had previously been no hill and place a palace fortress on its top, he could also build a port where there had never been a port and create a very unique breakwater. As he did so many times before in his long reign, about 22 BC Herod told his engineers and builders to create a seaport about half way between Joppa (II Chronicles 2:16) and Dora (Dor—I Chronicles 7:29) in honor of his patron at the time, Octavian Augustus Caesar. Located about 50 miles northwest of Jerusalem on the vital Egypt to Tyre (the great seaport in Lebanon) road, Caesarea would within Herod's lifetime dominate the sea trade in the region!

What made Caesarea so special for me was its location on a beach. Ever since I first moved to the coast of Maine in 1986 (I have lived nearly half my life now near the ocean. I will be honest with you. I hate being on the ocean, but I love living near the ocean.), I have fallen in love with the sea. Caesarea was for me one of the most beautiful spots in all of Israel. Despite the ruins and rubble, I enjoyed our three hour walk around this coastal city because of the sea breezes, the ocean sights, and the water vista. While taking in these magnificent sites, I learned this about the history of Caesarea by the sea:

1. Between 586–332 BC, the Phoenicians built a settlement on the site because the ground water level was high.
2. The village continued to flourish during the Hellenistic period during which it got its name: Straton's Tower (259 BC).
3. In 103 BC it was conquered by Alexander Jannaeus and was made part of the Hasmonean Kingdom.
4. By 30 BC, the town and the area had been conquered by the Romans and annexed to Herod the Great.
5. In Josephus' Jewish War, he writes this: "And he (Herod) chose on the coast one forsaken town by the name of Straton's Tower. . . . which thanks to its favorable location was suitable for carrying out his ambitious plans. He rebuilt it entirely of white stone and adorned it with a royal place of unique splendor, displaying. . . . the brilliance of his mind."
6. It took 12 years to build the harbor, a network of crisscrossing roads, a temple, a theatre, an amphitheatre, markets, residential quarters, and a defensive wall.
7. It was completed by 10 BC and by 6 BC the Romans made it their governmental headquarters for Palestine.
8. Caesarea was at the heart of the Great Jewish Revolt in 66 BC and was used by the Romans as a base for the legions that put down the rebellion. Interestingly, Vespasian was named Emperor (or Caesar) at Caesarea whereupon he traveled to Rome to claim his crown, and left his son Titus to finish the job. (Why, Titus is known for the capture of Jerusalem, and not Vespasian!)
9. Caesarea became a center of Christianity from the first century to the fourth century. It was at Caesarea that the Gospel officially came to the Gentiles with the conversion of the Roman centurion Cornelius (Acts

10). Philip the deacon, or evangelist had a great ministry there (Acts 8:40 and Acts 21:8). This is of course where Paul had some of his most famous trials (Acts 21, 22, 25).

10. During the Byzantine Period the city expended into the 6th century with a perimeter wall enclosing 400 more acres making it the largest fortified city in the country.
11. After the Arab conquest of 640 AD, the town lost its political and economic base and most of its citizens left, leaving it a small village again.
12. It wasn't until the Crusaders came that the port and city was once again refortified (1101-1251 AD). King Louis IX of France brought back its former beauty.
13. In 1265 it was conquered and destroyed by Baybars the Mameluke, and it remained that way until the 19th century when the Ottoman Empire began to rebuild part of the city.
14. 1873 was the year the site began to see its first archaeological work, and by the time we arrived the site was a massive archaeological dig!

Our trip through Caesarea took us through the theatre (seating capacity of 4,000), Herod's promontory palace (a group of half-submerged walls are all that is left of the fabled palace), the hippodrome (one of the largest in the Roman Empire, the massive stones that remain allow you to imagine its former size), the Roman and Byzantine streets through the commercial and administrative area, the bathhouse complex, the harbor (still surrounded by walls dating back to 1250), the old medieval fortified city, the temple platform, what they call statues square (all kinds of ancients statues, tombs, and pillars), the synagogue, and finally out through the Byzantine gate and walls. For me to imagine that I might have walked on stones that Philip, or Peter, or Paul might have walked on was enough for me. To see the expensive stones and the imaginative breakwater (that formed a large artificial harbor (Sebastos) using the 1200 foot breakwater as the base for the inner quay and anchorage area of mooring stones), and the simple architecture was breathtaking. I caught myself more than once thinking of how the Eternal God moved a wicked king to create an elaborate port, not for the export of goods, but for the export of the Gospel!

The more I saw the world of Jesus through the archaeological sites the more I understood Paul statement:

> When the fullness of time was come, God sent forth His son . . .
> (Galatians 4:4)

I had been taught that history was waiting for the Greek language to be in place, the Roman road system to be built, the Pax Romana (worldwide peace) to be in effect, and now I know for a harbor to be constructed on the Mediterranean Sea so that the evangelists and missionaries of the early church would have an exit from Palestine into the rest of the world. Our God worked out all the details, so that when it was time for the expansion of the Church to happen, the infrastructure to help with its rapid growth was ready. We certainly serve an amazing Planner that puts Herod to shame! He planned for the 'now' and the near future while our God prepared before *'the foundation of the earth'* (I Peter 1:20)!

50

A Lesson from the Theatre at Caesarea

Acts 25:13—And after certain days King Agrippa and Bernice came to CAESAREA to salute Festus.

The old pink jacket book had been in my library since my father gave it to me in the late 1970s. According to the copyright, the book was first printed in 1973. It contained the observations and devotionals of Vance Havner under the title of "Just a Song at Twilight". Over the years since getting this first book by this beloved author, I have read others inspirational books like: By the Still Waters, Day by Day, Repent or Else, Pepper 'n Salt, Lord of What's Left, Moments of Decisions, Though I Walk through the Valley, Rest Awhile, On This Rock I Stand, and many, many others. Last year on a visit to see our daughter at Dallas Theological Seminary, I had the privilege to spend many an enjoyable hour at their library reading from their extensive collection of Vance Havner books. Needless to say, Vance is one of my favorites, if not my favorite author. Now you can understand my excitement when after years, since I read these lines, I could see and understand for myself Havner's observation at the theatre at Caesarea:

> In Caesarea we saw an outdoor theatre, not an amphitheatre, but a semicircular stone auditorium. From the back row we could hear our leader speak in conversational tones from the platform. Moreover, he told us that a larger theatre in Ephesus that could hold twenty-four thousand was constructed centuries ago with the same marvelous acoustics. All this in a day when in my travels all over America I had congregations of a hundred or so complain that they could not hear in a tiny church! Larger

edifices wrestle continually with the problem. All our experts somehow cannot come up with the acoustics of antiquity!

What a thrill to have stood where Havner made this insight and to understand what he was getting at; and to say to myself, I was there—I see or hear more clearly his point!

I would like for you to hear a bit more of what Vance Havner wrote about the theatre of Caesarea:

> How many times have listeners in little auditoriums lamented that hearing was bad only a few yards from the pulpit! Could it be that we slaves of our own devices have become so accustomed to hearing aids of all sorts that we imagine we cannot hear without them? We limp on our crutches and if the amplifier does not work 'hearing we hear not' (Matthew 13:13). Once I listened to the veteran evangelist, Gypsy Smith. He was a preacher of the old days and abhorred all new devices. I thought I could not hear him and when he asked if any of us were having trouble about it, I raised my hand. 'You're not listening!' was his reply. Could it be that, conditioned as we are to mechanical aids, we just think we cannot hear the preacher? And of course those dear souls who come to church early to get a back seat could move up closer and fill the empty lumberyard of ten rows of seats right in front of the pulpit. But they never do, yet still insist that they cannot hear! 'Ears that hear not.' 'He that hath ears to hear, let him hear' (Mark 4:9). Ears to hear! All of us are equipped with ears but hearing is another matter. We hear and we do not hear. Our ears catch vocal sounds emanating from the pulpit, but the message escapes us. We hear (after a fashion) what the minister says but our Lord said, 'Let him hear what the Spirit saith . . . ' (Revelation 2:7). Of course sometimes the preacher is not saying what the Spirit says and if we listened ever so well there would be no word from God. Or the trouble may be not with the transmitter but with our receiver! There is a preparation to hear the sermon as well as a preparation to deliver the sermon. We live now in an ear-splitting age of amplified dissonance and some think the next generation will have to be equipped with hearing aids. The more our eardrums are bombarded with demonic waves of music (which is not music but only an excuse for not being able to make music), the deafer our souls will be. Something has gone wrong with our hearing—both physically and spiritually. We are not going to correct it by clever devices. We must get at the cause. We need to do something about how we hear as well as what we hear. There is a famine (Amos 8:11) of the hearing of the Word of God—a famine because in some quarters it is not

being preached and in others because our ears are not tuned and trained to hear it. God grant us more Samuels who can say, 'Speak, Lord, for Thy servant heareth!' (I Samuel 3:9)

As I recalled this devotional from a favorite book and a favorite author, I realized that I was also in a place where a similar event took place.

By the time King Agrippa showed up in Caesarea Paul had already been a prisoner there for two years (Acts 24:27). He had already stood before Felix and Festus, but I believe in order to fulfill prophecy (Acts 9:15) Paul had to stand before a king! King Agrippa and his wife Bernice had come to Caesarea to greet Festus, the new Roman governor. While on that state visit, Festus sought Agrippa's opinion on what to do with his most famous prisoner. What we have recorded in Acts 25–26 is perhaps one of the best appeals ever given by an evangelist to a needy sinner, yet at the end of Paul's discourse (Acts 26:2–27) it simply records this reaction of Agrippa:

Almost thou persuadest me to be a Christian! (Acts 26:28)

What was the problem? Agrippa wasn't listening. He had no spiritual hearing. His soul was so calloused that the Spirit's voice couldn't break down the barriers constructed there by the Devil himself. I have often thought, why? Then I found this:

In whom the god of this world hath blinded the minds of them which believe not, lest the light of the glorious gospel of Christ, who is the image of God, should shine unto them. (II Corinthians 4:4)

My conclusion: if Satan can blind, then Satan can make deaf! You can have the best acoustics and the most powerful amplifiers, but they are not enough to break through the deafness of one that will not hear. You can have the best salvation text proclaimed by the most powerful evangelist, but neither will penetrate the soul of a man like Agrippa. 'Almost' is never enough. Years ago I picked up a Gospel tract with a catchy title:

Missing Heaven by Eighteen Inches

The message of the tract was that many get the Gospel to their mind, but never get the message to their soul (the average distance between the brain and the heart). As I left the theatre at Caesarea, I realized that Vance's message was now fully settled in my mind, and that I need more than ever the Spirit to be working in my messages lest my sermons fall by the 'wayside' or on 'stony ground' (Matthew 13:4–5) or a deaf ear!

51

An Unexpected Lunch at Joel's House

I Chronicles 4:35 —... and JOEL ...

Did you know that there are 14 different men of the Bible named Joel? Probably the most famous is the prophet Joel (Acts 2:16), but Samuel also had a son named Joel (I Samuel 8:2) and David had a mighty man named Joel (I Chronicles 11:38). But the Joel I would like to introduce you to was the bus driver on our trip into northern Israel. An event took place on our first day on the road that told me a lot about the character of this Arab Christian from the village of Baka El Gharbiya.

To my sheer delight, our stay at Caesarea by the sea didn't stop with a tour around the ruins of that ancient seaport. We exited Caesarea through the eastern wall (a perimeter wall nearly a mile and a half around) gate of the old Byzantine section of the town. The gate contained an impressive tower and the moat was also spectacular, the best I had ever seen including some memorable moats from my wife's and my trip to England, Scotland, and Wales in 2003! As Joel drove away from the city limits of Caesarea, Greg pointed out the old Roman amphitheatre dating back to the second century, an arena where gladiatorial and animal combat was waged. On the other side of the road a massive Hippodrome (circus), also of the second century and Roman, was being uncovered. The structure was nearly 1500 feet long and 300 feet wide. They believe it could seat 30,000 spectators? A series of columns set along the wall through the middle of the race track have been uncovered, and a 75 foot obelisk has also been found. It was only an introduction to what was coming next.

I had seen pictures and had dreamed many times of visiting the most recognizable artifact of Caesarea: the high-level aqueduct. This marvel

An Unexpected Lunch at Joel's House   205

of ancient engineering still runs along an exposed beach just north of the city. Since Caesarea had no natural rivers or springs to supply the drinking water for this important center something had to be done. Because this city was a seat of the Roman government (Caesarea was the home of the Roman procurators, including Pontius Pilate, interestingly, whose name was discovered in Caesarea on an inscription naming him 'the prefect of Judah'.) for the region for 500 years, a water system was needed; started by Herod the Great and modified by the Romans. An aqueduct was a water carrying system where water was transported from one area to another by a series of canals. Because gravity was the means of powering this system, in low lying areas that section of the aqueduct was carried on arches. It was to a series of those arches we stopped to examine this amazing accomplishment. I had read about these structures for years, but had only visited one such place in my life: a relatively modern aqueduct system at Llangollen, Wales; a 46 mile long canal which only drops one inch per mile; it also contains the tallest navigable aqueduct in England. My wife and I were thrilled to have floated across this 126 foot high aqueduct in a narrow boat on our 2003 trip. Now I was going to get a chance to experience a nearly 2000 year old aqueduct on the shores of the Mediterranean Sea.

We stopped where the old aqueduct now comes to an end. Time had certainly taken its toll on the arches and canals. We could hardly imagine this structure running to the Shuni springs at the base of Mount Carmel nearly 15 miles to our north. I was told that along the route water from the Crocodile River (a smaller culvert carried water from an artificial reservoir that was formed with the damming of the river) was also added to the flow and that on the way a tunnel had to be hewn through the Kurkar Ridge. Where we stopped the aqueduct stood a good twenty-five feet over the beach, a perfect picture taking spot. Marnie and I got our pictures taken under the arch and by the aqueduct as we enjoyed the refreshing sea breeze. As I did at Caesarea, I walked the seashore to get an ocean side look at the conduit. We could only stay at the aqueduct for a few minutes because we were scheduled to be at Mount Carmel before dark. Again the visit was cut short in my opinion, but a few minutes were better than no minutes at all.

When we left the conduit at Caesarea around noon, we were surprised by the direction we took. Instead of heading north towards Mount Carmel, we headed east through a series of small villages. It was then we were told that we had been invited for lunch at Joel's house. Normally around noon, we would eat wherever we happened to stop along our planned path. Sometimes it was at a truck stop, a local restaurant, or we would pick up food at an Israeli market. On this our 13th day in Israel, we were going to be treated to an Arab barbeque (what I called it). To our surprise and delight, we pulled up to a modest two-story concrete house in an Israeli/Arab village. It was then we learned that Arabs fall into three categories in Israel: Christian Arabs, Moslem Arabs, and Jewish Arabs. Some Arabs have citizenship in Israel, and not all Arabs are hostile to Israel. Joel was one of those Arabs. My only question was who invites 40 people to lunch?

It was at Joel's home I learned that the Arab culture has at its root the honor of hospitality. They see it as an obligation and a privilege to invite strangers into their homes. When we arrived we were ushered to the top floor where Joel's wife, an aunt, and another lady (I never got the connection) were waiting to serve us coke, coffee, and a candy cookie of some kind. There were bananas, watermelon, peaches, apricots, and other fruits I didn't recognize. While we waited for the main course, Dr. and Mrs. Hilber played dress up in traditional Arab dress; oh, did the cameras flash! As we talked, the ladies were in the kitchen preparing our main meal. My best explanation is they were making Arab mini-pizzas for us. The dough was rolled into small portions, and these were then flattened into a round shape. After the dough was prepared, we were taken downstairs to a back garage where a wood stove was fired up. There was a round tray connected to the fireplace on which the dough could be placed. Before the dough was put into the oven, a variety of vegetables (like corn and peas and mushrooms—a first for me) were placed on the dough. About five pieces of dough could be put through the fire at once. Once the dough was cooked there was a table of other ingredients that you could add to your mini-pizza (now about six inches across).

While the ladies were preparing our pizza (for lack of a better title), Joel and Greg had gone to the local market and had brought back a number of boxes filled with chicken pieces on small sticks (like our shish kabobs). Then Joel brought out something that I hadn't seen in years, a hibachi. We ate our fill on Arab pizza and Arab shish kabobs and enjoyed the friendliness of Joel's entire family (a wife and two kids plus other relatives). Without a doubt one of the top five meals of the entire trip, but what impressed me was the openness and caring of this Arab family. Without a doubt the Arab people were the most hospitable people we met on the trip. Another key factor in this noontime meal was the fact that

Joel was an Arab Christian which made the visit to his home that much more enjoyable, fulfilling Paul's admonition:

> Distributing to the necessity of saints; given to hospitality."
> (Romans 12:13)

Thanks Joel for sharing your family and that wonderful lunch!

52

Mount Carmel

I Kings 18:19—Now therefore send, and gather to me all Israel unto MOUNT CARMEL

It was nearly four in the afternoon on May 23, 2010 when we finally left Joel's for Mount Carmel. I must admit, despite enjoying the special Arab lunch, I was getting a bit impatient as the feast lingered for over three hours. I was looking with great expectations towards an ascent up one of the most famous hills in Israel, and I knew with each extra minute we stayed in Baka El Gharbiya was one less minute I could spend on Mount Carmel.

As a Sunday school kid, I still recall the excitement of the story of Elijah on Mount Carmel. Lily Harris was my children's church teacher and she had a way of bringing the Bible stories alive. For many years I imagined myself standing on top of Mount Carmel and now I was just a few miles away. Our travels took us back on to Route Six until we came to Route 672. By the time we had turned off, we had started our climb up the slope that constituted the range of mountains in northern Israel called Carmel. This range is fifteen miles long and runs from the seaport of Haifa on the Mediterranean Sea to the Plain of Esdraelon in the Jezreel Valley. This region was given to Asher during the allotment of Joshua (Joshua 19:26). This range separates the Plain of Sharon to the south with the Plain of Esdraelon to the north forming a natural barrier, with its highest peak just under 2,000 feet. I was surprised by the trees that covered its slopes, the most we had seen since our travels to Azekah in the Shephelah. The mountain rises so sharply from the sea that the rapidly rising air deposits plenty of moisture on the ridge throughout the year making the area lush the year-around! It was on our trip up the ridge I learned that Carmel means 'fruitful place, or, 'garden land', certainly a fitting name!

On the winding road to the top, I recalled the Biblical history I remembered about Mount Carmel:

1. Joshua had defeated the king of Joknean (we saw the tel of this city from our vantage point on Carmel) of Carmel in his Canaanite campaign (Joshua 12:22).
2. Samuel met Saul here after the attack on the Amalekites (I Samuel 15:12).
3. Elisha traveled here after the event with the children and the bears (II Kings 2:25).
4. The Shunammite woman found Elisha here after the death of her son (II Kings 4:25).
5. Uzziah the king had a huge wine vineyard here (II Chronicles 26:10).
6. Solomon used the imagery of Carmel to describe his love for his beloved (Song of Solomon 7:5).
7. The prophets Isaiah, Amos, and Nahum refer to Carmel withering and languishing speaking of the judgment of God to come (Isaiah 33:9, Amos 1:2, and Nahum 1:4).
8. Jeremiah used Carmel to speak of the might and grandeur of Nebuchadnezzar (Jeremiah 46:18).
9. Elijah's famous encounter with the prophets of Baal on the summit of Mount Carmel is the most recognized Biblical story about this place (I Kings 18).

Few Biblical places have a more colorful history than Mount Carmel.

Greg told us as we climbed upward that the mountain range has three distinct parts: Rosh Ha-Karmel (headland of Carmel), also known as Cape Carmel. This is the area that borders on the Mediterranean Sea. This was our destination and, in particular, the Carmelite monastery of Stella Maris. Rom Ha-Karmel (summit of Carmel) is the highest point, near the Druse village of Isfiya. We would pass through this town on our way to the monastery. Finally, Keren Ha-Karmel (spur of Carmel) is a peak in the southeastern apex of the mountain range, the traditional site of Elijah's contest with the prophets of Baal (El-Muhraqa-the place of burning). A long Jewish tradition is attached to this section of Carmel because at the foot of this peak is the River Kishon where Elijah slew the prophets after the fire fell (I Kings 18:40). Nowhere else along the Carmel Range is there access to the River Kishon. There is also a terrace large enough to hold the crowd that was there to witness the contest, and a spring is near enough to provide the water that Elijah poured over his sacrifice (I Kings 18:33-34). Another disappointment of our trip was the fact that we didn't have time to stop there!

Once we arrived at the Stella Maris Monastery, I immediately knew why we had come to this particular section of Mount Carmel-- the view. My first sight of the Jezreel Valley was through a cluster of trees on the eastern slope of Mount Carmel. It was a clear day with just a few drifting clouds hovering over the valley. The vista made me forget about missing Elijah's Carmel, even though they had built a stature of Elijah in the courtyard of the monastery. Soon we were on the roof of the monastery and the view only got better. We could make out Nazareth (one of our stops the next day) Jesus' boyhood town and behind it Mount Tabor (Judges 4:6) of Deborah and Barak fame. We could clearly see Mount Moreh (Judges 7:1) of the Gideon story and Mount Gilboa (I Samuel 31:1) where King Saul and his sons died at the hands of the Philistines. The Jezreel Valley spread out before us in an unending patchwork of fields and ponds and rolling hills. We could see far into the upper Galilee. As we climbed up to the west side of the roof we could see the Mediterranean Sea in the distance. Once again the closeness of these famous sites was shocking to me. The Bible stories I knew as a child, both Old Testament and New Testament, were well within my sight!

The vision I saw from on top Carmel helped me understand Isaiah's observation:

> The wilderness and the solitary place shall be glad for them; and the desert shall rejoice, and blossom as the rose. It shall blossom abundantly, and rejoice even with joy and singing: the glory of Lebanon shall be given unto it, *the Excellency of Carmel and Sharon*, they shall see the glory of the Lord, and the Excellency of our God. (Isaiah. 35:1-2)

Without a doubt, this was the most naturally beautiful place I had seen in Israel. I had visited more memorable places, seen more meaningful sites, and experienced more exciting venues, but for sheer beauty, the view from the top of the Stella Maris Monastery was the best. From where

I am writing this chapter, directly behind me is a picture of Marnie and me taken with the Jezreel Valley behind us! The checkerboard fields of various shades of green and brown highlighted by a bright sun also filled me with joy and singing. Now I know what the glory and Excellency of God will look like. It will be like my visit to Mount Carmel on a spring day in May!

53

Sleeping On Carmel

Micah 7:14—Feed thy people with thy rod, the flock of thine heritage, which dwell solitarily in the wood, in the midst of CARMEL...

Our stay on Mount Carmel was only to last, I thought, for about an hour. Little did I realize that we were going to actually spend the night on top of Carmel Ridge!

Within the hour of our leaving Stella Maris, we pulled into the Bet Oren Guest House, our home away from home on our first night's stay during our northern tour of Israel. This guest house was located just a few miles from Haifa on Route 721. The guest rooms were located in a wooded area with plenty of flowering bushes and pleasant walkways surrounded by tall trees and budding shrubs. The thrill of all thrills was the fact that our fifth level apartment-like room had a porch that opened up on the Mediterranean. Through a gap in the tree line and the ridgeline, we could clearly make out the blue waters of that great sea. We had come to another inspirational place. After Marnie and I settled in, we took a walk around the area before supper. After supper, we enjoyed the cool ocean breezes and the wonderful sounds of the wind blowing through the trees (a sound of home). I also was challenged by the solitude of 'the valley and the mountain', and I wrote in my journal:

> From my porch high on the slopes of Mount Carmel in Israel I look out on the early evening sky towards the Mediterranean Sea. There in the distance I see clearly the sea Elijah sent his servant to watch (I Kings 18:43). At the same time I sense the

sheer joy of staying a night on this edge of Carmel that has, for most of my life, symbolized the place where the power of God was demonstrated. Despite the fact that the people who actually witnessed this amazing act of power and the impact a simple 63-word prayer (I Kings 18:36-37) rejected this powerful act of Jehovah. I am resting tonight on the summit of the hill that witnessed the answer to that prayer, but the rejection of another—that the people of God would stop halting between two opinions (I Kings 18:21)! They didn't and I fear the same result is happening today. Elijah wasn't the first and he certainly wasn't the last to be disappointed by the choice his people made. Even in the Church age we have a rebuke of a similar nature:

> I know thy works, that thou art neither cold nor hot: I would thou wert cold or hot!" (Revelation 3:15)

Elijah was looking for Baal or Jehovah, but the people wouldn't choose. Even after proving without a shadow of doubt that God, not Baal, controls the lighting and the rain, the people still wouldn't commit themselves to God. The fear of being politically incorrect in the kingdom of Ahab and Jezebel still haunted them. Surely if Elijah could pray down fire he could confront the king and the queen and prevail, yet even Elijah lost faith and fled when his name was put to the top of the list the nation's "Most Wanted". When he heard a price was on his head, he ran!

Could I share with you what I believe happened to Elijah? He got his eyes off the mountain and looked too long into the valley. If he had only remembered the second miracle on top of Mount Carmel—the rain. We forget that God not only sent fire, but he also sent rain (I Kings 18:45). After three and a half years (James 5:17), the rains returned. Elijah should have been on top of the mountain spiritually, yet he came down into the valley emotionally. It should have been encouraging to lift his eyes from the valley events (remember he had taken the priests of Baal there for their slaughter (I Kings 18:40). His enemies were dead except for two. We know that now the faithful outnumbered the faithless (I Kings 19:18), but it didn't seem to matter. I remember this from the teachings of Vance Havner:

> I think God set up the mountains to remind us valley dwellers of earth that there is Someone higher who looks upon our little doings in silent majesty. I remember reading about a poor factory worker who used to climb a mountain each evening after his day's work was done just to get away from the grime and

the gloom and the grind and remind himself that he had a soul. Mountains have an upward pull and the Almighty has graciously created an ample supply lest we succumb to a valley existence!

Interestingly, after Elijah's pity party outside Beersheba (I Kings 19:3), God lead Elijah back to a mountain—Horeb (I Kings 19:8). Don't get me wrong, I will not deny that God's men have accomplished some great things in the Jezreel Valley (Barak came off Mount Tabor to defeat Sisera—Judges 4), but the inspiring feats there towering above the plain event is Carmel. You stand in any valley and you look like a pygmy, but even a dwarf standing on a mountain looks like a giant! Every valley needs a mountain to balance the scales, geographically or spiritually. I believe Elijah too soon forgot Carmel.

Granted, we can't just built a tent on our mountain like Peter suggested (Matthew 17:4) and stay up there and never venture again into the valley, but we, like Elijah, will do very poor work in our valley if we fail to lift our eyes to the heights. The Psalmist knew of what I write:

> I will lift up mine eyes unto the hills, from whence cometh my help. My help cometh from the Lord, which made heaven and earth (mountains and valleys). (Psalms 121:1-2)

Just before I fell asleep on Mount Carmel, I read these lines from Vance:

> Nothing is more important than to keep our perspectives in order. Man is so constituted that he tends to spend all his time either in the valley or on the mountain. He becomes a lowlander without lifting his eyes upward. I have read of an old hillbilly who lived close to a great mountain. A new road was made that led clear to the summit. One day the old mountaineer was taken to the top to see the breath-taking view below. His comment was, 'Just think, I've lived here all my life with all this to see—and I almost missed it!' But there are some who want to stay on the crest away from the world and its needs. Our Saviour had the double perspective—He got away from the valley to the mountains and He returned from the mountains to the valley.

Tomorrow we will descend off Carmel to the Valley of Megiddo, but for now I am enjoying the thrill and chill that has come to my spiritual bones for being on one of God's mountains. Tomorrow I will put on my spiritual bifocals (working in the valley with my eyes to the hills) and press downward, for there are sites in the valley I must see as well.

It is important that with any devotional that we never lose sight of the big picture. It was on Mount Carmel I finally realized that I must live a balanced life. Paul was right when he wrote:

> Let your moderation be known unto all men. *The Lord is at hand.* (Philippians 4:5)

Never too high or too low; neither too long on the mountain nor too long in the valley, an even balance, and moderation that will allow a consistent and constant testimony to be seen!

54

A Rolling Stone Tomb by the Road

Mark 15:46— ... and laid Him in a Sepulchre which was hewn out of a rock, and ROLLED A STONE unto the door of the Sepulchre.

I woke unexpectedly at 2:30 on the morning of our 14th day in Israel. As will happen sometimes, I had to think twice to determine where I was. Within a few moments I realized that I was sleeping on Mount Carmel and that everything was fine. Our apartment style room was cozy. I was warm and the bed was comfortable, but why had I suddenly come awake? This was the first night in Israel I didn't sleep straight through. Each day had been filled with plenty of walking and hiking, and by the time bedtime arrived I was exhausted. As I fell asleep around 9:30, I thought this night would be like the rest.

Periodically throughout my life I have had times in which I have regularly been stirred between two and three in the morning. At first, these periods of sleeplessness have bothered me. However, a few years ago I realized the regularity of the timing of these periods of restlessness was too common to be chance or circumstance. It was then I recalled Samuel's experience as a boy (I Samuel 3), and I have come to the conclusion that God loves to talk to his saints in the wee hours of the morning. A time when the television is off, the wife is asleep, and the world has quieted down. I have found it to be a great time to meditate, pray, and listen. I have come to the place that I simply say:

Good Morning, Lord!

And pray this simple scriptural praise:

> O Lord our (my) Lord, how excellent is thy name in all the earth! (Psalms 8:1)

I then wait to see if the Good Lord brings something or someone to my mind that I need to pray for, or something I need to think through. Often, as in the night on Mount Carmel, the thoughts were few, the prayers were short, and the message was clear and I was soon back to sleep. Sometimes I lay in my bed for hours as I wrestle through difficult matters, life-changing decisions, or personal struggles. All I recall of that night was the anticipation of our next day's stops: Megiddo, Jezreel, Harod, and Nazareth.

I awoke again about 6:30. Despite the interruption, I felt rested as I got out of bed, went to the window, pulled back the shades, and looked again through the gap in the tree line and ridgeline to the Mediterranean Sea to the west. The light exposed a hazy sky, and the air was much cooler than other mornings in Israel. A few clouds could also be seen, but none "like a man's hand"! (I Kings 18:44). There would be no rain as we finished our second week in the Promised Land. By 7:15 both Marnie and I were ready for another day of spiritual adventure. We were all packed for we would not be returning to Carmel at the end of the day. If everything went according to the schedule, we would be sleeping on the shores of the Sea of Galilee on this night. By 7:40 we were back from breakfast, and by 8:00 we were heading for Joel's bus. The rest of the people in our party came trickling in over the next fifteen minutes, and by 8:15 we were on the road again. That old Willy Nelson tune came to my mind as we pulled out of the Bet Oren Guest House:

> On the road again, can't wait to get on the road again, can't wait
> to see my friends again; I can't wait to get on the road again!

I wasn't looking for new or old friends, but old Biblical places that had become as familiar to me over the years as an old friend!

As I have written before, one of the best parts of this DTS trip was the unexpected surprises; the stops not on the schedule. We came off Carmel pretty much on the same route that we had ascended Mount Carmel—route 672. In order to get to Megiddo, we had to take a few cross country lanes to route 66 (no, not the famous Route 66) where Tel Megiddo was located. About forty minutes into our journey Joel pulled the bus to the side of the road and stopped. Greg wanted to show us one of his favorite random places in Israel. Remember me telling you that Greg couldn't pass by a gravesite? His love of tombs, burial sites, and ancient graves was evident throughout the entire trip. I must admit that I was actually getting tired of these stops; that is, until we stopped in a heavily forested area just west of the Jezreel Valley. There directly on the side of the highway was a perfectly preserved 'rolling stone tomb'!

In Jerusalem we had gone to the Garden Tomb, but there was no stone. I had seen pictures of the kind of tomb Jesus was buried in, and at the Yad Ha Shmonah Biblical Park they had built a life-size model, but here beside the road was a real tomb and sure enough the rolling stone was still there. Greg told us that while they were building the road we were on they come across this piece of ancient history. Though the tomb didn't date back to the time of Christ, but probably back to the Byzantine Period, it was still the best preserved example of the rolling stone tomb design in all of Israel. They had not made a park out of it; they had not set a fence around it; they had simple built the road by it and left it as it was. Needless to say, we all got out and challenged the traffic to get our pictures taken by the tomb and in the tomb. It was exciting to me to finally see the scripture I have printed above come alive. My observation was this:

> It was smaller and shorter than I imagined.

Of course, we have no idea of the size of the one that Jesus was buried in, but it made sense to me that the cost of cutting such a tomb out of solid rock would dictate that you only remove the minimum!

We got back on the bus after about a ten minute walk around. We had to dodge a few cars, but we crossed the road and re-crossed the road without incident. As I reflected on our early morning discovery, I realized that no matter how much time I would spend in Israel that at best I would only scratch the surface of what could and would be seen. We had not only bypassed numerous Biblical sites because of the time factor, but there were interesting Scriptural places around every corner and beside every road we traveled. As we headed out again for Megiddo, I began to wonder about what I had missed on this trip. What great object lesson, spiritual insight, or Biblical meaning had I missed because I wasn't looking out the window of the bus? I was so excited to get to Megiddo that I almost missed a wonderful blessing. Thanks Greg!

It is similar to us not realizing on those sleepless nights that it might be the Lord calling. Perhaps, we have gotten so accustomed to looking ahead to the new day that we forget that God can also come in the night. Remember, the night Jesus left his disciples rowing while He prayed in the hills (Matthew 14:22–23). Do you recall when Jesus finally showed up? The account says: 'In the fourth watch of the night' (Matthew 14:25). The night in Jesus' day was divided up into four-three hour sections. That would mean that Jesus showed up between three and six o'clock. If they hadn't been looking they would have missed him. The Mark account also states *"and would have passed by them!"* (Mark 6:48). It is important that we stay alert both day and night, for we never know when a blessing, or a visit from the Lord will take place. Next time we are awakened in the middle of the night check to see if it is the Lord first, then maybe, the pizza you ate!

55

Arriving at the First Battlefield

Joshua 12:21— . . . the king of MEGIDDO, one.

Within twenty minutes of leaving the best preserved 'rolling stone tomb' in Israel, we had arrived at Tel Megiddo. I was more excited than normal because of my nearly fifty year love-affair with military history. I sadly admit, before I fell in love with the Bible I had fallen in love with history. It pains me to admit it but between the sixth grade and twelfth grade I read over 300 books just on the Second World War; maybe, an explanation is in order!

I never really learned to read until I was nearly a teenager. I was raised in a small rural town in northern Maine where our local school was located in a four room, eight grade building. Through my first five grades I pretty much faked my way through. It wasn't because I was stupid, just lazy! I hated school and preferred sports and being outdoors to the confines of a class room. I fooled everyone, my teachers and parents for years. I barely got by, but they thought I was doing the best I could do. In the early grades I never learned to sound out words, but I had a good enough mind to remember where I had seen that word and was able to get by. I thought I was doing fine cheating and coning my way through Perham Elementary. I can honestly say I don't remember ever reading an assignment, a book, or the Bible during those years. Oh, I would try, but instead of admitting my weakness and that I needed help I found other ways of making the grade. I was well established in the middle of the class by the time I moved into Mrs. Hallowell's sixth grade class. It wasn't long into the school year that my secret was exposed. I still remember the embarrassment when I had to admit I really couldn't read. Mrs. Hallowell was kind, but firm and determined that before the year was up I would be reading on a sixth grade level. She took away my recess times and made me stay in class for special tutoring. Her philosophy was simple—she didn't care what I read as long as I was reading. It was then we also got a new school principal and history teacher, Mr. Harper. An ex-marine with an amazing ability to make history interesting, and as they say the rest is history. Once Mrs. Hallowell taught me to read, I have never stopped. I still love to read an hour before I go to bed. I love to read a number of books at the same time, and I love non-fiction versus fiction. I am over sixty years old and I have probably only read a half dozen books of fiction in all those years. I love facts and reality and history, especially military history. Now you know why our arrival at Megiddo was so exciting, or do you? Did you know that the first ever recorded military battle in history was fought at Megiddo? And I now believe that the very last battle in history will be fought there as well!

The year was between 1481 and 1469 BC when one of the first great conquerors of ancient history, Thutmose III of Egypt, fought this important military battle. Historians don't believe, as I do, that this was actually the first; that mankind has been fighting and killing since Cain attacked Abel (Genesis 4) or Abraham armed his own household and defeated the Chedorlaomer confederacy at Dan (Genesis 14), but this is the first in which we have any recorded accounts. A rebellion by the kings of Megiddo (not the one mentioned in the verse above, but an earlier king; there are at least 20 archaeological levels of civilizations found at Megiddo) and Kadesh, or Qadesh against the authority of the Pharaoh of Egypt brought on this battle. According to the accounts left behind by Thutmose, the Egyptian Pharaoh marched his army nine straight days averaging 16 miles a day to reach Gaza where he regrouped before marching on toward Megiddo. Eventually, Thutmose arrived in the plain of Megiddo where he divided his forces into three 'battles' or divisions. One would attack the rebels coming down from Qadesh, the other would defend his route home to the south just in case the battle didn't go well, and the third under his personal command would strike at the Canaanite confederacy formed against him. Using his main battle weapon, the Egyptian war chariot, Thutmose swept away the coalition forces chasing the remnant behind the walls of Megiddo. The battle might have been over immediately, but Thutmose's forces decided to loot the enemy camp instead of pursuing them. It is recorded that 924 Canaanite chariots were abandoned outside the walls of Megiddo in order for the charioteers to be hauled up. It took seven months of siege before Megiddo was finally captured! Thutmose is recorded to have carried out 15 successful military campaigns in his 54-year reign, but the Battle of Megiddo was his most famous and a first for the world!

Now you know of Megiddo and Armageddon (Revelations 16:16), but did you know that at least two other major military battles were fought on this site?

1. In 609 BC Pharaoh Necho marched his Egyptian army north to help his Assyrian ally against a Babylonian attack. On the way he encountered an Israelite army under King Josiah blocking his way at Megiddo. In the ensuing battle King Josiah was killed (II Kings 23:29–30—II Chronicles 35:22) and the battle lost, but Necho would later be defeated by Nebuchadnezzar at Carchemish (II Chronicles 35:20).

2. In 1918 British General Allenby won the final battle of the Palestian Campaign at Megiddo by surprising the Turkish army by striking along the coast. Concentrating his forces after his capture of Jerusalem, Allenby divested a plan that convinced his enemy that he would be attacking inland. The plan worked and within days he had the Turks on the run. Upon Allenby's victory at Megiddo he was given the title of Viscount and Marshall of Megiddo!

Despite the peace and solitude we found at Megiddo, I believe the history of this impressive place is not yet finished. There is a day coming when the warrior will return to Megiddo. The tourist will be replaced by the soldier as the armies of the world once again come to the same conclusion Napoleon came to when he observed this place through the eyes of one of the greatest military generals ever to live. He is reported to have said that Megiddo was the most natural and best battlefield he had ever seen; although he never fought there himself!

As I stepped off the bus and made my way toward the knoll that is now the ancient city, I couldn't help but think, of not the past, but the future. Why will this mount of ruins of countless civilizations be contested over again? Why will this hill of rubble be fought over? What is there about this place that seems to draw the land hungry, the conqueror, and the powerful? We have already concluded that Israel is strategically located on the crossroads of the world, and for better or for worse the center of past history and future history will happen here, or around here! I have come to the belief that it all has to do with God using the pride of man to bring him to final judgment. Even the Psalmist asked:

> Why do the heathen rage, and the people imagine a vain thing? (that they can defeat God) The kings of the earth set themselves, and the rulers take counsel together, against the Lord, and against His anointed, saying, let us break their bands asunder, and cast away their cords from us. (Psalms 2:1–3)

I believe they will try to do this at Megiddo, but with all those who have come here it will not be to parley, but to do battle! This time mankind won't be up against his fellowman, but against the Almighty Himself!

56

Tel Megiddo and a Manger

I Kings 9:15—And this is the reason of the levy which King Solomon raised; for to build the house of the Lord, and his own house, and Millo, and the wall of Jerusalem, and Hazor, and MEGIDDO and Gezer.

We spent over two hours walking around Tel Megiddo. It was a welcome reprieve from the often hurried visits we had made at other tels. As we wandered from ruins to ruins, the history of this famous crossroad town began to be revealed in the rubble. Its location on the main trade route between east and south could clearly be seen in the sloping landscape to the even more famous plain (Esdraelon) that surrounds the hilltop.

After Joshua's capture of this town (Joshua 12:21), the territory was given to the tribes of Issachar and Manasseh, but they were unable to ultimately drive the Canaanites out (Joshua 17:11–13 and Judges 1:27 and I Chronicles 7:29) of the region. The proof of this is seen clearly in the days of judge Deborah when Barak was called on to fight Sisera (Judges 4:1–24), the general of King Hazor's infamous chariot corps (Judges 4:2–3), near this historical site. In the recording of Barak's famous battle in song, Megiddo (Judges 5:1) is mentioned in context to 'the waters of Megiddo'. Interestingly, one of my most memorable memories at Tel Megiddo was a walk through the 9th century BC water system still preserved to this day. It consists of a large shaft sunk through the rock to a depth of 120 feet, where it meets a tunnel cut through from a distance of 215 feet to a spring outside the city. Most feel that the tunnel was built to insure the city of a water supply during a siege, much like what Hezekiah did at Jerusalem to get the water from the Gihon Spring into the holy city. The spring is hid by a camouflaged covering, but in the days of Barak and Deborah it was probably known simply as 'the waters of Megiddo' and opened!

The extensive archaeological excavations we walked through belonged mostly to King Solomon's (see verse above) chariot city (I Kings 9:19) built around 1000 BC. So by the time of David and Solomon this city seems to have been completely under the control of Israel. The Bible tells us that one of Megiddo's officers was appointed Solomon's commissary (I Kings 4:12), a man by the name of Baana. Solomon's building trademark, the triple gate, can be seen clearly at Megiddo, much like the one we saw in Lachish. At the southern end of city we walked through the ruins of stables, some built by Solomon and others built by King Ahab when this city was a part of the northern kingdom. In the center of the city we saw an 8th century BC sunken grain silo, with a staircase against the circular wall curving down to the bottom. The rock work was simply amazing; whether the outside walls of the city, the rocks forming the gates of the city, the storage silo walls, or the rockwork leading down into the water system, one could see the time and effort it took to make this city one of the best in the land.

We also came across in the eastern edge of the ruins three ancient Canaanite temples, including a huge round, raised altar, the largest we saw in Israel. It simply reminded me of the pagan history that was Megiddo both pre-Israeli and in Israeli history. Even when Israel was in control of this town, the town wasn't always faithful to Jehovah, especially when the nation split in two; which brings me to the last Biblical event recorded with Megiddo being mentioned. God was bringing judgment down on the house of Ahab whose family had controlled Megiddo and the region for years. God's appointed assassin was a man by the name of Jehu (II Kings 9:1–3). When Jehu came to the town of Jezreel (interestingly, our next port of call), he discovered that King Ahaziah of Judah had come to visit King Joram of Israel. Joram was in Jezreel recovering from a wound he had received while fighting the Syrians (II King 9:14–16). As Jehu rode up to Jezreel, both Joram and Ahaziah rode out to meet him not realizing he had come to kill King Joram. When they realized their mistake they tried to flee but Jehu was a good shot and with one arrow killed King Joram (II Kings 9:24). Meanwhile King Ahaziah tried to flee but with a second arrow he was wounded. The Bible simply says that he survived to Megiddo, but there he died! (II Kings 9:27).

For me, the most inspiring find at Megiddo were the 'mangers' we saw. Scattered near the ruins of Solomon's stables were these stone mangers, the only ones we saw in Israel. I still remember when Greg stopped by one and said, "If you want to know what the baby Jesus was probably laid in here is your chance!" It was then this verse came to a new understanding for me:

> And she brought forth her firstborn son, and wrapped him in swaddling clothes, and *LAID HIM IN A MANGER*, because there was no room for them in the inn. (Luke 2:7)

I know I had heard this truth about Jesus' first resting place before. I knew deep in my mind that unlike the wooden mangers of the many Christmas Sunday School plays I had witnessed over the years the real manger was made of stone, yet it was only after the mangers of Megiddo that I fully understood that part of the Christmas story. The carved out slab of stone is for me one of the best examples of this verse penned by Paul:

> For ye know the grace of our Lord Jesus Christ, that, though he was rich, yet for your sakes he became poor, that ye through his poverty might be rich. (II Corinthians 8:9)

In our modern world where we try to make everything soft and comfortable, Jesus' first night of sleep was in a stone-cold container made for animal water or feed. Don't get me wrong, I do believe Mary and Joseph made that manger into the most comfortable bed they could probably by adding straw or hay, yet it remained a stone manger. The stark reality that came to me in Megiddo was just how far my Saviour was willing to condescend to be like me, and even more, to be lower than me. I have never to my knowledge ever slept on rock, the ground maybe, but never solid stone. This was just the first of a series of illustrations of just how poor Jesus was willing to be for me. Would He not later tell some would-be disciples?

> The foxes have holes, and the birds of the air have nests; but the Son of man hath not where to lay his head. (Matthew 8:20)

Now we understand this statement better because we know that the first place he laid His head was on the side of a stone manger! I walked away from Megiddo humbled by a simple rectangular stone manger. The ones I saw were empty, but in my spiritual imagination I saw Mary, after wrapping her baby-boy, laid him down to rest in a manger. As with the rolling stone tomb, I had in a short two hours witnessed the first and the last resting places of my Lord and King, and both of them had been carved out of stone!

57

Armageddon and the Valley of Megiddon

Zechariah 12:11—In that day shall there be a great mourning in Jerusalem, as the mourning of Hadadrimmon in THE VALLEY OF MEGIDDON.

Located about fifty-three miles (as the crow flies) to the northwest of Jerusalem is the Valley of Megiddon (the Biblical name—II Chronicles 35:22). Interestingly, it simply means 'place of God'. Better known in history as the Valley of Esdraelon, this plain filled with rich soil and beautiful landscapes was a peaceful place the day we viewed it from Tel Megiddo and drove through it as we explored the Old Testament sites that surround its fabled past and fateful future. Yet as we have already mentioned, this place, perhaps, more than any other plain on this planet, is stained with the blood of just about every army that ever marched through or fought in this picturesque valley. Canaanites, Hittites, Israelites, Syrians, Egyptians, Midianites, Assyrians, Babylonians, Greeks, Romans, Arabs, Crusaders, Turks, and the English have fought over this plain. Both the famous and infamous commanders of world history have come here seeking control of 'the crossroad of the world' and personal glory. Some have been victorious and some have been vanquished as we have seen from Thutmose of Egypt to Viscount Allenby of England. Since 1918, the battlefield has been quiet, but we know from prophecy that there is one battle (Revelation 16:16) yet to be fought here and there is much blood yet to be shed (Revelation 14:20), dare we say, more than the combined volume so far?

Armageddon and the Valley of Megiddon

As we drove from the Tel of Megiddo to the Tel of Jezreel, I read again this article by Vance Havner written after his ride through the Valley of Megiddon in the early 1970s:

> Teddy Roosevelt said, 'We stand at Armageddon, and we battle for the Lord' (Teddy was referring to the beginning of the First World War). Douglas MacArthur said at the surrender of Japan, 'If we do not now devise some more equitable system, Armageddon will be at our door' (Douglas said that just 65 years ago). The word (Armageddon: which is a corruption of the Hebrew 'Har Megiddo'-hill of Megiddo) has taken on many meanings in many minds. The interpretation of it ranges from a mere symbol of the final clash between good and evil to detailed programs of extreme literalists who read in or read out of the record more than it contains. I rode through the world's last battlefield today. No one with any degree of Bible understanding can visit the Valley of Esdraelon without a sense of being where strange things have happened and where strange things lie ahead. . . . Dr. George Adam Smith wrote: 'What a plain! Upon which not only the greatest empires, races, and faiths, East and West, have contended but each has come to judgment and men felt they were fighting with heaven (perhaps, a reference to 'the stars in their courses fought against Sisera'—Judges 5:20)!' Mighty forces converge on the Mediterranean today. One would have to be blind and brainless to see no significance in the confrontation of the Communist colossus (remember Vance wrote at the height of the Cold War) and the free world. In the midst of it all lies tiny Israel. God's chosen people are back in their land, but the future is not as lovely as some imagine. Antichrist will be accepted first before Israel looks on Him whom they have pierced and receive the true Messiah. Our Lord said, 'If another comes in my name, him ye will receive' (John 5:43). The time of Jacob's trouble is still future. The final clash—however one may line up the participants—will be at Armageddon. A look at the valley is enough; there is room here for the battle of all battles. I am glad I have had a preview. I don't expect to be there when the holocaust comes but I like to know where it will be. Armageddon is God's answer to all the progressionists who dream of a new age ushered in by legislation, education, and social reformation. That dawn will break only after a mighty confrontation-not a conference of diplomats. My Lord is not coming back to negotiate. He will put all His enemies under His feet. All the way through the New Testament there is the message of final judgment, fire and brimstone, a great gulf fixed, a bottomless pit

and a lake of fire, earthquakes and falling stars, and men praying for rocks and mountains to hide them from the wrath of God (Revelation 6:15–17)? History does not end in idyllic storybook form. It comes to a head in a valley of slaughter. But it does not end at Armageddon. It comes to its climax—not with the Alas of fallen Babylon, but with the Alleluia of the redeemed-a new heaven and the new earth. I am glad to have had a look at the Last Battlefield. Armageddon is more than vivid imagery. It is grim reality, and some who laughed at its meaning a few years ago are beginning to sober up a bit. Some old-timers are coming into their own, and Bible prophecy is becoming respectable in some quarters. Some who once laughed now stand in somber awe in the presence of this silent valley quietly waiting that awful day after which we 'ain't gonna study war no more.'

What can I add to that practical observation and spiritual insight? Vance Havner has hit the prophetic nail squarely on its scriptural head. I too agree that this world has only one end, God's final act. For all those who feel that mankind is in some kind of control of his destiny; a visit to the Valley of Megiddo will sober him up. It is a haunting place despite the lovely vista that rolls on before your searching eyes. The only hint that this was still a battlefield was the sound of F-16s roaring over our heads as we wandered through the rubble and ruin that is Megiddo today. The land was quiet and still, but the air vibrated with the noise of war. A stark reminder for those of us who were listening, that war is coming back to the Middle East, and that another battle:

The true mother of all battles

will be fought on this ancient battlefield again.

Like Havner, I was glad to visit this horrible place in a time of peace. I am glad I can say I have been there, but I don't want to be there when the slaughter begins. For me the most ghastly imagery of the entire Revelation is the description of the blood that will one day literally fill this idyllic dale. I have photographs I took between Megiddo and Jezreel that would make you believe it was the most tranquil place on earth. The rolling hills surrounding a pasture land of colorful fields invoke delightful and dreamy thoughts. Sometimes I think I know, or should I say, believe, too much about the Bible. Once again I'm glad I went, and I'm glad I saw, but the Valley of Megiddo wasn't the best place I saw because of what I know of its future. By contrast, the Mount of Olivet certainly didn't have the beauty of the Jezreel Valley, but for me its appeal was more of a draw because of what I believe of my Lord's return (Acts 1:11). Do I believe that my Lord will come to the Valley of Megiddo, I do, but with entirely different results:

> And I saw the heaven opened, and behold a white horse; and he that sat upon him . . . And I saw the beast, and the kings of the earth, and their armies, gather together to make war against Him that sat on the horse, and against His army. . . . and the remnant were slain with the sword of Him that sat upon the horse, which sword proceeded out of His mouth: and all the fowls were filled with their flesh. (Revelation 19:11, 19, 21)

Megiddo will be revisited and the horror of war will once again plague its serene setting.

58

Jezreel and Naboth

I Kings 21:1—And it came to pass after these things, that NABOTH the Jezreelite had a vineyard, which was in JEZREEL, hard by the palace of Ahab king of Samaria.

We left Tel Megiddo for a short ride over to Tel Jezreel around eleven o'clock on our second day in the north country of Israel. I was excited about this stop because of one of my favorite unsung heroes of the Old Testament; a man by the name of Naboth!

When you hear the name Jezreel, one immediately thinks of 'the valley of Jezreel' (Joshua 17:16), where this town is located. There is also confusion because there is another city in the territory of Judah with the same name (Joshua 15:56). The Jezreel we were heading for was given to the tribe of Issachar (Joshua 19:8), but came under the control of the tribe of Manasseh mostly because of the dominion of the brothers Ephraim and Manasseh, Joseph's heritage! Located between Megiddo and Bethshean, this city rose to influence when Ahab and Jezebel built a palace there (I Kings 21:1). The capital of their kingdom was in Samaria, about twenty miles southwest of Jezreel, but Jezreel was probably a summer palace because of the lush, fertile country that surrounded this hilltop. As we drove up the roadway into the parking lot at Tel Jezreel, I could see why these two wicked people would like this place. I liked this place; it reminded me of my boyhood home in northern Maine, a simple hamlet called Perham.

As we walked up the pathway to the exposed foundation stones that once housed Israel's most notorious couple, I recalled the Biblical events that took place on this spot:

1. After the death of King Saul on Mount Gilboa (which is located not far from Jezreel), Abner, the surviving captain of his army, made Saul's son Ishbosheth king over this region (II Samuel 2:8-10).
2. When Solomon became king he divided the kingdom up into twelve districts and one of them was Jezreel and the surrounding towns (I Kings 4:12).
3. After the amazing events of Mount Carmel, the fire and the rain, it was to Jezreel Elijah made his famous run beating Ahab, who was riding in a chariot, to the entrance of the city (I Kings 18:45-46).
4. Jezreel would become a place of recovery for Ahab's son Joram after he was wounded in a battle with the king of Syria (II Kings 8:29).
5. It was at Jezreel that Jehu killed both the king of Israel and the king of Judah as well as Jezebel herself (II Kings 9).
6. It was here that the heads of the seventy sons of Ahab were piled up as Jehu finished the annihilation of the house of Ahab and Jezebel (II Kings 10:1-11).
7. It was here that one of the greatest injustices of the entire Bible took place when Naboth was killed for a vegetable garden (I Kings 21:1-14)!

I must admit that the entire time we stayed in Jezreel my mind was on the sacrifice of this righteous man, and the haunting question that has always troubled me—why does God allow the righteous to be sacrificed at the hands of the unrighteous?

Why is it that sometimes the wicked seem to win? Naboth was not the first to fall into this category of unexplainable deaths. The patron saint of this group is Abel, killed by his brother Cain (Genesis 4:1-10). Time would fail me to write of James the disciple and the wicked Herod (Acts 12:1-2), and what of Antipas (Revelation 2:13) and, yes, Jesus himself (John 19:30). The Bible is filled with these righteous, just individuals that meet their end at the hands of wicked men and women like Ahab and Jezebel. Church history is also filled with a list of names that also seemed to die an ignoble death at the hands of evil and vile men, but why? Why were they expendable? About ten years ago I wrote a book trying to answer this profound question that I simply called "Expendable". In it I used fifty scriptural examples of individuals that seemingly died too young, or too soon. What provoked this search was the information I had found about my grandfather Barton's brother, Benjamin Stanley Barton, a young man who after serving this country in the First World War volunteered for a pioneer missionary work to Peru in 1925. Within a year and a half, he died of tuberculosis. In 1934, Vance Havner wrote his first devotional book entitled "By The Still Waters". In that book he wrote an article with this title "When The Good Die Young"! There might be a debate just how old Naboth was when he died, but there is no debate that his was an unjustifiable death!

As I tried to imagine in my mind just where Naboth's vineyard was in relationship to Jezreel, I remembered the conclusion I had come to after my in depth study into this thought-provoking question. It was the soul-thrilling teaching of Jesus that at last set to rest my weary soul on this matter:

> For whosoever will save his life shall lose it: and whosoever will lose his life for My sake shall find it. (Matthew 16:25)

Naboth took a stand against King Ahab and Queen Jezebel because they were trying to buy his family's inheritance. To the Jew the land was a sacred trust, passed down from generation to generation. My family's farm in northern Maine has been passed down six times and soon, maybe, a seventh. I know of this concept, a precept worth dying for? For Naboth, and the many like him life isn't as valuable as obeying a God-given instruction. It was the great American missionary Jim Elliot, another of God's seemingly expendable saints, who wrote:

> He is no fool who gives up what he cannot gain to gain what he cannot lose!

Did Cain get away with killing his brother? Did Ahab and Jezebel get away with killing Naboth? Not a single crime against the righteous goes unpunished, and in the end the glory of God remains and we know that physical death doesn't mean eternal death. Abel remains to this day as does Naboth and James and Jim Elliot and so too my Uncle Ben. As I finished my book I came up with this paraphrase of Jesus classic statement:

> For those of us who will not see our lives as 'expendable' will ultimately fail, but those of us who will count our lives as 'expendable' will never, ever lose!

I left Jezreel that morning with a renewed understanding of my unsung hero. His stand against the wickedness that was the house of Ahab was honorable and godly. Naboth was no fool and the loss he suffered can't be compared to the gain he received when he stood before His God. Oh, that we might have more like Naboth in our age; a generation that believes that life isn't about the things we possess (Luke 12:15), but simple obedience to God even if that obedience costs us everything (Luke 14:33), including our life!

59

Drinking at the Well of Harod

Judges 7:1—Then Jerubbaal, who is Gideon, and all the people that were with him, rose up early, and pitched beside THE WELL OF HAROD: so that the host of the Midianites were on the north side of them, by the hill of Moreh, in the valley.

To show you how close we were to Jezreel, this verse in the Gideon story will define the 'valley' mentioned above:

> Then all the Midianites and the Amalekites and the children of the east were gathered together, and went over, and pitched in the valley of Jezreel. (Judges 6:33)

Once again the land became small as we, within miles, traveled between the Old Testament stories I had heard about since childhood. Within minutes we had made a leap in time from the days of Elijah and Naboth back to the days of the famous judge Gideon and his well-known encounter with the Midianites. What I was most excited about was the fact that I would get a chance to drink from the stream where God had Gideon test the courage and loyalty of his famous 'three-hundred'!

In the few miles from Jezreel to Harod, we passed the small town of Shunem (II Kings 4:8), where the lady of that town made a prophet's chamber for Elisha in her home. I recalled the grand tale of the Shunammite woman and her son and the amazing resurrection story (II Kings 4:18–37). Since we had left Mount Carmel our journey had taken us through countless Biblical stories, and now before us was one of the most famous 'mounts' of all: Gilboa, the battlefield that claimed another one of my favorite Old Testament characters, Jonathan (I Samuel 31). It was there under the shadow of this infamous place that 'the well of Harod' could be found.

Ma'ayan (the Harod Spring) Harod National Park is one of sixty-three national parks in the Israeli park system. During our journey through Israel we stopped at twenty-eight of these parks, and while Ma'ayan Harod wasn't the most inspiring or most amazing, it was the most beautiful. Acre for acre it contained the most beautiful flowers and flowering trees we saw in all of Israel, and the clear flowing stream through its heart only added to the tranquil atmosphere already there. There is a series of large springs that flow from the westernmost foot of Mount Gilboa. Harod Spring actually bubbles out of Gideon's Cave at the base of Gilboa Mountain. At the mouth of the cave a pool is formed before the water flows eastward along a narrow creek. It was at this creek its greatest call to fame happened. This is how the Book of Judges tells the story after God had already whittled Gideon's army down from 32,000 to 10,000 (Judges 7:2-3):

> And the Lord said unto Gideon, the people are yet too many; bring them down to the water, and I will try them for thee there: and it shall be, that of whom I say unto thee, this shall go with thee, the same shall go with thee; and of whomsoever I say unto thee, this shall not go with thee, the same shall not go. So he brought down the people unto the water: and the Lord said unto Gideon, every one that lappeth of the water with his tongue, as a dog lappeth, him shalt thou set by himself; likewise everyone that boweth down upon his knees to drink. And the number of them that lapped, putting their hand to their mouth, were three hundred men: but all the rest of the people bowed down upon their knees to drink water. And the Lord said unto Gideon, by the three hundred that lappeth will I save you, and deliver the Midianites into thine hands: and let all the other people go every man unto his place. (Judges 7:4-7)

The rest of the story is very familiar as God uses these 300 commandoes to eventually defeat the Midianites and their allies in a surprise night assault (Judges 7:16-25).

While at Harod we also learned that another important battle of history was fought at these springs in 1260 AD. This was the Battle of Ayn Jalut (the Arabic name for the spring) in which the Mameluke Sultan Kotuz of Egypt stopped the Mongolian attempt to take over the Middle East and Europe. It was just a month after this victory that one of Kotuz's commanders, Baibars, killed Kotuz and made himself sultan. Baibars would become one of the great military leaders and conquers in history. For me the place was filled with historical evidence of what I had been taught since Sunday school. I could see the army of the Philistines chasing King Saul and his sons onto Mount Gilboa as they made their last stand against the onslaught. There was certainly no way of finding the exact spot where Jonathan and Abinadad and Malchishua (I Samuel 31:1) fell, or where their father took his own life (I Samuel 31:3–6), but from Harod Spring I could look up to the top of the barren hill and imagine I saw them fall. Their story has such reality now since I have seen the place and that was one thing I could be sure of!

As our group gathered with others around the stream that flowed out of Gideon's Cave, I stepped down into the shallow water. They told us that at certain times of the year the water flows over the banks of the streambed, but on the day we were there the stream was but a trickle. The water barely came up to the shoelaces of my boots. It was then I announced that I was going to demonstrate the two methods of drinking water out of Harod Spring: the bowing method and the lapping method. So there before my companions I first got down on both my knees and drank the water straight from the stream. Then I got on one knee and cupped some water in my hands and brought the water to my lips. I had for most of my life understood why God had chosen the famous three-hundred. By bowing to the stream you leave yourself open to a surprise attack for there is no way you can look around and stay alert by drinking this way. By bringing the water from the stream to your mouth you can not only quench your thirst, but you can also stay vigilant to any possible attack by the enemy. God was looking for sober-minded, serious soldiers who by their very character were men of alertness and vigilance. Is not the Lord looking for such men and women to this day?

> *Be sober, be vigilant*; because your adversary the Devil, as a
> roaring lion, walketh about, seeking whom he may devour.
> (I Peter 5:8)

Harod was another wonderful place that I was able to act out a familiar Biblical story, and see and experience firsthand the importance of the lessons taught there. I will never forget my drink at Harod Spring for as long as I live, and the picnic we ate on the banks of Harod Stream and under the shade trees along its shore will also be remembered for the warm spring noon I shared with Marnie under the shadow of Mount Gilboa. The cool breeze through the trees and the sound of flowing water over rocks only added to the peace and serenity of Ma'ayan Harod. For just a moment I thought I heard from a distance the shout of three hundred voices:

> The sword of the Lord, and of Gideon. (Judges 7:20)

And was that a trumpet I heard?

60

Journey to Nazareth

Matthew 2:23—And he came and dwelt in a city called NAZARETH: that it might be fulfilled which was spoken by the prophets, he shall be called a Nazarene.

At one o'clock on May 24, 2010, the final leg of my journey to Nazareth began. Since childhood I had wondered what Jesus' boyhood hometown was like. Certainly born in Bethlehem, but Jesus was raised in Nazareth (Luke 2:39, 51). Jesus spent more time in the village of Nazareth than in any other place in his short life here on earth. Its draw was strong because I have come to the belief that I too was raised in a similar place.

Just before we got back on the bus at Ma'ayan Harod to go to Nazareth, I wandered again through the open fields and blooming bushes of that beautiful and fragrant park. On the backside of the area I found a man selling bees honey, a favorite of mine. My father and I had raised honey bees in my childhood, and I have always liked to sample the product of the bee wherever I have found it. In our southern trip we had been exposed to date honey, but this was the first bee's honey I had discovered in Israel. I bought a jar to take home to share with my dear wife—our favorite topping on toast. I also finished a fascinating conversation I was having with Brennen Searcy, one of the members of our team. Brennen is an independent missionary to the Arabs of the Middle East. He had spent some time in Iraq and was now working in Afghanistan. I was interested because I wanted his opinion on the place I knew my son would soon be deploying too. (As I write this article, I have just gotten a phone call from my son. He has been in Afghanistan for nearly six-weeks now, and the combat has already been more violent than anything he experienced in his fifteen-month deployment to Iraq. My son would return after a year on the battlefields of Hellman Province having experienced three concussions from bomb blasts, the loss of four close bubbies, and the Purple Heart on his chest!) I admire men like Brennen who are willing to go to the difficult and dangerous place on this planet with the Gospel of Christ without the backing of a mission board. I have been down on the modern mission board movement for years because of their abuse and misuse of God's people—both missionaries and the people they have been sent to evangelize. Brennen, for me, is another example that God is doing just fine finding and sending His own missionaries! Did not God the Father send His own Son alone to this world to evangelize without a fancy organization located in a fancy building complex with a fancy staff to support Him?

Our travels took us northwest up Route 71 to 65 and eventually to Route 60 into Nazareth. Nazareth is considered to be in the Lower Galilee just north of the Plain of Esdraelon. Nazareth is about seventy miles from Jerusalem, and is not found by name in the Old Testament. Its only call to fame is its being the home of the 'holy family': Joseph, Mary, and Jesus. The first mention of Nazareth is recorded because of the visit of the angel Gabriel to the Virgin Mary (Luke 1:26). Gabriel would return to Nazareth to tell Joseph that it was alright for him to take Mary as his wife because the baby she was carrying was of the Holy Ghost (Matthew 1:18–25). Then Joseph and Mary would leave Nazareth for Bethlehem (a journey of about 75 miles) for the birth of the Child (Luke 2:4). After some time in Bethlehem to meet the 'wise men' and a trip to Egypt to escape Herod (Matthew 2:1–18), the new family would return to Nazareth to live (Matthew 2:19–23). Here Jesus lived out a simple and obscure existence until He was nearly thirty (Luke 3:23). For most of my life I believed that Jesus also lived in isolation, but our journey to Nazareth changed that understanding because of what I learned while touring the area.

For example, near Nazareth the ancient trade route that ran from Dan in the north to 'the way of the sea' (Via Maris) in the west in found. As a boy Jesus would have seen and probably interacted with the caravans and the merchants and travelers that passed by Nazareth. The one story of his childhood recorded in the Gospels tells me that he could have easily mingled with people of all races that passed through his region. Remember, the time Jesus' parents took him to Jerusalem at twelve years of age. Jesus was not a shy lad, for he boldly debated and questioned the priests (Luke 2:41–52). If he did that then why not to those he came in contract with on a daily basis. I also learned that Nazareth was only three miles from the capital of Galilee during the Roman period; a place called Sepphoris. This city came under the control and was rebuilt by Herod Antipas (Herod the Great's son) during the childhood and young adulthood of Jesus. There are even some that believe that Joseph and Jesus could have worked on the reconstruction because of their trade as carpenters (Mark 6:3). The misapplication often with this job description is that Jesus only worked with wood. The term in the Greek means 'artificer' which can refer to one that works with a numbers of materials. Jesus might have been a mason, or a number of other professions besides a carpenter!

On the way into Nazareth we passed the little town of Nain where Jesus would perform one of his most spectacular miracles, the resurrection of the widow of Nain's son (Luke 7:11). We also came close to Endor where King Saul sought out Samuel through the witch of Endor (I Samuel 28:7–25). As we climbed the new bypass (a huge road ramp leading through a ridge tunnel) into the city, we could make out Mount Tabor in the distance; the very hill Barak gathered his troops (Judges 4:6) for his final assault on Sisera's elite chariot corps (Judges 4:2–3). But much like our entrance into Bethlehem, the minute we drove into Nazareth my heart went sad. Nazareth is no longer a small family town of about 300 people, or so the experts think it was in the days of Jesus. I still remember the first time I read those figures and determined that Jesus was brought up in a small town—a town like Perham, Maine, my hometown. It was this reality that helped me understand why Jesus lived the way he did and stayed for so long in Nazareth. New insight into the experiences of Jesus came quickly when I remembered many of the same things from my boyhood. The Scriptures came alive when I could see and understand Jesus' use of certain objects to illustrate his lessons. Like with Bethlehem, Nazareth has become a tourist town and the savor and favor of small town, rural Israel is gone.

Sure enough, like with the birth place of Jesus, they have built a church over the spot where they think the angel Gabriel came to Mary. We passed it as we worked our way through town. Our original plan was to just drive through Nazareth to Mount Tabor for a bird's eye view of the area. (There is a roadway up the side of Mount Tabor, and they say the view from the top is outstanding, but we never got to see it!) After working our way through the narrow streets of Nazareth, Joel suddenly stopped at the foot of a very steep hill. After a close inspection of the bus, it was discovered we had two flat tires. They had been deliberately cut by someone, maybe, at Ma'ayan Harod? We were struck in Nazareth until the tires could be fixed. Joel thought it might take the rest of the afternoon. We still had to travel to the eastern shore of the Sea of Galilee before night fall, so what to do? Sometimes the most blessed events happen when you are detoured because less than a few hundred yards from where the bus was setting was 'Nazareth Village'. Little did we realize that our journey to Nazareth was going to take us back to the days of Jesus and to the village He called home for over two decades!

61

Nazareth Village and Detours

Mark 1:9—And it came to pass in those days, that Jesus came from NAZARETH of Galilee . . .

Who of us hasn't been driving down a pleasant or not so pleasant roadway when we have come across a detour sign? Or maybe, we have started our day with a certain goal in mind, a certain destination, and because of circumstances (circumstance is not chance) beyond our control we have been detoured in another direction; that loathsome reality that has forced us away from our planned route of travel? More often than not, we have to turn abruptly onto some dirt side road that leads us over a very rough lane. Unlike our super, smooth interstate highway, our detour is narrow, full of curves, and hilly. We grumble at first as we have to slow down, and we growl because of the time we are losing. As for me, I like detours—just like the one we had to take on our 14th day in Israel. For often those drab trails will lead us through colorful meadows and blossoming orchards that we would have missed if we hadn't been detoured; open country, away from the rushing traffic and man-made signs that blight God's wonderful creation, another world. There have been times that I have wished the detour would not end; much like the time our Israel Study Tour was detoured through Nazareth Village!

As Joel took care of the two flat tires on our bus, we departed the bus and walked to a very unique attraction that had been created on a hillside on the northeast corner of modern-day Nazareth. This is what the brochure said about Nazareth Village:

> Step into the life Jesus knew. Nazareth Village brings to life a farm and Galilean village, recreating Nazareth as it was 2,000 years ago. Combining archeology and recreation, it is a window into the history and the life of Jesus, the city's most famous citizen. Philip said to Nathanael, 'Come and see!' (John 1:46) Don't just come and see. Come and meet Him. Come to this Galilean village as the first-century town is brought back to life. Cultivated terraces and vineyards, an ancient winepress, stone quarries, the village residents, a watch tower, a working olive press, a threshing floor, the village well, the town synagogue, a shepherd and his sheep, the carpenter's shop—all these are seen along the Parable Walk that leads you through the teachings of Jesus.

It was like stepping back in time. From the noisy streets of modern Nazareth (70,000 citizens now), we were transported back to the dusty lanes of Jesus' Nazareth of only a few hundred souls.

Not very far from my home in Northern Maine, just across the border in New Brunswick, Canada is a similar village called King's Landing. This attraction is the reconstruction of an Acadia village two hundred years in the past. At this site on the Saint John River, the creators built houses, barns, a saw mill, a floor mill, a church, a store, and countless other buildings that could have been seen when the area was first settled from England. The attraction is filled with people dressed in the era clothing, and they are all doing the normal things people did back then. Such was the concept and reality of Nazareth Village, but instead of going back two hundred years, ten times that long. As we strolled through the byways of Nazareth we came across the shepherd, the watchman, the weaver, the farmer, the carpenter, and numerous other individuals, dressed and working as they would have in the days of Jesus. The lanes were lined with olive trees, fig trees, pomegranate trees, and grape vines. We saw a wheat field and the old instruments used to plow the field and winnow the grain. We saw sheep and goats and donkeys. It wasn't long before we couldn't hear the sounds of modern Nazareth and we were all caught up in the atmosphere of Jesus' Nazareth. I was touched by the synagogue most. We know from the Gospels that Jesus spent a lot of time there (Luke 4:16). For the first time I was able to visualize how the worship of a synagogue was conducted. I was able to set in Moses' seat (where the Torah was read-Matthew 23:2), and pretend that I was Jesus on the day He revealed Himself to the people of Nazareth. Unlike Jesus, I wasn't taken to the brow of the hill to be killed (Luke 4:29), but Nazareth does rest on a hill!

Life itself has detours. An old preacher once said:

> We set out upon the highway of some fixed course we have chosen and mapped and planned for ourselves. Then one day around some sudden bend of the road, we find our thoroughfare blocked and the side road in its place. Business crashes, health fails, dear ones die, disaster comes; we must abandon the way we meant to go and try some shabby trail of shattered dreams and fallen hopes and breaking hearts. We start out wearily upon it and find to our surprise that it leads to treasures and beauty we never would have found elsewhere!

That is what happened to us in Nazareth, and now I see that is what happened to Jesus in Nazareth. How He must have grieved over the rejection He had from those he had spent his childhood and young adulthood with, yet His detour took him to the harvest fields of Galilee, Samaria, Decapolis, Judea, and eventually to Calvary for us. When John Bunyan was detoured through Bedford Prison, he found "Pilgrim's Progress". When Paul ran into the Damascus detour (Acts 9:3), he was lead down glorious roads of service for the King of Kings he never would have traveled, if not for that detour. And so it will be and is for us if we allow the Master of Detours His way!

At nineteen, I was traveling down an easy road, but I was asleep at the spiritual wheel. I was speeding down the road of life with no direction or destination, but the scenery was pleasant and the road was smooth. It was then I came upon my detour, and I was sent in an entirely different direction. At first, I was unsure of its virtue over the main road I had been traveling, but the further I follow this slow road, the more I am sure it is the better road. Unlike the road I was on, this detour can't be traveled quickly. There is time to stop and look around and see the world around me, including FOUR detours to India in the last eight years. Much like what happened at Nazareth Village, because of the flat tires, somebody's evil act, we spent three hours (the most in any one stop on the trip) of unhurried pleasure. Even Greg couldn't push us onward because the time schedule had been taken out of his hands. On the super-highway of self-will, the scenery is nothing but a blur (as were many parts of our trip). But at Nazareth Village the road was clear, and the way was lined with wonderful blessings that could only have been enjoyed at a slower pace. How many times have we missed God's greatest blessing because we have rushed through His ordained detours?

We must believe, as I do about Nazareth Village, that despite the detour God's side roads in life do hold their own compensations. Whether a crushing detour that takes you from a rosy road to a drab driveway of infirmity, or a running path of success to a plodding along a narrow lane with one misfortune after another, when the journey is over and we look back on this burdensome boulevard of detour, we will be able to say with Paul, *"I have finished my course,"* (II Timothy 4:7) detours and all! For me, the best detour on our travels through Israel was the afternoon we were diverted from Mount Tabor to Nazareth Village.

62

Another Day In Nazareth

Luke 2:51–52—And He (Jesus) went down with them, and came to NAZARETH, and was subject unto them: but his mother kept all these sayings in her heart. And Jesus increased in wisdom and stature, and in favour with God and man.

Nearly two years before I visited Nazareth, I spent a year writing a book with the same title as this chapter in my Israel journey. It contained the parallels I felt I had experienced in my boyhood town of Perham, Maine as I thought Jesus might have experienced them in his boyhood town of Nazareth, Israel. This is how I introduced the series of articles (100) I wrote under this topic:

> I once dreamed of pastoring a big church in a big place and making a big difference. As I near my fiftieth spiritual birthday (June 4, 1958), my dreams and desires have changed. I haven't and will never pastor a big church. I haven't and will not live in a big place. And as for making a big difference, the verdict is still out. What has made this dramatic change in my basic philosophy? It all happened quite suddenly when I came to the realization that my dear Lord and Saviour Jesus Christ had lived nearly ninety percent of His life on earth in Nazareth! Remember what Nathanael said to Philip when hearing Philip's testimony about finding the Messiah:
>
> Can there any good thing come out of Nazareth? (John 1:46)

How often have we thought that greatness is geographical? Because a man is born in a big place where he finds great opportunities for grand advancements that is the reason he becomes important. Greatness however does not depend on location or largeness. When Alexander marched out of the insignificant Greek province of Macedonia there were those who probably asked, "Can any one great come out of Macedonia?" And yet before he was done he would be known as Alexander the Great of Macedonia. Most would have thought he should have come from Athens or Sparta, but greatness is not geographical! Greatness also doesn't take into consideration how long one stays in Nazareth. I see now that I have spent most of my nearly sixty years in Nazareth, or places like Nazareth. I was born in a small farming community in Northern Maine. In the first century in Galilee, Nazareth was a typical farming village where agriculture determined nearly every aspect of daily life; just like in Perham. Jesus' boyhood home was located in a sheltered basin nearly 1,300 feet above sea level just miles from the Jordan River Valley. Perham is also located in hill country just above the Aroostook River Valley. My four pastorates have taken me to rural hamlets in Southern New Hampshire, back to Northern Maine, to an small island off the Downeast coast of Maine, and now to the riverside (Union River) and seaside (Gulf of Maine) town of Ellsworth, Maine. Even in His hometown Jesus was trying to demonstrate to the world that God looks at people, not places! I like this from an unknown poet:

> 'Father, where shall I work today? And my love flow warm and free.' He pointed out a tiny spot and said, 'Tend this place for me.' I answered Him quickly, 'Oh, no, not that. Why no one would ever see. No matter how well my work was done; not that little place for me!' The word He spoke, then, wasn't stern; He answered me tenderly, 'Nazareth was a little place, and so was Galilee.'

Nazareth was the extent of Jesus' life, for the bulk of His life. Just three short years were given to ministries among the multitudes, and thirty years were given to the 'few'. I too have spent my life among individuals, small groups, and tiny congregations. For years I thought I was somehow losing out, wasting my time, accomplishing little. Then it came to me like a revelation: what of Jesus' time in Nazareth? It was then I began to ponder just how blessed a life I have had: a life much like Jesus' life. Who better to know what 'another day in Nazareth' is like than one who has spent most of his days in small country towns? I have often speculated what the silent years in Nazareth were like for Jesus; then it came to me—much like my days! Dr. J. H. Jowett writes:

Our Lord Jesus lived for thirty years amid the happenings of the little town of Nazareth. Little villages spell out their stories in small events. And He, the young Prince of Glory, was in the carpenter's shop. He moved amid humdrum tasks, petty cares, village gossip, trifling trade, and He was faithful in that which was least. If these smaller things in life afford such riches of opportunity for the finest loyalty, all of our lives are wonderfully wealthy in possibility and promise. Even though our house is furnished with commonplace it can be the house of the Lord all the days of our lives.

Once I realized that my Lord had called me to 'His lifestyle', I became more content, more confident, more thankful, and more determined to be found as faithful in my Nazareth. Nettie Rooker put it this way:

When I am tempted to repine that such a lowly lot is mine, there comes to me a voice which saith, 'Mine were the streets of Nazareth.' So mean, so common and confined, and He the monarch of mankind! Yet patiently, He traveleth those narrow streets of Nazareth. It may be I shall never rise to place or fame beneath the skies but walk in straitened ways till death, narrow as the streets of Nazareth. But if through honor's arch I tread and there forget to bend my head. Ah, let me hear the voice which saith, 'Mine were the streets of Nazareth.'

It is with this message ringing in my ear and singing in my heart that I give you this series of thoughts on 'another day in Nazareth'. My goal is to share with you the experiences of my own life that I feel might have paralleled the Life of Jesus in Nazareth. I have determined to write each as a diary entry, or a journal, so that you my reader might use them to challenge yourself in your Nazareth days. Most of us will never know the greatness of a great accomplishment, the creation of something totally new, or the success of changing the world like Christ did, but we can all experience 'another day in Nazareth'. Let us come to the conclusion that our best days will probably be our Nazareth days, and that there is service to be done; there is duty to be performed; there are people to be helped even in Nazareth. Can any good thing come out of another day in Nazareth?

Seeing that I have only spent literally one afternoon in Nazareth, I will let you be the judge. But my prayer is that each of us will realize that we have spent more time like Jesus spent than we realize. Our day in Nazareth ended when Joel returned with the bus tires fixed. We still had an hour ride to the eastern shore of the Sea of Galilee, so we had plenty of time to reflect on what we had seen in Nazareth Village. For me it was the common things that would eventually come out in Jesus' sermons: a speck of sawdust on the carpenter's bench (Matthew 7:3–5), a house built on a ledge (Matthew 7:24–25), a yoke to make a burden lighter (Matthew 11:29–30), a broom to sweeping a dirt floor (Luke 15:8–10), drawing water from a well to quench a thirst (John 4:5–13), the mending of a garment (Matthew 9:16), boys and girls playing in the streets (Matthew 11:16), a merchant in the market looking for something valuable (Matthew 13:45–46), a father giving bread and fish to his children (Matthew 7:9–11), a man hiring day laborers for the fields (Matthew 20:1–16), the birds flying above and the flowers in the surrounding meadows (Matthew 6:26–30), an olive-oil lamp (Matthew 5:15), a shepherd and his sheep (John 10:1–14), and a city set on a hill (Matthew 5:14); just another day in Nazareth!

63

Sunset Over the Sea of Galilee

Mark 1:16—Now as He (Jesus) walked by THE SEA OF GALI-LEE, He saw . . .

Our second week in Israel was drawing to a close as we slowly made our way from Nazareth to the En Gev Resort, our home for the next three days and nights in Northern Israel. On the way to the Sea of Galilee, we passed through Jonah's hometown of Gathhepher (II Kings 14:25). One of the reasons I believe that Jesus used Jonah as an illustration (at least four times-Matthew 12:39, 40, 41, 16:4), more than any other Old Testament prophet, was the closeness of Jesus upbringing to Jonah's place-of-birth. Like Jesus, Jonah was a prophet from Galilee. We also passed through the town of Jesus' first miracle: Cana (John 2:1–11). The changing of the water into wine now has a new dimension because now I have seen the town. Once again it was easy to see how Jesus could reach all these places, for they were only a few miles apart.

Then, even more exciting to the military history part of my being, was our drive by the Horns of Hattin. Located just off Route 77 and just west of Tiberius is this world famous geographical landmark. On July 4, 1187 King Guy of Jerusalem squared off with the era's most famous warrior, Saladin, by and on this unique rock formation. The crusader army from Jerusalem was marching to the relief of Tiberius on the Sea of Galilee, which was under siege by Saladin's Saracens. The armies were well matched, about 20,000 on each side, but Saladin knew the terrain and the vital ingredient in any battle in the region—water. Rejecting the wise counsel of his men-at-arms, King Guy decided to advance across the

Sunset Over the Sea of Galilee 253

arid region at the hottest time of the year. Saladin's mounted archers harassed Guy's column most of the way, and just when the army was within sight of water (Sea of Galilee), Saladin blocked its advance before the twin peaks of the Horns of Hattin. Saladin had sent two wings of his army to encircle Guy's crusaders and deny them access to a second source of water at Turun. The Saracens then set fire to the shrubs surrounding the crusader's camp which only aggravated their torment. On the primary day of battle the crusaders tried to break through the Saracen's line to a spring at Hattin, but they were stopped and had to retreat to one of the Horns. The battle waged on all day, but finally Guy's army degenerated into a thirst-crazed mob. One final assault was all Saladin had to launch. I had read of this battle for years, but only after passing the battlefield could I understand just how the battle unfolded in 1187!

Our ten miles journey from Nazareth to Tiberius was cut short when just before we got to Tiberius we turned on to Route 768. This roadway would take us to the southern tip of the Sea of Galilee and Route 90 and eventually Route 92 which runs up the eastern shore of the Sea. I still remember coming over a brow of a hill and a bend in the road and there it was—the most famous body of water in the world. As we traveled down its western shore we learned these characteristics of the sea that is really a lake! It is pear-shaped or heart-shaped in its 13 miles in length and 7 miles at it's widest. Its widest and deepest part is in the northern basin, and it is completely surrounded by hills making it like a bowl. This is the reason for its history of sudden and violent storms. Periodically the winds will sweep down through the narrow gorge which opens up to the lake, which will in turn whip up the water into a fury. Remember, Jesus and His disciples faced a few of these storms (Mark 4:35-41). The Sea of Galilee is a fresh-water lake fed primarily by the flow of the Jordan River which enters the lake between Bethsaida and Capernaum on the north shore. The river exits on the southern shore continuing its travel until it finally empties into the Dead Sea.

The lake is 680 feet below sea level; making it the lowest freshwater lake in the world, and like its bigger brother, the Dead Sea, the Sea of Galilee is called by a number of names in the Bible:

> Tiberius (John 6:1), Gennesaret (Luke 5:1), and Chinnereth (Numbers 34:11)

The lake was on the very rich trade caravan route that ran both along the King's Highway on the eastern shore, and the Via Maris which passed on the north shore. Josephus, the Jewish historian during the time of Jesus, tells us that about 40,000 people lived around the shore and that 2,300 boats (one was Peter's) fished the lake. He also wrote this:

> Now this lake of Gennesaret is so called from the country adjoining it. Its breadth is forty furlongs and its length one hundred and forty. Its waters are fresh, and very agreeable for drinking. The country that lies over against this lake has the same name of Gennesaret; its nature is wonderful as well as its beauty; its soil is so fruitful that all sorts of trees can grow upon it, and the inhabitants accordingly plant all sorts of trees there; for the temper of the air is well mixed, that it agrees very well with those types, particularly walnuts, that require the coldest air. There are palm trees also, which grow best in hot air; fig trees and olive grow near them, which require an air that is more moderate. One may call this place the ambition of nature, where it forces those plants that are naturally enemies to one another to agree together, it is a happy contention of the seasons, as if every one of them laid claim to this country, for it not only nourishes different sorts of autumnal fruit beyond men's expectation, but preserves them a great while; it supplies men with the principal fruits, with grapes and figs continually, during ten months of the year, and the rest of the fruits as they become ripe together through the whole year; for besides the good temperature of the air, it is also watered from a most fertile fountain (the Jordan River).

We found this two thousand year old description as accurate on May 24, 2010 as then!

We arrived at the resort just before seven. We checked into our private cabin, went to supper, and then just before sunset put on our swim suits for our first of three dips into the warm waters of the Sea of Galilee. Marnie and I were the first ones to take the plunge. Less than a hundred yards from the front door of our bungalow was the shoreline of the lake. Directly across the lake we could see the lights of Tiberius, and there just to the right of the lights were the Cliffs of Arbel. Each night we were there the sun sat directly over the cliffs. The sight was divine, but to witness the setting of the sun from the waters of the lake was heavenly. The water was the warmest lake water I had ever experienced (only cold-water lakes in Maine), and the wind was blowing just enough to create small waves. Marnie and I made our first pilgrimage to the water just as the sun touched the Arbel Cliffs. The rule at the resort was no swimming in the dark. We only had about a half an hour that first night, but thirty minutes was enough to satisfy the urge we had upon our first sighting of Jesus' Sea. As we walked the rocky, sandy beach to the water's edge all we could remember were these lines from Matthew 4:18:

> And Jesus, walking by the Sea of Galilee, saw . . .

Now we too had walked by that same sea, and now we had seen what Jesus had seen!

64

A Stranger In Galilee?

Obadiah 12— . . . the day that He became a STRANGER . . .

When I was a teenager, our church youth group had a choir. One of the songs we learned was Leila Morris', 'The Stranger of Galilee':

In fancy I stood by the shore one day,
of the beautiful murmuring sea;
I saw the great crowds as they thronged the way
of the Stranger of Galilee.
I saw how the man who was blind from birth,
in a moment was made to see;
the lame was made whole by the matchless skill
of the Stranger of Galilee.

And I felt I could love Him forever,
so gracious and tender was He.
I claimed Him that day as my Saviour,
this Stranger of Galilee
His look of compassion, His words of love,
they shall never forgotten be,
when sin-sick and helpless He saw me there,
this Stranger of Galilee.
He showed me His hand and His riven side,
and He whispered 'It was for thee!'
My burden fell off at the pierced feet
of the Stranger of Galilee.

I heard Him speak peace to the angry waves
of that turbulent, raging sea;

and lo! At His word are the waters stilled,
this Stranger of Galilee.
A peaceful, a quiet, and holy calm,
now ever abides with me;
He holdeth my life in His mighty hands,
this Stranger of Galilee.
Come, ye who are driven, and tempest-tossed,
and His gracious salvation see;
He'll quiet life's storms with His 'Peace, be still!'
this Stranger of Galilee.
He bids me to go and the story tell;
What He ever to you will be
if only you let Him with you abide,
this Stranger of Galilee.

And I felt I could love Him forever,
so gracious and tender was He.
I claimed Him that day as my Saviour,
this Stranger of Galilee.

Oh, my friend, won't you love Him forever?
So gracious and tender is He.
Accept Him today as your Saviour,
this Stranger of Galilee!

On our 15th day in Israel, Marnie and I woke on the shores of the Sea of Galilee, and before the morning was over would relive the message of this song, and would understand why Jesus was a stranger in His own country (Luke 4:24).

During the days of Jesus, Palestine was divided up by the Romans into three districts: Galilee, Samaria and Judea (Luke 17:11—Jerusalem was found in Judea). Galilee was the northern section of the division of Israel. This territory measured 25 miles from the Mediterranean Sea to the Jordan River, and 60 miles from Mount Gilboa to Mount Hermon to the north. Originally this area was given to the tribe of Naphtali (II Kings 15:29) as their allotment of the Promised Land. Interestingly, King Solomon offered King Hiram of Tyre twenty Galilean cities in payment for his help on the Temple project, but the king refused (I Kings 9:11–13). In that day they were seen as low class, no good compared to other areas in Solomon's kingdom. Solomon was giving Hiram his worst; while today this area is considered the best Israel has! We remember Galilee best because this was the province of Mary and Joseph and the boyhood and adulthood place of Christ. Jesus was fulfilling one of Isaiah's great prophecies (Isaiah 9:1-2) by spending the bulk of his ministry and performing the bulk of his miracles in Galilee.

Our small cabin at En Gev Resort (an old kibbutz converted into a tourist resort) was homey and comfortable. For the first time on the trip Marnie didn't have to sleep in the same room as her habitually snoring father. With separate rooms, Marnie got a good night's rest, and we both felt energized for our day traveling around and across the Sea of Galilee. Breakfast was pretty much what we had experienced in other places, but the walk back to our cottage was very different. Our stroll overlooked Israel's primer sea. The sun had just come up over the eastern hills, and we knew another warm, pleasant day was before us. The trees that lined the pathways to our bungalow were filled with singing birds. The large city of Tiberius could be seen seven miles across the lake glittering in the sun. We could even see on the lake a few boats, where they fishing or taking tourists on a ride? So much of what I remember of Jesus took place around this shore. From the calling of the brothers Andrew and Peter, James and John (Matthew 4:17-22), to their final fishing trip together (John 21:1-23), it was upon these very shores that the multitudes sought healing and understanding from 'The Stranger of Galilee'!

As was our custom, we were at our bus and on the road by around eight. Our first stop of the day was just a few miles from the entrance to En Gev. I didn't recognize the place when we pulled into the parking area of the Kursi National Park. Located at the junction to the road that leads to the Golan Heights, Kursi is the traditional site for Jesus' classic miracle of the 'swine' (Luke 8:26-39 and Mark 5:1-20). It was then I realized that we had entered 'the country of the Gadarenes'. It was here, or near here, that Jesus cast the 'legion' of demons out of a man and allowed them to enter a herd of swine grazing nearby. The pigs were so enraged that they raced into the Sea of Galilee and were drowned, preferring death to demon possession (who says pigs are dumb animals?). Once the inhabitants saw what happened to their treasured swine they exhorted Jesus to leave their country—a perfect example of why Jesus was 'a stranger in Galilee'. The Gadarenes preferred their swine to the Savior—sound familiar? Economics over Emmanuel, pigs over the Prince of Peace—they were more comfortable living and dealing with a demonic than dealing with the Daystar (II Peter 1:19) and a demon less man!

Of course, there was no evidence that this mighty miracle and the miraculous change in the demonic of Gerasa actually took place in Kursi,

A Stranger In Galilee?

but what we saw in Kursi was the largest known Byzantine monastery in the Holy Land. Uncovered accidentally in 1970 during road construction in the area, this monastery was surrounded by walls nearly 500 feet long and 400 feet wide. Most archeologists believe the monastery was built in the 5th century and destroyed in 614 when the Persians invaded the land. It was rebuilt, but destroyed by fire again in the 8th century. After that it was lost in time until its ruins were opened to the public in 1982. The area reminded me of Jesus' two great natural loves—hill country and sea shores. Numerous times the Gospels speak of Jesus walking along the sea and climbing into the surrounding hills. Kursi was a prime example of the rolling hills around Galilee touching the sea. It certainly takes men of the masses, the city, to reach the crowded centers of humanity, but Jesus pattern and pace can be seen in His Galilean gait and the salvation of the demonic of Gerasa!

Vance Havner wrote of Jesus' example like this:

> Jesus rose long before day, found a solitary place, and there prayed. He found both time and place for communion with God and so must we. Both are hard to come by today in this rat race-this madhouse we misnamed Progress. If you find such a spot for solitude you must pay a price. The places grow fewer and harder to reach, and a minister must devise ways and means to find his hiding place unknown to telephones and committees and those pests who steal his time to no good purpose at all. And time is the scarcest commodity ever. Crowded calendars filled with appointments made in church offices leave no time for God. Much of our 'church work' could be done-maybe is done—without the Holy Spirit.

But even in Jesus' love of solitude and silence, He still had time for a 'soul'. What I remembered at Kursi was that Jesus sailed across the Sea of Galilee for just one convert. Jesus left at the request of the citizens of Gerasa (Jesus will never stay where He is not wanted, where people chose to keep Him a stranger), but he left a missionary behind:

> Howbeit Jesus suffered him not, but saith unto him, Go home to thy friends, and tell them how great things the Lord hath done for thee, and hath had compassion on thee. And he (demonic) departed, and began to publish in Decapolis (the wider region) how great things Jesus had done for him: and all men did marvel. (Mark 5:19–20)

Jesus might have been a 'stranger', but the demonic was well known, a perfect missionary to spread the Gospel. Church history tells us in the earliest days of the church counsels there was always a Bishop from Kursi present. A lasting testimony of the work of one man who simply spread far and wide what Jesus did for him. Our stop at Kursi was inspiring when I realized that 'the Stranger of Galilee' doesn't care whether or not He is received, but whether the truth of His message is received. In the case of the Gadarenes, a demonic spreading the message was better than 'the Stranger of Galilee"!

65

Bethsaida Brotherhood

John 1:44—Now Philip was of BETHSAIDA, the city of Andrew and Peter.

After a short walk around Kursi, enough time to smell the blooming bushes (Harod and Kursi were the two best places to experience the brilliant colors and marvelous aroma of Israel in spring), we left for Tel Bethsaida. While the rest of the group headed back to the bus, I took a few minutes to wander beyond the ruins of the monastery and, as happened often on this trip, discovered something unique. This time it was a sand pit that contained a cone shaped, coping instrument. On the sides of the steel cone were printed, in a number of languages, the story of the demonic (Mark 5:2) and the Legion (Mark 5:9). Taking the iron handle at the end of the cone, one was able to roll the cone around the sand pit. Once you pass over an area of sand the Biblical story was stamped into the sand. There was no explanation of who created this unique method of sharing Jesus' miracle, but it was one of the most unusual objects I uncovered while in Israel!

Our second leg of this day took us just a few more miles up Route 92 until we came to the intersection of 92 and 87. By this time we had arrived to the northern shore of the Sea of Galilee. At the time of Jesus and His disciples, the city of Bethsaida was located on the shore of Galilee, but by the time we found it the tel was over a mile from the water's edge. We were told that in 363 AD a massive earthquake actually plugged the flow of the Jordan River for a period of time. Because the Jordan flows into the Sea of Galilee just west of the town, when the dammed up river finally broke through it deposited a lot of sediment in front of the town. Added to this has been the gradual drop in the height of the Sea of Galilee, so now instead of being on its shore, Bethsaida has a lush plain between it and the water. Archeological evidence now suggests that the Sea of Galilee in ancient times was much larger than its present size and may also to have included a series of estuaries leading off of a large lagoon just north of the shoreline today!

Tel Bethsaida is one of the largest artificial mounds yet discovered in Israel. Once we reached the top of it we had a commanding view of the entire northern section of the Sea of Galilee. We learned that some believe that Bethsaida was the ancient Naphtali town of Zer (Joshua 19:35). The archeologists have discovered a massive fortification system that once surrounded the area which has no parallel in the military architecture of the period. Two large towers once flanked the entrance. A four-chambered city gate was also found complete with a cultic 'high place'. The evidence seems to suggest that the gate was destroyed during the Assyrian invasion of 732 BC. The city gate led to a huge palace complex with a very spacious paved plaza. At one time this city was a very important place, perhaps, a stopping off place for the trade route that passed along the northern tip of the Sea of Galilee. Among other things discovered on site was a small figurine of the Egyptian fertility god Pataikos which reveals the pagan past of Bethsaida.

Still others connect Bethsaida to the kingdom of Geshur (II Samuel 3:3). David married a lady by the name of Maachah, the daughter of Talmai, the king of Geshur. This wife gave David his troubled son Absalom (I Chronicles 3:2)! Bethsaida means 'house of the fisherman', or 'the place of nets'; both meanings underline the primary enterprise practiced in the town by the time Jesus called Peter, Andrew, and Philip to be fishers-of-men. Two of Jesus most famous miracles were performed in or near Bethsaida—the feeding of the 5,000 (Luke 9:10) and the healing of the blind man (Mark 8:22). It was also near here that Jesus walked on the water (Mark 6:45–49). Bethsaida, Chorazin, and Capernaum made up the triangle of cities where Jesus performed the bulk of his miracles (Matthew 11:20). Sadly, Bethsaida was numbered with the other two towns in Jesus' curse because they were without repentance (Matthew 11:21 and Luke 10:13). Today, all three cities, in which Jesus spent the majority of his time, are nothing but a pile of rubble!

I found this history in the pamphlet given to me at Tel Bethsaida:

Bethsaida Brotherhood

The ancient Jewish historian, Josephus Flavius, recounts than in the year 30 AD Philip, the son of Herod the Great, raised the village of Bethsaida to the status of a Greek city (perhaps, the reason for its moral decline) and renamed it Julias, after Livia-Julia, the wife of the late Emperor Augustus. Four years later (shortly after the death of Jesus), Philip died and was buried at his beloved Bethsaida. According to Josephus, Bethsaida also played a role in the opening battles of the First Revolt against Rome in 67 AD. Bethsaida was well-known in rabbinic literature as a town at the historic borders of the land of Israel. According to second century figures, Rabbi Shimon ben Gamliel and the Emperor Hadrian (had to mention him) speak of the abundant fish and fowl present at the city. Despite the large number of literary accounts in the Hellenistic and Roman periods, Christian pilgrim accounts throughout the Middle Ages could not pinpoint its location!

When Christ brought a curse upon this city, the city was literally removed from history. Not until 1838 was the site relocated by an American named Edward Robinson, and not until 1987 was excavations begun and the site was verified.

For me the history was fascinating and the tel was geographically appealing, but inspirationally it was the brotherhood that began at Bethsaida that thrilled me the most. Granted, the town never turned to Christ but at least three of its most famous residences did: Peter, Andrew, and Philip. If you haven't read this part of the story recently I would encourage you to reread John 1:35–51. I believe one of the aspects of Christianity that is missing today is the brotherhood Jesus established first among his disciples. We all love the imagery of the 'bride of Christ' (Ephesians 5:24–33), and the intimacy of the 'body of Christ' (Ephesians 1:20–23). We preach and teach on the instruction clearly seen in the 'building of Christ' (Ephesians 2:19–22), but what of the 'brotherhood of Christ'? Peter would write in his first epistle:

> Love the brotherhood! (I Peter 2:17)

He would also write of 'brotherly kindness' (II Peter 1:7). Paul would write of 'brotherly love' (Hebrews 13:1). For me this aspect of Jesus' teaching began with three friends from Bethsaida, a bond that would lead them from the north shore of the Sea of Galilee to an area-wide ministry that would test their brotherly love and kindness!

I found these thoughts on 'brotherhood' many years ago in the writings of F. B. Meyer. I share them here to highlight what I remember best about Bethsaida:

> Between a man and his brother there is a special tie. It may be truly said, in the case of brothers, that a doorway has been made through the walls which ordinarily part men, which may be bricked up or filled with debris; but the wall there will always be thinner than anywhere else, and someday the doorway may be opened for the messenger of peace. Men are always more inclined to follow the man of whom they can say, 'He is our brother!' As soon as Andrew had found Jesus, he started off to find his own brother Simon; and Simon was glad to follow him because he was his brother. Had another tried, it is as likely as not that he would have repelled him. But what could he say to the man who had shared his childhood's sports, and had helped him haul in a net of fish many a time after a night of hard work?

Jesus is still looking for brothers from Bethsaida!

66

Capernaum

Matthew 4:13—And leaving Nazareth, he (Jesus) came and dwelt in CAPERNAUM, which is upon the sea coast . . .

Our next stop along the northern shore of the Sea of Galilee was the truly Biblical city of Capernaum, Jesus' adopted town. On the way to this seaside city we crossed the Jordan River for the second time. During our trip from Nazareth to En Gev the day before, we had crossed the Jordan just south of where it exits the Sea of Galilee. This morning we crossed the Jordan just north of where it empties (Capernaum is about two and a half miles away) into the Sea of Galilee. What amazed me most was the difference in the volume of water coming into the lake versus the flow of water going out of the lake. I could see clearly why the water level of the Sea of Galilee was dropping!

Did you know that Capernaum is mentioned more times (sixteen) in the New Testament than any other site with the exception of Jerusalem? One can't read the Life of Christ without wondering why and what brought Jesus to this coastal community. For me, I believe it was the rejection by the people of Nazareth (Jesus' hometown-just a few miles to the southwest) to Jesus' claim to be the Christ. Remember, they tried to kill him (Luke 4:16–30). Following that event the text simply reads:

> And He came down to Capernaum, a city in Galilee, and taught them on the Sabbath days. (Luke 4:31)

I also believe that Jesus knew in order to get his astonishing doctrine (Luke 4:32) out, he needed to be in a crossroad town (Capernaum was on the main trade route, the Via Maris, from Damascus to the seacoast and Egypt) like Capernaum. Most of Jesus' closest disciples lived either in Capernaum, or nearby, so it was an ideal, central place in which to spread His message. Even Peter had moved from Bethsaida to Capernaum (Matthew 8:14)! (Recent excavations have exposed a 5th century church complex that was believed to be built over Peter's Capernaum home.) Some believe that Capernaum was the largest and richest city along the Sea of Galilee at the time with a custom station (Where Matthew worked-Matthew 9:9) and the residence of the leading Roman official in the region.

Like we saw at Bethsaida and later at Chorazin, Capernaum is mostly just an archeological site today. As one commentator put it:

> Today Capernaum is no more than a heap of ruins in the midst of palm trees beside the lake shore!

Unlike Bethsaida or Chorazin, the area around the ruins does have a few dwelling places, mostly a monastery and a church. Right in the middle of the rubble they are building a modern sanctuary. When we arrived the place was crawling with scores of tourists, one of the busiest sites we explored. After a quick lesson, we had about an hour to walk around. This is what I remembered about Capernaum:

1. Jesus often taught in the synagogue in Capernaum (Mark 1:21, 2:1, John 6:59). The site was first excavated in 1905, and the most significant find was 'the synagogue". Most feel that the synagogue ruins we explored was of a later synagogue than Jesus' time, but that Jesus' synagogue is probably beneath the current site. Romans destroyed all synagogues in the holy land after the Jewish Revolt. The one in ruins today appears in a more Greco-Roman style and reminds us of another story from Capernaum and that being that the original Capernaum synagogue was built with funds from the Roman centurion of Capernaum (Luke 7:1-10).

2. Jesus performed some of His most famous miracles in Capernaum, including the healing of the centurion's servant (Matthew 8:1-15), the healing of Peter's mother-in-law (Matthew 8:14-17), the palsy man who was let down through a roof by his friends (Mark 2:1-13), the raising of Jarius' daughter from the dead (Matthew 9:8-26), the healing of the woman with the issue of blood (Matthew 9:20-22), the healing of a demon possessed man in the synagogue (Luke 4:31-37) the two blind men received their sight back (Matthew 9:27-35), the man with the withered hand was healed (Matthew 12:9-14), and it was near Capernaum that Jesus walked on the water (John 6:15-21).

3. Jesus proclaimed a curse on Capernaum because of its lack of belief and repentance. He said that the citizens of Sodom would have responded if they would have seen His miracles and heard His teachings (Matthew 11:23–24). Eventually, Capernaum was destroyed and lost until the twentieth century.

4. Jesus preached his famous 'fishers-of-men' (Matthew 4:13, 18–20) sermon to His followers here, as well as His equally important message "I Am the Bread of Life" (John 6:1–59), and the enlightening illustration of a 'child' (Mark 9:33–37).

The ruins we walked through (some of the best in the trip and one of the earliest and best preserved of the Galilean synagogues) were believed to have dated back to 4th century, probably dating from the time of Emperor Julian, when the imperial government gave permission to the few Jews that remained the authority to rebuild a synagogue on site. The archeologists believe that some of the stones of the first synagogue (the centurion's synagogue) were built into the later synagogue. What was confusing at first was finding Roman symbols and Jewish carvings together. As we walked around the rows of cut stones that had been assembled after excavation, we could make out the menorah, the shofar (the ram's horn), the star of David, the palm tree (often the symbol of the land of Israel itself), and yes, they even found on site 'the ark of the covenant' carved in stone. At the same time we also saw the Roman eagle, lion, dates, and shells. For me, as with so many of the other sites we had visited, the simple reality was this was another place my Saviour had been. The stones might be different, and the layout changed, but one truth was the same: the spot and the view overlooking the Sea of Galilee!

As we passed from one basalt stone to the other and relived Jesus' time in Capernaum, I was stuck most by the huge statue of Peter placed directly in front of the main gate. I watched as monks instructed pilgrim's under the shade trees, and in all of the remaining carvings and symbols, no reference of Jesus. Oh, the Jews were there in their symbolic carvings. The Romans were there in their imperial symbols. The Christian influences could be seen in the monastery and the modern church, but where was the Christ of Capernaum? Still a stranger it seems!

67

Unimpressed In Tiberias

John 6:23—Howbeit there came other boats from TIBERIAS nigh unto the place where they did eat bread, after that the Lord had given thanks.

After a short walk along the water's edge at Capernaum, we boarded our bus for the short ride to the city of Tiberias. The morning by the Sea of Galilee had restored my soul, and had, as I would soon realize, given me the needed inspiration to endure what was about to take place until a mountain revived me again. All my life I have been a rebel to anything that smells of 'city'. I praise God for the Sea of Galilee that has made up the bulk of my life, but on every shore others have built a Tiberias. That morning, traveling the north shore of the Sea of Galilee, had brought me back to the source of my love affair with the country versus the city. As I overlooked the sea from the slopes of Capernaum, I half expected to see Andrew and Peter mending their nets and James and John washing their boat. And when life gets busy in the city and the storms begin to build, it is nice to know a 'Man' who can still the waters and calm the seas. The Sea of Galilee was peaceful and tranquil the day we walked its shores from Kursi to Tiberias, but even that Sea is not immune to stormy waves and boisterous winds. Sometimes walking in the city is as difficult as walking on water as Peter learned. "Toiling in rowing" (Mark 6:48) can be the same on land as on the ocean, especially if a city is involved. But like Peter, sometimes we are called to walk in uncharted places, like cities, but I am confident that if we start to sink the Good Lord will reach out His hand and pull us back in the boat, offshore.

John writes, "*But when the morning was now come, Jesus stood on the shore. . . . .*" (John 21:4), not in the street! I believe God calls us from the shore, not the streets, but sometimes we have to walk the streets as we did that morning in Tiberias!

We drove into the modern city of Tiberias about 11:30 AM. It was lunch time and Greg thought we might like to get a good meal. Most of our previous noontime stops had been at fast food or snack food places. Tiberias would offer us the best in Israeli dining. While others jumped at the chance, I had my doubts; after all it was a city, a tourist city. Once again Marnie and I teamed up with Chris Hanchey and Jeremy Pendergrass, our best friends on the trip. Our team work in Jerusalem convinced us that we might be able to navigate the busy streets of Tiberias during our one hour lunch break. Joel parked the bus on a side hill, just west of the business and commercial district of Tiberias. Our walk down the hill and our periodical stops at the numerous eating places along the way revealed that eating in Tiberias would be very expensive. Even our walk through a fruit market proved unproductive. The closer we got to the seashore, the price of lunch only soared. All we wanted was a simple meal, but was there a simple meal to be found in this tourist Mecca?

As we began to retrace our steps, Marnie suggested we take one of the side streets away from the main street. Marnie had learned in her many visits to foreign places that the further you get away from the heart of a city the cheaper things are, and sure enough after walking about three blocks we found a small café with good food and cheap prices. As we sat outside in the plaza to eat our lunch, I had these thoughts. That night back at En Gev I wrote this observation in my trip journal:

> From my table in a small plaza in the heart of a city, I look out on the teeming masses of Tiberias. One could imagine he is in any modern city: America, Europe, or Israel. Exciting and interesting to most, I am afraid I have another opinion to offer. Even in its modern building and well-planned streets, an echo of the past still haunts this place. Even though a new city in the days of Jesus (built between 18-20 AD by Herod Antipas in honor of Tiberius Caesar), there is no record that Jesus ever visited this city of Galilee. Why? Could it be for the same reason I was unimpressed in Tiberias? Vance Havner put it best when he wrote:
>
> The only thing we learn from history is that we learn nothing from history!

I couldn't escape the weird feeling, the eerie impression I got as my daughter and her friends and I watched the crowds pass us by. In my imagination I saw the ghosts of a past civilization parading by with the same ignorance. Remember, Tiberias carried on like nothing important was happening while the Son of God lived, taught, performed miracles just a few miles away. You can't tell me the news of Christ's exploits didn't make it to Tiberias? But like the Gadarenes across the Sea, Jesus remained a 'stranger' because they really didn't want what He had to offer. To me, Jesus failure to visit Tiberias wasn't an oversight, but the insight of the Son of God who wouldn't waste His time on a city that wouldn't believe in Him anyway (John 2:24-25)!

Tiberias was already in Jesus' rearview mirror when He walked the shores of Galilee. Aflame with one purpose, Jesus was never impressed with statues, marble streets, ornate buildings, and the culture of His day, no matter how civil it claimed to be. Jesus bore not the slightest resemblance to the average tourist I saw on the streets of Tiberias. No 'oohs' and 'ahs' came from his lips as he sailed by Tiberias in Peter's boat. I believe what moved Him, as with Jerusalem, was their ignorance and lack of understanding that the Almighty was living next door. So caught up in the latest fashions and social events, when somebody important would visit their city, the citizens of Tiberias didn't care to know 'a carpenter from Nazareth'. The tragedy is that most today are more impressed with Tiberias than 'the teacher' that chooses to pass it by. More concerned about art appreciation (after we left Tiberias we stopped at the Hamat Teverya National Park where we saw a massive mosaic floor that had been excavated from the Severus Synagogue), the world laments that Christianity isn't cultured enough, that we are too dull and boring in our obsession with the need of personal salvation (Romans 10:13)!

History tells us when Herod Antipas rebuilt this city that he placed in it beautiful palaces, a theatre, temples, and public baths (long before Herod built his city, the seventeen hot springs of Hamat, located right next door, were famous all over the Roman world for their healing properties). Each of these places represented the vital religions of that day: politics, entertainment, spirituality, and medicine. Sound familiar? From where I sat in Tiberias just a few hours ago, I must admit nothing seemingly had changed since Jesus' day. I fear that the same fate awaits Tiberias as the cities of Bethsaida, Chorazin, and Capernaum. As we wandered back through the bustling boulevards and back alleys of Tiberius to our waiting bus, I thought of this statement by Vance Havner:

We are too easily impressed by the phony grandeur of our time!

Now that I have had a few more months to ponder my time in Tiberias, I have only this one thing to add:

A grand place holds no grandeur without God.

I wrote that about my impression of Paris (a complete set of observation can be seen in the book "Rendezvous in Paris") after a short visit to pick up my daughter from a mission's trip to Togo, West Africa, another city filled with the trappings of godliness, but without God! When Paul wrote of the characteristics of 'the last days' (II Timothy 3:1-4), he added this last prophetic observation:

> Having a form of godliness, but denying the power thereof: from such turn away. (II Timothy 3:5)

I had no problem in doing just that as we left Tiberias that afternoon in Galilee!

68

A Mountaintop Experience

Matthew 28:16—Then the eleven disciples went away into Galilee, into a MOUNTAIN where Jesus had appointed them.

After an hour in Tiberias (the company was pleasant but the atmosphere was citified), we boarded our bus for what I thought would be a quick trip out of town. Instead of more antiquity, we came face to face with an advertisement. My city ordeal would continue a bit longer!

Within five minutes of leaving our parking spot, we had stopped again. Instead of being outside the city limits of Tiberias, we had stopped on a street corner by a side alley in a very busy section of town. The building beside the bus looked pretty much like the other building in the block, but what was inside this concrete structure? We got off the bus and walked into a large room in which a lady had set up a display of Dead Sea Beauty Products. Even before we could check out her wares we had to listen to a fifteen minute promotional pitch. I left! If there is something I hate worse than cities, it is shopping! To think that I was going to waste an hour of my Israeli time on face cream and foot cream made of mud from a dead sea made me mad! I was beginning to believe that maybe Joel was getting a cut in the profits by having us stop at such places. I know there were a few on the trip that enjoyed the tourist aspect of our tour, but I wasn't one of them. I can honestly say it was the only segment of the trip that I could have done without. It was two o'clock before we finally left Tiberias behind us.

Our next official stop was at the Hamat Teverya National Park (this was our 20th national park on the tour). This area was just south of

Tiberias (about a mile) and was known for its healing hot springs—even before the country was conquered by Joshua! The city became the southernmost of the fortified towns of the tribe of Naphtali (Joshua 19:35—Hammath). The Romans were not the first, but they did build the most elaborate and sophisticated spas there, and many traveled from all over the Roman Empire to visit the seventeen springs eventually found in the area. Even up to the 18th and 19th centuries, people were coming to the spas at Hamat Teverya. The area was left to itself until 1921 when it was rediscovered by a road crew paving the Tiberias-Zemach Road. During excavation of the site, a small synagogue was found dating back to the 5th century. In 1961, the remains of another synagogue were found in the southern part of the dig. Under further excavation, a huge mosaic floor was uncovered in what became known as the Severus Synagogue. The magnificent mosaic contains three inscriptions in Greek and one in Aramaic, and partly damaged Hebrew words inlaid on a zodiac. The type of design indicates a Hellenistic influence. For me, the artistry was amazing, but the mixture of the zodiac with the sun god Helios next to a depiction of the Ark of the Covenant only verified to me the Jewish people's desire to co-exist with the people of the land; some things never change in the Promised Land; my 'Tiberias' attitude wasn't improving at Hamat! By the time we left Hamat it was nearly three. According to Greg we were heading for the Arbel Cliffs, but we still had another stop to make before we could view the Sea of Galilee from the famous peak. From our cabin window at En Gev, we first saw the Arbel Cliffs. I couldn't wait, but I still had another commercial stop to make before I could "scale the utmost height and catch a gleam of glory bright".

As we slowly climbed the high ground behind Tiberias and Hamat, I was thrilled to recognize a familiar rock formation. I had seen the Horns of Hattin on our way in from Nazareth, and there they were again on my left. Surely we would stop, but instead of turning left we turned right onto a dirt road that lead us away from the Horns of Hattin. Sure enough we were returning back to modern versus antiquity. We had stopped at an old kibbutz (an agricultural, communal farm) which specialized in olive oil. The tour might have been interesting if it was the season for making olive oil, but it wasn't. We basically got a tour of the machinery, and of course, the store where we could buy the world's most expensive olive oil! While the others looked around and drank tea, I walked back down the road we had followed to get as close as I could to the Horns of Hattin. I at least can say I got to within a half mile of the famous rock formation before I heard the call to board the bus. I really needed a mountaintop experience to pull me out of the worst Israeli 'blues' I had experienced during the entire trip.

It was nearly four in the afternoon before we finally arrived at Mount Arbel. As we made our way up the steep pathway leading to the top, I was determined to beat everybody to the top. Like with my descent to the palace of Herod at Masada, I wanted to be the first to view the Sea of Galilee and the Plain of Gennesaret (Mark 6:53)—I was! Almost instantaneously my attitude changed. A light wind was blowing and the sky was clear and so too was my soul and spirit. I quickly forgot the nearly five hour ordeal I had been through as I looked down on the famous international truck route from the Horns of Hattin through the Wadi Arbel (better known as the Valley of the Doves) onto the Plain of Gennesaret (Matthew 14:34). By the time the rest of the group had made the summit, I had wandered around enough to regain my Israeli composure and my antiquity smile. Once Greg started to give us the history of the Cliffs of Arbel, I was back in my element-history. It was in the caves of Arbel that Jewish resistance to the rule of Herod was best exemplified. Josephus recorded that in the years 39–38 BC Herod brought under control the regions of Judea, Samaria, and later, Galilee. He captured Sepphoris (the capital city of Galilee) in a snowstorm, and finally cornered the last Jewish brigades in the caves of Arbel. He had his soldiers lowered in baskets over the sides of the cliff to either smoke out the final rebels, or his soldiers threw large hooks over the side into the caves to pull the rebels out of the caves. It was on top of the hill that I learned that the day before the study group from Master's College had actually climbed the snake path down the Arbel Cliffs from the top to the Wadi below. Oh, what I would have done to have taken that climb—maybe, next trip!

From the top of Arbel we could look back into Jesus' past again. Our tour guide pointed out Magdala (Matthew 15:39) where Mary Magdalene was from. We were shown the Plain of Gennesaret (Luke 5:1), and why the Sea of Galilee is sometimes in the New Testament called the Lake of Gennesaret. We could see Capernaum and Bethsaida, and yes, back to En Gev. Our entire day could be reviewed from this mountaintop platform. It was even suggested that this might be the 'mountain' where Jesus gave us "the Great Commission" (Matthew 28:16–20). There are those who even think this could be the place Jesus preached his classic Sermon on the Mount (Matthew 5–7), and the place he prayed before picking the Twelve Apostles (Luke 6:12–16). None of these events can be with certainty proven to have happened on Mount Arbel, but this one thing I know—it was on top of that hill I had one of my nicest mountaintop experiences in Israel. Before, the trip I didn't know about Arbel, but after this experience this hilltop was added to places like Olivet, Masada, Carmel, Lachish, Azekah, Megiddo, and Jerusalem. Arbel was another place I was able to view the past and see what the people of the Bible once saw!

69

Simon's Ship

Luke 5:3—And he (Jesus) entered into one of the ships, which was SIMON'S (Peter), and prayed him that he would thrust out a little from the land. And he sat down, and taught the people out of the SHIP.

One of the locations Greg Behle pointed out to us from the peak of Mount Arbel was the very dock we would be leaving from for our cruise across the Sea of Galilee. The last scheduled event on our 15th day in Israel was to experience what it felt like to ride on the waves of this world famous inland sea!

Our land travel from Arbel took us once again along the coastal road until we came to the tiny fishing village at Ginosar. We were heading to the Yigal Allon Center to view a very unique artifact from the 1st century, a rare item even in Israel—a fishing boat from the Sea of Galilee. This is the story as written in a pamphlet they gave us at the museum:

> In 1986 two brothers from the Kibbutz Ginosar discovered the Galilee Boat when a severe drought resulted in the lowering of the waters of the Sea of Galilee (Hebrew: Yam Kinneret). The vessel had been buried in, and thus protected by, the seabed's sediments. The Israel Antiquities Authority, assisted by many volunteers, rescued the boat in a remarkable eleven-day excavation. Excavators packaged the weak and waterlogged hull in a cocoon of fiberglass and polyurethane foam, and then successfully floated it to the nearby Yigal Allon Center, where it underwent an extensive carefully monitored eleven-year-long conservation process in a specially-built pool . . . The boat is

preserved to a length of 26.9 feet, a breadth of 7.5 feet, and a height of 3.9 feet. It is built in the typical ancient Mediterranean 'shell-based' construction, employing pegged mortise and tendon joints to edge-join the planking. Iron nails hold the frame to the hull. Numerous repairs, the reuse of timbers and a multiplicity of wood types (twelve) evident in the hull, suggest that this vessel had a long work life and an owner of meager means. Based on several criteria the Galilee Boat is firmly dated to the first century BC!!! An analysis of crew size suggests that this is the type of boat referred to in the Gospels in use among Jesus' Disciples, as well as that used by the Jews against the Romans in the nautical Battle of Migdal in 67 AD. This humble vessel is, thus, a remarkable porthole into the past providing a clearer view of the Galilean seafaring that forms the backdrop to both Jesus' ministry and the Battle of Migdal. In February 2000, fourteen years after its excavation, the boat was moved to its permanent home, a new wing of the Yigal Allon Center, which is devoted to the story of man in the Galilee.

It was in that new wing we got to see the old ship, and a scale model of what it looked like when it sailed the Sea of Galilee in the days of Simon Peter and his famous passenger!

Being a fisherman by heart, I was fascinated by the information we received on this aspect of the Gospel story. I had read the various 'fishing' stories of the Bible for years, but now visualization had filled in the gaps in those stories. We were told of the types of fish in the Sea of Galilee. Basically three kinds: sardines, perhaps, the small fish in the lad's lunch (John 6:9); barbels (barbs at the corners of the mouth-like our catfish), 'Biny' in Arabic, perhaps, the fish of the great haul (Luke 5:6–7), and Musht, or 'comb', sometimes called Saint Peter's fish. This is the largest of the Sea of Galilee fish growing upwards to 18 inches and weighing in at four to five pounds, perhaps, the great fish mentioned in John 21:11. We also learned of the four fishing methods used on Galilee: the seine net method, perhaps, the oldest type of fishing (Habakkuk 1:15 and Ezekiel 26:5) which used lines over 250 feet in length (Jesus used this method of fishing in one of His parables of the Kingdom (Matthew 13:47–48); the cast net method, perhaps, the most popular type of fishing (Ezekiel 32:3) which used a circular net, some measuring 15 by 25 feet, lead sinkers take the net to the bottom trapping the fish inside, then the net is pulled in much like the Gospels describe the disciples of Jesus doing (Mark 1:16–18 and Matthew 4:19–20 and John 21:4–11); the gill net method, the preferred fishing method of today was also used in Jesus' day especially at night (Ecclesiastes 9:12), as recorded in the stories of the disciples fishing John 21 and Luke 5:1–10, and finally there is the method I like, a hook and a line (Matthew 17:27).

While Marnie and I were enjoying the sea breeze at Capernaum, we actually saw fish swimming in the clear waters just off shore. Always quick to spot fish, it was a pleasant surprise to actually be taken to a place where we learned more of the fishing industry that was such a vital occupation of the region of Galilee and such a part of the makeup of the disciples of Jesus. I have come to believe that at least seven of the original apostles were fishermen (John 21:1–3). In a study of the twelve disciple's years ago, I came to these conclusions why Jesus would call fishermen to become fisher-of-men. They were typical (Acts 4:13); just ordinary men, like you and me. They were a team; they knew how to work together (Luke 5:7). They were comfortable working two by two (Luke 10:1), the method Jesus used to pair up his disciples and deploy them. They were teachable (Matthew 5:1–2); Jesus was able to reprogram their old understanding of fishing for fish into a new understanding of fishing for men. They were trainable (Matthew 10:5); Jesus was able to adapt their old skills into new skills. They were transformable (John 17:22); Jesus was able to take simple fishermen and others and mold them into a force that would literally turn the world upside down (Acts 17:6). We also would see a number of the fish of the Sea of Galilee in the Jordan River when we stopped for a baptism, as well as fish in the upper Jordan in Banias Stream. My only regret was I didn't have my fly rod and a few flies to test my skills on the fish of Galilee!

Our stay at the Yigal Allon Center included a walk about the different displays and a short film on the uncovering and restoration of the Galilee Boat. Our wait for our own ride across the Sea lasted about an hour, but it was well worth the wait as we had time to ponder the stories of Jesus in Simon's ship. I know that the boat found in the mud wasn't Simon's, but it probably wasn't far off. For years I had seen artist attempts to draw Simon's ship, but now I have a wonderful image in my mind just what it looked like. Now I can see much clearer Jesus stepping into Simon's ship and making it his preaching platform just before the miraculous catch of fish. I can see him sleeping in the bow of Simon's ship during the storm, and getting into that same boat after his walk across the water. Perhaps, the best lesson I learned at the center was just how small that ship really was. Despite the fact I love to fish, I don't like fishing from a boat; I prefer wading and flies to nets. I understand now just how and why the disciples were scared in the midst of the storms they faced because they were not very well protected in that boat. And I still marvel at the miracle of the first storm when it says, *"insomuch that the ship was covered with the waves: but he was asleep!"* (Matthew 8:24) The miracle is that the ship didn't sink, but could it with the Son of Man in it? Now I understand the uplifting, preserving power of my God just a bit better because of seeing that ancient first century ship!

70

The Sea of Galilee

John 6:1—After these things Jesus went over THE SEA OF GALI-LEE, which is the Sea of Tiberias.

I have mentioned before that one of the thrills of traveling through Israel was the opportunity to do Biblical things: riding a camel, walking through a water tunnel, drawing water from a cistern, riding a donkey, picking stones from Elah brook, drinking water from Harod Stream, and taking a boat ride across the Sea of Galilee!

We boarded our tourist boat (sometimes called a pilgrim boat) from a dock just behind the Yigal Allon Center. Other than a few other boats similar to ours there was very little activity on the lake. I remember reading this once from the pen of George Adam Smith about the Sea of Galilee:

> Where there are now no trees there were great woods; where there are marshes, there were noble gardens, where there is but one boat, there were fleets of sails!

Certainly the Sea of Galilee has changed since the days Peter plied his trade on its waters, and certainly the tourist boat has replaced the fishing boat, but Marnie and I were about to embark on a trip that Jesus took, and that was good enough for us.

The Sea of Galilee is 32 miles in circumference, and lies within the Great Syrian-African Rift Valley. We had now traveled completely around the lake in the last two days. The time had come to return to our cottage by the lake and what better way than to take a boat ride across the widest part of the sea from Ginosar Harbor to En Gev Harbor, a trip of just over seven miles. We would be traveling from the northwest corner of the lake towards the southeast. We would be sailing over the deepest part of the lake, depths reaching 157 feet. We had picked a calm day to make our journey though there was a slight breeze that did ripple the surface just a bit. It was easy to see just how quick the Sea of Galilee could turn into a raging ocean. The lakes in the northern tip of Maine have similar characteristics. I have been caught out on such lakes a number of times while salmon fishing with my father-in-law, Stacy Meister, and the experience is not pleasant. One minute the water is as smooth as glass, and within minutes you are fighting three foot swells all because of the change of the wind direction and speed. We had no such event on our trip, but deep down we all knew that a sudden change in the weather could stirred the sea into a cauldron of fury. (Did secretly we wish it?)

As we got underway (a motorized craft), our boat was filled with not only our group but other tourists making the trek from west to east. The first thoughts that came were these verses about Jesus making a similar trip:

> And when he (Jesus) was entered into a ship, his disciples followed him. And, behold, there arose a great tempest in the sea. . . ." (Matthew 8:23) "And he (Jesus) entered into a ship, and passed over, and came into his own city (Capernaum). (Matthew 9:1)

In the instruction booklet they gave us for our classes in Israel I learned that the predominate winds comes from the west, from the Mediterranean. The strongest wind, however, comes from the Golan in the winter which was probably the case when Jesus and the disciples came up against 'a great wind that blew' (John 6:18). I was told that waves as high as 12 feet have been recorded at Tiberias. For those of us who live on the ocean, those are ocean heights! We know that Jesus was familiar with maritime weather forecasting for he makes mention of them when he was debating with his skeptic about the signs of the times (Matthew 16:1–4).

Halfway across the lake, the operator of the ship stopped the engines and we floated in the middle of the sea for about ten minutes. We could see clearly the outcropping that was the Arbel Cliffs directly to our west. Looking more southwestward we could see Tiberias in the late afternoon haze. To the north we couldn't make out Capernaum or Bethsaida but we knew basically on the shoreline where they could be found and the Lower Golan Heights rose gently upward directly to our east. It was then Greg pointed out a distinctive mount directly in front of the bow about three miles away. It stood out even against the higher hill of Bashan behind it. This was the Decapolis city of Hippus, a dominate town in the region just a few miles from En Gev Resort. I had noticed its distinct cone shaped hill when we drove into the resort, but only on our ride across the Sea of Galilee was its history revealed. Greg said that some believe that this might have been the city Jesus was referring to when he said:

> A city that is set on a hill cannot be hid. (Matthew 5:14)

It certainly stood out as a ruin hilltop. I couldn't imagine what it must have looked like when fully lit up at night. It was just another imagery that now fills my mind when I read Jesus' Sermon on the Mount, and yes, you can make out Hippus on a clear day from Mount Arbel.

As I took in the sights from the middle of the lake, I could understand why Josephus described the landscape around the Sea of Galilee as 'the ambition of nature.' The mild climate, natural beauty, and the presence of therapeutic thermal springs still make it a favorite tourist destination for health and holiday to this day. Eugene Hoade once described the lake like this:

> I believe that there are more beautiful lakes in the world set in a more enchanting surrounding, but I still believe that there is not in the world a more fascinating lake. Look at its azure blue in deep sleep without a ripple on its bosom: the little sailing boats as if just painted on the canvas; not a breath of air to disturb in its waters the great reflections of the surrounding mountains. It is a joy that leads on to hour less contemplation.

And contemplating I was as the engine started up and we headed for a landing just a couple of miles north of our resort. The plan for the evening was a fish fry at a well-known eating establishment in En Gev Harbor. We were to taste Saint Peter's fish, or Musht; sometimes called Peter's perch. The lake was still extremely rich in fish, and according to Greg and Joel this restaurant was the best place to experience Galilee's favorite fish, or was it?

I was having mixed feelings about the special supper for two reasons. After you taste fresh fish from the Gulf of Maine any other fish in the world is second rate at best, and in Maine 'perch' is a trash fish, only used for bait! Second, if we stayed for supper we would miss swimming in the Sea of Galilee. Because we got in late the night before, Marnie and I only had a few minutes to enjoy the warm water of the lake. In the end,

Marnie and I decided to skip supper and swim. Of our group only one other, Ike Spiker, made the same choice. Ike is a diabetic and he knew that he could only swim once in the Sea and this night was that night. So after a 45 minute boat ride across the Sea of Galilee, we walked 35 minutes back to En Gev Resort to enjoy another Galilee sunset and swim. I will never regret our decision to forego a meal of Galilean perch, to the pleasure we had on the beach at En Gev. Marnie, Ike, and I had the place to ourselves for nearly an hour. A few of our comrades who had supper did make it back to watch the sun set behind the Cliffs of Arbel. We talked of our day and the great sights we had seen, and soaked in the sunset and the warm waves lapping in around us. It was then that we learned that the man who had pushed so hard for us eating a supper of fish actually ate pizza!!!!!

71

Completing the Triangle

Matthew 11:20–21—Then began He (Jesus) to upbraid the cities wherein most of his mighty works were done, because they repented not: Woe unto thee, CHORAZIN!

After another pleasant evening at the water's edge on the shore of the Sea of Galilee, Marnie and I retired to our private cabin. Marnie was quick to sleep (two weeks on the go was catching up with her), but I still had plenty of journal work to do before I could rest. I was determined not only to keep a personal record of my observations and opinions, but I was determined to keep a second journal of the information I gleaned from our teachers as well as other information I picked up along the way. The only reason I have been able to compile this book of memories is because of the late nights I spent recording! This is what I finished writing on our 15th day in Israel:

> Tomorrow we make the final climb. We have a 4,000 foot ascent to the base of Mount Hermon (9,232 feet, the highest in the land), and before the day is through we will have found Dan. We are scheduled to go beyond Dan to the Golan Heights (the Old Testament Bashan) along the Syrian border, so this will be the day we reach the northern most corner of Israel just as we reached the southernmost corner of Israel in Eilat.

I went to bed by 10 p.m. and was up by 7 a.m. for our 16th day. By 8 o'clock we had gathered at Joel's bus, and we were off 'to complete the triangle'!

Completing the Triangle 285

On our travels around the northern shore of Israel's inland sea, we stopped at Bethsaida and Capernaum. On our way up the Hula Valley our first stop of the morning would be at Chorazin, the apex of the triangle of Jesus ministry. As with Bethsaida and Capernaum, Chorazin is a massive archeological dig today. Nobody lives there except for a family of conies. Now I understand Solomon's illustration when he wrote:

> The conies are but a feeble folk, yet make they their houses in the rocks. (Proverbs 30:26)

These grey-backed creatures have white bellies with long hair, short tails, and round ears. As we walked around the ancient ruins these groundhog like animals watched us from the rock walls that surround the site. Others see the hare, or rabbit like characteristics, I wonder if they knew the Bible calls them 'unclean'? (Leviticus 11:5) Even the Psalmist uses the conies as example of how God protects the smallest of His creatures, and His mode of refuge the rock (Psalms 104:18); just like us (I Corinthians 10:4)! The conies of Chorazin were in no danger as we walked through their world. We enjoyed watching their heads popping up and out of the stones, rocks that once housed a vital city in the region, but now just a home for hedgehogs!

As with other historical and Biblical sites, we walked to a spot in the ruins where Greg share what he knew of the site. We were given, as with most Israeli national parks, a pamphlet that filled in the details not shared by Greg or John. One of the interesting items we saw on site was a single hand-turned mill. According to the information I learned, Chorazin was renowned for the excellent wheat grown in the area. We also saw ancient olive presses, and other objects (all make of basalt stone) that suggested to us that this town was a major producer of agricultural products. We also saw a ritual bath and the ruins of an ancient synagogue. It was here we saw our first, but not our last example of a stone "Moses Seat" (Matthew 23:2); the place the individual would sit to read the books of Moses. Like with Bethsaida and Capernaum, Chorazin was a large town and a very well laid out community. The village was divided into five quarters with the central quarter containing the synagogue, the remains of three large buildings, and a paved square in the middle of the quarter. From what the archeologists have uncovered, they believe the town was fairly new at the time of Christ and would be lived in until the 16th century. One of the fascinating things to me was the dwellings of ordinary people and how their homes were grouped along family lines. A father would help his son build next door with common walls and in time families would have their own group of buildings sometimes holding a number of generations. According to the Korazim (their spelling) National Park (our 24th park) pamphlet, the first excavations made at Chorazin took place in the early 1900s and they continue to this day. As a matter of fact, there were a few people digging around while we were there. Our stay lasted just under an hour but was well worth our time.

As we left the tel, my mind went back to why Chorazin is Biblically important, a city condemned by Jesus because of their lack of repentance (Luke 10:13). When Jesus cursed Capernaum he invoked the ancient city of Sodom (Matthew 11:23), but when he cursed Bethsaida and Chorazin he mentioned the cities of Tyre and Sidon (Matthew 11:21). I believe this was because of the twin nature of the two Phoenician towns and the parallel of Bethsaida and Chorazin, for they are also located just a few miles apart. Jesus also mentions in the indictment 'the mighty works'. To a people who wanted a sign (I Corinthians 1:22) Jesus went out of his way to show to them through great exploits just who He was. Only God could do what Jesus did and He did what He did more in the 'triangle' than any other region in Israel, and yet they didn't repent. He even makes the point that if the very same works would have been done in Tyre and Sidon they like Nineveh (Jonah 3:6) would have repented 'long ago in sackcloth and ashes.' (Matthew 11:23) This is a telling argument against the attitude of the people of Chorazin. For me it was a message to a people who saw their economy more important than their spiritual wealth. Oh, there was a synagogue there, but was it only for 'show'? We live in a similar time and seem to demonstrate a similar attitude when it comes to the things of Christ. Has there been a more blessed nation on this planet in the last two and a half plus hundred years? Yet what are we more concerned about; our place in the world as the number one economy on the planet? Chorazin certainly has no such place, yet in their little world they were important, and when a 'greater' came along and chose to bless them with His miracles and teachings and, yes, His very presence, yet they did not take advantage of it and for this Jesus said of them:

> But it shall be more tolerable for Tyre and Sidon at the judgment, than for you! (Luke 10:14)

I have come to believe in the judgment of nations and cities as well as individuals. Places (collective decisions) and people will be judged on their actions according to what they did with Christ. Chorazin will one day give an account of the time they had with Christ, as will its citizens. So with them, so with us:

> To whom much is given, much will be required!

Is this still a precept in relationship to Christ? Jesus never visited Sodom, Tyre, or Sidon, but he did visit Bethsaida, Chorazin, and Capernaum and for 'much', they will have to give answer too. As with Capernaum, *"Which art exalted to heaven, shalt be thrust down to hell?"* (Luke 10:15) I believe that Jesus also warns other countries and cities with these words:

> He that heareth you heareth me; and he that despiseth you despiseth me; and he that despiseth me despiseth him that sent me. (Luke 10:16)

We know who Chorazin despised and we know what is left of them today, but America who are you despising? Will one day a study group be touring your rubble and ruin and find only tiny animals living in your homes, churches, and government buildings?

72

Hazor and the Hula Valley

Joshua 11:1—And it came to pass, when Jabin king of HAZOR had heard those things . . .

We left Chorazin a little after nine on the morning of May 26, 2010. Our journey north into the Hula Valley (a region of northeastern Israel 16 miles long and 4 ½ miles wide, rising about 1,000 feet above the Sea of Galilee) followed Route 90. Our next destination was the mighty Canaanite fortress of Hazor, the major city-state that controlled the area in the days of the conquest of Canaan (Joshua 11:10). The king of Hazor would be numbered in Joshua's list of kings and kingdoms he captured (Joshua 12:19).

Within ten miles, we drove into the parking lot for Tel Hazor. From where we parked we could make out the Galilee Mountains. Hazor had been a major crossroad town in the ancient road between the empires to the east and the trade routes to the south. Two major roads linked up at Hazor, the northeast road that joined Israel with Babylon through the Beka'a Valley and the northwest road that joined the trade route through Phoenicia. The fertile land and a natural spring provided the perfect conditions to make Hazor one of the greatest cities in the land, but on the day we arrived the site was almost void of people and the once impressive city was nothing but piles of rubble. The site consists of the discovery of an upper city (the acropolis) and a lower city (the enclosure). The upper section stands on a mount about 120 feet above Hazor Stream. The lower section, just north of the acropolis, is surrounded by an earthen rampart, while the upper is surrounded by stone walls. Here are some bits of history I learned about Hazor:

1. Little is known about Hazor's earliest history. It is first mentioned by name in Egyptian documents from the 18th century BC called the Execration Texts.

2. Hazor's history seems to be divided into two main periods: the Canaanite Hazor and the Israeli Hazor. The Canaanite Hazor seemed to encompass both the upper and lower cities, but the Israeli Hazor only the upper city.

3. During it period of growth, its link to the great empires brought it prosperity. The Mari Archive discovered in a city by the same name on the banks of the Euphrates River speaks of the importance of Hazor on the commercial caravan route between east and west. The Mari documents also mention a king of Hazor by the name of Ibni-Addu, or Jabin. Some feel this is a title because every mention of the king of Hazor in the Bible uses Jabin (Compare Joshua 11:1 and Judges 4:2). Between the manuscript's Jabin and Joshua's Jabin was about three hundred years!

4. Just before the conquest of Joshua the city of Hazor is mentioned in a list of military conquests by the king of Egypt. At the height of its power, Egypt controlled the important cities along the vital trade route. We have already seen Egyptian influence on Megiddo, and Hazor certainly would have been another important conquest in the northern region of Canaan.

5. By the time Joshua saw this city it was at its zenith in power, influence, and development. Archeologists have uncovered massive walls, ramparts, palaces, temples, and dwelling places for perhaps 40,000 people, without a doubt the largest city in Canaan. The gigantic city was filled with pottery, statues, weapons, jewelry, and many other artistic pieces from Syria, Egypt, Babylon, Crete, Cyprus, and as far away as the Hittite and Greek Kingdoms.

6. Biblical history teaches us that Joshua confronted a Canaanite confederacy lead by Hazor after he had brought southern and central Canaan under control (Joshua 11:1–12). The battle took place near the Waters of Merom (most feel in the days of Joshua there was a lake in the Hula Valley just north of Hazor), and after Joshua defeated the combined armies of the north he burned Hazor (Joshua 11:11). Archeological evidence has discovered that this once mighty city had indeed been destroyed by a massive conflagration in both the upper and lower sections of the city.

7. The site was seemingly abandoned for a while, but by the time of the judgeship of Deborah Hazor was once again in dominion of the region. The text also gives us this insight: "And the Lord sold them into the hand of Jabin KING OF CANAAN that reigned in Hazor..." (Judges 4:2) Instead of the king of Hazor, Jabin was king of the whole land. But as before, Hazor was defeated by Barak at the Battle of the Kidron River (Judges 4:15) and once again went into a period of decline and possible abandonment.

8. Its next mention in Scripture was during the days of King Solomon when he fortified Hazor (I Kings 9:15); no doubt to once again control the very rich caravan trade through the region. The city was recaptured during the Assyrian invasion (II Kings 15:29) of Tiglath-Pileser in 732 BC and the citizens that survived were sent into exile.

9. The last mention of Hazor in any historical document is in I Maccabees 11:67 which describes a battle between Jonathan and Demetrius, which takes place on 'the plains of Hazor'; probably around the year 147 BC.

During our tour around this impressive archeological site, we walked through the lower city and entered the upper city through the Solomonic Gate, his trademark six chamber gate. The gate is a carbon copy of the gates at Megiddo and Gezer I Kings 9:15). We then passed on through the palace area of the Canaanite King Jabin. We entered the throne room through a massive door structure. The mud-brick walls could still be seen. We then found the water system and another thrilling experience underground. Hazor's (most feel probably constructed by King Ahab) water system was in three parts: the first part is an access structure that leads to the vertical shaft; then a vertical shaft nearly 150 feet deep (now accessible by five flights of metal stairs); the third part is a nearly 100 foot long sloping tunnel that eventually ends at a small pool filled by ground water. Finally we passed through what they feel was a citadel (a fort within the fortress) until we came to an Israelite tower on the western edge of the tel. The archeologists believe this tower was built just before the Assyrian invasion (II Kings 15:29). Quite a bit of the tower is still standing and from its summit one can see clearly up the Hula Valley. The way the hills to the north wrap around the hills to the west, one can see why this became the important city in the region. Like we learned in the Shephelah, every valley needs a guard city and Hazor was certainly the guard city for the Hula Valley.

As we wandered around the ruins, we also found a cultic 'high place' and a standing stone idol which told us of the other side of Hazor. Hazor was not a godly place in its pre-Israeli days or during the wicked reign of Ahab and Jezebel. Could that be the reason Jeremiah prophesied:

> And Hazor shall be a dwelling for dragons, and desolation for ever: there shall no man abode there, nor any son of man dwell in it. (Jeremiah 49:33)

This is how we found it!!!

73

From Dan . . .

Genesis 14:14—And when Abram heard that his brother was taken captive, he armed his trained servants, born in his own house, three hundred and eighteen, and pursued them unto DAN.

We left the strategic city of Hazor located on a well-defined mount that used to straddle the old international highway near the Jordan River after about an hour of exploration. We could see clearly why Hazor was the first line of defense against any enemies coming down from the north. It was certainly the door into Galilee, and vital to anyone who would control the region. Beside its strategic value, we could also see why it had a huge economic value to whoever owned it.

Our travels took us another ten or so miles northward further into the Hula Valley. We were heading for Tel Dan, but before we could get there Greg and Joel had another stop for the tourists among us. The pitch was we were going to stop at an outlet where we could buy the best sandals, not just in Israel but the world, cheap? Near a place called Ramot Naftali we made a 45-minute stop at the Naot Outlet, and the cheap sandals were not cheap! These very expensive sandals were made in an old kibbutz by highly skilled craftsmen, or so the story went. Marnie and I had noticed that we had made more tourist stops on our five-day northern tour than all the stops we had made in our other twelve days in Israel, or was it just a Joel thing? Yes, Israel has many 'tourist traps' and most of them seem to be in northern Israel. It was nearly noon before we were on the bus again for Tel Dan.

About five miles north of the sandal factory, we left Route 90 for a smaller highway, 977. We crossed the Jordan River again just north of the Hula Valley. We had now entered into the foothills of Mount Hermon. About 105 miles northeast of Jerusalem, we finally arrived at the old borderland of ancient Israel. Now I knew the extent of 'from Dan to Beersheba'; as the crow flies only 150 miles stand between these two distinct Old Testament places. Before we could explore Tel Dan, we had to stop for lunch. Once again I must admit I got a little impatient as we lingered for over an hour at a truck stop just outside Tel Dan Nature Reserve. I spent 25 shekels on some junk food to eat and wondered what we would find behind the tree line. It was by far the thickest forest we had seen, even more forested than Mount Carmel and the Shephelah. If I didn't know better, I was back into the woodlands of Northern Maine. Finally, at 2:45 PM we entered the best natural site we had visited or would visit on this Israeli excursion.

Dan Nature Reserve is a naturalist paradise. A singing brook immediately draws your attention to a stand of trees that literally blocks out the sky—a rare place in Israel. Our plan was to make a walking tour through the reserve following the marked trail that would eventually lead us to Jeroboam's high place (I Kings 12:25–30). Our first steps took us over a small foot bridge across the Dan River. Now before you imagine the Mississippi River or the Hudson River, Dan River is more a brook or a stream to most of us. As with the Jordan River, I never saw it any bigger than a brook, or a creek. So it was with the Dan River. As we walked along its banks, we learned that of the three streams that make up the headwaters of the Jordan River that Dan Brook is the largest and most important. The springs that feed this stream come from the snow melt and rain that falls on Mount Hermon. The water that drops on Hermon seeps into the mountain and comes out in places like Dan. The reserve itself only covers about 120 acres, and despite the attempts to turn the park into a water source (in 1966 there were plans to siphon the water from Dan into the Hula Valley, but in 1969 the conservationists won the debate and Tel Dan Reserve was preserved) it remains in its natural state to this day. Praise the Lord!

Our wandering walk took us through a tree-lined canopy path that gradually lead us upward and deeper into the forest. For the first half mile we pretty much followed the river until we came to Dan Spring. It was here we had our picture taken beside the stream to signify the beginning of the Jordan River. Before our journey would be completed, we would travel the entire length of the Jordan from the foothills of Hermon to the Dead Sea. One of the beautiful sights along the trail was the variety of flora that could be seen. Vibrant colors from these flowering planet and bushes only highlighted the massive Syrian ash behind them. About halfway through our walk to the 'high place', the individuals Marnie and I were with got separated from the main group. Some of us wanted to linger a bit longer at certain places than the others, so it wasn't long before we came to a cross-path and didn't know which way the main group had gone. One of two choices, but as often happens we chose wrong, but for me getting lost in the forest of Dan wasn't a bad thing!

One of the great thrills of this trip was the times when we left the team and ventured out on our own. I knew that we would eventually catch up, but for the time being we had a chance to stroll 'a path less traveled'. After we got back to the main gate of the reserve, we were given a pamphlet of the park. In that pamphlet was a map of the trail system of Tel Dan. It was only later when we got back to En Gev did I discover where we had gone wrong and what we got a chance to see the others didn't. After passing En Dan (Dan Spring), the path forks to the left toward 'the high place' and right towards En Leshem (Leshem Spring), a series of natural springs that literally bubble out of the side of the hill below 'the high place'. We had a chance to witness this amazing flow of water under our feet, and came to understand why this was a favorite site for settlement even long before the Danites showed up. We also passed what they call Pooh Bear's Tree, a massive and picturesque Syrian ash likened to the home of the famous literary bear. We were also in the section of the park they call 'the garden of Eden'. Despite the hot day we were experiencing outside the park, the shade trees and cooling springs made this side trip into the undergrowth pleasant, peaceful, and cool. My tranquility was soon however interrupted by a call that the right path had been found by Professor Hilber.

My biggest regret at Tel Dan was once again time. Our time was limited because, in my opinion, of a wrongful use of our little time in other endeavors, like sandals. Our walk basically took us around the outside of the reserve. Other than the short trip into the heart of the park while we were looking for the right trail, we failed to see the 'flour mill' (a mill built over 150 years before operated by the water of the stream and containing two large millstones), an old Byzantine tunnel (you know of my love of tunnels), and a wading pool, the only place in the park where visitors are allowed to get in the waters of Dan. How 'cool' would that have been to experience? Despite the places we didn't see, and the experiences we didn't get to enjoy, the trip through a forest by a stream was added to the other fabulous adventures Marnie and I had on this trip. One of my favorite family photographs of Israel is of Marnie and me standing on the bank of Dan Stream. Next to our picture at Masada, our Dan picture is a favorite. Who says you can't find peace of heart and mind and soul in a forest by a brook?

I recommend Tel Dan Nature Reserve!

74

The High Place At Dan

I Kings 12:28–29—Whereupon the king (Jeroboam) took counsel, and made two calves of gold. . . . And he set the one in Bethel, and the other, even unto DAN.

They tell us that around 930 BC, Jeroboam, the first king of the northern ten tribes of Israel after the split with the Kingdom of David, built one of two high places for his version of the 'god' that brought the Jews out of Egypt. If this sounds familiar it is! When Moses tarried on Mount Sinai while getting the famous tables of stone with the ten commandments written on them by the very finger of God (Exodus 31:18), the people got impatient and tempted Aaron into making an image of their God. The result was a golden calf (Exodus 32:1–6). Aaron even built an altar to set the calf on, just like Jeroboam. It was Jeroboam's way of keeping the people at home, and under his control, and the two shrines were the boundary of his land—from Dan to Bethel. Jeroboam set up his own priesthood, and the perversion was finished with the one and only true God being carved into 'a god' that looked like a cow! The Apostle Paul described this wickedness this way:

> Because that, when they knew God, they glorified him not as God, neither were thankful; but became vain in their imaginations, and their foolish heart was darkened. Professing themselves to be wise, they became fools, and changed the glory of the un-corruptible God into an image made like to corruptible man, and to birds, and four-footed beasts (calves), and creeping things! (Romans 1:21–23)

The High Place At Dan

By the time we caught up with our group, they had already arrived at the exposed 'high place of Dan'. But before I share with you my impressions of this well-defined area, let me highlight and underline the history of Dan from the first Jewish settlement to the time of Jeroboam's golden calf. Do you remember your Dan history?

1. Dan was first a Sidonian town called Laish at the northern extremity of Canaan (Judges 18:7) just west of Mount Hermon. The same city as Leshem according to Joshua 19:47.
2. When the Danites were unable to conqueror their own allotted territory in the south, they sought a new land (Judges 18:14) and settled on the town of Laish and the surrounding area (Judges 18:27-29).
3. This became the northern boundary of the Kingdom of Israel (II Samuel 3:10).
4. This was one of the first towns to fall when foreign powers (Syria) began to invade the land (I Kings 15:20). Instead of being well protected in the heart of the land, their original allotment, Dan chose to go out on its own to the edge of the Promised Land, and become the first to face and fall to foreign invaders.
5. And of course, it's only real call to fame was the site of one of Jeroboam's golden calves (II Kings 10:29).

Dan ought to be a warning to any who would believe or even imagine that God doesn't know best—both in the present and in the future.

And sure enough, there on a high knoll overlooking the border with Lebanon was a large area surrounded by stone walls. We walked through a stone gate and before us was the actual altar area. The archeologists believe the stonework is of the Jeroboam period of history. We could clearly see the surrounding buildings that were created to house this sacrificial high place. The experts believe that in the entire time this site was used for the purpose of worshipping the golden calf these stones were in use. As the shrine increased in popularity with other kings, the people simply added more walls, chambers, and courtyards. The altar we saw stood in front of an elevated platform created out of well chiseled rocks. To give tourists an idea where and what the altar looked like they have created a metal frame that was similar to the original stone altar. Despite the capture of Dan by foreign armies, the place remained a worship site into the Hellenistic period. The archeologists discovered an inscription in both Greek and Aramaic which reads: "to the god who is in Dan". Some feel that the shrine was used into the Roman era.

After walking around the site, we next followed the trail to what is called in the park pamphlet 'the command-post lookout'. There just above the 'high place' was a series of trenches that could be traced back to the earliest days of Israeli independence (1948). From the top of the ridge we could see into Southern Lebanon (the border was just a few miles away) to the northwest and the border with Syria to the northeast. According to the history given to us, the Israeli Defense Forces used the post until the famous Six-Days War of 1967. Because this was the first actual trench system I had ever had a chance to walk through, I took advantage of the opportunity. However, I was so excited to get into the trench that I didn't watch my head and within a few feet I smashed my head into an iron rod that periodically crosses over the trench. Despite the gash on the top of my head, and yes, a bit of blood, I was not discouraged from finishing a walk through the system; which included a bunker about half way through. By the time Marnie (who also hit her head) and I and a few others got through we were once again alone. The rest of the group had headed towards the ruins of the actual town of Dan.

As we worked our way down off the high place of Dan, we once again encountered massive trees and beautiful flowering bushes and shrubs. Eventually, we caught up with the group that had stopped in the Israelite Gate. What caught my eye first were the smooth stones that made up most of the walls that remained of the old city. The street or lane leading up to the gate was also stone, the best cobblestone walk I had seen since Jerusalem on Herod's Street. We were shown a judge's seat, a place by the entrance were people would come to find justice. I immediately remembered that Lot held such a position in Sodom (Genesis 19:1) and that is where Boaz went (Ruth 4:1) to settle the issue with Ruth. Most of us got our pictures taken sitting in the gate of Dan. We were told that an archeological team began digging in 1966 lead by a Professor Avraham Biran, and that it was that team that had uncovered the city site as well as the ritual site that dated back to the events described in the Bible. The earliest findings placed human activity at Dan at 2700 BC. One of the historically important discoveries at Dan was a fossilized tablet with the name of Hazael of Damascus on it boasting of his victory over the king of Israel and the house of David (they say that this was the first time the words 'house of David' were found outside the Biblical account). This was the very king Elijah was appointed to anoint (I Kings 19:15, 17)! Could this be the same Hazael of II Kings 8:29 and II Kings 9:14? More of God's Word coming alive!

Our last stop at Dan was a short walk up to the Canaanite gate. They have dated this gate from the days of Abraham (1800 BC). The gate is still intact after all these years, and is considered one of the oldest complete arches in the world. The site is so fragile they have built a steel dome over it to protect it from eroding. Made out of bricks, the gate and wall was the best we saw in our travels, and to think Abram might have passed through it on his travels from Haran to the Promised Land? Was that the reason Abram knew where to find the Army of Chedorlaomer after his nephew Lot had been captured? (Genesis 14:13-14).

75

Caesarea Philippi

Matthew 16:13 — When Jesus came into the coasts of CAESAREA PHILIPPI, he asked his disciples, saying, Whom do men say that I the Son of man am?

Dan continued to be inhabited until the Roman period in Canaan, and then it was abandoned with the center of the settlement moving to Banias, or Caesarea Philippi, our next stop on our northern study tour of Israel.

Within a few miles due east of Tel Dan Nature Reserve, we drove into the ancient worship center for the god Pan during the Hellenistic Period. Sometimes called Panias (Banias is the Arabic spelling), the site today is just a tourist stop, but at one time it was an active center of pagan worship. Small niches in the rock face once contained the imagines of the god Pan; the images are gone but the niches remain to this day. The most impressive aspect of the tel is a large cave; once considered the entrance to underworld! Besides the temple area and the stream that once flowed out of the cave mouth, the region is known for a famous military battle in which the Seleucid king Antiochus III won an important battle over Ptolemy IV of Egypt for control of the vital area in 198 BC. This battle set the stage for the oppression of the Jews by Antiochus IV and the famous revolt of the Maccabees. Some see Antiochus as a type of the Anti-Christ because he was the one that defiled the Altar at the Jerusalem Temple that provoked the revolt of the Maccabees brothers. During the time of Christ, Herod Philippi (Herod the Great's son) rebuilt the site. It became Philippi's capital. Remember, when Herod the Great died his kingdom was divided up between his sons. Philippi got the northern tetrarchy (Luke 3:1). Originally, the city was called Caesarea after the Roman emperor, but it eventually was known as Caesarea Philippi (Philippi's Caesarea) to distinguish it from other cities by the same name. Caesarea Philippi seems to mark the northernmost limit of Jesus ministry (Mark 8:27) as well.

It was mid-afternoon when we stepped off the bus into the lush terrain around Caesarea Philippi. What impressed me most was the volume of water coming out from under the rock face just below the temple site. We were told that after an earthquake, the flow of water changed from the mouth of the cave to small springs from under the hill. Banias Stream does materialize before your eyes into a wide brook that helps to feed the Jordan River just a few miles away. We walked along a concrete path to a shady area for our introduction lecture on Caesarea Philippi. As the others waited for Greg to start, I spotted a fish in the stream. The water coming down Banias Stream was as clear as any I have ever seen. It reminded me of a favorite salmon stream in Washington County, Maine. Grand Lake Stream is one of the best landlock salmon fisheries in the world. Known for its fly fishing only, the crystal clear water draws fishermen from all over the world to try their skills on a very aggressive, but illusive fish. What makes the stream so appealing to fishermen like me is that it is one of those rare places you can literally stock your prey. The water is so clear you literally can pick out the salmon even in deep water. Banias Stream didn't seem deep, but the trout of Banias could be easily seen. A group of them were hanging near some small rocks just beside the bank where Greg was giving his lecture. I am afraid I didn't hear much. I took some of the nicest pictures of fish in the water I have ever taken! Oh, for a fly rod and a few flies. The banks were void of trees or any other obstacles, an ideal situation for casting a fly!

Soon we had to move on to the raised platform that once housed Pan's Temple. You could see the huge amount of work it must have taken to carve the platform out of the solid rock of the cliff face. We walked up the stairs into the well laid out area. We could make out the outline of rooms, and a picture with an artist conception of how it might have been only helped us picture the vast temple area that once rested beside the huge cave mouth. It was then I began to imagine why Jesus would have brought His disciples here to take the first public opinion poll in history:

Who do men say that I the Son of man am?

There was a variety of answers, "Some say that thou art John the Baptist: some, Elias; and others, Jeremias, or one of the prophets" (Matthew 16:14). As with most polls the answered were varied, but Jesus also wanted to know what their answer would be—"But, whom say ye that I am?" (Matthew 16:15). It was then Peter came to the forefront, and just maybe, put himself into the leadership position of the disciple band. There in the shadow of the statue of a pagan god Peter made his confession of Christ's deity; Jesus was God!

It was then that Jesus handpicked Peter to lead His Church after His departure back to His Father. It was this statement: "Thou art the Christ, the Son of the Living God" (Matthew 16:16). that provoked Jesus to first speak of His Church:

> That thou art Peter, and upon this rock I will build My church; and the gates of hell shall not prevail against it. (Matthew 16:18)

For me the doctrine of the Church begins here. The foundation of the Church is built on this simple statement, yet if we take time to ponder what Jesus was saying we can glean from it the very cornerstone of truth that began the Church. Some misunderstand 'upon this rock'. Some feel it is speaking of Peter (John 1:42), but Cephas means stone not rock! Others feel that Jesus was speaking of the very site, for certainly Caesarea Philippi was built on a rock, a massive rock, a foothill of Mount Hermon. We will not say Jesus' Church didn't include Caesarea Philippi, but if you are to choose a place where the Church began you would have to name Jerusalem (Acts 1:8). I have no doubt that the Rock Jesus was speaking about was Himself (I Corinthians 10:4). Rock is a name and description given to Jesus and Paul teaches us that it all started with Him:

> For other foundation can no man lay than that is laid, which is Christ Jesus. (I Corinthians 3:11)

Paul also taught, "And are built upon the foundation of the apostles (including Peter) and prophets, Jesus Christ Himself being the chief corner stone" (Ephesians 2:20).

I also love the imagery Jesus used when He spoke of 'the gates of hell shall not prevail against it (church)'. There beside the mouth of a cave that some believed was the entrance into hell itself, He promised His disciples that they would even conqueror here. This pagan place would not resist their onslaught. Remember, as a professor of mine once taught me, gates don't attack, they are attacked. Jesus was speaking of the offensive nature of His Church. We have forgotten this today. We seem to be a more defensive church than the offensive juggernaut we ought to be. Instead of attacking the Caesarea Philippi's of the world we are holed up in our temples awaiting the assault of the world. There in the heart of a pagan town, Jesus was calling his troops to battle. It is interesting, that it was at Caesarea Philippi that Jesus began to tell His closest followers of His up and coming death (Matthew 16:21). The road to Calvary began at Caesarea Philippi as far as the disciples knew it. I was impressed with the place, not because of the remains of an ancient pagan temple area, or the impressive stream that flowed from it. I was impressed because I finally had a visible understanding of Jesus classic sermon at Caesarea Philippi:

> Upon this rock I will build my church!

76

Viewing Mount Hermon from the Golan Heights

Deuteronomy 3:8–9—And we took at that time out of the hand of the two kings of the Amorites the land that was on this side Jordan, from the river of Arnon unto MOUNT HERMON; which HERMON the Sidonians call Sirion; and the Amorites call it Shenir.

We left Caesarea Philippi just after four on the afternoon of our 16th day in Israel. It was time to start our descent back to En Gev by way of the Golan Heights. In order to gain the summit of the famous heights, we traveled eastward along Route 98 towards a town called Masada (not the famous hilltop fortress by the Dead Sea). It was here we would take a southern track along the spine of the Golan Heights.

The verse by the hand of Moses that I have printed above is repeated by the hand of Joshua in his recording of the conquest of Canaan (Joshua 12:1). Before Israel ever crossed the Jordan, the armies of Israel under the command of Moses through his general Joshua brought under subjection all the city-states from Moab to the south to Bashan to the north and all the way to Mount Hermon. Because little is written of this campaign, we sometimes miss the truth that long before the west bank of the Jordan was captured the east bank of the Jordan had been subdued all the way north to the highest mountain in the region, the 9,232-foot Mount Hermon (which means prominent or rugged). This was the large area asked for and given to the tribes of Gad, Reuben, and half of the tribe of

Manasseh (Numbers 32:1–5). Mount Hermon is the crowning jewel of the northeastern border of Israel today. Now I can see why after the Yom Kippur War of 1973 that Israel kept these heights. To the west of Hermon is Lebanon and to the west Syria, two of Israel's Arab enemies. Whosoever controls the heights of Bashan and the hill of Hermon controls the region!

Mount Hermon rises majestically above the ancient cities of Dan and Caesarea Philippi. As we traveled along the narrow foothill road, we watched in awe as the mountain came into view rising high above us, certainly the highest mountain we had seen on our trip. What makes Hermon so impressive is the suddenness of it rise. In the State of Maine we too have a Mount Hermon we call Katahdin (5,268 feet). Half the size of Hermon, Katahdin is awe inspiring because it rises unexpectedly from the very low surrounding hills. You come around a corner and there it is rising nearly a mile above you. I have seen this mountain from all sides having traveled around it to some favorite fishing spots, and when I saw Mount Hermon I knew they were alike. Most high mountains have other high mountains around them, but Katahdin and Hermon have no equals anywhere near them. They stand alone. Is there any wonder that in the Bible Mount Hermon symbolizes beauty, fertility, and plenty? When the Psalmist was writing of the fullness of the creation of God, he uses Hermon as an example (Psalms 89:12). When David was writing of the blessings of God, he wrote of 'the dew of Hermon' (Psalms 133:3). When Solomon was writing of his beloved spouse, he invoked 'the top of Hermon' (Song of Solomon 4:8). We didn't get a chance to climb to the top, but we were able to see the top. There was no snow left, but I have seen pictures. The source of the Jordan and the life it brings to the Promised Land is all because of this 'high mountain'.

Check the context of Matthew 16 and Jesus' trip to Caesarea Philippi with his disciples and these words:

> And after six days Jesus taketh with him Peter, and James, and John, and leadeth them up into *a high mountain* apart by themselves: and was transfigured before them. (Mark 9:2)

Was that 'high mountain' Hermon? Tradition places the site of the transfiguration on Mount Tabor, but Tabor is only a 1,850 foot hill compared to Hermon at 9,232 feet. I now have seen both 'mounts', and because nobody can be sure it comes down to this classic precept of Paul:

> Let every man be fully persuaded in his own mind.
> (Romans 14:5)

As for me, I believe it was on the top of Mount Hermon that Jesus meet with Elijah and Moses, and it was there they spoke of his coming 'departure'-"decease", the Greek work for 'exodus' (Luke 9:30-31). Most miss this word and replace it with death. Remember, even Paul used 'departure' instead of death in his eulogy (II Timothy 4:6). It was on Mount Hermon that Peter tried to persuade the Lord to stay (Mark 9:5), but was rebuked by the Almighty Himself when a voice from out of a cloud said, "This is My Beloved Son: hear him!" (Mark 9:7) Peter had so quickly lost focus. Just six days before in Caesarea Philippi Peter had proclaimed that Jesus was the Christ, God's anointed one, but now less than a week later Peter wanted a mountaintop experience instead of a hill called Mount Calvary! I believe that it was at the foot of Mount Hermon that Jesus healed the lunatic (Matthew 17:14–20), and taught his other disciples the value of fasting and prayer (Matthew 17:21).

For about a half an hour we were able to see the mighty mountain up close and personal as we wound our way around its foothills. From the window of our bus, we looked upward against the rocky crags of its southern slope. One of the impressive sites that was pointed out to us was a distinct mount called Nimrod's Fortress. Not to be confused with the Nimrod (Genesis 10:8–10) of the Bible, this was a castle built by a Moslem to control the region during the Islam invasion. I also learned that we were only 120 miles from Jerusalem and that another name for Hermon was Sion (Deuteronomy 4:48), not to be confused with Zion. It was then that we turned our backs on Hermon and headed south along Route 98 into the land of Bashan. I must admit I looked over my shoulder a couple of times to take a few final glimpses at Hermon and the land of the Hermonites and I said with the Psalmist:

> O my God, my soul is cast down within me: therefore I remember Thee from the land of Jordan, and of the Hermonites, from the hill of Mizar (most feel a hill near Mount Hermon, maybe, Nimrod's hill). (Psalms 42:6)

What made my heart so sad was for the first time I realized that my travels in Israel were coming to an end. As we made the turn southward, I realized that I had now covered the Promised Land from north to south- from Dan to Beersheba and beyond. I would be going no further in either direction and that within a short three days I would be leaving this fabled land. I didn't want to go. I didn't want this trip to end but it was. Mount Hermon became for me a symbol of the height, the zenith of the trip. I still had a number of great spiritual adventures ahead of me, and I had certainly enjoyed the grand times we had already shared; but when I lost sight of Hermon, I knew the end was near. It was then I realized why Peter asked what he asked, for I too wanted to stay. I spoke of my home state mountain Katahdin earlier in this memory. What I never told you is the quest of most to climb it. Along the east coast of the United States is a famous trail called the Appalachian Trail which stretches from Georgia in the south to Maine in the north; a path that snakes its way through the Appalachian Mountain Range? Over two thousand miles long, this trail is the ultimate challenge for the avid hiker. While Marnie and I was in Israel, a young girl in our church, Sarah Carter, was hiking the Appalachian Trail alone! The trail ends at the summit of Mount Katahdin. I have yet to make the climb though I had my chances, but preferred fishing instead of climbing each time I have come close to its slopes. On our travels around Mount Hermon, I didn't have the opportunity to make the climb, but if I ever have another chance I will. I can' wait to see the view from the top like Peter did, and experience my own 'transfiguration'!

77

The New Bulls of Bashan

Psalms 22:12—Many bulls have compassed me: strong BULLS OF BASHAN have beset me round.

We had seen them first in Tel Aviv at the Ben Gurion Airport standing like sentinels guarding our entrance into the country. Next we encountered them in groups of four at various places in Jerusalem, like New Gate and on the Via Dolorosa. We were surprised to see them again in Jericho, on the West Bank, forgetting that despite the West Bank being under the authority of the Palestinians; it was still under the control of the Israeli Army. Within forty-eight hours, we would come face to face with another four-man patrol on the top of Mount Gerizim and be ordered to leave. Throughout our sixteen days in Israel we had seen the Israeli soldier in small numbers, but on the Golan (Golan was a city given to the sons of Gershom (I Chronicles 6:71) for a Levitical town in Bashan and was also named one of the three refuge cities (Joshua 20:8) on the east side of the Jordan) Heights we found them in great numbers. We saw military base after military base as we traveled Route 98 to Route 91. We saw warning signs for mine fields all along our highway, and field after field where army maneuvers had been held. We saw no tanks of their famous Armor Divisions, but were told that on other such tours many had been observed traveling through the rolling knolls of the Golan. What we did see were the offspring of the 'bulls of Bashan', and it hit me as we traveled through the ancient land of Bashan a new breed of 'bull' now inhabits the land now known as the Golan Heights.

Over sixty times the name Bashan is mentioned in the Bible. It was the old Amorite kingdom of King Og, the last of a race of giants (Deuteronomy 3:11) that once inhabited the land from Mount Hermon to the north to the land of Gilead in the south. "The way of Bashan" (Numbers 21:33) was part of the famous 'King's Highway', the ancient trade route that ran down the east side of the Jordan. Before the Israelites crossed the Jordan in front of Jericho, they conquered this land to leave no enemies at their back. The land was eventually given to the half tribe of Manasseh (Joshua 22:7) as their allotted piece of the Promised Land. Besides being known for its gigantic king (his coffin was 13 feet long and 6 feet wide—Deuteronomy 3:11), the land of Bashan was famous for its massive oak trees (comparable to the cedars of Lebanon—Isaiah 2:13), and its animals. The broad plateau was known in the Bible as a great country for grazing (Numbers 32:4). Renowned among its animal husbandry were its rams (Deuteronomy 32:14) and its bulls (Ezekiel 39:18). As we traveled southward through the middle of Bashan, there beside the road was a reminder of the military importance of the 'heights'. There sitting alongside the highway was the turret of a Russian made T-55 tank. I was excited when Joel pulled his bus into an overlook rest area just a hundred yards north of the military artifact.

The Arab-Israeli conflicts started shortly after the Second World War when the British mandate in Palestine began to wane. Between 1945 and 1948 Israel struggled to create an independent state in the heart of an Arab Middle East. The Israeli War of Independence demonstrated the importance of IDF (Israeli Defense Force) both in the struggle for a sovereign nation as well as a means to hang onto that nation in the increasing hostility of its neighbors. In 1956, the region exploded in what history would call the Suez Crisis. This war was fought mainly between Israel (with Israel being helped by France and England) and Egypt, but despite the capture of the Sinai Peninsula international pressure put the borders back where they were before the war (March of 1957). By 1967, the Israeli Armed Forces realized that it was about to be attacked from three sides: Syria to the north, Jordan to the east, and Egypt to the south. In a lighting preemptive six-day campaign, the Israeli Army and Air Force destroyed the Egyptian Air Force on the ground and easily occupied the Sinai for a second time with equipment superior in every way to their enemy's forces. At the same time other elements of the IDF occupied Jordan territory on the west side of the Jordan (the infamous West Bank today), and defeated a Syrian invasion into the Golan Heights. It was also during this war that Jerusalem came under the control of Israel for the first time in two millenniums. I have come to believe that in June of 1967 'the times of the Gentiles' (Luke 21:24) ended. And then there was 1973, the Yon Kippur (the Jewish holiday that celebrates the Day of Atonement—Leviticus 16:29–34) War.

This time it was the Israeli Armed Forces that were caught by a surprise two-pronged attack by her neighbors. From the south Egyptian forces crossed the Suez Canal into the Sinai and at the same time a massive Syrian force struck northern Israel at the Golan Heights on October 6, 1973. It took three times longer (18 days) than in 1967, but eventually both fronts were stabilized and a cease-fire was negotiated on October 24, 1973. Syria's attempt to recapture (lost in 1967) the Golan Heights ended in a bloody defeat because of the better training and more determined aggressiveness of the Israeli mechanized units. The masses of Soviet tanks (1,500) proved to be no substitute for the better American and Israeli equipment used against them. Even when a force of 300 Iraqi and Jordanian tanks tried to stop the Israeli advance on Damascus half way through the battle, the outcome was the same. The main battle of that war on the Golan Heights took place at 'the valley of tears' between October 7 and 9. When I returned home I got out my military battle books and discovered that the Damascus Road observed on that late afternoon in May of 2010 was in the very middle of that battlefield! By 1982, Egypt would regain the Sinai Peninsula from Israel, but Israel has yet to give back the Golan Heights. As we stood on the turret of that old Soviet tank and looked down on the Damascus Road (the ancient city was only twenty miles away and they told us on a clear day you can see it from where we were standing)), I could see clearly the advantage the occupier of the ridge had against any attack from the east.

But as I stood on that knoll overlooking the border with Syria, I thought of another battle that was fought not far away on that very road. Saul had just gotten permission from the Jewish leadership to take his campaign against the Church to Damascus.

> Breathing out threatenings and slaughters against the disciples of the Lord. (Acts 9:1)

Saul journeyed up the road we were looking at to make a frontal attack on the infant church at Damascus. And just as the IDF did to the Syrians, Jordanians, and Iraqi armies Jesus met Saul on that road and stopped his aggressive advance cold. In an amazing turn-around, the main general for the opposition defected. I have often preached it would have been as if General Robert E. Lee would have switched sides at the height of the Battle of Gettysburg! Instead of arriving in Damascus as the Church's warring enemy, he arrived as its newest convert. I was reminded of two promises of God as I stood transfixed on the battlefield in the Valley of Tears; that God has promised to protect his people, the Jews (Genesis 12:3), and He has and continues to do so, and that He has promised to protect His Church as well:

> If God be for us, who can be against us? (Romans 8:31)

78

A Final Salute to En Gev

Matthew 10:12—And when ye come into an house, SALUTE IT.

Our trip off the Golan Heights took us down Route 98 until we came to the crossroad town of Ein Zivan where be turned southwest onto Route 91. We followed Route 91 just before another crossing of the Jordan River near the junction of Route 91 and Route 888. This road took us directly southward along the Jordan River until we came to Bethsaida. We had finished another circle in our travels through Israel. It was just a short ride down Route 92 to reach our Galilean Resort at En Gev. We had dropped nearly 4,300 feet in elevation and we could feel the difference in the air as we left the bus and walked to our cabin. The climate on the summit of the Golan Heights was cooler, but that doesn't mean that the wind of the Sea of Galilee wasn't also pleasant. Supper was scheduled for 6:30, so we had a chance to get a short nap and refresh ourselves before our final evening on the shores of the Sea of Galilee.

One of the great aspects of staying in the same place for three-straight days is the down time that is possible. Instead of packing each night, and unpacking the same day, you get a chance to be still and ponder what you have experienced. Instead of rushing about, you can take the time to mediate on what you've seen and heard. Overlooking the Sea of Galilee I rethought through our 16th day and the joys of Dan and Banias. Covered in woodland green instead of the desert brown of the south, the gurgling sound of water and waterfall were wonderful to my ears. The song of stream and spring could still be heard as I listened to the rolling of the waves onto the beach at En Gev. I loved the natural sanctuary that was Dan, tucked into the sloping foothills of Mount Hermon. I know the first to inhabit (Canaanites) the region of Hermon worshipped the water gods and later the Greeks came to dedicate Banias to the cult of Pan, another god of nature. How sad it is when mankind fails to see the God of creation, and can only see the creation. For me, I heard again the hills declaring the glory of God (Psalms 19:1) and the headwaters of the Jordan showing His handiwork. Eventually, God had enough of the pagan worship and destroyed the area with an earthquake. When will we ever learn?

One of my regrets on our northern trek was not being able to visit Nimrod's Castle. After I got back to the States I learned that in 1130 AD the Crusaders moved into the region and captured the fortress of Subeiba (Nimrod's Castle). The hill-top fort was built, according to local legend, by the first king of Babel (Genesis 11:1–9) Nimrod of Biblical fame, but historians believe it was constructed by a convert to Islam. Interestingly, after the Crusaders were kicked out of the area the fortress fell into the hands of a secret sect called the Hashshashin. At the heart of this sect was the taking of hashish. The addiction to the drug made its members experts in political murder. Their very name became synonymous with assassinations; where we actual get our word assassin. I can verify that the imposing remains of the fortress can still be seen to this day, and it stands as a silent witness to the mysterious and fascinating past of the northeast corner of the Israel.

After another typical Jewish supper, Marne and I were off to enjoy our final swim in the Sea of Galilee. As with the previous two evening, we were the first from our group to reach the seashore. The water was as nice as before, and the sun was still high in the western sky. We would have over an hour to bask in the site and sea that is the beach of En Gev. After a quick dip, I pulled a beach chair into the surf. I sat down and got great pleasure out of the waves cascading over my sore feet and tired legs. As I treasured the gentle breeze and the warm surf, I thought again of our trip from Mount Hermon (snowcapped from November to March) to the Lower Golan. Again it wasn't until after I got home that I learned a bit more of this vital area of Israel. Famous for its fertility, over twenty Jewish settlements (kibbutz) have been established on its heights since it came under the control of Israel after the 1967 war. Alongside these Israeli farmers are a few Druse and Circassian farmers that stayed after the Syrian withdrawal. It seems that we passed through some of their villages on our way back to En Gev. It was a dream trip, but as with all such adventures, they have to end!

Marnie and I and a few of our traveling companions stayed on the beach at En Gev until the sun had slipped once again behind Mount Arbel. What made this sunset so special was the fact that the moon rose from behind the Golan Heights minutes after the sun had set. It was one of those unique events that I have enjoyed a number of times in my life. I still remember the first time I witnessed such a celestial happening. I was setting beside another lake, but this one was in the deep woods of Northern Maine. I was lake trout fishing with a group of young men (I was the oldest) from our church at Alagash Lake. The spruce trees were high blocking out the eastern and western sky, but there through the branches a full moon came up shortly after the sun had set behind the ridge on the opposite side of the massive lake. The heavenly glow bathed our entire campsite in its warm reflection of the sun. Such was the case at En Gev as Marnie and I walked back to our small cabin. I have in my picture collection of our Israel trip the two photographs back to back of a sunset over Arbel and a moonrise over En Gev.

I chose carefully the verse I have printed for you at the head of this chapter. The context of the Scripture is Jesus' instructions to His disciples as they went out to minister before him. He was giving them instruction of how they were to react to the places they visited, and what their response would be concerning those who would welcome them and those who would not. They were to place a blessing on the places that received them (Matthew 10:13), and a cure on those who wouldn't receive them. It is in this cure the famous exhortation of 'shake off the dust off your feet' (Matthew 10:14) is invoked. I could only find one occasion in which this was actually practiced. When Paul and Barnabas left Iconium they 'shook off the dust off their feet' (Acts 13:51)! It was also in this admonition Jesus repeated again the warning of Sodom and the Day of Judgment (Matthew 10:15) we had seen at Bethsaida, Chorazin, and Capernaum. I am happy to report that I performed no such ritual at En Gev. If anything I wanted to take the place with me. The peaceful sanctuary that was the En Gev Resort was by far the best place we stayed in all of Israel. I have highlighted our various stops and most were wonderful and special in their own way, but if only one can be chosen for the 'best' then En Gev was the best. For me it was the private cabin and the lakeside location that put it over the top.

So here is my final salute to the solitude and serenity of a cottage by a sea. It will remain until I return to the Promised Land the best home we had for the three wonderful days we explored the Galilee. The staff was pleasant and helpful. The accommodations were homey and comfortable. The food was enjoyable and plentiful. The scenery was spectacular and satisfying. The water was warm and worth wading. The sunsets were unforgettable and the surf was therapeutic. The company was family and friendly. The next morning the goodbye was heartfelt and sad. I took the dust in my shoes with me when I departed the En Gev Resort on the Sea of Galilee!

79

A Baptism at the Jordan River

Matthew 3:13 — Then cometh Jesus from Galilee to JORDAN unto John, to be BAPTIZED of Him.

Our last night at En Gev was restful and relaxing. There was time to kick back and enjoy the warm breeze from the Sea of Galilee. Marnie and I were both in bed by nine and we were able to sleep in an extra thirty minutes. Our 17th day in Israel would be slow paced with just a few stops on the schedule. We would be outside of Jerusalem before the sun would set; a trip of just over 100 miles. We woke to a few sprinkles, a rarity on our travels, and a shift in the wind. Instead of blowing from the Mediterranean, the wind was coming directly off the Jordanian Plateau. We were warned that probably before the day was through we would experience a dust storm. I woke with the reality that within three days we would be back in Texas and within five days I would be back in Maine!

After the seven o'clock breakfast Marnie and I returned to our cottage to finish packing. My suitcase was getting a bit full so I took the opportunity to throw away a few things I wouldn't be returning to the States with. By 8:30 AM, we were loading Joel's bus for the last time on this trip. Just before we left En Gev, we were given our test papers from the first two quizzes. I got 89 on the first and 70 (as an excuse most of the questions I missed on the test had to do with geology, not a strength of mine) on the second; pretty sad when you consider that the Bible has been my life for the last 40 years. It just reminded me that I still had a lot to learn about God's Word. We were on the road before nine, but hadn't gone very far when we stopped for coffee; another one of those wasted times for me, but we did have many on the trip that needed their morning start-up juice, especially Greg. While we were waiting for the coffee click, we were told that our first stop would be at the Jordan for a baptism. The secret had been kept from us until then, but I was excited to think I could witness this highlight of the Christian faith at the actual Jordan River.

Being a minister of the Gospel for nearly forty years, I have had the privilege of participating in numerous baptisms since my own in 1964. The thrill of actually baptizing somebody is one of the great joys of pastoring. Despite the fact it is difficult to baptize all year around in the northern hemisphere, I still enjoy the outdoor baptism best. In a stream or a lake, the experience is more Jordan-like than in the baptistery of a church. My best experience at a baptism took place in 2006 when I was asked to participate in an Indian baptism. It was my first trip to India and to be given the honor of actually baptizing someone was beyond a thrill. It became even more meaningful when I saw the venue for the baptism. For me, at that time, it seemed like the Jordan. On January 15, 2006, nearly two hundred people walked nearly a mile in 100 degree temperatures to a small stream just outside the village of Edayappara, Kerala. The palm trees and other tropical plants that grew along the banks of Big Stream appeared to me just like the pictures I had seen of the Jordan River. That morning I baptized six individuals 'in the name of the Father, and of the Son, and of the Holy Ghost' (Matthew 28:19), of the nearly twenty-five that were baptized that morning. When we finally arrived at the Yardenit Baptismal Center, I felt like I had already been there.

We parked the bus in a huge parking lot near the main entrance into the site. There were ripening date trees surrounding the area, the best I had seen up to that time. The place we had stopped was called Kibbutz Kinneret. We were told that a Christian organization from the United States had developed the site to give Christian pilgrims a place to baptize in Israel. The grounds were well maintained, and the complex ran for hundreds of yards along the Jordan. As you walked into the center, a concrete wall on your right had the baptism of Jesus from the Matthew account recorded on the wall in various languages. I got a picture of Marnie by the Greek inscription (Marnie had taken Greek that year at Dallas Theological), and I can still hear the excitement in her voice when she said, "Bubby, I can read this!" I am afraid, however, that from that point on my experience at the Yardenit went downhill.

As with so many of the Christian religious sites we had visited, the Yardenit was nothing but a commercialization of 'baptism'. There were shops for buying things, and the actual baptisms we witnessed before Julie's baptism had more of a country fair atmosphere than the solemn and serious nature of a Christian Baptism. Some of the tourists were getting into the Jordan and baptizing themselves. Some were swimming in their white robes. Instantly, a sore spirit descended on my soul. We wandered around watching this display as we waited for Julie Waters and Dr. Hilber to come out from the dressing rooms. Granted, the Jordan was easy flowing and the tree-lined banks were appealing. There were beautiful flower pots everywhere, and the song of the bird only added to the pleasant surroundings. What I couldn't get over were the scores of people frolicking in the baptismal areas. There seemed to be no orderliness (I Corinthians 14:40) to it all, and I am not one to judge the heart intent of another, but I did question what kind of message this might be giving to someone who wasn't a believer?

Within ten minutes, Julie Waters and Dr. Hilber emerged and we followed them down to the water's edge. The creators of the Yardenit had built concrete walks down to the bank of the Jordan at various sites along the shore. They had built handrails out into the stream so the candidates for baptism and the one officiating the baptism could comfortably get in and out of the water with ease. The slope of the ramp gradually went out into the deeper part of the river, so a proper immersion could take place. It was then we heard the story of why Julie wanted to be baptized in the Jordan. Julie had never been baptized and when her husband Ben told her of this Israel trip she decided to have her baptism in the Jordan. Dallas Theological Seminary doesn't baptize, but if permission is given by the home church of the individual and there is an ordained minister on the trip they will allow it. Dr. Hilber was an ordained minister and was happy to fulfill Julie's request. In a simple service at the water's edge, Dr. Hilber shared the truth of baptism and then taking Julie into deeper water administered the rite of baptism. For just a few minutes I shut out what was going on upstream with the other groups that had gathered at Yardenit. In those brief seconds, I pictured in my mind the Lord coming to John and the crowd looking on. In that fleeting event, I relived why my Lord got baptized and why I got baptized and why I still baptize to this day. It is the most sacred of times when we identify with Him as He identified with us. It was Jesus' public coming out, as it is for us. Salvation takes place in the heart between God and man, but baptism is the public profession of our faith when we start our ministry for him.

Despite the negative observations I made at Yardenit, I am glad I had a chance to witness a baptism in the Jordan. I am pleased that some time was set aside to accommodate the desire of Julie Water's heart. I know it is only an outward expression of an inward experience, but to actually see it done in the very river where John and Jesus first set the example will always be a cherished memory of this trip.

80

The River Jordan

Mark 1:5 —And there went out unto him all the land of Judaea, and they of Jerusalem, and were baptized of him in THE RIVER OF JORDAN, confessing sins.

Despite the fact they had turned the Jordan River into a product, I was thrilled to have spent a bit of time on its banks, and yes, even to have dipped my foot into it. Unlike the priests of Joshua's day (Joshua 3:15), the Jordan didn't divide but I did get to see Saint Peter's fish swimming around in the baptismal pools. As the group wandered back through the gift shops waiting for Julie and John to change into dry cloths, I took one final walk down the shore of the Jordan to an area where there were no pilgrims. I knew this would be my last stop beside the great river of Palestine. I had first seen it from afar at Jericho. I had been able to float in its waters at the Dead Sea. I had found its headwaters at Dan and Banias, and had crossed its course a number of times while exploring Galilee. I had seen its source on the rocky cliffs and crags of Mount Hermon. I swim in its waters at En Gev, and boated across its back on the Sea of Galilee. Now it was time to say goodbye to this ancient waterway.

For me it seems strange to call the Jordan a river. When you come from a state with as many brooks and streams and creeks and rivers as Maine, you question the title of River? Its twists and turns only carve a 223 mile riverbed from Mount Hermon in the north to the Dead Sea in the south. If that distances were not curves and corners it would only be 133 miles long. In some places the 'river' is only a few feet across with, according to the experts, the average distance being 100 feet (the width of the river where I was standing on that Thursday morning in May)! In Maine that is a small brook, or stream. Despite its length and size, the Jordan is one of the most famous rivers in the world. The name Jordan simple means 'go down', or 'the descender'; certainly a fitting description for a waterway that starts with rain or snow from the top of a nine thousand foot mountain and that eventually empties into a dead sea thirteen hundred feet below sea level. The snaking path in ancient times was lined with thick vegetation (Jeremiah 12:5, 49:19, and 50:44) and a habitation for wild animals. The modern stream is open with most of its water being drained for irrigation or drinking. The exception to this rule was the section of river at Yardenit. The banks were still full of trees and the river was wide and deep. A dam at the southern end of the Sea of Galilee controls the flow, and there the water is kept at a desirable height for the tourist trade! The water entering the Sea of Galilee was only a trickle, but there seemed to be plenty of water at the Yardenit Baptismal Center.

To show you the importance of the Jordan to the Biblical story, the river or the plain or the land of Jordan is mentioned over 200 times. The Jordan River is the life-blood of the Promised Land and the story of the Bible happened along its shores; truly, an eastside and Westside story. The river itself served as the borderland between the ancient kingdoms to the east (Moab and Ammon and Edom) and the nations to the west (Amorites and Canaanites and Jebusites). Even today the Jordan is the nature border between the State of Israel to the west and the State of Jordan to the east. In the Old Testament the nation of Israel was divided by this waterway when the tribes of Gad and Reuben and the half tribe of Manasseh desired the land on the east bank of the Jordan (Numbers 34) whereby splitting the nation. It is my opinion that this dividing of the nation happened because of God's permissive will not His perfect will. As we know from our history, these tribes were the first to fall into captivity (II Kings 10:32–33). It has become my opinion that the Jordan was intended to be a defender not a divider; a defense for the land, not a division of the land. Long before the nation of Israel was split north and south (in the days of Rehoboam and Jeroboam—I Kings 12), it was split east and west. How often have we pleaded to God for something we thought we must just have, and after God gives us what we want we discover that that desired thing becomes a barrier between us and God (read carefully the story of Joshua 22)? The east bank tribes would curse the day they decided to stay across the Jordan rather than move their families across the Jordan (Joshua 1:13) with the rest of the nation.

As I looked for a final time down the Jordan, I thought again of the Scriptural stories that had as a focus the Jordan River: the great crossing at Jericho when the Jordan literally dried up for a time (Joshua 3:16 and 4:18); then there was a time during the civil wars of the judges when the Jordan was a military frontier (Judges 7:7-25 and 12:1-7); and then there was Elijah and Elisha and the famous chariot of fire at the Jordan (II Kings 2:1-15). My mind floated back to the days of Naaman and his famous seven-fold dip in the Jordan that cleansed him of leprosy (II Kings 5:1-27). David used the Jordan to distance himself from his rebellious son Absalom (II Samuel 17:22). And of course this was where John the Baptist spent much of his time preaching and baptizing those who were looking for the coming Christ (Matthew 3). Tradition tells us that John's Jordan was probably nearer Jericho (we were about 60 miles north of Jericho at Yardenit). Yet in the picturesque setting of Yardenit, I could see in my mind's eye an austere looking man across the Jordan, cloths of camel's hair, an eater of locust and wild honey (Matthew 3:4), step into the water. As I listened I could hear the echo down the stream:

> O generation of vipers, who hath warned you to flee from the wrath to come? Bring forth therefore fruits meet for repentance: and think not to say within yourselves, We have Abraham to our fathers: for I say unto you, that God is able of these stones to raise up children unto Abraham. And now also the axe is lad unto the root of the trees: therefore every tree which bringeth not forth good fruit is hewn down, and cast into the fire. I indeed baptize you with water unto repentance; but he that cometh after me is mightier than I, whose shoes I am not worthy to bear; he shall baptize you with the Holy Ghost, and with fire; whose fan is in his hand, and he will thoroughly purge his floor, and gather his wheat into the garner; but he will burn up the chaff with unquenchable fire. (Matthew 3:7-12)

I now have a new understanding of that Jordanian Sermon.

The remarkable river of the Promised Land is still an inspiration to those who get a chance to walk its shores or step into its flow. I left Yardenit that morning with a new insight not only to its geography but its grandeur in the light of the Scriptures. The Psalmist was right when he asked:

> What ailed thee, O thou sea, that thou fleddest? Thou Jordan, that thou wast driven back? (Psalms 114:5)

Despite the fame and the flow of this river (because of the overflow (Joshua 3:15) of its banks in the spring few towns are found along its length), its course is controlled by the Almighty. The history of the Jordan is the history of God and how, no matter the obstacle, its flow is under His command. What is true of a river is true of a life. I left the Jordan with a new reality that as the Jordan flows through the middle of the Promised Land and refreshes and restores the life of the land, so too does the Spirit of God in my life. Jesus taught:

> He that believeth on me, as the Scriptures hath said, out of his belly shall flow rivers of living water. (But this spake he of the Spirit, which they that believe on him should receive: for the Holy Ghost was not yet given; because that Jesus was not yet glorified.) (John 7:38–39)

Do you know you have a Jordan flowing through your life?

81

A Walk Through Beth Shan

I Samuel 31:12—All the valiant men arose, and went all night, and took the body of Saul and the bodies of his sons from the wall of BETH-SHAN . . .

After witnessing Julie Water's baptism at the Yardenit Baptismal Center, we traveled southward on Route 90 about 12 miles to the Bet She 'an (Beth-Shan or Beth Shean of the Old Testament) National Park. This would be our 27th park of the trip, and this site is just about four miles west of the Jordan River. What a thrill to walk through this massive archeological site. I was looking forward to the stop because of one of my favorite Old Testament heroes—Jonathan, the son of King Saul.

Our first stop was actually just outside the main park to see firsthand a gladiatorial arena. Originally built as a hippodrome for horse races in the 2nd century AD by the Romans, it was converted into an amphitheater in the 4th century; this complex is still much in tack to this day although grass and small bushes have invaded the site. Only three rows remain of the original seating that could have held upwards of six thousand spectators. There is some debate whether or not bloody gladiatorial contest were actually held in this venue, but its haunting similarity with others around the Roman Empire was enough to conjure up imaginations of our brothers and sisters in Christ facing martyrdom in places like this. Marnie and I agreed that it was one of the saddest places we visited in Israel. The cold high stone walls were a sober reminder of the final resting place of some of God's beloved children; men like Antipas (Revelation 2:13). For me, I was looking for the place where the body of Jonathan was nailed to a Philistine wall.

What we saw when we actually entered the park was impressive, even more impressive than Caesarea. Our first stop was at the seven thousand seat theater. Not quite as big as the one in Caesarea, but just as well preserved. After a short talk Greg left us to ourselves to explore the massive site on our own. We had until lunch to see as much as we could see. The pamphlet given to us at the gate helped us understand the ruins and what we were observing. The huge city site in front of the theater was in actuality the Decapolis city of Beth-Shean, or Bet She'an. The site extends to well over 400 acres and includes the ancient city of Bet-She'an-Scythopolis (the New Testament city) and the imposing Tel Beth Shan (the Old Testament city). They started uncovering the site in the 1920s and continue to this day. Our walk took us down Palladius (named after the governor of the province at the time of its construction) Street, the broad main artery through the middle of the town. The colonnade was over a football field long from the theater to the tel; originally built by the Romans, it was renovated during the Byzantine period. Lining the street were areas where shops (some two-stories high) once stood, a typical retail street of ancient times. Half-way down the street on the left hand side was a semicircular concourse called the Sigma (named because of an inscription found on site). The concourse was also lined with small rooms that were no doubt used as shops. At the end of the street was a Roman semicircular temple. All that is left is the collapsed columns. There were numerous standing pillars still along the street, but there were even more toppled pillars from the 749 earthquake that leveled the lower city.

Our walk took us past the old temple at the junction of Palladius, Northern, and Silvanus Streets. We turned right at the crossroads passing the Nymphaeum, a public fountain of the 2nd century. Just a short walk brought us to Valley Street a Roman paved street that took us to the foot of Tel Beth Shan. Our goal, or should I say my goal, Marnie was just about finished with climbing to the top of tels, was to ascend to the top of the tel and see the old city of Beth Shan. According to the pamphlet, twenty settlements have been uncovered on the Tel. Discovered among the ruins of the Canaanite city were five temples, public and residential buildings, a governor's house, and monuments with inscriptions from the period when Egypt controlled this vital city. The mount was just south of the Harod River in a fertile area that enjoyed plenty of water and good land as well as being on a major crossroad. The city was given to Manasseh in the allotment (Joshua 17:11, 16), but the tribe was not able to drive out the Canaanites that occupied the site (Judges 1:27). By the time of Saul, the Philistines controlled the town.

After the Battle of Gilboa (I Samuel 31), in which King Saul was defeated, the bodies of Saul and his three sons (I Samuel 31:2) were brought to Beth Shan and tacked to the walls of the city. The displaying of their bodies in this manner so infuriated the men of Jabesh-gilead (probably because Saul had helped this town earlier in his reign-I Samuel 11) that they staged a night attack on Beth Shan and recovered the bodies of the fallen (I Samuel 31:11–13). This admirable feat is often overlooked in the story of Jonathan. It was nice to stand on that knoll and remember the bravery and courage it took to honor Saul and his sons in the manner of the men of Jabesh-gilead, an event that David would honor many years after the exploit (II Samuel 21:12). By the time of King Solomon the city was under Israeli control (I Kings 4:12). By 732 BC, it was destroyed again by the Assyrians when their king Tiglath-Pilneser III (II Chronicles 28:16–21) captured the northern kingdom of Israel. From the top of that tel I was once again able to see back into the Old Testament and understand what happened to Jonathan. We had visited Gilboa at the start of our Galilean trip, and now the story of Jonathan was finished at the end of our northern tour. Tel Beth Shan would not be my last climb up an Israeli hill; I enjoyed every one!

Also from the summit of Tel Beth Shan we were able to look down on Bet She 'an. The bird's eye view allowed us to make out the Truncated Bridge and the old city gate area at the end of Valley Street. The street runs across the Harod River via a triple vaulted bridge (truncated) which leads into the city from the northeast. We were able to see the eastern bathhouse, a huge cold water bath hall built by the Romans and renovated by the Byzantines. In the center of town we could clearly make out the Byzantine Agora, a concourse surrounded by porticoes which served as the commercial center for the Byzantine Bet She 'an. The most unique structure on the mount was a tree on the edge of the tel overlooking the lower city. We were told that it was actually a movie prop from the making of the 'Jesus' film. It was the tree Judas hung himself on. It appears the filmmakers were looking for a better shot than historical accuracy! We reversed our steps and descended the tel around noontime. We walked back up Valley Street to Silvanus Street and halfway back up Palladius Street before exiting at the Sigma. Our next stop would be at the western bathhouse of Bet She 'an.

This Byzantine bath complex contained both hot and warm bathing halls. The construction was amazing as they had removed the floors in some sections of the bathhouse to expose the heating elements. It was large enough to accommodate hundreds of people at one time. Its walls were coated with colorful plaster and its floors were paved in beautiful marble slabs and artful mosaics. The main structure opened up on all sides onto rooms where the people could relax after a refreshing bath. We left the bathhouse by way of one of those rooms returning to the visitor's center to have lunch. As we worked our way up the hill to the tourist area, I thought again of how the ancients are similar to our modern way of life. Shopping malls and theaters and pleasure filled halls dominate our culture as well. Was it not Paul that described the people of 'the last day's as being:

> Lovers of pleasure more than lovers of God? (II Timothy 3:4)

82

Hot Springs and a Dust Storm

Psalms 107:35—He turneth the wilderness into a standing water, and DRY GROUND into WATERSPRINGS.

After a very warm walk (nearing 100 by noontime) around the Bet She 'an National Park, Marnie and I bought a cold drink (twenty shekels for two small juices—or $5.72) and found a shady spot to enjoy our final moments overlooking the most extensive archeological dig we had explored in Israel. We certainly didn't cover every inch of the site, but from the peak of Tel Beth Shan we were able to see it all! As with the other guard cities (Megiddo, Azekah, Jericho, Lachish, Hazor), we now could visualize why this site had been chosen by its early settlers as an important defensive town. The Harod Valley (the northwest by southeast valley that comes down from the Jezreel Valley) and the Jordan Valley (the north to south valley) meet at Bet She 'an, making this place the primary geographical entrance gate into Galilee in the region. As Jericho is the geographical entrance gate to central Canaan, Beth Shan is the door into the heart of Galilee; so whether Old Testament or New Testament this city was a major player in the area and remains so to this day! We could see that the residents of Bet She 'an took great pride in the amazing remains of the ancient cities that once rested within the boundary of their town. The grounds were clean and well taken care of, and the shopkeepers were friendly and accommodating. We left Bet She 'an around one in the afternoon for a short drive over to Gan Hashlosha National Park, another surprise stop on our trip.

It was only after I returned to the States that I learned that we had bypassed an Israeli national park that is now on my Promised Land 'bucket list', if I should ever get a chance to return: Kokhav Hayarden, or the Crusader Fortress of Belvoir. But as it happened at the Dead Sea when we stopped to swim instead of going into En Gedi Falls, it was the swimming at Gan Hashlosha that distracted me from knowing just how close I was to Belvoir Castle. Because this stop wasn't on our trip agenda, we had no idea why we were stopping. We didn't recognize the name, and the surrounding trees hid the real reason for the park. We had been warned to have our bathing suit in our carryon before we left En Gev, but we thought we might swim in the Jordan. When that didn't happen and with the distraction at Bet She'an, we had forgotten about bathing suits and swimming. As the bus stopped in the parking lot at Gan Hashlosha, we were told that we had come to the best hot springs area in all of Israel, and that for the next couple of hours we could kick back and relax and enjoy the waters of Gan Hashlosha. We had deserved a few hours off from the rigid schedule we had kept since leaving Yad Ha Shmonah nearly five day before.

As I have told you, I am not much of a swimmer and swimming isn't a favorite pastime, but like our swim in the Red Sea, or swim at Gan Hashlosha was wonderful. The springs were crowded when we finally emerged from the changing rooms just south of the first pool. As we had done at the Dead Sea, we left our personal affects with Ike Spiker (he was unable to swim because he is a diabetic). Marnie was the first to jump in as I took a few pictures, then I left my camera with Ike and took the plunge. I thought 'hot' springs' were supposed to be 'hot'? They were lukewarm at best, but maybe it was because of the hot air that was surrounding the springs. The contrast in temperature between the water and the air actually made the swim pleasant. Instead of being hot, the water was cooler and thereby refreshing. The springs were actually a series of small pools cascading into each other by a set of waterfalls. The first pool was the largest of the three I visited, but I could see below us a few more. The water was deep in the middle and the rocky shore was sharp on your bare feet. You had to be careful when getting in and out, but other than that the experience was amazing. We eventually worked our way to the second pool to experience standing under the waterfall that separated the two bodies of water. Ike walked along the shore and was able to get pictures of Marnie and me under the falls with a few of our swimming companions.

For the next ninety minutes we swam in the warm water of the hot springs at Gan Hashlosha. Just as we were getting out, we began to notice that the air was beginning to grow dark. At first we thought it might be that clouds were just settling into the Jordan Valley, but then we noticed that the air was thick with dust. We had been warned on a number of occasions that the weather in Israel can change in a moment with the winds shifts from a westerly breeze to an easterly breeze. Up until our 17th day in Israel the wind, if there had been a wind, was always out of the west, blowing in from the Mediterranean Sea. What had happened at our stay at Gan Hashlosha, the wind had switched from blowing in from the sea to blowing in from the Jordanian Plateau. In my journal I have two pictures of the very same site. The first was taken on a clear day, and the second was taken in a dust storm. The contrast is beyond description. As I made my way back to the dressing room at the head of the first pool, I could make out that brown haze engulfing Gan Hashlosha. My first thought was I was thankful that it didn't happen on a day we were sightseeing; swimming and a sand storm can go together!

After a couple hours of play, we were back on the bus and heading south on Route 90. We had a few hours of driving ahead of us before we got back to Yad Ha Shmonah for supper. The further south we traveled the thicker the dust got. I was disappointed because it blocked out everything we could have seen as we journeyed along the Jordan River towards Jericho. We passed the Damia Bridge (the old Biblical site of Adam where the Jordan River stopped flowing in the crossing of the Israelites in Joshua's day-Joshua 3:16) Crossing into the country of Jordan. We did make our 3rd stop at the truck stop outside Jericho where Marnie and I rode the camel. By late afternoon the temperature was well over a hundred degrees and the dust was so thick you couldn't see a mile in any direction. The drinks were cold and the camels were still waiting for someone to ride them. Our climb up the Jericho Road into Jerusalem was slow with afternoon traffic. The sites that we had already seen were a sandy brown in the haze. Once again I rejoiced that we hadn't had this weather any other time on the trip. Greg told us that he had lead some groups in past years when they were in a dust storm their entire time. How good our Lord had been to us on this trip:

> Great is the Lord, and greatly to be praised . . . ! (Psalms 145:3)

By five o'clock, we had returned to our home on a hill, but unlike five days before we couldn't see anything. The thick dust had blotted out the Mediterranean Sea, the hills around Jerusalem, and the tree line after about a hundred yards. Our prayer would be that overnight the wind would switch back to the west and blow the dust of Jordan back to Jordan. This time Marnie and I moved into Room 203 facing the sea. As before, the room was roomy and comfortable with all the trappings needed for rest and recovery. We would be staying here until we left for the airport in forty-eight hours. Supper was at six, and then another highlight of the trip would begin our last two days in the land of Israel—a lecture by Dr. Bryant Wood in preparation for our early morning archeological dig at Ai. Even a dust storm couldn't discourage me from digging around in the dirt and dust of Israel.

83

Memorable Lecture

*Joshua 7:2—And Joshua sent men from Jericho to AI . . . .
. . . and spake unto them, saying, Go up and view the country. And the men went up and viewed AI.*

Before we would go up and view Ai, we had the privilege of sitting in on a lecture by one of the top archeologists on ancient pottery in the world today. One of the side benefits of this trip to Israel through Dallas Theological Seminary was the contact we had with other groups already working in Israel to uncover the Biblical truth found in the ruins of places like Ai. Our plan was to spend the morning of our 18th day in Israel actually digging at the archeological site at Ai, the second city in Canaan to fall to Joshua's forces. In preparation for that dig, Dr. Bryant Wood shared with us his insights on why the site we would be going to was the ancient tel of Ai. It seems that there is some debate among the archeologists of just where the old Amorite city is? Other sites had been located, but evidence found in the ground has disqualified their authenticity. This new site under consideration is believed by some to be the place that resisted Joshua and inflicted on his forces their first and only Canaanite defeat.

I will never forget my walk to the lecture hall at Yad Ha Shmonah that late May evening. I was not only excited to hear what Dr. Wood had to say, but I was amazed at what I saw around the campus. The dust storm had only increased in thickness since our arrival and had literally turned the sun 'white', a sight I had never seen before. It was a celestial omen to the nature of the lecture I was going to hear. I can honestly say that the hour I spent with 50 others was spell-binding to me. I had never had the privilege of actually hearing a professional archeologist before. His knowledge of pottery from ancient times and the methods and techniques used to understand dates and times and reasons why this places or that places fits into the Biblical text was fascinating. This would be our seventh lecture on the trip, but for me the most memorable and insightful because of the spiritual lesson I gleaned from Dr. Wood's talk.

Before I share that lesson, I would first like to quote Dr. Bryant Wood. We were given this in some introduction material to understand why Dr. Wood and his organization were so passionate about the Christian Church supporting archeological digs. He writes:

> The Bible has been under attack in the Western world for over 200 years, but never more intensely than today. These attacks have taken different forms and have come from many different corners of the academic world-from philosophers, to scientists, to textual critics. In the specialized world of archeology, the attacks have increased dramatically in the past 50 years. Once a field dominated by Bible-believing individuals, it is now overrun by atheists and skeptics, agnostics and those committed to the destruction of the Bible as a source of true historical information. These attacks on the Bible are part of a sweeping movement in Western culture. Spearheaded by academic elitists in the university and the public educational system, the news and popular media, and the entertainment industry, these revisionists cloak themselves with supposed objectivity, purity of motives, and the superiority of science over the 'uninformed' and 'unscientific' religious community. They regularly mock those who question their worldview and their conclusions by name-calling and the worst forms of anti-Bible and anti-Christian propaganda. They have powerfully infected the Church by turning Bible-believing Christians against the very Scripture which is the foundation of truth and life in this world. Instead of contending for the Bible, Christian academics, pastors and lay-persons make egregious accommodations to these destroyers of faith and truth. In these days of intense spiritual battle, God called ABR (Archeological Biblical Review) to step into the gap, to contend for the truth, and to assist the Church in this critical hour. ABR is a non-profit ministry demonstrating the historical reliability of the Bible and giving answers to questions being asked by believers and non-believers alike. We do this through original archeological fieldwork and research along with studies in other apologetic disciplines. We take on the bold claims of skeptics and critics. We challenge the bizarre, anti-biblical propaganda that is

purveyed upon the public as gospel through television and the print media.

As I sat waiting for Dr. Woods lecture, I read what I have just printed. I have been on another frontline my entire adult life as a local pastor. I knew that there were men like Dr. Wood fighting for the authoritative truth of the Bible on other fronts; now I would be able to hear him personally and be challenged to continue the struggle.

If I could shrink what I learned in that hour lecture into three words it would be:

Paralysis by Analyses.

Because we have had two thousand years to dig and dissect and debate, we in the Christian community have lost focus on the one undeniable truth of the Scriptures—it must be taken by faith. Instead of taking God's Word at its word, we have switched to the human method of doubt before belief, versus belief first. For all of my life I have believed in Noah's Ark, not because they have found some evidence in Turkey, but because the Bible speaks of Noah's ark. Whether or not they ever find the 'ark' on Ararat will never change my mind on the historical truth of Noah and the Flood. In Wood's lecture he mentioned that there are some in the Christian community that are even doubting Joshua's conquest of Canaan because they can't find evidence in the rocks, the pottery, or their carbon dating. We have gotten the cart before the horse. Pure Biblical archeology must start from a belief in the reliability of the Scripture, and then the study of rocks and pottery and carbon dating will make sense. For me the biggest problem today is those who want to somehow marry the Bible and Evolution. Man's view and God's view, but they are like oil and water; they cannot be mixed (Isaiah 55:8–9). Before we dig in the ground we need to first dig into the Bible, as men like Dr. Merrill and Dr. Wood have. That is what I loved about Dr. Merrill and Dr. Wood and Dr. Behle and Dr. Hilber's lectures. Before we ever set foot on site, we spend some time in the Scriptures!

I came to the conclusion after Dr. Wood's lecture that we are analyzing too much and believing to little. Isaiah gives those of us who believe in the Bible this amazing promise:

> So shall my word be that goeth forth out of my mouth: it shall not return unto me void, but it shall accomplish that which I please, and it shall prosper in the thing whereto I sent it. (Isaiah 55:11)

It was refreshing to hear a highly educated man acknowledge his belief first in the Bible then in archeology; first in the pages of God's Word and then in pottery, and first in the Scriptures and then in the soil he has for most of his life turned over; not to prove God's truth but to verify God's truth. Not since my days at Bob Jones University had I spent as much time with intelligent men who have not only become well-known in the Christian community but well known in the academic community. Men who are able through Biblical knowledge and archeological evidence stand toe to toe with the world's best critics and beat them at their own game. I was honored to have at least shook the hands of a number of men on this trip who face in my opinion the 'goliaths' of this day, and armed with a single scripture attack boldly. Willing to believe that if God said it then that was good enough for them; no matter the archeological evidence! And if it is good enough for them, it ought to be good enough for us as well!

84

Archeological Dig at Ai

Joshua 8:28—Joshua burnt AI, and made it an heap for ever, even desolation unto this day.

Long before May 28, 2010 came along, I had looked forward to this day on our Israel schedule. Months before we left Dallas for Tel Aviv, we had gotten a calendar highlighting the events of each day on the trip. On the first line in the block for May 28th were these three words:

Archeological Excavation Ai

I went to bed the night before with Dr. Bryant Wood's lecture still rolling around in my head. The evidence he shared convinced me that our group was going to the very site of Ai that next morning. The location was right in conjunction with 'beside Bethaven, and on the east side of Bethel' (Joshua 7:2). The timing was right (1406 BC) in relationship to the evidence of the time of Ai's destruction and the Canaanite conquest of Joshua. The archeological site was fairly new, so we would be working on some virgin soil and would perhaps help to prove that Ai had indeed been found. It took me awhile to fall asleep in anticipation and expectation for what our last official study day in Israel would reveal? I was also amazed over the opportunity we were being given to dig at Ai when I learned at supper just how much the group already digging at Ai had paid to be on Dr. Eugene Merrill's archeological team. While at supper Marnie and I had once again run into Dr. Merrill and his wife. They and their team were also staying at Yad Ha Shmonah for the two weeks they were in Israel. This had not been the first time Dr. Merrill had brought a digging team from DTS for the sole purpose of an on-hands experience digging at an archeological site. That night at supper Dr. Merrill told me that each member of his team had paid $7,000 for the privilege of digging at Ai (can you imagine a vacation in which you simply spend your days digging in the dirt in ninety degree temperatures) for two weeks! Most of the team was older, and Dr. Merrill was looking forward to getting some young blood onto the site. Fresh backs and energetic youthfulness were valuable assets on a dig site according to Dr. Merrill.

I woke just as excited as I was the night before. It was around six when I opened my eyes and realized again that today I would be an archeologist. I opened the blinds in our apartment and sure enough there was the Mediterranean Sea again. Over the night the wind had shifted again and had blown the sand storm back to Jordan. The air was clear and a bit crisp as I walked out on the porch overlooking the western side of Yad Ha Shmonah. It was beautiful with only one thing missing, the Sea of Galilee. By seven Marnie and I were off to breakfast where I had my typical Israeli first meal of the day: corn flakes, white toasted bread with real butter, a glass of milk and a glass of orange juice. I questioned whether or not this would be enough for a morning of digging in the hot sun in an Ai hole? Because there wasn't anything else I like to eat on the tables, and they were full of stuff, I decided to have an extra bowl of cereal. By seven-thirty we were back in our apartment where Marnie borrowed Chris Hanchey's computer to check her e-mail account. It was then we learned that my wife hadn't as yet received any of the postcards I had sent to her. I had religiously, daily sent her a postcard with the highlight of my day. Seventeen had been put in the mail and not one had yet arrived?

We loaded up our bus (with Joel still our driver) around eight and headed out for the Ai dig site. We retraced our route on our fifth day when we traveled to Nebi Samwil and Gibeah, but instead of turning southeast towards Michmash and Jericho we headed north on Route 60. Just before nine we stopped beside the road and got off the bus; we were going to have to walk to the Ai site. Much like we did at Michmash, we walked up the side of the road about a hundred yards before we crossed the busy highway. Once on the other side we climbed a small hill before we started down the other side. The terrain was again much like Michmash with small shrubs and rocky paths. You could see that sheep had grazed here (before we left a shepherd did come by with a few sheep). The side hill was isolated and the field covered maybe ten acres. Within fifteen minutes of our leaving the bus we had arrived at the dig site. We were told that we were in an Arab section of the West Bank and that for some years they had not been able to dig because of hostilities in the neighborhood. Opened in 2000, but only six squares were in the process of being explored. Perhaps, an explanation is on order; forgive my amateurish description!

When a tel is discovered the archeologist makes a survey of the site (there were others there that day doing a survey on some new sections of the tel), and makes an educated guess where to start digging. He then maps out certain areas to explore by marking off a square, and it is within that square the digging begins. Everything found in that square is recorded and mapped out where a particular item is found. Using simple tools, each inch of the square is excavated downward until something (like a wall) is found. When something of significance is found then the process becomes labor intensive so that no valuable finds are either overlooked or destroyed in the digging. We were told that anything, like a piece of pottery (potsherd), must be collected for analysis. From the lecture the night before I had learned that the reason that pottery was so important in archeology was that after thousands of years few items survived except for pottery. If you know your ancient pottery you can tell not only the time but the type. Our job was to carefully work down through the strata (layers of dirt) and see what we could discover. After a short talk on what the site boss wanted us to do, we were divided up in groups and sent to a square where they believe they had found the western wall of Ai. Some of us dug while others carried away the dirt. I wanted to dig; I wanted to find something!

It would be hard for me to explain what I felt when I started to remove dirt and rocks from the trench I was in. The goal according to the square master was to find the bedrock, so that the foundation on which the wall was made could be discovered. The rocky terrain made them believe that the walls of Ai had been built on the bedrock of the side hill we were digging on. Below us the team that had been at the site for nearly a week had already uncovered a loose rock wall about four feet high. You could easily see that the stones were not there naturally, but had been placed on top of each other by a human hand. How does one explain what you feel like when you realize you are uncovering history, a civilization that 3,500 years ago decided to build a city on this very site, and now you are unearthing the rocks they stacked up for a defensive wall. With each swing of my small hand pick and with each sweep of my small hand brush, I was exposing thousands of years of history to the sunlight of my day. It wasn't long before we did start uncovering the potsherds of the past. Before our morning was over those who dug with me had filled a small jar. My first significant discovery was a potsherd about the size of two quarters side by side. Within three feet we had found the bedrock they thought was there, and then along the western side a small rock wall began to emerge that we could see was connected to the east/west wall at the end of the trench. For an hour and a half we dug away at the walls of Ai. Despite the heat and the dust, it was exciting and thrilling at the same time. That morning as an archeologist was the best on-hands experience of the trip! Once again I thought of my trip verse:

> That which was from the beginning. . . . and our hands have handled . . . (I John 1:1)

85

Doctor Merrill's Square

Psalms 22:15 — My strength is dried up like a POTSHERD . . .

About halfway through our digging at Ai, we were encouraged to take a break. The sun was hot and the dry air was taking its toll on our strength. We stopped for water and a snack, and while we did Marnie and I also explored the rest of the archeological site. Both of us were excited over what we had already found and experienced. Marnie, within minutes, had found a piece of a handle of a clay pot, a rare find they said. I had uncovered a number of small potsherds (a little piece of clay pottery) but nothing to really brag about. They were just flat, unmarked pieces of pottery found by the thousands throughout Israel. It was on Tel Ai that I finally understood Job 2:8:

> And he (Job) took him a potsherd to scrape himself withal; and he sat down among the ashes.

Just about every tel we explored on the trip we came across potsherds. The only difference was these we had found underground versus simply laying on the ground. At the other tels we were able to keep a souvenir or two in remembrance of the stop, but at Ai we were told to return all pieces until they could be examined. What I saw as common might in the eye of an expert be something truly uncommon!

We walked down the hill towards two large squares being excavated near a small hillock. The survey team was surveying two new squares for future exploration just to the side of the small mount. I noticed immediately what Dr. Merrill had talked to me about the night before. Each individual we came across looked like they were in their seventies. We saw no younger people in that area of the dig. There were a number of twenty year olds in the trench below us, so there certainly were some college students on the team, but the majority was senior citizens (perhaps the only ones that could afford such a trip). As we worked our way from square to square our favorite question was "have you found anything?" Like us, most were uncovering the typical potsherd, but no major finds had yet been unearthed that morning. Eventually, we came upon another group of older diggers who had also stopped for a mid-morning break, and there in the midst was Dr. Merrill. Marnie and I went up to him to thank him for allowing us the archeological experience and he asked, "Would you like to see my square and the amazing discovery we found this morning?" We said, "Certainly!"

We worked our way to the far western corner of the tel, and there before us was a square measuring about twenty feet by twenty feet. We could see that they hadn't dug very deep, perhaps, eighteen inches. My first question was why he had picked that spot to start. His explanation was simple. Once the site had been surveyed, like a puzzle, it is easier to try to find the corners and work from the outside to the inside. They felt that where they had started their square was the southwestern corner of the city site. They couldn't be sure, but they had already made an extraordinary discover in the square. One of the young ladies (of the young people at the site there were more women than men) on Merrill's team had unearthed a tiny stone arrowhead. I was surprised, an arrowhead, I asked? Reaching into his pocket, Merrill pulled out a small tan envelop. Opening up the flap, he allowed the arrowhead to fall into the palm of his hand. Sure enough, it was a miniature arrowhead. What made Merrill so excited was the fact that at the time of Joshua's destruction of Ai, it was the Late Bronze Age (1550–1200 BC). The people had stopped using stone in their weapons and had switched to bronze weaponry. To find a stone arrowhead on site meant that the area had been inhabited long before the time of conquest. It was such an unusual find the team was excited. It was then I tried to pull off 'the trade of the century'.

Unknown to my fellow diggers and my daughter, I had pocketed a potsherd earlier in the morning (that night at Yad Ha Shmonah John Nuxoll approached me with a picture he had taken with his digital camera of me putting the potsherd in my pocket, you never know who is watching today). I was determined to take a remembrance back to the States of my one and only archeological digging exploit. As Merrill was explaining the arrowhead, I reached into my pocket for the potsherd.

I confessed my transgression, but asked boldly, "How about a trade?" I will never forget the smile that came to Merrill's face; we both laughed as he put the arrowhead back into the envelope. The young lady (Tabitha, I am sorry I never got her last name, but we learned that she was an engineer and was on vacation) who had discovered the arrowhead was standing beside Merrill as I attempted the swap. She took my potsherd and looked it over and then told me that I could keep it for it was nothing extraordinary. It was then she pulled a grooved potsherd from her pocket and said:

> This potsherd would make a better souvenir from Ai!

I graciously accepted her gift. It was a thrill to listen to Dr. Merrill explains his square, and to see the excitement of a man who for a lifetime has taught the Word of God. You would have thought that this was Merrill's first archeological dig the way he talked of the joys of archeology. He taught us how to properly record a find like the arrowhead. What the different marks on the envelope meant, and why it was important to check each piece of the past carefully, for in such finds was the evidence that will provide the proof that the town of Ai had been rediscovered!

It was also while we were at Merrill's square that I discovered that Doctor Merrill was from Maine. He was born in a city (Bangor) about twenty-five miles from where my pastorate is; a very small world indeed. Dr. Merrill had taught at Bob Jones University before I attended, and later taught at a college where my cousin Clayton (also a pastor, our mothers are sisters and our fathers are cousins) had attended. He knew people from my hometown of Perham, and my Uncle Roy (my mother's youngest brother) who worked at Bob Jones. We had a great talk and to think that our many connections had been linked at an archeological excavation site on a windswept hillside in an Arab section of the West Bank! After about a half an hour, Marnie and I returned to our square and continue to dig. We even started a new trench that opened up the northern corner of the site. We found a few more potsherds, but nothing as spectacular as Tabitha's arrowhead and the potsherd she gave me. It was a joy digging with the other members of our team and around noontime we were called together to leave. We still had two more sites to visit before the day was through, so we had to be on our way. We said goodbye to the people we met, especially Dr. Merrill, who invited us back on a future trip; what a thrill that would be.

As we climbed back up the hill, and headed back to the bus, I put my hand into my pocket and rubbed the potsherd that Tabitha had allowed me to take off the Ai site. I thought of this verse from Isaiah:

> Woe unto him that striveth with his Maker! *Let the potsherd strive with the potsherds of the earth.* Shall the clay say to Him that fashioneth it, What makest thou? Or thy work, He hath no hands? (Isaiah 45:9)

I now know the insignificance of the broken clay, the single piece of pottery that has broken away from the whole. Who are we that we would think ourselves something when we are nothing; that we would question our Maker and why and how He made us? Yet this is the attitude of most today, and most will one day be buried in the ground as the potsherd of Ai, but unlike the potsherd of Ai nobody will be searching for them!

86

The Field at Shiloh

Joshua 18:1—And the whole congregation of the children of Israel assembled together at SHILOH, and set up the tabernacle of the congregation there...

Shortly after noontime on May 28th, we boarded our bus again. We were going to head strait north up Route 60 until we came to the ancient crossroad city at Shechem, a trip of about twenty miles. As was our custom, we stopped for a truck stop lunch just south of the famous Biblical site of Bethel (Genesis 28:19), or Beitin today. It would be the closest I would get to this prominent city in Palestine, second only to Jerusalem. As Joel fixed Arab sandwiches, I ate crackers, an apple, and wandered around the truck stop parking lot wishing I was at Bethel. Many asked why I was not eating Arab, and I would say "I have meat to eat that ye know not of!" (John 4:32) As my companions feasted on Joel's spread, I thought of my Bethel history and was upset we had chosen a truck stop parking lot for our noontime stop instead of 'the house of God' and 'the gate heaven' (Genesis 28:17):

1. Abraham first visited Bethel on his way down through Canaan—Genesis 12:8.

2. After Abraham's visit to Egypt he returned to Bethel—Genesis 13:3–12.

3. It was here that Jacob dreamed his famous dream of a ladder reaching up to heaven and raised his stone pillow for an altar and made his vow—Genesis 28:10–22.

4. Jacob returned to Bethel after serving his Uncle Laban for twenty years; for two wives and a flock of sheep—Genesis 35:1–15!

5. Samuel would judge Israel from Bethel—I Samuel 7:15–16.

6. This is where King Jeroboam would desecrate the spot with one of his golden caves (I Kings 12:25–33) and would make it a place of idolatry that would be condemned by the prophets—Amos 3:14, Jeremiah 48:13 and Hosea 10:15.

7. Elisha and Elijah passed through Bethel as they traveled to the Jordan for Elijah's famous departure—II Kings 2:1–3.

8. It was at Bethel that the young men mocked Elisha and the bears attacked them for their disrespect of God's prophet—II Kings 2:23–24.

As my comrades finished lunch, I sang to myself:

> We are climbing Jacob's ladder; we are climbing Jacob's ladder; we are climbing Jacob's ladder, soldiers of the cross! Every round goes higher, higher; every round goes higher, higher; every round goes higher, higher, soldiers of the cross. Rise and shine and give God the glory, glory; rise and shine and give God the glory, glory; rise and shine and give God the glory, glory, soldiers of the cross!

We left the truck stop shortly after one o'clock. We could make out Mount Ephraim (II Samuel 20:21) on our left as we worked our way northward on Route 60, and twenty miles due north of Jerusalem we drove into the parking area for Tel Shiloh.

One of the strangest events on our Israel tour took place in the parking lot at Shiloh. We were making our way to a grove of trees for our introduction lesson on Shiloh when another tour bus pulled in. A group much like ours got off their bus and headed towards the tel. I fell in step with a tall, heavy-set man in his fifties. We began to exchange information as we walked. He told me he was from South Carolina leading a group from a church in Greenville. I immediately informed him that I had gone to school at Bob Jones University between 1969 and 1973. He asked my name and after I told him you would have thought that we were long separated cousins. He told me his name but I couldn't place him, yet he was sure we had gone to school together. He soon called over another member of his group who had also gone to BJU in the early 70s. We even had to stop to get a picture taken with the three of us. For a few minutes, there under the shadow of Shiloh, we had a BJU reunion. Soon however, they were off in one direction and I was off to find my team. The more I pondered the encounter, I realized that his timing was a bit off and the man he thought I was probably was my cousin Bob who had attended BJU at the time and had lived in the dormitory this South Carolina pastor spoke about. He recognized the last name, but not the face!

Our lecture at Shiloh was short with the main highlights of the importance of this site: where the wilderness tabernacle finally came to rest (Joshua 18:1–10), where Joshua finished dividing up the land (Joshua 19:51), and where Samuel served God as a child (I Samuel 1–3). We then climbed the very steep hill to the summit of a plateau that over looked the region. One could see why this place had been chosen; not just because it was a central location in the heart of the Promised Land, but because it was a place that could be easily defended. There is nothing left at Shiloh, but a few rock walls around a field of only a few acres. There is an old cistern and a modern watchtower that helps you get a feel for the region. The Shiloh site sets between slightly taller hills on three sides. You can see down through the valleys between the hills, but the tel is isolated from the broader areas in all four directions. After viewing the area, we walked down to the field were the archeologists believe the tabernacle may have rested. After seeing the mockup at Timnah, it was easy to imagine the tabernacle setting in the field at Shiloh. The day we were there the small field was full of ripening wheat. The golden grain against the granite stone walls surrounding the field made for an amazing picture. Some of my favorite pictures of Marnie on this trip are ones of her setting in that field of grain at Shiloh. We also had Mark Trahan take pictures of us together setting on the walls at Shiloh. As we set on those walls and looked into the field, we could see the tabernacle and its 400 years on site through the age of the judges. It was only after I got back to the United States that I found this verse and understood the meaning of what I experienced at Shiloh:

> So that He (God) forsook the tabernacle of Shiloh, the tent which
> he placed among men, and delivered his strength into captivity,
> and His glory into the enemy's hands. (Psalms 78:60–61)

To think, that the Glory of God once rested on this place? I will be honest with you. I was surprised that the site wasn't more popular with the Jewish people. It certainly had been neglected in comparison to other sites we visited in Israel. For me, it was peaceful and appealing. I could see in my mind's eye the days of Eli and the great decline. Of Eli's sons and the wickedness they played out in Shiloh (I Samuel 2:12–17). I knew in my theological heart why God left and why He would write through Jeremiah:

> But go ye now unto my place which was in Shiloh, where I sat my name at first, and see what I did to it for the wickedness of my people Israel. (Jeremiah 7:12)

Now that I have been to Shiloh and now that I have seen the desolation and the ruins, I understand God's anger at His people for their sins and transgressions against His holy site. Before the Temple there was the Tabernacle, the home of God on earth; God's desired dwelling place with mankind, and look what they did there. Even a Samuel couldn't change God's mind and He left. Shiloh was added to my 'sad' list of stops. Like the Wailing Wall and 'the burnt house', Shiloh had a somber effect on my spirit. As with Shiloh, so with Jerusalem:

> Therefore will I do unto this house (temple), which is called by my name, wherein ye trust, and unto the place which I gave to you and to your fathers, as I have done to Shiloh? (Jeremiah 7:14)

What we saw on Temple Mount we saw on Tel Shiloh!

87

Overlooking Shechem

Psalms 108:7—God hath spoken in His holiness; I will rejoice, I will divide SHECHEM, and mete out the valley of Succoth.

One of the inspiring aspects of our travels in Israel was the opportunity to experience obscure Biblical verses like this one:

> Then they said, Behold, there is a feast of the Lord in SHILOH (where we had just left) yearly in a place which is on the north side of BETHEL (which we had just passed), on the east side of the highway that goeth up from BETHEL to SHECHEM (where we were going), and on the south of Lebonah. (Judges 21:19)

This verse is found in the narrative of how the nation of Israel got wives for the surviving men of Benjamin after the bloody civil war over the sins of Gibeah (Judges 19–21). After our solemn experience at Shiloh, we took that highway from Bethel to Shiloh to Shechem. We were on our way to the vital city of Shechem (called Nablus today), and to a surprising twist in our final journey into central Israel and the West Bank.

As we neared the city limits of Shechem, we suddenly turned left onto a side road leading us away from the center of town. The road began almost immediately to climb sharply upward. It was then Greg informed us that we wouldn't be able to travel into Shechem because the town was a hotbed of Palestinian hatred towards Israel and towards Americans that support Israel. There was a major Palestinian refugee camp on the southern end of town, and it was, like Hebron and Gaza, a very dangerous place to go. The best that he could do was to take us to the top of Mount Gerizim (2,900 feet), for a bird's eye view of Shechem and beyond. By mid-afternoon, we were standing on a cliff-face overlooking the wide valley that separates two of Canaan's most famous mountains: Gerizim and Ebal (3,100 feet). Then I remembered where I was in Biblical history:

> And it shall come to pass; when the Lord thy God hath brought thee in unto the land whither thou goest to possess it, that thou shalt put the blessing upon mount Gerizim, and the curse upon mount Ebal. (Deuteronomy 11:29)

Moses even gave instruction on which tribes would stand where on these two central Canaan Mountains. (Deuteronomy 27:12) Joshua would obey this instruction when the territory was firmly under his control (Joshua 8:33)!

I also remembered another obscure Biblical story that comes out of the self-proclaimed kingship of Abimelech (Judges 9). Abimelech was one of the sons of the judge Gideon. His flight of grandeur started in his hometown of Shechem where they crowned him king; something his father refused to allow (Judges 8:22–23). To cement his title and rule, Abimelech killed all his half-brothers except for one, the youngest by the name of Jotham (Judges 9:5). When Jotham heard of his brother's rise to power the Scriptures record:

> And when they told it to Jotham, he went and stood in the top of *mount Gerizim*, and lifted up his voice, and cried, and said unto them, Hearken unto me, ye men of Shechem, that God may hearken unto you. (Judges 9:7)

Jotham goes on to preach one of the great parable sermons of the Old Testament; the Parable of the Trees (Judges 9:8–15). Now I can see clearly the advantage of being on the top of these hills. They create a natural amphitheater, not to mention the vista. I felt like shouting myself just to see how far my voice would carry, but we were encouraged to keep a low profile. Besides, that four-man Israeli patrol I told you about in a previous chapter was working their way up a hilly path towards us.

Standing on the brow of Gerizim, I could see back in time and watch men like Abraham as they travel through this valley. It was here that God first promised Abraham the land, and it was here that Abraham built his first altar (on Gerizim?) in the Promised Land (Genesis 12:6–8). It was in this town that Jacob settled and quickly got in trouble with the inhabitants of the town of Shechem (Genesis 33:18—35:4). Two of Jacob's sons (Simeon and Levi) would wipe this town off the face of the earth for their prince's rape of their sister Dinah (Genesis 34). Joseph would travel through Shechem in search of his brothers (Genesis 37:12-17), but would only return home through Egypt. Joshua would deliver his last message to the nation of Israel from Shechem (Joshua 24). It was to Shechem that Solomon's son, Rehoboam, went to claim his rule over the ten northern tribes of Israel (I Kings 12) upon their revolt against his reign. From our perch overlooking Shechem, I could see all these events unfold. Then Greg pointed out the tel of Shechem; clearly visible on the western side of town, and after that the church which was built over Jacob's well in the center of town. It was then another disappointment on this trip was realized -- so close yet so far away; how often had that happened on this trip?

When we were told we would see Shechem, I thought we would be able to actually visit Shechem, not just see it from a mountaintop. One of my favorite stories out of the life of Christ is His encounter with the Samaritan woman at Jacob's well (John 4:5-6). The well was dug (they say the well is 90 feet deep) during Jacob's brief stay in the area, and to Jesus' day and to this day the name has been connected to the patriarch. It was at that well that Jesus preached one of his greatest messages: The Water of Life (John 4:10-24). I wanted to set at that well and read the story again, but I could only make out the red-roof church and imagine what it might look like. Most scholars believe that the mountain the Samaritan woman spoke about (John 4:20-24) was Mount Gerizim. (Ezra refused to let the Samaritans help rebuild the Temple in Jerusalem (Ezra 4:1-5), so the Samaritans built their own temple on Mount Gerizim in 432 BC. It was destroyed by a Maccabean ruler in 128 BC, but they continue to worship on this mountain to this day. There is a Samaritan synagogue in Nablus today which contains an ancient copy of the Pentateuch (the first five books of Moses) which according to their tradition was written by a grandson of Aaron!) Hopefully, on another trip I will be able to visit these missed sites on my first visit.

Our journey north into the heartland of Israel would stop at Mount Gerizim. We didn't have the time or the guards to take us any further into this hostile land. We were just a few miles from Samaria, the capital of the northern tribes after the nation split (I Kings 16:24). (The city of Samaria was strategically located on a round, isolated, three hundred foot hill which allow Omri and his sons to control a vital connection between the International Coastal Highway on the Mediterranean shore and the trade routes from the east. Overlooking this vital valley, the area was surrounded by three mountains which serve as natural fortifications for the city. The Hebrew prophet Amos rebukes Samaria for trusting its

Overlooking Shechem

mountains instead of its God (Amos 6:1). They told us that, next to Jerusalem, Samaria was the best defensible city in the Land! This place was finally destroyed by the Assyrians in 721 BC. Herod the Great rebuilt the city and named it Sebastia or Sebaste today, in honor of Augustus: Sebastos being the Greek for Augustus.) We were just a few more miles from Tirzah, Omri's first capital; before he built Samaria (I Kings 16:23); so all three capitals of the northern kingdom of Israel were within miles of each other; including the first, Shechem—I Kings 12:25. We were just a few miles south of Dothan, where Joseph finally found his brothers (Genesis 37:17) and Elisha and his servant saw the invisible army of God (II Kings 6:1–23). Thebez was just behind Mount Ebal where the false judge and king Abimelech meet his end (Judges 9:50). So much Biblical history yet to explore, but our time on Gerizim was suddenly over with the order of that Israeli patrol to leave the site.

It was nearly four in the afternoon when we started our trip back to Yad Ha Shmonah. It would take us nearly an hour and a half to cover the thirty miles. We hit heavy Jerusalem traffic, and we also had to pass through the West Bank security wall. The Jews are very careful who they let into Jerusalem. I was able to get some amazing pictures of this barrier, and came to the conclusion that if you really want to secure your borders there is a way! It was a bitter/sweet trip back to our hilltop retreat outside of Jerusalem. Our official travels in the land of Israel were over, but after eighteen days the body and mind were on overload. It was time I knew to end the trip, but there was so much more to see and know about this land. Our tour had only touched the surface and had only given me a greater thirst to drink more from the fountain that is Israel!

88

Doctor Wood's Lecture On Jericho

Joshua 6:26—And Joshua adjured them at that time, saying, Cursed be the man before the Lord, that riseth up and buildeth this city JERICHO: he shall lay the foundation thereof in his firstborn, and in his youngest son shall he set up the gates of it.

Our next to the last day in Israel had one more blessing. After the thrill of digging in Ai, finding Shiloh, and viewing Shechem from Mount Gerizim, our day ended with another lecture by Dr. Bryant Wood. The night before our archeological experience at Ai, Doctor Wood had shared his insights into the evidence behind the theory that the site we would be digging at was actually the ancient city of Ai. He would follow up that lecture the next night with his Biblical views on the archeological site at Jericho. This was going to be our 8th and last lecture on the trip:

1. May 11—Dr. Greg Behle on our Jerusalem Field Study Tour.
2. May 13—Dr. Greg Behle on our Benjamin Field Study Tour.
3. May 14—Dr. Bill Schlegel on what has been unearthed at Jericho.
4. May 17—Dr. Greg Behle on our Southern Israel Field Study Tour.
5. May 21—Dr. Eugene Merrill on the archeological site at Ai.
6. May 22—Dr. Greg Behle on our Northern Israel Field Study Tour.
7. May 27—Dr. Bryant Wood on the archeological site at Ai.
8. May 28—Dr. Bryant Wood on the archeological site at Jericho.

The first blessing I got from Dr. Wood's talk was this affirming precept:

Doctor Wood's Lecture On Jericho

Instead of archeology verifying the Bible; it is the Bible that verifies archeology!

Archeologists like Doctor Wood have come to the conclusion that excavations done at the ancient mound of Jericho (a site we had the privilege to walk through on May 15th) have revealed amazing finds that fit nicely with the Biblical account in Joshua 6. The only surviving record of "Joshua fought the battle of Jericho, Jericho, Jericho; Joshua fought the battle of Jericho and the walls came tumbling down" is found in the Bible and at Tel Jericho. For years, the critics have denied the story because it could not be verified by other written accounts. No book other than the Bible speaks of this classic siege and conquest, but now even the greatest skeptics have to recognize the archeology of Jericho; that the Biblical account is an accurate, eyewitness description of the events that took place at Jericho thousands of years ago!

According to Dr. Wood, this is the list of the extraordinary finds and their correlation with the Bible:

1. At the time of the Israelite conquest (1406 BC), Jericho was heavily fortified, as the Bible implies—Joshua 2:5, 15.
2. Piles of mud bricks from the collapsed city wall were found at the base of the tel, verifying that 'the wall fell beneath itself'—Joshua 6:20.
3. An earthen embankment around the city required the fighters to go 'up into the city'—Joshua 6:20.
4. Houses were built against a portion of the city wall that did not collapse, verifying that Rahab's house was built against the city wall, and that her house was spared—Joshua 2:14-21, 6:22-23.
5. A layer of ash three feet thick with burned timbers and debris demonstrates that the Israelites 'burned the whole city and everything in it'—Joshua 6:24.
6. The destruction occurred at the beginning of the 15th century BC, precisely the time of the Conquest of Canaan according to the internal chronology of the Bible—I Kings 6:1, Judges 11:26, I Chronicles 6:33-37.
7. Many large jars full of charred grain were found in the destroyed buildings. This is very rare find since, because of its value; grain was normally plundered from a vanquished city. The large amount of grain at Jericho indicates:
    a. The harvest had just been taken in—Joshua 2:6, 3:15.

b. The siege was short, just seven days—Joshua 6:15.

   c. The Israelites did not plunder the city—Joshua 6:18.

8. There was evidence of earthquake activity, possibly the agency God used to dam up the Jordan (Joshua 3:16) and bring down the wall-Joshua 6:20?

Dr. Wood went on to also explain that the site was abandoned for a number of decades. Then in the rubble, an isolated palace-like building seemed to have been built (1334-1316 BC)—not the entire city, but a single structure. This would fit in nicely with the Biblical story of King Eglon of Moab (Judges 12-14) who used Jericho as an advance base to subjugate Israel during the judgeship years of Ehud (Judges 3:15-30). David seemed to have occupied Jericho (1000 BC) during his reign (II Samuel 10:5), but there is no indication he tried to rebuild it and test Joshua's curse (Joshua 6:26). That was left to a man by the name of Hiel, the Bethelite (I Kings 16:34). And sure enough he sacrificed his oldest son to build the walls and his youngest son to raise the gates! More often than not Joshua is left off the prophet's list, but he proclaimed one of the most amazing prophesies in the Old Testament and its fulfillment is verification he was indeed a mighty prophet as well as a brilliant general.

Once again I was transfixed as Dr. Wood weaved his way through the archeology and the Bible in relationship to Jericho. I had known the story of Jericho since childhood, but now I would see the story unfolding in the rock and pottery evidence that fell in step with Joshua's account of what happened that fateful day. Only an eyewitness to the happenings could have written with such detail, and now nearly 3,500 years later the stones and soil of Jericho are telling the same story. I am no archeologist, and I do prefer digging into scripture versus digging in soil; but it was refreshing to my Biblical belief to hear an academic like Dr. Wood tell the same story through archeological evidence. Not that I needed such a confirmation, but in this world were the media is questioning every aspect of The Faith, it is encouraging to know that God not only recorded the story of Jericho in the pages of Divine Writ, but He also left a lasting recorded in the tel at Jericho. As with the Dead Sea scrolls of Qumran, the archeological squares of Jericho have for nearly 150 years exposed the world to the reliability of the Word of God. Dr. Wood told us that the first site was opened in Jericho in 1868 by Charles Warren. It was Ernst Sellin and Carl Watzinger in 1907 and 1908 that continued the excavations. John Garstang followed between 1930 and 1936. The famous woman archeologist Kathleen Kenyon dug at Jericho between 1952 and 1958. Since 1997 the University of Rome and the Palestinian Department of Antiquities have headed up the dig. There has been much debate and much disagreement over the years, but one undeniable truth remains: the Jericho site is the location of one of history's most famous conquest, a conquest in which the hand of God and not the hand of man was the primary instrument involved. I left the IBEX classroom that night with a new insight into the workings of God, not only in the Bible, but in archeology as well.

My final conclusion was this—because of the omniscient God, the all-knowing God which includes foreknowledge, forth knowledge, and full-knowledge (Psalms 139:1-6), this makes the Scriptures authentic and authoritative whether your speaking about Geology (Genesis 1:1), History (Daniel 5), Astronomy, (I Corinthians 15:41), Geography (Luke 19:28), Biology (I Corinthians 15:39), Prophecy (II Peter 1:20-21), Anthropology (Genesis 1:27), or Archeology (Joshua 2:1)!

89

Last Day In Israel?

Nehemiah 8:18—Also day by day, from the first day unto THE LAST DAY . . .

It had come too quickly, our last day in the Promised Land. Marnie and I were up by seven o'clock and decided to skip breakfast (raw fish and dessert didn't appeal to us). Instead, we decided to study for our third quiz and final exam. To give you a taste of the academic side of this trip, I will reprint for you the piece of paper we received to prepare us for the finals under the title of "Regions and Routes Examination Study Guide":

> Below is a list of regions and routes that will appear on the 25-point final matching test. This test is an open Bible test (with the exception that one is not allowed to use any maps printed in the Bible). You will look up assigned passages in the Bible, and match the passages with a region or a route. For the Regions part of the test, know the region in which major cities are located. For instance, know that Nazareth is in the Lower Galilee. Regional maps in the Satellite Atlas can be helpful for review. For Routes, know which site locations are along each route. For instance, Penuel, Adam, Tirzah toward Shechem utilize the Wadi Far'a (Nahal, which means 'Wadi', Tirzah) route.

REGIONS	ROUTES
1) Biblical Negev	A) Road of the Patriarchs (Judean/Ephraim Ridge)
2) Samaria	B) Ascent of Adumin
3) Jezreel Valley	C) International Coastal Highway

REGIONS	ROUTES
4) Central Benjamin Plateau	D) Husan Ridge Route
5) Mount Hermon	E) Jericho-Ai-Bethel Ridge Route
6) Hill Country of Judah	F) Megiddo-Tabor-Arbel Pass-Hazor-Dan
7) Wilderness of Judah	International Route
8) Philistine Coastal Plain	G) Harod Valley-Beth Shean-Lower Gilead
9) Sharon Plain	International Route
10) Plain of Akko/Asher	H) Beth Horon Ridge Route
11) Upper Galilee	I) Nahal Zin International Route
12) Lower Galilee	J) Tekoa-En Gedi Route
13) Hulah Valley	K) Aijalon-Beth Shemesh-Azekah-Maresha
14) Shephelah of Judah	Lachish Route
15) Jordan Valley	L) Wadi Far'a (Nahal Tirzah Route)
16) Harod Valley	
17) Aravah	
18) Trans-Jordan	

Now you know what we were up against that last morning in Israel.

By eight o'clock we were all in the IBEX classroom to take our Northern Israel Study Tour quiz followed immediately by our final exam which covered all aspects of our study trip. It took me about a half an hour to complete both tests and once again I did not do very well. Just before we headed for the airport we were given our final grades. I got 62 on the final quiz and 77 on the final exam. Once again, a serious reminder that no matter how long you study the Bible there is plenty of room for improvement. This book is a record of just how much I did learn in my nineteen days in Israel, even though overall I only got a C in the course; I hope I get an A on the book! My daughter did just a bit better than I did, but she was troubled over her grade because it would go on her record at DTS, and bring her grade point average down a bit. I am happy to report Marnie has rebounded nicely from that low grade in Israel and has nearly a 4.0 grade point average into her fourth year at Dallas Theological Seminary (Marnie graduated on May 10, 2014).

At nine-thirty, we boarded a bus for a final shopping trip into Old Jerusalem. I have shared with you in a previous chapter our desire to meet the merchant Moses again. We also had a few more items on our list to pick up, like tea for my wife, a hat for myself, some postcards for my friend Mark Honey, and a few other personal things. I had nearly 200 shekels left and needed to get rid of them. I spent some of my final shekels (except for those I would take home for souvenirs) on Jacob's Pizza. It was only fitting that pizza would be our last meal; seeing it was out first meal in Jerusalem. Pizza was my last meal in the holy city, but not my last food. One of the items I was determined to have was the famous 'Jerusalem bread' that can be bought on just about every corner in the old city. As we worked our way back to the bus at the Jaffa Gate, I noticed that a bread merchant I had seen numerous times in our walks through and around the Jaffa Gate was still in his strategic spot. Just to the right of the entrance of the gate, this merchant could get people both coming and going from the vital exit or entrance. I handed over seven shekels and I got a huge loaf of bread. In the bag with the bread were some seasonings that could be sprinkled on the bread. I would have preferred real cow's butter!

As I ate my bread on the trip back to Yad Has Shmonah, I thought of the wonderful Biblical application that I could make on the real Bread of Jerusalem that had been rejected by this city nearly two thousand years before. Jesus taught:

> I am the bread of life: he that cometh to me shall never hunger;
> and he that believeth on me shall never thirst. (John 6:35)

He would go on to make the application that unlike the 'manna' that once fed the Jews (John 6:48–58), He was the true Manna that would feed them and they would never hunger again. I ate Jerusalem 'bread' to say I did it, but I long ago ate of 'that bread of life' and I hunger no more. Such was the feast that I ate in Jerusalem and the rest of Jewry in May of 2010. It was a spiritual feast that lasted nineteen days and you can see that I am still enjoying a full soul!

We had returned to our apartment at Yad Has Shmonah by late afternoon. At five we took our group picture. Rarely can you take a picture of nearly 40 people and call it a good picture, but ours came out wonderful. After that we had another picture taken with our group and the Master's group together. Even rarer is the good picture with nearly seventy people, but that came out nicely as well. The pictures were taken on the porch overlooking the valley that leads away to the coastal plain. It was a fitting keepsake for a grand trip with a great group of people. I will treasure that photograph along with all the other treasures I brought back from Israel. At supper we had a testimonial service as we shared with each other the blessings we received on the trip. I didn't get up and say anything because I knew if I got started I wouldn't stop. That is one of the reasons for this book, so that I might say thanks for the marvelous memories to those that I shared this trip of a lifetime with. My hope is that a copy of this record will eventually make it into the hands of every person in the trip photograph.

After supper, each of us returned to our rooms to pack. We would be heading to the Ben Gurion Airport around seven-thirty. I had already basically packed, so I had a few minutes to walk around the area before the sun slipped into the Mediterranean Sea. Those final views, parting breaths, and quiet sounds were a fitting end; the frosting on the cake. My final desire is that my last day in Israel wasn't my last trip to Israel; to return to that beloved land would be another prayer answered! And if I never get to return in this life, I have the 'blessed hope' that I will return with Jesus in that future day of His Return.

90

Finishing My Lists

Revelations 1:19—WRITE THE THINGS WHICH THOU HAST SEEN...

We left Yad Has Shmonah for the airport outside of Tel Aviv in the early evening of May 29, 2010. We were still waiting our flight when May 30th rolled around. We were nearly five hours from leaving our apartment at Yad Has Shmonah before the wheels of our jet left the ground at Ben Gurion International Airport. So what did I do while waiting? I finished my lists.

I have for most of my life loved to keep records, especially statistical records. Numbers have fascinated me, for to me they bring a sense of accomplishment to a job, a project, or a trip. How many miles, how many stops, how much something cost, and recording the facts has been a part of my routine. So it is not surprising on this journey of a life-time, I would keep such interesting figures. In the back of both of my trip journals is a series of lists I compiled to help remember the highlights of my Israel adventure. What better time to record your 'top ten' than waiting to leave the Promised Land. For your interest let me share with you these lists:

The Top Ten Non-Biblical Things That I Got to Do in Israel

1. Climb the mount of Masada with my daughter and a few of my companions.
2. Went snorkeling in the Red Sea with Marnie and a new friend named Ron.

3. Went swimming in the Sea of Galilee for three evenings in a row.
4. Ate Domino's Pizza in Beersheba with seven wonderful comrades.
5. Went swimming at the hot springs at Gan Hashlosha for over an hour.
6. Went to visit the Yad Vashem, the holocaust museum in New Jerusalem.
7. Went swimming in the Dead Sea, the strangest thing we did on the trip.
8. Went shopping with Marnie on two consecutive Saturdays in Old Jerusalem.
9. Walked the beach at Caesarea on the Mediterranean Sea.
10. Ate dates under the palm trees in the ancient city of Jericho.

The Top Ten Non-Biblical Places That I Got to See in Israel

1. HERODIUM—Herod the Great's amazing fortress and burial place.
2. WARREN'S SHAFT—The great archeological find in Hezekiah's tunnel.
3. THE BURNT HOUSE—The archeological discovery of a 70 AD house.
4. THE WESTERN WALL—Being able to walk by it, under it, and over it.
5. ALLENBY'S MONUMENT AT BEERSHEBA—Honoring his famous victory.
6. GORDAN'S CALVARY—Not the real Calvary, but a blessing nevertheless.
7. CRUSADER'S FORT AT NEBI SAMWIL—Where Richard the Lionheart stayed.
8. YAD VASHEM—The holocaust museum that records the death of 6 million Jews.
9. THE HORNS OF HATTIN—The famous battlefield of the Crusades of 1189 AD.
10. CORAL REEF AT EILAT—My first ever snorkeling experience was wonderful.

The Top Ten Biblical Things That I Got to Do in Israel

1. Drink water from the Gihon Spring while walking through Hezekiah's tunnel.
2. Go for a boat ride across the Sea of Galilee like Jesus and His disciples did.
3. Walk down Herod's Street next to the Temple like Jesus often did.
4. Pick up five stones out of the brook of Elah just like David did.
5. Ride a camel with Marnie just like Eliezer did with Rebekah.
6. Ride a donkey down a hill just like Jesus did at His triumphal entry.
7. Drink water out of Harod Spring just like Gideon's famous 300 did.
8. Able to see the conies in the rocks at Chorazin just like Solomon described.
9. Draw water from an old shepherd's cistern at Michmash like Jacob did at Haran.
10. Push a mill stone around like Samson did after he was blinded in Gaza.

The Top Ten Biblical Places That I Got to See in Israel

1. JERUSALEM—The holy, eternal city; God's center of the entire world.
2. MOUNT OF OLIVET—Where Jesus spent so much of his time near Jerusalem.
3. CLIFFS OF BOZEZ AND SENEH AT MICHMASH—Jonathan's battlefield.
4. HEZEKIAH'S TUNNEL—Greatest man-made project I have ever witnessed.
5. BEERSHEBA—Abraham's Promised Land city, and, maybe, one of his wells?
6. VALLEY OF ELAH—To walk where David killed Goliath was amazing.
7. MOUNT GERIZIM—Now I can see why the blessings where proclaimed there.

8. CAESAREA PHILIPPI—Where the CHURCH was born in Jesus' teachings.
9. JORDAN RIVER—To be able to travel from its source to its end at the Dead Sea.
10. CAESAREA—Herod's seaside seaport was amazing to walk through.

The Top Ten Pieces of Artifacts I Was Able to Pick Up on the Trip

1. Five, not so smooth, stones from the Wadi in the Elah valley.
2. A grooved piece of pottery out of the archeological dig at Ai.
3. A piece of granite from the gladiatorial arena at Beth Shean.
4. A smooth stone from the Sea of Galilee near En Gev Beach.
5. A date pit from the sweetest dates I ever ate from Jericho.
6. A white pebble from the floor of Hezekiah's tunnel.
7. A piece of flat stone from Beersheba near Abraham's well.
8. A piece of wood from an acacia tree from the Wilderness of Paran.
9. A piece of coral from the beach of Eilat (Ezion-Geber) on the Red Sea.
10. A small stone from the Spring of Harod where Gideon tested his soldiers.

The Top Ten Biblical Animals I Was Able to See on the Trip

1. CONY—the rock-dwelling creature mentioned in Proverbs: saw in Chorazin.
2. ANT—the little creatures Solomon sought for wisdom: saw in Jerusalem.
3. DONKEY—the animal of burden: saw the best ones in Nazareth.
4. CAMEL—the nasty animal with a mean disposition: saw the best ones in Jericho.
5. SPARROW—the small bird Jesus spoke about: saw in Beersheba.
6. VIPER—the snakes of Jesus' and John's sermons: saw at Hai Bar Refuge.
7. SHEEP—the classic animal of the Bible: saw the best ones in Bethlehem.

8. GOAT—the often used symbol in the Bible: saw the best ones in the Negev.
9. BULL—the symbol of Bashan: saw them on the Golan Heights.
10. FOX—the animal Samson used to destroy the Philistine fields: saw at Hai Bar.

As I waited to return to the States, I also compiled my favorite food and drink lists which included honey, dates, fresh bread, butter, chocolate milk, water from the top of Masada, and of course shawarma! (See the next chapter) I also put together the number of miles we had traveled in Israel: 1,099 miles by bus and 100 miles by foot. When I finally got back to Maine I would have traveled 18,353 miles. I compiled 120 actual Biblical sites we either visited, or we were able to see from our bus in my Biblical Place List. I listed 37 names on 'the people I got to know' list; one of the joys was to meet these brothers and sisters in Christ in the setting of Israel. I recorded the seven places we stayed, the sixteen 'tels' we visited, and the six water tunnels we went through. John was told to write about the things that he saw, and to do the same about Israel has been for me a pleasure also.

91

My Israeli Meat

John 4:32—But He said unto them, I HAVE MEAT TO EAT THAT YE KNOW NOT OF.

I have already mentioned my encounter with falafel and shawarma on this Israeli trip, but as I finalize this adventure to Israel in written form, I felt it was necessary for me to share my other eating experiences. Every morning and evening for nearly three weeks we were exposed to the cuisine of Israel through the variety of foods in the cafeterias' at the seven different places we spent our nights. It was always cafeteria style with a multitude of choices each meal. I am no food expert, but I did check out a book after I returned to the United States to see exactly what I did eat, or didn't eat on this trip!

Here are some of the foods I saw, but passed up for more Western kinds of foods. I saw a lot of vegetables on the food carts; vegetables like carrots, peppers, cauliflower, cabbage, beets, zucchini, pumpkin, and eggplant. I don't think I eat a single vegetable on the entire trip. You shouldn't be surprised by this, for I rarely eat a vegetable when I am home! It seems that every night we would have at least three soups to pick from, but I couldn't tell you any of them other than ones that looked like some kind of bean soup. I saw nothing like a chicken soup, or split pea and ham soup, or the classic tomato soup. So as with the vegetables, I didn't have soup on this trip either. It also seemed that each collection of foods had what I called dips. Bowls of mixtures that you could either use bread or checkers to dip into were found at the beginning of the long tables the food was placed on. I found the names of two: tabuleh, a mixture of bulgur wheat with finely chopped mint, parsley, spring onion, tomato and cucumber seasoned with oil and lemon, and tahini, a sesame seed paste, often with parsley, oil, lemon and garlic. Needless to say, I didn't try any of these meal starters!

Every meal we had some kind or a variety of meats. I saw lamb, chicken, rarely beef, and lots of fish; I never saw pork! Often the meat for the meal was in some kind of sauce, but we did have some meats roasted and other meats grilled. There seemed to be a lot of garnish with the meats, and often the meat was spicy, not India spicy, but sometimes too hot for me. I like no heat other than cooking heat! I understood before I went to Israel that other cuts of meat could be found like chicken livers and hearts, but I saw none, and was thankful. Probably the most room on the food tables was reserved for fruits. Because of the climatic variations in the country a variety of fresh grown fruits was always available. Whether at breakfast or at supper, the fruits were plentiful, including, dates, figs, grapes, pomegranates, mangos, and melons. I did try the fruit, but again I am not a big fruit person so I passed them by more often than I indulged. There was also a variety of sweet, sticky pastries at every meal many of them covered in nuts and smothered in honey or some other syrup. Now don't get me wrong I love my desserts, but rare was there an Israeli dessert I eat, but then there was the bread.

I think I would have starved in Israel if it hadn't been for the bread. There was plenty of falafel and shawarma to fill your pitta bread, but I am not a big pitta bread fan. I like bulky bread, not flat bread. Deep-fried chickpeas (falafel) loaded with salad on pitta bread might have been a national favorite, but as for me 'no-thanks'! I have told you already my shawarma stories, so that leaves bread. I always had toast at breakfast and plenty of bread at night. Fresh bread is manna to me, and there was enough of it to satisfy my every craving. I did have problems getting enough butter for my bread, and I could never find peanut butter, or jam, but the bread alone was enough to fill my belly, and then there was that other thing that filled me all the time!

Israel was not the first nor will it be the last place I experience what Jesus meant when he told His disciples "I have meat to eat that ye know not of". I too have faced the wonderment of others who wonder how I was surviving in a strange land without much food. I still remember my first trip to India when I didn't know nor would stand the hot dishes of Kerala. I still recall the first meal I had in Australia wondering whether or not I had made the biggest mistake of my life. How was I going to survive ten-weeks in Australia if I couldn't eat the food? How was I going to spend 40-days in India if I could stand the food? Was Israel any different? I know there are people who travel all over the world for the cuisine, but not me. I never think of the food, not that food isn't important, but like Jesus at Jacob's well, there are other things that can fill you besides food.

Remember, Jesus had sent his disciples away to get food (John 4:8) while he rested by the well (John 4:6). The famous encounter with the Samarian woman took up Jesus' time until the disciples had returned (John 4:27). Following the woman departure back into town, Jesus' disciples said, "Master, Eat!" (John 4:31). They knew he must be hungry and he probably was, but because Jesus wouldn't pass up an opportunity to teach His followers something he boldly made the statement printed at the beginning of this remembrance. The disciples were puzzled asking themselves, "Hath any man brought Him ought to eat?" (John 4:33). Overhearing there question Jesus replied, "My meat is to do the will of Him that sent me, and to finish His work" (John 4:34). I have always believed that if you are in the middle of doing the Father's will food will be the farthest thing from your mind. Sometimes when I am focused on the study of God's Word I work through lunch, and hardly ever eating breakfast one would think I would be hungry but I'm not. I learned in Australia in 1972 that when you are involved in something wonderfully spiritual food is the last thing you think about. Spiritual food can be very nourishing!

Israel was a constant banquet, a continual feast for me. I did stop to eat, but more often than not I didn't want to stop and eat. Every noon lunch was an interruption of something I wanted to continue. I remember the time we stopped in the Elah Valley for lunch. We had just walked the brook where David picked up his five stones, and we needed to stop to eat? I remember just outside Dan we stopped at a small mall for our noon meal; the last thing I wanted to do was eat just a few hundred feet away from the headwaters of the Jordan River. I would have rather had an extra hour walking the stream than eating a bag of chips! I felt so much time was wasted on eating when we could have been exploring. Don't get me wrong, others needed to eat, but as for me I could have gone on because I was already being feed by the places I saw and the experiences I was having reliving Biblical events. Jesus' meat was the realization that He had just led the Samarian woman into a relationship and a faith in Him. My 'meat' was just being there. I only saw the chapel over which Jacob's well now rests, but that view from Mount Gerizim was a full course meal for me, one of hundreds of such feasts I enjoyed in Israel.

When was the last time you skipped a meal to read your Bible?

> As newborn babes, desire the sincere milk of the word that ye may grow thereby. If so be ye have tasted that the Lord is gracious. (I Peter 2:2–3)

> *God taught Moses,* "... that man doth not live by bread only, but by every word that proceedeth out of the mouth of the LORD doth man live." (Deuteronomy 8:3)

Have you ever experienced being filled with spiritual food? I am reminded as I finish this Israel chapter of Paul's admonition in Hebrews:

> For when for the time ye ought to be teachers, ye have need that one teach you again which be the first principles of the oracles of God; and are become such as have need of milk, and not of strong meat. For every one that useth milk is unskilful in the word of righteousness: for he is a babe. But strong meat belongeth to them that are of full age, even those who by reason of use have their senses exercised to discern both good and evil. (Hebrews 5:12–14)

My Israel trip in May of 2010 was nothing other than meal after meal of 'strong meat' my favorite meal of all.

92

Going Home From School

Judges 19:9—. . . and to morrow get you early on your way, THAT THOU MAYEST GO HOME.

I will admit that I found the verse that headlines this chapter when I got back to the States. Found in the story of the Levite and his concubine, this phrase describes exactly what happened to us on our way back to Dallas from Israel. Just after midnight on May 30, 2011, we were still at the Ben Gurion International Airport waiting to board El AL #029 for Newark. We had gotten to the airport around eight. It took us 45 minutes to get through Level One security and another 45 minutes to get to D7, where we would board our plane. An hour and a half to work our way through the SIX check points; they told us that was quick! A few of our group got their bags flagged, but overall it was a smooth process. (While in line I learned one final fact about the money of Israel and that being that a 10 piece is called a 'grotto' and that it takes ten grottoes to make a shekel.) For the two and a half hours before midnight, I finished updating my journals and compiling my Israel 'lists'. Marnie did some e-mailing and the rest of our group talked and visited and others napped. It was five hours after Yad Ha Shmonah that we finally boarded our flight home. Marnie and I got to set together in row 51. The team was pretty much scattered throughout second-class, and as Marnie and I always say each time we come through a first-class cabin—someday!

I have quoted him in numerous chapters of this book, and it is only fitting that I share this with you. One of the activities in my last moments in Israel was to finish again "Song at Twilight", Vance Havner's

1973 devotional book in which he shares with his readers some of his experiences in Israel. The last chapter in that journal is titled "Home from School" and Vance writes:

> This morning I slipped back sixty years into the past and strolled along the paths of my boyhood. I returned to Jugtown, and what is left of old scenes that fond recollection has enshrined in the temple of memory. I made my way through woods once familiar and across the little stream where often I lingered in gentler and simpler days. It was about the time I had my first automobile ride, holding on for dear life while we must have made thirty miles an hour. Last week I crossed the Atlantic in six hours on a 747 (interestingly, we also flew a 747 back from Israel, the first one I had been on since 1972 when I did my short-term mission's trip to Australia). A lot of water has run down that creek I crossed this morning since I looked for crawfishes in it in the early years of this century. I tried to find the place where Hog Hill School used to stand. I had no success, but on my jaunt I made a precious discovery. New hard-surface roads are everywhere, but I found several hundred years of old dirt road-the same old road I walked as a boy to and from that little one teacher school. It came back to me like yesterday, that little band of country kids who didn't have much and didn't know much and didn't want much. I remember the old slate for writing, and the few books, and my tin dinner box with the sweet potato and hunk of fatback. I had good health and a good home and good friends. We were not spoiled brats who had tried everything. There were things wrong with the Establishment but we weren't out to burn it down. Life was wholesome and plain, and we were just ordinary young'uns with not a wild and woolly freak in the crowd. We trudged that old road fresh and happy of a morning. I enjoyed the hour at noon when we could play. By afternoon we were a bit worn from arithmetic and geography and spelling and playing ante-over and what passed for baseball. So we sort of loafed along as a languid pace home from school. The decades have passed, and that old gang of mine has few survivors. I stood quietly on that old road this morning and reflected. I'm passed threescore and ten but I'm still in school. It is the school the Saviour meant when He said, 'Take my yoke upon you and learn of me . . .' (Matthew 11:29). I've been a student a long, long time. I'm afraid I've been a poor learner, and I don't think I'll make magna cum laude. My homework has often failed, and my report card has not shown many A's. But I'm not a dropout, and I'd like to finish at the Great Commencement Day with the

Master's, 'Well done.' I must be getting pretty close to graduation, and I'd like to finish my course, and, as Sam Jones put it, 'Go home to God as happy as any schoolboy ever went home from school.' So I walked that old, old road this morning, deeply conscious that I'm still coming home from school. With sixty years to study I should have made better grades. I ought to be in graduate school whereas I am barely out of kindergarten. But there is an eternity ahead, and the contrast between now and then will be greater than the difference between this little schoolhouse of my boyhood and the great university. And I am upheld by that sweetly solemn thought that comes to me o'er and o'er-that I am nearer home than I've ever been before.

As I read Vance's last thoughts, I realized just how close they were to my last thoughts as I sat and waited our departure flight. I too had been raised in a country setting; not in a one room, one teacher schoolhouse, but in a four-room, four-teacher country school. I too have had opportunity to return to my hometown, and like Vance the school building is no longer there but the field where it once rested is. I too have imagined and relived those school days in my mind and have come to the same conclusion—my school days didn't end at Perham Elementary, or at Washburn High School, or at Bob Jones University. My trip to Israel reconfirmed that I was still in school. My nineteen days in Israel were all a classroom experience and as I have shared so often, I still have so much to learn whether in the area of Biblical archeology or Biblical geography, I am still in kindergarten. Oh, in some areas I might have reached elementary school and others high school, but I am a long way from graduate school and I have such little time left. Vance wrote his book at seventy. I finished writing the rough draft of this book the day before my 60th birthday. How many more years of education will I have before I 'go home from school'?

At 12:40 AM, local time, we lifted off from the land that flows with milk and honey under a nearly full moon. It was a heavenly sight the moonshine reflecting off the Mediterranean Sea as we climbed to 32,000 feet and a smooth ride home. Eleven hours later we had landed at Newark International Airport in New Jersey. On that flight I caught a few winks of sleep, and on one of my waking moments I confirmed the title for the book I would write of my Israel adventure first thought of in Eilat: From Dan to Beersheba and Beyond. My key verses for the book would be I John 1:1–3. I also determined that I would share more than I received on the tour—my insights and observations and spiritual lessons (see the postlude). After three hours at Newark we boarded American Airlines Flight # 365 for Dallas, and by 9:40 AM, Dallas time, we were back to Texas. Before noontime, we had gotten back to Marnie's apartment on the campus of Dallas Theological Seminary. Marnie was home, but I still had a ways to go, both trip wise and figuratively. Two days later I would board a plane for Detroit, and from Detroit to Bangor. My mid-afternoon on June 1, 2010, I was home on the coast of Maine. The first phase of my Israel adventure was over!

Since I returned home I have played teacher and not student. I have been able to share my Israeli adventure with my church family and my family (I even took my experiences to India in the fall of 2012 to share my insights with the students of Kerala Baptist Bible College), various other brothers and sisters in Christ in other churches as well as young people's groups. I have relived my trip through a series of power points in an Evening School class I taught throughout the winter of 2010-2011 under the title of ISRAEL (the winter of 2011-2012 I would do another series under the title of EXODUS and the winter of 2012-2013 another series under the title of CHURCH, overall nearly 90 lessons on what I saw and learned from my Israel trip), and then there is this book. It is my hope that my Israel trip will end with the publication of this book, so that a wider audience might be challenged by this schoolboy's lessons 'from Dan to Beersheba and beyond'! Norman B. Kellow in his great devotional book, Daily Will I Praise Thee, makes this application to the precept I have tried to underline and highlight in this chapter of my Israel book:

> I am one who believes it is virtually impossible to get too much instruction in any discipline. A physician may have graduated from an excellent college and medical school; he may have interned at the finest hospital in the country; he may have had quite a few years' experience in his profession, but if he is not continually learning and reading and studying, he will not be my physician! A CPA who passed his exams in the thirties and never cracked another book will be of no use today in this world of intricate federal, state, and municipal tax structures. The whole congregation soon knows that their preacher does not have regular study habits. Life must be a constant schooling, a continual learning process. This is particularly true of the Christian. He will continually attend the school of God to receive instruction in His way!

That is why I went to Israel, and that is why I am still in school. My hope is that this text book has helped you in your spiritual education.

93

Israel Pilrimage

I Peter 2:11—Dearly beloved, I beseech you as strangers and PILGRIMS...

As I ponder my last few observations on our incredible trip to the Promised Land, I realize that what I have just experienced was a pilgrimage. For most Christians Israel and especially Jerusalem is a utopian belief, a spiritual Shangri. The Holy Land and the Holy City have been the destination for countless well-known travelers; even those we wouldn't consider Christian today. Most think of the archaeologists and the biblical scholars, yet the region has been a magnet for writers, poets, artists, and painters for centuries, and then there is the common man like me. The history of a Palestine pilgrimage is a well-documented event throughout the era of the Church.

When Christianity was established as a religion of the Roman Empire in the 4th century, this event triggered a wave of of visitors and visitations to the Holy Land that hasn't stopped to this day. The first noteworthy pilgrim was Helena, the mother of Constantine the Great, the Roman emperor that outlawed persecution on the Christians and elevated Christendom to a state religion. In 326, this stately woman embarked on one of the first recorded pilgrimages to the Holy Land. She undertook this trek to discover the places of her Savior's life and to build churches to honor Him. With the support of her son she did just that and some of her work, if only in certain sites, remains to this day. Others took their pilgrimage to atone for a sin, or sins, while others were there to put in place the events of the Bible. A little known nun by the name of Egeria traveled to the Promised Land between 380 and 415. Thought to be a

Spaniard, Egeria left to the world a journal that wasn't rediscovered until 1884. It contained a copy of her travel diary which made mention of many historical sites like Jerusalem and the Sinai. As I read of her journal, I thought that I had only followed in the footsteps of those who had for the last 1500 years did what I was doing with my pilgrimage -- writing their experience down!

Time would fail me to speak of John Moschos, a 5th century monk who traveled the Holy Land and wrote a book called "From the Holy Mountain". Even the famous world-traveler, Marco Polo, took time to stop in the Holy Land before he headed east to China. It is recorded that he dined with crusaders in their fort at Acre. Jerusalem is mentioned in "The Book of Marvels" documenting Marco Polo's travels. As we have said Christians were not the only visitors, for there was one El-Muquaddasi, a 10th century Muslim historian, who is recorded to have described Jerusalem as 'a golden basin filled with scorpions'! Then there was the Moroccan scholar Ibn Batuta, a 14th century traveler to Palestine who wrote of the tomb of the prophets in Hebron and of Jerusalem's Dome of the Rock, saying, "It glows like a mass of light and flashes with the gleam of lighting." I too saw the brilliant light of Old Jerusalem and the wonderful afterglow of centuries of change that has transformed the citadel of Israel into an inspiring place. I doubt my works or observations will ever be remembered far beyond my own life, but I will remember well my pilgrimage to that fabled land.

Another great event in the history of pilgrimages to Israel happened after Napoleon's invasion of Egypt in 1789. Most fail to remember that the emperor himself made a subsequent expedition north into Palestine after his famous victory at the pyramids. When he came back a flood of Europeans started a new era of pilgrimages. First came the explorers and archaeologists, like Johann Ludwig Burckhardt who in 1812 rediscovered Petra, a place on my 'bucket list' for my next pilgrimage. Men were not the only ones of this age to travel and live in Palestine. An eccentric English aristocrat by the name of Lady Hester Stanhope actually moved to Palestine and because she didn't want to wear the veil (Palestine was under Muslim rule at the time) wore men's clothing. Her greatest adventure was an excavation in Ashkelon, one of the five Philistine cities just north of Gaza. In 1838, the American clergyman, Edward Robinson, traveled to Palestine because of his interest in biblical geography. He was one of the first to document Biblical sites. His name is also attached to the south arch on the Western Wall (Robinson's Arch). One of my favorite pictures of Marnie and me on this trip was taken of us on a pile of rocks under Robinson's Arch. And then there was Lieutenant Charles Warren of the Royal Engineers, a man who would be best known for being the lead investigator into the infamous serial murders in London of the still unknown and uncaught Jack the Ripper. For those of us who love Biblical mysteries versus murder mysteries, it was Warren who discovered the famous shaft that connected the Jebusite well (Gihon Spring) with the ancient city of Jebus (Jerusalem's second name (I Chronicles 11:4), if you believe that Salem was the first-Hebrews 7:2). His discovery of a sloping tunnel, accessed by spiral stairs, leading to the vertical shaft at the bottom of which is a pool fed by the Gihon Spring, made possible one of my most memorable mornings in Jerusalem—a walk through Hezekiah's Tunnel. It was also at this time one of the most remarkable watercolors of Jerusalem was painted by Edward Lear in his famous "Jerusalem from the Mount of Olives" painting of 1859.

Then there were the writers that used the Promised Land as a source for many a book. Francois Rene de Chateaubriand sojourn in Jaffa, Jerusalem, Bethlehem, Jericho, and the Dead Sea resulted in a book in 1811 entitled "Journey from Paris to Jerusalem". Some feel it was this book that made traveling to Palestine fashionable. Alponse le Lamartine followed in Chateaubriand's wake and in 1832 wrote "Remembrances of a Journey to the East". Inspired by the historical and geographical landmarks, these men wrote great accounts of their travels and pilgrimages to the Holy City. Not all were so impressed because in 1850 Gustave Flaubert wrote in his diary of the eternal city, "It seems as if the Lord's curse hovers over the city." The great American writers Herman Melville and Mark Twain had similar impressions, with Melville, the author of Moby Dick, writing of the Holy Sepulchre, "a sickening cheat"! Twain writes in his "The Innocents Abroad", "There will be no Second Coming. Jesus has been to Jerusalem once and He will not come again." Such was Mark Twain's impression of Jerusalem. I too had some negative observation in my trip, but all the negative impressions couldn't dampen the soul-stirring excitement generated by simply being there. My pilgrimage was mostly pleasant.

Billy Graham once wrote, "Aliens are rarely shown the welcome mat." We certainly were not by the inhabitants of the Holy Land and Holy City in our pilgrimage. I have already made comment of the lack of friendliness shown to us by the residents of Jerusalem and the citizens of Israel. This was one of the valuable lessons I relearned in Israel. As the hymn writer put it, "This world is not my home I'm just passing through." Whether through Maine or through Israel, with my citizenship in Heaven (Ephesians 2:19) I am at best a 'peculiar' (Titus 2:14) person, a stranded 'stranger', and a pilgrim on a pilgrimage. Like the saints of old we must confess that we are but "strangers and pilgrims on the earth" (Hebrews 11:13). Our real life is not here, but there, and "Our Conversation is in Heaven" as Paul wrote to the saints in Philippi (Philippians 3:20). That is why Peter also beseeches us 'strangers and pilgrims', for he learned as we all must that we are an enigma to the earth, even to the beloved Promised Land and God's chosen people. As a left-handed man in a group of right-handed people, we are out of place, we are backwards because we are different; we threaten the norm; we are not politically correct, and we can't overlook or ignore what is wrong with this world. What my trip to Israel ultimately taught me is that I can never trust in a land over the Lord, God's people over my Potentate (I Timothy 6:15). I will always be a stranger, I will always be a pilgrim, and I am still on a pilgrimage and will be on one until I get home to Heaven.

I will close with a comment by my favorite devotional writer, a man I have quoted often in this book, Vance Havner:

> The Christian is a citizen of eternity walking through time. He follows in the footprints of the heroes of faith catalogued in Hebrews 11, also called 'strangers and pilgrims.' The pilgrim-and-stranger concept has almost disappeared from a church comfortably settled in this world. A lot of water has run under the bridge since John Bunyan wrote Pilgrim's Progress. The travelers in that immortal book were not at home in Vanity Fair. They and those who kept the Fair seemed barbarians to each other. But lines of demarcation have been erased until a Christian pilgrim is now viewed as a rare specimen. The Book still calls him a pilgrim and a stranger-'. . . *let God be true, but ever man a liar . . .*' (Romans 3:4)*!*

POSTLUDE

Instructive Teachings from Israel Trip

Proverbs 9:9—Give INSTRUCTION to a wise man, and he will be yet wiser: TEACH a just man, and he will increase in learning.

One of the first categories I set up in the back of my journey journal was 'spiritual insights in Israel that taught me something in the Bible'. I had taken this Israel trip not just to see the sights or experience the environment, but to learn concepts from the Bible that I had missed in my first sixty years. At the time of the DTS tour, I had read the Bible through over thirty times. I was just months away from a complete study of the Bible (by the end of 2010, I had book studies completed on all 66 books of the Bible), not counting the 215 spiritual studies of over 2500 lessons and 1500 general sermons I had finished in my profession as 'pastor-teacher' (Ephesians 4:11) that I started in 1973. I am no expert on the Bible, but I know a few things about it and its application to the Christian life. Yet I knew from day one that new insights and understandings would come my way on this adventure. To end "From Dan to Beersheba and Beyond", I would like to share with you some of my favorite instructive teachings from my Israel trip:

1. MATTHEW 23:27—As we looked over the largest gravesite in Israel on the slopes of Mount Olivet, I understood what Jesus meant by 'whited sepulchers'. The Jewish headstones had been bleached snow-white by the Jerusalem sun!

2. LUKE 15:4—On our way from Beersheba to Arad across the Negev, I saw a lone sheep in the desert. It reminded me of Jesus' parable, and just how easy it was to get lost in that vast wilderness.

3. MATTHEW 27:51—According to Jewish culture, if a son dies before his father, the father will tare his cloths to symbolize his grief, just like the Heavenly Father tore the veil of the Temple at the time of His Son's death on Calvary!

4. EXODUS 25:8—When God had the Israelite build for Him a 'sanctuary' that He "may dwell among them", the Hebrew word isn't 'among them' but "in them'; reflecting more the coming of the Spirit (I Corinthians 3:16) than the coming of Christ (John 1:14).

5. LUKE 5:4—The 'nets' Jesus is speaking of were for night fishing in shallow water, but Jesus was asking Peter to let down these same nets in deep water; a different kind of net altogether, making this miracle catch even more miraculous!

6. I KINGS 18:43—When Elijah told his servant to go view the Mediterranean Sea, it was not as difficult an act as I had before imagined. When we got to the top of the Carmelite monastery of Stella Mars, we too could see the Mediterranean Sea.

7. MARK 6:3—The word 'carpenter' doesn't mean just a wood-worker. The true meaning of the word is 'builder', and implies that Jesus and Joseph could have worked with stone as a mason just as much as with wood as we often use the word carpenter. During the time Jesus was in Nazareth, the city of Sepphoris was being built by Herod; just three miles from Nazareth.

8. GENESIS 8:11—One of the reasons that the dove probably brought back 'an olive leaf' was the nearly indestructible nature of olive trees; immune from fire, water, and insects. We saw trees in Gethsemane they claim had roots dating back to the time of Jesus and beyond.

9. LUKE 4:16-30—When Jesus revealed Himself as Messiah to the residents of Nazareth, He also used the faith of two Gentiles (the widow of Zarephath and Naaman) to support that He was the Christ to the entire world. Was this the reason they tried to kill Him?

10. MATTHEW 11:20-24—When Jesus cursed the three cities of Chorazin, Bethsaida, and Capernaum for not believing in Him; little did they know they only had a few hundred years to exist. In 363 AD, an earthquake dammed up the Jordan River and when it let loose it destroyed these three towns; they are still dead today!

11. MATTHEW 24:41—We saw in numerous towns around Galilee the 'mill', and why its takes 'two'. So many activities in Jesus day required at least two people to do the work, yet one is taken and one is left.

12. MATTHEW 3:4—Outside Tiberius we came across the 'locust' tree whose fruit is shaped like a 'locust'; resulting in the question, did John eat insects or fruit?

13. JOSHUA 11:7—When Joshua marched north to defeat the strong confederacy of nations under the command of King Jabin of Hazor, he actually bypassed Hazor to meet the Canaanite army in the Hulah Valley.

14. I KINGS 6:1—Is a key chronological verse to the understanding of the time of the Exodus and the time of the conquest of Canaan? 480 years from the year of the start of the construction of Solomon's Temple would make the start of the Exodus in 1446 BC, and the beginning of the capture of Canaan in 1406 BC.

15. JOSHUA 6:20—The city of Jericho was actually quite small. A thirty minute walk will take you around the old tel. Most of the size of things and places I imagined to be so large now are very small in my mind!

16. JOHN 19:17-18—That cross-level is eye-level; when they crucified people they were not raised on high poles but short poles, about the height of a man. We saw such a display at Nazareth Village.

17. DEUTERONOMY 31:20—Then the country of Canaan was described as 'a land flowing with milk and honey', Moses was referring to goat's milk and date honey, not cow's milk and bee's honey!

18. EXODUS 40:17—Our visit to Timnah helped me see the tabernacle in a desert settling, and how it was raised and taken down with each journey through the wilderness wandering.

19. PSALMS 23:1-6 AND JOHN 10:1-16—In the Negev we saw the rock folds of the shepherd with the one entrance, and at various places on our trip we found 'still water' (cisterns) and 'green pastures, not knee high clover like on my father's farm in Northern Maine, but green in comparison to the brown ever other place. We saw valleys of death where the sheep could be caught in a flash flood, and how they are constantly going in and out to find pasture.

20. LUKE 2:21-22—It might have been a hard journey from Nazareth to Bethlehem (Luke 2:4), but it was less than an hour's walk from Bethlehem to Jerusalem!

So there you have it. My insights and observations and instructions from my May 10-30, 2010 trip to Israel. It is my hope and prayer that you have been inspired to pick up your Bible and learn more of the Land of our Lord; that if you have opportunity, you might yourself find a team heading to the Promised Land and go along. You will be changed in your own "from Dan to Beersheba and beyond' spiritual adventure I am sure! Could I leave you with this final observation connected to the Bible and the Land? Not only is the Bible and the Land inspiring (human in penmanship, but divine in authorship) and inerrant (that they can be totally, absolutely believed), but they are infallible as well. Distinctly, decisively, definitely of God; they both have stood the test of time and tyrants!

Bibliography

Boyd, Bob. *Footsteps in Bible Lands*, Johnson City, NY: Gibson & Gibson, 1972.

Chambers, Oswald. *My Upmost for His Highest*. Grand Rapids, MI: Discovery House Publishers, 1963.

Havner, Vance. *Songs at Twilight*. Old Tappan, NJ: Fleming H. Revell Company, 1973.

Inman, Nick, editor. *Jerusalem and the Holy Land*. London, England: Dorling Kindersley, 2000.

Josephus, Flavius. *The Works of Flavius Josephus*. Edinburgh, Scotland: T. Nelson and Sons, 1880.

Spurgeon, Charles. *Morning and Evening*. Mclean, VA: MacDonald Publishing House, 1969.

www.ingramcontent.com/pod-product-compliance
Lightning Source LLC
Chambersburg PA
CBHW071143300426
44113CB00009B/1070